COMPLETING THE
UNION

To Ken,
With my best wishes
and the hope that y
my story of the

[signature]

Athens
Folio club
October 25, 2005.

Histories of the American Frontier

Editor:
Howard Lamar, Yale University

Co-editors:
William Cronon, University of Wisconsin
Martin Ridge, The Huntington Library
David J. Weber, Southern Methodist University

COMPLETING THE
UNION

Alaska, Hawai'i, and the
Battle for Statehood

JOHN S. WHITEHEAD

University of New Mexico Press
Albuquerque

10 09 08 07 06 05 04   1 2 3 4 5 6 7

Library of Congress Cataloging-in-Publication Data

Whitehead, John S.
Completing the union : Alaska, Hawai'i, and the battle for statehood /
John S. Whitehead.
    p. cm. — (Histories of the American frontier)
"The book had its origins in 1981 as an oral history project for the Alaska
Statehood Commission"—Acknowledgements.
  Includes bibliographical references and index.
  ISBN 0-8263-3636-1 (alk. paper) —
  ISBN 0-8263-3637-X (pbk. : alk. paper)
  1. Alaska—Politics and government—1867–1959. 2. Hawaii—Politics and
government—1900–1959. 3. Constitutional history—Alaska.
4. Constitutional history—Hawaii. 5. Statehood (American politics)
I. Title. II. Series.
  F909.W53 2004
  979.8'03—dc22

                                        2004013685

Design and composition: Maya Allen-Gallegos
Typeset in Bembo 11/13.5
Display type set in Onyx BT and Schadow BT

*For the Statehooders of Alaska and Hawai'i
and to the memory of
George H. Lehleitner of New Orleans
and his dream of a more perfect union*

Contents

List of Maps

Foreword

I am delighted to write a brief Foreword for John Whitehead's splendid book, *Completing the Union*, for many reasons. First, because it is a thoroughly researched original history of how our two most far western states, Alaska and Hawai'i, evolved from frontier and/or undeveloped conditions after American acquisition, to territorial status; and then only in 1959, how they finally gained statehood.

The statehood movement was a long and hard one. Each state had to overcome congressional and presidential resistance, just as the other western territories had done. Thus the achievement of statehood for these last two "Wests" was the culmination of a territorial system begun in 1787 with the enactment of the Northwest Ordinance. Frederick Jackson Turner said that the frontier ended in 1890, but we did not acquire Hawai'i until 1898, nor did Congress give Alaska even territorial status until 1912 because it was considered such an unpopulated frontier.

What is most significant about Whitehead's *Completing the Union*, however, is that he was able to personally interview most of the principal movers and shakers working in behalf of the statehood in Alaska, Hawai'i, and in congress. In a way he is in the grand tradition of H. H. Bancroft, who was able to interview many of the principal figures who were still alive when he wrote his massive history of the acquisition and evolution of the western states.

Because of John Whitehead's exhaustive research and extraordinary interviews over many years, he has been able to introduce us to a whole new set of western leaders. In Alaska, for example, former Territorial Delegate, E. L. Bartlett, and former Territiorial Governor, Ernest Gruening, finally saw their dream realized when they became Alaska's first U.S. Senators. Similarly, Hawai'i's Territorial Delegate, John Burns, a western pioneer who had moved to Hawai'i, worked tirelessly for statehood. Once admission was achieved, John Burns, a Democrat, then served as Hawai'i's governor for twelve years. These men and American settlers brought American values and institutions to the very different regions just as earlier pioneers had brought them to the older western states.

Whitehead has also addressed four other unique factors in the movement to gain admission. He demonstrates that both territories had been greatly affected as American outposts facing Asia during the Second World War; and then later as parts of a strategic defense system against Russia during the Cold War years. As a result the two territories shared a common national experience during the mid-twentieth century, and so their stories deserve to be told together.

Whitehead also points out how Alaska with its Indian, Aleut, and remnant Russian population, and Hawai'i with its native Hawaiian, and more recently arrived Asian immigrants, were factors shaping congressional resistance to statehood, just as the presence of a Hispanic population in territorial New Mexico caused congress to resist admission for many years.

Because Whitehead knew so many of the principal leaders, he has been able to tell the story of the two constitutional conventions in a "you-are-there" gripping narrative made all the more attractive by a smooth, engaging style throughout the book.

Finally, a book about the coming of statehood for these two states is badly needed. As one enthusiastic reader commented, "The book will stand as a lasting contribution to the histories of both states." Such a book not only marks a political closure of the long-lived territorial system, it is a wonderful example of what Ray Allen Billington sought in the Series: a history of American westward expansion.

Howard R. Lamar, Yale University, for the editors of the *Histories of the American Frontier Series.*

Co-editors:
William Conron, University of Wisconsin
Martin Ridge, The Huntington Library
David J. Weber, Southern Methodist University

Acknowledgments

For a book that took two decades to write and relied heavily on personal interviews for its basic research, my debts to friends and associates are many. Those people interviewed for the book are listed and acknowledged in my bibliography, and in many cases acknowledged directly in the text. Still others were more the "backstage" crew in the development of the book rather than the "actors" in the statehood story. I would like to acknowledge their contributions here.

The book had its origins in 1981 as an oral history project for the Alaska Statehood Commission in collaboration with my University of Alaska Fairbanks (UAF) colleagues Claus-M. Naske and William Schneider. Jack de Yonge at the Statehood Commission was always supportive of the original oral histories. Later grants from the Alaska Historical Commission and the Alaska Humanities Forum continued this research. I am grateful to Jo Antonson at the Historical Commission and Steve Lindbeck and Steve Haycox at the Humanities Forum for their support. My friend and former student Mead Treadwell of Anchorage introduced me to the statehooders of Alaska when I first arrived in 1978. He has kept me in touch with every twist and turn of Alaska politics for over twenty-five years and opened doors I did not even know were there.

At the Rasmuson Library in Fairbanks, archivist Renee Blahuta was a constant source of encouragement. In the history department at the University of Alaska, Sheri Layral was my original typist. Charles Mason of the UAF journalism department provided photographs of his father's service as an engineer on the Alaska highway. Others at UAF who tracked down illustrations were Barry McWayne and Terry Dickey in the University of Alaska Museum, and Caroline Atuk Derrick in the Rasmuson Library. Roger Pearson of the UAF geography department and the Alaska Geographic Alliance drew maps of Alaska and Hawai'i during World War II. The maps of the two territories during the Cold War were drawn by Jacqueline Nolan and first appeared in a chapter I wrote for Kevin Fernlund, ed., *The Cold War American West, 1945–1989* (1998).

I am particularly indebted to my colleague Dr. Mary Mangusso, who has been the principal reader of the manuscript for decades now and has constantly offered tips and insights. I hope that the book will aid her in expanding the knowledge of the many students in Alaska history whom she has prepared to teach in the public schools of Alaska.

Even before going to Hawai'i I was greatly aided by H. Brett Melendy of San Jose State University. The voluminous set of documents that he compiled and opened to me is discussed in the bibliography. My physical introduction to Hawai'i in 1984 was arranged by George H. Lehleitner, who put me immediately in contact with his many statehood friends, particularly George Chaplin at the *Honolulu Advertiser* and Dan Tuttle Jr., who had "invented" the Tennessee Plan. Once on my own in Hawai'i, Dan and Elsie Tuttle were regular hosts and aides. I was greatly aided in my original oral history ventures in Hawai'i by Warren Nishimoto at the University of Hawai'i Mānoa (UH). Dan Boylan, one of the interviewers for the John Burns Oral History project (JBOH), has also been a constant source of advice over the years. He provided numerous insights into what was not necessarily evident in each of the JBOH tapes. Haunani-Kay Trask at UH aided me in understanding the views of native Hawaiians toward statehood and the modern Hawaiian movement.

At the Hamilton Library of UH, I was particularly aided by Michaelyn Chou in the Special Collections Department. Michaelyn arranged numerous introductions to interviewees in Hawai'i and guided me through the use of the JBOH under her care at UH. Her role in the national Oral History Association also broadened my knowledge of oral history techniques. Chieko Tachihata succeeded Michaelyn Chou in the Special Collections Department and guided me through my second decade of work there. As the UH library, like almost every library in the United States, shifted from card catalogs to computer files in the 1984–2003 period, Chieko constantly rescued volumes for me that somehow computer searches could not find. Not a week goes by that I do not get a care package of "clippings" from Chieko that keep me posted on each political twist and turn in Hawai'i politics.

As the manuscript entered the writing phase, I have been aided by helpful comments from Eileen Tamura at UH and by Franklin Ng of California State University, Fresno, who have sat on several professional conference panels with me.

Toward the end of my research days in Hawai'i, I was indeed fortunate to meet Hawai'i political writer and video producer Tom Coffman, who was also engaged in a project on Hawai'i's postwar political development. Coffman has been an insightful reader of my drafts and supplied documents and numerous illustrations for the project.

My family's annual Christmas research trips to Honolulu over the past decade were made all the more enjoyable by the constant hospitality of our good friend Nancy Henry, who has also been a regular supplier of newspaper clippings, often with the comment, "Did you interview this person?"

At Yale University I want to thank my friends and colleagues Howard Lamar and the late Robin Winks and George Pierson, all scholars of the frontier. They encouraged me to seek the last frontier and first saw me off on my journey from New Haven to Alaska. At the University of New Mexico Press I want to thank my editor David Holtby for his incredible patience in waiting for this manuscript, which at times I am sure he never thought would appear.

Finally I must thank my dear wife, Patty, who left the East Coast to marry me in Alaska. She began the journey with me to find the statehooders and sat through so many of the interviews. Along the way our son, Andy, joined us and shared the best of Alaska and Hawai'i. This is their story too.

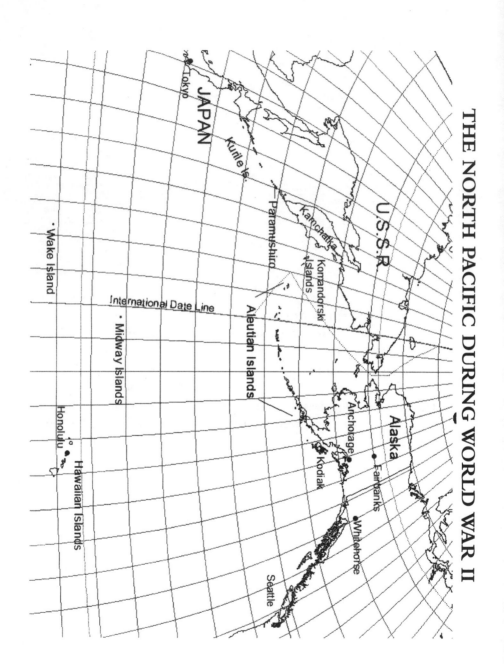

THE NORTH PACIFIC DURING WORLD WAR II

JAPAN
Tokyo
Kurile is.
Paramushiro
Kamchatka
Komandorski Islands
U.S.S.R
Wake Island
International Date Line
Aleutian Islands
Midway Islands
Honolulu
Hawaiian Islands
Anchorage
Fairbanks
Alaska
Kodiak
Whitehorse
Seattle

THE ALEUTIAN ISLANDS IN WORLD WAR II

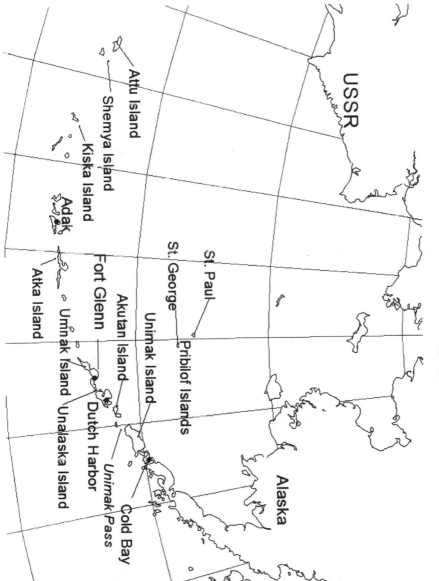

USSR

Attu Island
Shemya Island
Kiska Island
Adak
Atka Island

St. Paul
St. George
Pribilof Islands
Unimak Island
Akutan Island
Fort Glenn
Umnak Island
Dutch Harbor
Unalaska Island
Unimak Pass
Cold Bay

Alaska

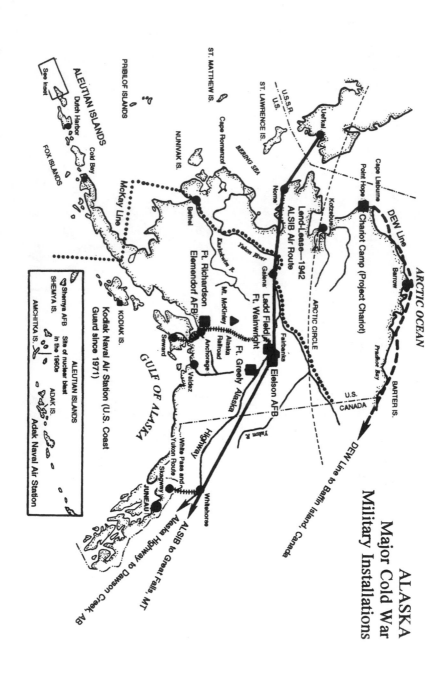

ALASKA
Major Cold War
Military Installations

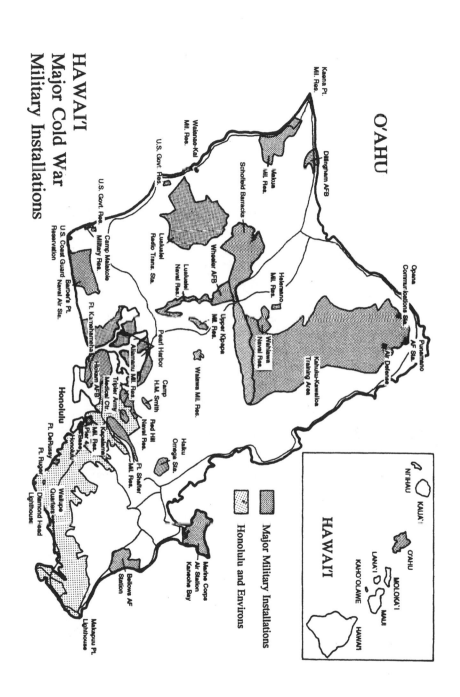

HAWAI'I
Major Cold War
Military Installations

O'AHU

HAWAI'I

NI'IHAU

KAUA'I

O'AHU

MOLOKA'I

LANA'I

KAHO'OLAWE

MAUI

HAWAI'I

Major Military Installations

Honolulu and Environs

Kaena Pt. Mil. Res.

Dillingham AFB

Opana Communications Sta.

Punamano AF Sta.

Air Defense

Waianae-Kai Mil. Res.

Makua Mil. Res.

Schofield Barracks

U.S. Govt. Res.

Helemano Mil. Res.

U.S. Govt. Res.

Camp Malakole Military Res.

Lualualei Radio Trans. Sta.

Wheeler AFB

Upper Kipapa Mil. Res.

Wahiawa Naval Res.

Kahuku-Kawailoa Training Area

U.S. Coast Guard Reservation

Barber's Pt. Naval Air Sta.

Ft. Kamehameha

Lualualei Naval Res.

Pearl Harbor

Aliamanu Mil. Res.

Waiawa Mil. Res.

Camp H.M. Smith

Red Hill Naval Res.

Haiku Omega Sta.

Hickam AFB

Tripler Army Medical Ctr.

Kapalama Mil. Res.

Pier 42

Honolulu

Ft. Shafter

Ft. DeRussy

Ft. Ruger

Waikapu Quarters

Diamond Head Lighthouse

Bellows AF Station

Marine Corps Air Station Kaneohe Bay

Makapuu Pt. Lighthouse

Introduction
Apathy and Ecstasy

When I see the flag flying and I look at the stars,
two of 'em arc mine.
—*Leo O'Brien, on his feeling for Alaska and Hawai'i, 1981*

A lbany, New York, was a long way from my home in Fairbanks,
Alaska, and it was seemingly a strange location in which to interview the man known as the "quarterback" for the Alaska and
Hawai'i statehood bills. But New York's Thirtieth Congressional District,
encompassing Albany and Rensselaer counties, had long been home to
Leo W. O'Brien. First elected to the U.S. House of Representatives in
the spring of 1952 to fill a vacated seat, O'Brien was reelected for seven
full terms before his retirement in 1967. Upon arriving in Washington,
he may well have wondered how his first committee assignment would
help his district or his reelection. He was appointed to the Interior and
Insular Affairs Committee and soon became chairman of the subcommittee on territories. By 1955 he assumed responsibility for the bills proposing the admission of Alaska and Hawai'i to the union. O'Brien held
hearings in remote villages in the Arctic and on the shores of the mid-
Pacific. He achieved ultimate victory for the peoples of Alaska and
Hawai'i in 1958 and 1959 when the House of Representatives passed the
statehood bills that admitted the forty-ninth and fiftieth states.

What impact had the admission of the nation's last two territories had
on this eastern congressman? The voters of Alaska and Hawai'i could
never help him get reelected and were unlikely to send him campaign
contributions. Had his work on the territories' subcommittee simply been
one of those onerous tasks assigned to a freshman congressman to deflect
him from the needs of his own district? Would he remember Alaska or
Hawai'i at all? Such were the thoughts going through my mind as I drove
to meet Leo O'Brien at his home in Albany in 1981. A commission created by the Alaska legislature had sent me to record the memories of those

1

people involved in the struggle for Alaska's admission and to ask if they considered their work a success two decades later.[1]

The answers to my questions soon became clear as the kindly eighty-year-old former congressman led me into his den. Memorabilia from those far western states adorned the walls. O'Brien pointed proudly to a picture of a mountain named for his grandson in southeastern Alaska. As our conversation progressed, he spoke with increasing enthusiasm for the remote western regions he had brought into the union. He confessed that he had known almost nothing about Alaska before he went to the Congress, but he was fond of a couple from Albany who had migrated there. To him they had been born again, not, he said, as "born-again Christians" but as "born-again pioneers." O'Brien first went to Alaska in 1955 to hold statehood hearings. The people there fascinated him, and his interest in Alaska's admission to the union soared.

When I asked him where the admission of the forty-ninth and fiftieth states ranked in his congressional experience, he replied that he had worked on two very memorable committees: the first committee to consider space exploration and the subcommittee on territories. Which was the more important? There was no hesitation in his reply: "The states by far. It does something to you. When I see the flag flying and I look at the stars, two of 'em are mine."

Those two stars did something to the congressman from Albany. Half a world away in Honolulu, Robert Oshiro, a respected chairman of the Hawai'i Democratic Party, expressed a feeling much like O'Brien's. When historian Dan Boylan asked him in 1974 to explain what statehood meant to him, he replied, "That gets to be almost emotional with me." He told Boylan that being born in a territory always made him feel second-class. He remembered working as a clerk on the floor of the territorial legislature on the day in 1959 when the telephone call came from Hawai'i's territorial delegate, John Burns, announcing the passage of the statehood bill. "That news was so electrifying," said Oshiro, "that I had goose pimples. I wanted to cry. I would say that right then and there, I made a decision. I'm going to run [for political office]. I'm going to run because I wanted to share and participate in laying the foundation for a new state."[2]

Reports of ecstasy came not only from O'Brien and Oshiro but also from otherwise sanguine participants in the statehood movement such as political scientists Emil J. Sady and John E. Bebout. These men had been hired as professional consultants by the 1955–56 Alaska Constitutional

Convention to offer advice on the drafting of a state constitution that could help Alaska win admission. Describing their experience to their professional colleagues at a 1956 meeting in Gatlinburg, Tennessee, the men felt compelled to explain, "If some of our hearers are suspect that we have been a bit 'touched' by our experiences in Alaska and perhaps elsewhere, let them believe it for it is true. To be close to a constitutional convention that approaches the greatness of which such a body is capable is to have something akin to a religious experience. There can be no doubt that in such a body many members attain heights of statesmanship seldom equaled in their political or private lives."[3]

The creation of the last two states filled politicians Leo O'Brien and Robert Oshiro, as well as political scientists Emil Sady and John Bebout, with ecstasy. But what about the nation at large? Did its enthusiasm and interest reach similar levels in the years between the end of World War II and 1959, when the various statehood bills wound their way through Congress? Surely completing the union was a unique experience for postwar Americans. There had been no new states admitted since Arizona and New Mexico in 1912. The admission of Alaska and Hawai'i would all at once relocate the northernmost, southernmost, easternmost, and westernmost points in the union of states. There would be a fully self-governing state in the middle of the Pacific and another on the Arctic Circle. A distance of only a few miles in Bering Strait would separate an American state from the Soviet Union. Surely such changes in the shape and character of the republic would have been uppermost in the minds of the general population and certainly of the Congress.[4]

Though in theory such changes were momentous, the reality for the public, as I would learn in many subsequent interviews, was another story. While a few members of Congress were decidedly for or against statehood, most of their colleagues and the bulk of the American public were decidedly apathetic or indifferent. Members of Congress whose committee assignments did not take them to America's last two territories knew little about Alaska and Hawai'i and wondered why they should be concerned with their admission. Typical was Louisiana Senator Russell B. Long's response to a plea for support of the Hawai'i statehood bill in 1950. When World War II veteran Spark Matsunaga tried to convince Long of Hawai'i's qualifications for statehood, the senator responded, "Young man, a senator has two major interests. One, to be elected, and two to be reelected. I don't have anyone from Louisiana interested in this at all. So I don't see why I should get involved." Long would later become a convert to the cause of Hawai'i and Alaska, but his initial reaction was typical of many of his colleagues.[5]

Congressional apathy was matched by that of the American public, though the surface of this indifference was deceptive. Successive Gallup polls after World War II showed that a majority of Americans favored statehood for Alaska and Hawai'i. George M. Gallup himself became so intrigued with his statistics that he chastised the Congress in 1956 by announcing, "The stalemate that has developed in admitting the two territories is a classic illustration of the gap which often exists between public opinion and Congressional action." Gallup's words might better have been directed at the people he polled. While the public might respond favorably to a pollster's unsolicited question about the two territories, this response did not mean they would exert any particular effort to influence their congressmen to admit the two states. Representatives and senators, like Leo O'Brien and Russell Long, reported little if any interest in the territories among the bulk of their constituents. The correspondence files of members of Congress were as likely to contain requests from schoolchildren asking for information about Alaska and Hawai'i as from voting-age adults demanding that the two be—or not be—admitted.[6]

Public apathy was also registered by the response to television treatment of the two territories. In March 1958, only two months before O'Brien won the vote for Alaska in the Congress, CBS-TV aired an edition of Edward R. Murrow's *See It Now* on statehood for Alaska and Hawai'i. Murrow concluded the program with the remark, "There has been no great public debate on the matter of bringing these two territories into the union. Also the Congress has not appeared to feel any sense of urgency about the matter. We have presented this report in the hope of starting a small argument about it." Even Murrow could not move the public. In the week after the program aired to an estimated audience of seven to eight million people, CBS reported virtually no popular reaction. The network received "less than one hundred letters and only a half-dozen telephone calls." In contrast, other recent *See It Now* programs had elicited thousands of letters and hundreds of phone calls. In reporting this response from CBS, the *Honolulu Star-Bulletin* sadly concluded, "the Statehood question—at least on the Eastern seaboard—just isn't one about which the ordinary public has any deep feelings."[7]

The contrast between the ecstatic enthusiasm of O'Brien and Oshiro and the collective apathy of most congressmen and the American public was enormous. Such were the parameters of the saga of completing the union. Adding Alaska and Hawai'i to the union of states was all at once the story of an American passion for democracy and an American apathy for it. Fundamental questions about the very nature of American government arose in the course of this saga. Could the union include a state where Caucasians were a minority? Could members of the Congress bear the names of Fong or Inouye? Could American citizens in Alaska be denied their full political rights simply because the territory was economically underdeveloped? On the day before the House took the final vote on the Alaska statehood bill, James C. Wright, a young congressman from Texas, rose on the floor of that chamber and told his colleagues that the Alaska issue forced them to face up to some searching questions about the future of the nation. "What is to be our destiny?" he asked. "Is the United States finished with growing? Are we still young and vibrant and vital with a message and a mission and a future to the world? Or have we reached the state of maturity from which the only road leads downhill?" Though some members of the public would respond vigorously to these questions, most placed their attention elsewhere.[8]

Congressional and public apathy was not necessarily a negative phenomenon. It shaped the statehood movements in a number of fascinating ways. Since statehood did not consume the interest of a large part of the nation, the momentum for admission stayed in the hands of the relatively small populations of the two territories, a few members of Congress, and an occasional extraordinary stranger like New Orleans businessman George H. Lehleitner, who assigned his wholesale appliance dealership to a manager for thirteen years while he walked the halls of Congress seeking support for his personal crusade to end, as he saw it, the fundamental injustice of territorial government. His goal, he told me over and over, was simple—to create a more perfect union.

Apathy shaped not only the number of people involved in the movement but also the manner in which the final congressional majority for statehood was achieved. Few congressmen saw the completion of the union as a crucial concern in their districts. Since they did not seem to be constrained by their constituents, they frequently gave or withheld their vote for statehood as a matter of personal liking for the statehood advocates they met. The final majority for victory was collected, it seemed at times, by a series of anecdotal incidents. To a considerable extent the union was completed, not as the result of a searching discussion on the shape of the nation, but as a personal favor to a few good friends.

The saga of apathy and ecstasy that I first encountered in the 1980s continued to perplex me for years after my initial interviews in Alaska and later in Hawai'i. I dutifully reported my findings to the Alaska Statehood Commission that had contracted the interviews. The commission had asked for an evaluation of how the statehooders felt about statehood in 1981. I was able to respond that the statehooders were overwhelming pleased with the progress of the state since 1959. I took some satisfaction in the knowledge that the commission, using these as well as other findings, decided not to recommend secession to the Alaska legislature as a viable option to resolve the complaints the forty-ninth state had with the federal government.[9]

But when I tried to move farther afield to audiences outside of Alaska or Hawai'i, I often encountered the kind of apathy that so confounded Edward R. Murrow in 1958. The achievement of statehood in two remote western parts of the United States did not interest even historians of the American West. Occasionally oral historians showed an interest, but more for interview techniques than for the actual historical saga. Why did others find so dull what I found so interesting, even exciting?

Part of the apathy may well have stemmed from the fact that the statehood battle was always described by the participants as a legislative battle. After all, there was only one way to achieve statehood for Alaska—or for Hawai'i. A statehood bill, either an enabling bill authorizing a constitutional convention or a direct admission bill, had to be introduced into both houses of Congress; hearings had to be conducted; committee recommendations had to be made, and above all a majority vote had to be achieved in both houses in the same session of Congress. The president of the United States then had to sign the statehood bill into law. My statehood interviews were filled with stories of how Lyndon B. Johnson and Sam Rayburn were won to the cause of statehood. There were passionately told stories of parliamentary maneuvers in the House of Representatives to thwart the control of the dictatorial Rules Committee chairman, Howard Smith of Virginia, and to bring the statehood bill to a floor vote. Other stories described attempts to convince a reluctant President Dwight Eisenhower to support statehood. Though such legislative intricacies were indeed studded with the names of leading politicians, audiences outside of Alaska and Hawai'i were more interested in how Lyndon Johnson, Sam Rayburn, and Dwight Eisenhower reacted to pieces of legislation affecting their own states. In searching for a wider audience, I had to admit that the reaction of Sam Rayburn or Lyndon Johnson to the Alaska and Hawai'i statehood bills was probably not the essential key to understanding the full political character of either man.[10]

Given the apathy that I encountered, I began to wonder if there was a context larger than legislative history into which the Alaska and Hawai'i statehood sagas might fit. For the moment I shelved my interviews, thinking that a time might come when Alaska and Hawai'i would be in greater demand. The elusive context gradually came to me from sources other than my interview tapes. I received a request from a colleague to write a chapter on the impact of the Cold War on Alaska and Hawai'i. My colleague said that several other western historians had refused to explore this topic. So much for any new interest in Alaska or Hawai'i! In writing this chapter it became clear to me that the statehood movements were entwined with the buildup of both territories as major Cold War defense installations. Alaska's population soared in the late 1940s and early 1950s as a result of the military buildup. In both territories defense spending was the base of their postwar economies. The Cold War created a critical role for both Alaska and Hawai'i in postwar America. The importance of that role raised the visibility of the two distant territories and made the case for statehood all the more urgent and compelling.[11]

Why had this Cold War role not been obvious to me before? The answer was simple—my interviewees rarely ever mentioned it. Their memories were not of Cold War America, but of the legislative battle. In 1996 I pointedly asked a group of Alaska statehooders if the Cold War military buildup of Alaska was on their minds during the statehood battle. Their initial response was "No, they didn't think of it at all." However, after a little reflection some of the statehooders did come out and admit that it was the Cold War buildup that gave Alaska a population and an economy to demand statehood. Gradually I came to see that Leo O'Brien's memory of his role in both the statehood movements and the space race was not a pairing of apples and oranges. Both were outgrowths of the same forces propelling the direction of Cold War America. However, neither O'Brien nor any other statehooder directly made that connection in my interviews.[12]

If statehood for Alaska and Hawai'i had been an integral part of the Cold War, it also had its origins in the history of the Cold War's predecessor, World War II. Though Edward R. Murrow did not provide a clue to a broader context for Alaska and Hawai'i statehood in 1958, another television news anchorman—Tom Brokaw—did so forty years later. In his book *The Greatest Generation* (1998), Brokaw described the personal impact of interviewing veterans at the fortieth anniversary of D-Day in 1984. Prior to meeting the veterans he had expected that this would be no more than an ordinary interview assignment. "Instead," wrote Brokaw, "I underwent a life-changing experience. As I walked the beaches with the American veterans who had landed there and now returned for this anniversary, men in their sixties and seventies, and listened to their stories in the cafes and inns, I was deeply moved and profoundly grateful for all they had done." Brokaw, it seemed, had the same experience of ecstasy with his veterans that Emil Sady and John Bebout had had with the delegates at the Alaska Constitutional Convention.[13]

As I paged through Brokaw's book, I realized it was no coincidence that I found a statehooder among the veterans—Daniel Inouye of Hawai'i. Though Inouye was the only major player in the statehood battles that Brokaw noted, he could easily have named others. He included Senator Mark Hatfield of Oregon. He could just as easily have mentioned Hatfield's predecessor in the U.S. Senate from Oregon, Richard L. Neuberger. As a young lieutenant in 1942, Dick Neuberger worked on the construction of the Alaska Highway. Elected to the Senate in 1954, he became a devoted supporter of statehood for both Alaska and Hawai'i. On the night of June 30, 1958, Neuberger was the presiding officer of the Senate when the Alaska statehood bill was approved. Statehood for Alaska and Hawai'i was clearly one of the achievements of Brokaw's "Greatest Generation."[14]

The impact of World War II had not been as muted in the state-hooders' stories as the role of the Cold War. Because many of the state-hooders were veterans, the interviews often began with, "When I got out of the service I knew I wanted to make things different." At times the statehooders even indicated that the statehood battle, as they called it, was another World War II veterans' fight. George Lehleitner, who had served in the Pacific with the navy, told me that he always looked to veterans in the Congress, like Russell Long and Jim Wright, as statehood supporters. He noted that those members of Congress who "sat out the war" were more difficult to persuade. However, the initial linkage of statehood to a broader World War II legacy usually gave way in the interviews to a much more detailed history of getting the Alaska statehood bill out of the House Rules Committee.

With the passage of time I was able to get beyond the legislative story of the interviewees. Statehood for Alaska and Hawai'i was both a legacy of Brokaw's "Greatest Generation" and a marker in the nation's Cold War struggle to create a wider presence in the world. This was indeed a context with much broader connotations than the passage of statehood bills for two distant western states. The saga of completing the union was an integral part of the changes that took place in the American nation as a result of both World War II and the Cold War.

That broader context, however, in no way made the ultimate outcome of the statehood saga inevitable. The statehooders made it clear that they could not sit back and wait for broad national and international currents to sweep the two territories into the union. The myriad twists and turns of the Congress were the crucial elements to them. They emphasized that such twists and turns had to occur within a finite period of time. The statehood bills could not simply come before Congress forever. The statehooders worried that after a certain period of time Congress would simply lose interest in the issue if a positive vote were not achieved. And that loss of interest could well extend for decades, they feared. Thus it should come as no surprise that the statehooders talked so insistently about the legislative battle that they hoped to control rather than about any broader movements over which they had no control.

During the years in which I sought a wider audience and context for statehood, I also came to see the need for a renewed telling of the story in Alaska and Hawai'i, where the voices of the statehooders are growing weaker. When I first arrived in Alaska in 1978 the statehooders were all around me. I stayed in touch with the delegates to the 1955–56 Alaska Constitutional Convention, who called themselves the "55 Club," throughout the 1980s and 1990s. Whenever a constitutional amendment appeared for a popular vote on the Alaska general election ballot, the delegates would come out en masse to explain what they had intended in 1955 and to recommend acceptance or rejection of the amendment. As the millennium approached and then passed, the statehooders were increasingly a passing breed. By no means had they all died by the turn of the century. In 2003 Daniel Inouye of Hawai'i and Ted Stevens of Alaska were among the most powerful members of the U.S. Senate. But in both Alaska and Hawai'i the statehooders' story became one of a few solo voices rather than the majestic chorus of the early 1980s.

The death in 1997 of statehooder Robert B. Atwood, publisher of the *Anchorage Times,* drove the message home to me. I had participated on panels with Bob Atwood at historical meetings and conferences. How ridiculous it was, I thought, for me to comment on the "mood of Alaska" in the 1950s when the man who had created much of that mood was sitting next to me. Bob Atwood and many others like him are no longer around to tell their story. So like the gullible accomplice at a robbery who finds himself holding the gun when the major players have fled, the oral historian can find himself holding the tapes after the historical actors have passed from the scene. For the accomplice and the oral historian, the inevitable time must come to explain our story to the judge.

In preparing that story, I realized there was also something that the statehooders rarely ever told their local audiences. Alaska and Hawai'i were inextricably joined in the battle for statehood. One could not have entered the union without the other. For some reason, this truth, which I learned by playing both sides of the territorial fence and venturing to the center of the battle in the nation's capital, never seemed to make the return journey from Washington back to the territories. As a result, the statehood story in each has often been presented as a singular movement. The politicians and statehooders of each territory have been portrayed as the prime, even the sole, agents of securing admission for their respective homes. The "other" territory is seen, if at all, as a background echo. The great mistake of the battle, each thought, had been the joining of the two in a single bill in 1954. Thus the statehooders in Alaska and Hawai'i rarely spoke of each other. When Bob Atwood's memoirs were published posthumously in 2003, there was not even a mention of the word "Hawai'i." The Anchorage publisher described his many trips to Washington in the 1950s, but never once does it appear that he even paid a courtesy call on his Republican newspaper publisher counterpart, Joseph Farrington, the territorial delegate from Hawai'i.

However, most members of Congress came to see the two as one. Hawai'i, the more mature of the territories, usually attracted their first interest. But their interest in one territory quickly was directed to the other, if only because Hawai'i was seen as Republican and Alaska as Democratic. As the years wore on, Hawai'i seemed to accumulate more political baggage and attract a greater level of obstruction in the Congress. As in a relay race, the baton in the final stretch passed to

Alaska, which then pulled in Hawai'i. Members of Congress realized all along that when they admitted one territory, they were giving a signal to admit the other. Speaker of the House Jim Wright told me in 1988 that there were a number of ironies in the statehood story. "One irony," he explained, "is that it was initially the appeal of Hawaii, which led us to consider Alaska, but in reality it was Alaska statehood which preceded and opened the way for Hawaiian statehood." When George Lehleitner asked Leo O'Brien which territory was the more responsible for the two admissions, the New Yorker replied, "Hawaii was the thread, but Alaska was the needle." This was the way "his" two stars were sewn to the flag.[15]

For citizens of both states, and of the nation at large, the story of each star requires the story of the other. When I first contacted George Lehleitner to interview him about Alaska, he told me I had to go quickly to Hawai'i. Lehleitner knew the truth of Lord Byron's poetic lines:

> "All who joy would win
> Must share it—Happiness was born a twin."

Such was the twin story of the two territories that completed the union in 1959.

A great transformation overtook Alaska, Hawai'i, and the nation during World War II and the Cold War. It slowly but surely entwined the two territories in the mind of the nation. To understand this transformation, we must first look at the status of the two territories in the decade before World War II. As I began to delve further into this background, I discovered that both Edward R. Murrow and I had misjudged the nature of the broad public "apathy" for Alaska and Hawai'i in 1958. Apathy in the 1950s, which registered as a positive public attitude toward statehood but a lack of interest in actively promoting it, was actually a giant step forward. In the decade before 1941 one would have found a decidedly negative national attitude toward Hawai'i that threatened to curtail even territorial status for the islands. As for Alaska, the national public knew so little about the northern territory that it had virtually no opinion at all.

Part I

Far-off and Distant Territories:
Hawai'i and Alaska on the Eve of World War II

Acquired in 1867 and 1898 respectively, the two territories of Alaska and Hawai'i went largely unnoticed by Americans in the mainland states in the nineteenth century and the first four decades of the twentieth century. No westward surge of migration from the continental United States brought the two into the national fabric. However, the populations of both territories were their defining marks. In Hawai'i the population was notable for its racial and ethnic diversity. In Alaska the population was notable simply for its scarcity.

Both territories held strategic geographic locations in the mid-Pacific and the North Pacific. During the twentieth century, and particularly in the decade before 1941, the U.S. government built substantial military fortifications in both Hawai'i and Alaska. In the two years prior to American entry into World War II, a number of reporters for mainland magazines began routine trips to examine these new and enhanced fortifications. The attention of the mainland began to focus on the two distant territories as never before.

Chapter 1
Hawai'i: A Gibraltar Worth Defending?

Obviously they do not think as we do . . .
— *Clarence Darrow,*
describing a multiracial jury in Honolulu, 1932

Residents of the territory of Hawai'i were disheartened in January 1941 when a Gallup poll revealed that only 48 percent of Americans favored the admission of Hawai'i as a state, though Hawai'i's citizens had voted 2–1 in favor of joining the union in a 1940 plebiscite. The poll was in line with the sentiments of a 1939 survey by *Fortune Magazine* revealing that "fewer people in the U.S. were willing to go to war to defend the Hawaiian Islands . . . than Canada." Some island businessmen responded, "So the mainlanders voted that way. Don't they know that we exist to defend them?"[1]

The islanders were correct. By 1940 the territory, particularly Honolulu and the island of O'ahu, had become the Gibraltar of the Pacific, one of the most heavily fortified military positions in the nation. Over $125 million had been invested in defense installations there; total military personnel stood at thirty thousand in 1940, and annual defense expenditures had reached $60 million.[2]

The strategic importance and military buildup of Hawai'i had not taken place overnight. In the days of the Hawaiian kingdom, prior to the 1893 Revolution, the islands' strategic location in the mid-Pacific prompted a series of reciprocity treaties between the kingdom and the United States. Raw Hawaiian sugar could be exported to the American mainland duty-free in exchange for guarantees of exclusive American rights to Pearl Harbor, though no military facility was built there.[3]

After the United States annexed Hawai'i in 1898, the buildup of military fortifications began. Army and naval forces began arriving in Honolulu soon after 1900, first to man a series of forts constructed to protect Pearl Harbor. Fort Shafter opened in 1907; Schofield Barracks followed in 1909. The installation of a naval base at Pearl Harbor was finally authorized in 1908, but the fortification was not completed until 1919. In the interwar years, Pearl Harbor became home to an increasing portion of the Pacific Fleet, which was finally headquartered there in 1940. Military aviation grew in the 1920s and 1930s with the construction of a series of airfields, the largest of which, Hickam Field, opened in 1937. From 1925 to 1935, Hawai'i's military population was fairly stable, fluctuating between seventeen thousand and twenty thousand. Those numbers grew steadily by ten thousand over the ensuing five years.

Though the military presence in Hawai'i was substantial by 1940, the island territory had a much broader economic and political structure. It was no isolated military outpost and was in many ways as mature as the states on the mainland. The Organic Act of 1900, passed by Congress, created a territorial government for Hawai'i similar to those established on the mainland in the previous century. Following the pattern set in the Northwest Ordinance of 1787, the new mid-Pacific territory had an elected legislature and a territorial judiciary. The governor was appointed by the president of the United States, but the Organic Act required that an appointed governor be a resident of the islands. As in previous territories, the residents of Hawai'i could elect a voteless delegate to the U.S. House of Representatives. Though Congress held the right to veto territorial legislation, it never once used that authority. The federal government did acquire the title to certain public lands but delegated administration of those lands to the territory. As political scientist Norman Meller noted, "Once having established the broad frame of government for the territory, and after a few watchful ministrations during the initial years of the territory's life, Congress permitted the Territory to manage its own affairs."[4]

The normality of Hawai'i's political life was matched by its population growth and economic development. Hawai'i's population grew steadily each decade after annexation, from 154,000 in 1900 to 428,000 in 1940. Annexation spurred the islands' sugar production, which surged from its 1895 level of 150,000 tons to 426,000 tons by 1905 and then to one million tons annually by 1932. The Hawaiian Sugar Planters' Association (HSPA), organized in 1895, modernized the industry and established an experiment station to enhance crop yields by controlling insects and improving soils. Agriculture in Hawai'i was as scientifically advanced, if not more so, as in many mainland states.

Mainland journalists who visited the islands from 1910 to 1940 regularly commented on the advanced state of the sugar industry.

The pineapple industry was also a modern feature of Hawai'i's economy. James B. Dole arrived a year after annexation and began to raise pineapples on a small homestead. In 1901 he organized the Hawaiian Pineapple Company. Dole and other growers created the Hawaiian Pineapple Growers Association in 1908 and orchestrated a massive marketing and advertising campaign for "Hawaiian" pineapple on the mainland. Dole further revolutionized the canning of pineapple in the years 1911–13, when one of his employees, Henry Ginaca, designed and perfected a machine that could peel, core, and slice one hundred pineapples a minute. The production of pineapple, which stood at 1,893 cases of canned fruit in 1903, rose to one million cases by 1912 and to 4.5 million cases by 1930.

By the late 1930s the Hawaiian sugar and pineapple industries, as well as the shipping lines to the mainland, were controlled by a group of local companies known as the Big Five. These firms had begun their existence as general merchandise companies and then branched into sugar factoring. Though their specific function as factors was to provide supplies and services to the sugar plantations, the Big Five often used their profits to establish a controlling interest in the companies that owned the plantations. In addition they owned a refinery in Crockett, California, that refined the raw Hawaiian sugar shipped to the mainland. The Big Five's profits from sugar and pineapple remained in Hawai'i. Though still a territory, Hawai'i was not a colonial preserve of mainland corporations.

The growth of the sugar and pineapple industries so strengthened Hawai'i's economy that the territory generated substantial federal taxes. By 1940 statehood supporters proudly announced that from 1900 to 1937 Hawai'i had contributed $144 million more to the federal government than it received in benefits—a record matched by only sixteen mainland states in the same period.[5]

Given the maturity of Hawai'i's government and economy as well as its importance as a military base, why were mainland Americans in 1940 so indifferent—and among some elements so hostile—to its admission as a state or even to its defense as a part of the nation? The principal cause of concern to mainland Americans—particularly national politicians, labor unions, and the American military—was Hawai'i's predominantly Asian and Asian American population. Longstanding anti-Asian prejudice on the mainland by civilians as well as military fears of a subversive local population led to the hostile approach to statehood for Hawai'i.

The Ramifications of Hawai'i's "Different" Population

Hawai'i's population had taken on its Asian complexion before annexation. Asian workers, first Chinese and later Japanese, were recruited in the last quarter of the nineteenth century to man the islands' sugar industry. By 1900 the islands' population was 25.7 percent Hawaiian and part Hawaiian, and 17.3 percent Caucasian, including Portuguese immigrants as well as those of American ancestry. Chinese composed 16.7 percent of the population. Most important of all, the Japanese were the largest single group in Hawai'i at 39.7 percent. Between 1900 and 1940 the population grew, but with a new dynamic. Further Chinese immigration was halted after annexation because of the Chinese Exclusion Acts. The Chinese and Chinese American proportion of the islands' population dropped to 6.8 percent by 1940. Japanese immigrants continued to enter Hawai'i in the first decade of the 1900s. In 1907–08 a series of notes between the governments of the United States and Japan, sometimes called the Gentlemen's Agreement, limited further entry of male workers. Females continued to arrive until the Immigration Act of 1924 halted all Japanese immigration to the United States. Still, Japanese and Japanese Americans accounted for 37.3 percent of Hawai'i's population in 1940. The Philippines, acquired by the United States in 1898, was the principal new source of population after 1900. Filipinos, who were virtually unrepresented in Hawai'i in 1900, rose to 17 percent of the population by 1930 before declining to approximately 12.4 percent by 1940. By 1940 Caucasians comprised 23 percent of the population and Hawaiians or part-Hawaiians 15.2 percent. The growth of the American military had been the greatest source of increased Caucasian presence in Hawai'i.[6]

The makeup of Hawai'i's population had dramatic ramifications in shaping the islands' political electorate and posture. Federal law prohibited Asian immigrants from becoming naturalized; however, their children born in Hawai'i were American citizens who could vote upon reaching age twenty-one. As a result Hawaiians and Caucasians dominated the islands' electorate at the time of annexation. The Caucasian business elite—or "haoles" as they were called in the islands—generally controlled political life through their domination of the Republican Party, which held the majority in the territorial legislature before World War II. The appointed territorial governor often came from their ranks before the election of Franklin Roosevelt in 1932. The elected territorial delegate to Congress was usually Hawaiian or part-Hawaiian, the most noted of whom, Prince Jonah Kūhiō Kalaniana'ole, served from 1902 until 1922.[7]

During the late 1920s and the 1930s an increasing number of Chinese Americans and Japanese Americans, educated in the public schools of the territory, reached voting age and ran for public office. Yew Char became the first Chinese American elected to the territorial legislature in 1926. In 1930 the first Japanese Americans, Andy Yamashiro and Tasaku Oka, won seats in that body. Hiram Fong, who would later become the first U.S. senator of Chinese ancestry, was elected to the territorial house of representatives in 1938. By 1941 that thirty-member house contained two Chinese Americans and six Japanese Americans. The fifteen-member territorial senate had one Japanese American and one Chinese American. Most of the prewar Asian Americans in the legislature were members of the dominant Republican Party.[8]

Hawai'i's Asian and Asian American populations and their role in territorial political life were a constant source of comment by mainland journalists. As early as 1911 Progressive journalist Ray Stannard Baker wrote a series of articles on Hawai'i that described island politics as undemocratic because of the high proportion of disenfranchised Asians in the population. Baker and others also criticized the Caucasian business elite for recruiting these disenfranchised Asians and thus giving the haoles undue political influence. Baker thought the haoles and the Big Five had consciously restricted the immigration of Caucasian homesteaders in favor of the Asians to preserve their "semi-feudal" political power. Baker did, however, see glimmers of a brighter, more democratic future for the islands when the industrious Asian Americans reached voting age.[9]

Other mainlanders did not see such a bright Asian American future and criticized Baker for his optimism. President Theodore Roosevelt was an ardent proponent of Asian exclusion. He became particularly critical of Hawai'i during his presidency because Japanese immigrants often used the islands as a way station for migration to the mainland. He halted Japanese immigration from Hawai'i to the mainland a year before the Gentlemen's Agreement was enacted.

Labor activity also stoked mainland fears. Strikes by Japanese work-ers on the sugar plantations in 1909 and by Japanese and Filipino work-ers in 1920 particularly alarmed mainlanders. The strike of 1920 was particularly bitter. Despite an appeal by the Reverend Albert W. Palmer, minister of Honolulu's elite Central Union Church, for negotiations, the planters rejected any form of bargaining with the workers and launched a racially charged anti-Japanese campaign in the local news-papers. They linked the strike to a Japanese "plot" or "conspiracy" to take over the islands. Editorial cartoons in local newspapers displayed workers waving the Japanese flag in the fields.[10]

The planters prevailed in the 1920 strike, though they granted most of the strikers' demands once the labor action ended. However, their constant anti-Japanese rhetoric prompted mainland investigations of Hawai'i's "problems." By "screaming Jap" the haoles opened the door to more virulent anti-Japanese investigators from the U.S. military and the U.S. Congress. The onset of worker militancy in 1918 triggered the U.S. Army's concern with the "Japanese problem." The 1918 Merriam Report stressed the anti-Americanism of Hawai'i's Japanese population, particularly as evidenced by the lingering of Buddhism and Japanese lan-guage schools, and concluded that a national security problem existed.

In 1922 the congressionally appointed Hawaiian Labor Commission, composed of prominent mainland trade-union officials, visited the islands and reported that the domination of Hawai'i by alien Japanese posed a grave national problem. The commissioners claimed that white women lived in an atmosphere of fear, a theme that would reach epic proportions a decade later in the Massie rape case. The Hawaiian Labor Commission's report included yet another assessment by the military, the Summerall Report, that stressed the failure of acculturation among the Nisei, as the second-generation, or Hawai'i-born, Japanese Americans were called. The military again saw both the Nisei and their parents, known as the Issei, or first generation, as a threat to national security.

By the early 1930s the constant scrutiny of Hawai'i by the mainland press and the alarms raised by the military over the islands' racially mixed population began to threaten the islands' political and economic lead-ers. The local business elite had at first welcomed the generals and admi-rals with the confidence that they shared the same economic, political, and racial goals. Leading haole businessman Walter Dillingham amassed a fortune from the construction of military fortifications. Territorial del-egate Victor Houston, a part-Hawaiian, was an Annapolis graduate who had served for almost thirty years as a naval officer prior to his election to Congress in 1926. Given such a comfortable relationship, the haole business and political elite, including the HSPA, did not advocate statehood before the 1930s. Many thought that active political lobbying in Washington was sufficient to achieve the political advantages they desired. This method had proved effective in maintaining the equal treatment of Hawaiian sugar with mainland sugar for thirty years. They feared that further mainland scrutiny, which would inevitably come from congressional statehood hearings, might well jeopardize the economic and political status quo. The more the mainland looked at Hawai'i's multiracial population, the more likely it might be to limit or curtail territorial home rule.

Beginning in late 1931, island leaders began to change their views on the status quo and subsequently on statehood. In September of that year the military's oft-shouted concern for the safety of white women erupted into an island scandal, the Massie-Fortescue murder trial or Massie rape case. This sensational case focused the attention of the mainland on Hawai'i and attracted America's most prominent lawyer, Clarence Darrow. The Massie case would be a watershed in both the internal history of Hawai'i and the territory's relation to the mainland. It would launch the statehood movement. As such it deserves a closer look.[11]

The Massie Case and the Intrusion of the Mainland

The safety of the white woman in question was that of Mrs. Thalia Massie, the twenty-year-old wife of a naval lieutenant stationed at Pearl Harbor. On the evening of September 12, 1931, Mrs. Massie left the Ala Wai Inn near Waikiki unaccompanied, evidently becoming bored with the party she and her husband were attending. Whether she wanted some air or whether she intended to walk home is unclear. Several hours later she was picked up on the side of a road, battered and bruised, by helpful motorists who took her home. She later told her husband that she had first been abducted by a group of "local boys" in a car, raped, and then left on the side of the road. Coincidentally the Honolulu police had taken five young men—two Japanese, two Hawaiians, and a Chinese Hawaiian—into custody that evening for an argument and fistfight with a motorist in another part of town. Mrs. Massie eventually identified four of these five men as her abductors. All five were brought to court in November for the first of two trials involved in the drama.

Throughout the first trial there was always doubt about Mrs. Massie's testimony. The only certain evidence was that she had been beaten. It was not clear that she had been raped, that she had been attacked by any of the five men on trial, or that she had been attacked by "local boys" at all. There was always the suspicion that someone from the party had followed her when she left the inn. There were also questions about the accuracy and techniques of the police investigation and interrogation. The number of suspects Mrs. Massie could identify increased as the police talked with her. For these reasons and because of conflicting testimony at the first trial, the all-male jury, composed of six part-Hawaiians, one haole, one Portuguese, two Chinese, and two Japanese, could not reach a verdict. The case against the five men was declared a mistrial. The suspects were released on bail awaiting a new trial.

The navy and its local commandant, Admiral Yates Stirling, reacted bitterly to the mistrial. For the admiral, Hawai'i was no longer the paradise of the Pacific but a primordial jungle where white women were subject to wanton racial attack and where the local police proved inadequate for their job. The navy suggested replacing the territorial government with a commission containing military representation. Walter Dillingham added what seemed to be local support to these assertions by calling for a reorganization of the police department. Matters might have rested with the racial rhetoric of the navy and a few conservative haoles had this remained a Honolulu affair. But Hawai'i was not insulated from the mainland. Mainland newspapers carried sensational coverage of the trial. Events in Honolulu were also complicated by Thalia Massie's mother, Mrs. Grace Bell Fortescue of Washington, D.C., who arrived in Hawai'i shortly after the attack on her daughter. The local haoles would soon have trouble controlling both the navy and Mrs. Fortescue.

In the weeks following the mistrial, the navy and then Mrs. Fortescue took matters into their own hands. Operating under the impression that the only way to convict the "boys" was to obtain a confession, several navy men kidnapped one of the suspects, Horace Ida, and beat him in a cane field. No confession was forthcoming. The vigilante impulse gained force in the ensuing weeks. In early January 1932 Mrs. Fortescue, Lt. Thomas Massie, and two other navy men kidnapped another of the suspects, native Hawaiian Joseph Kahahawai, and took him to Mrs. Fortescue's rented house to obtain a confession. During the interrogation, supposedly after Kahahawai had offered a confession, a shot was fired and Kahahawai was killed. The four Caucasians then wrapped his body in canvas and departed by car for the shore to dispose of the evidence. En route to the sea the car was stopped by Honolulu police on a tip following the kidnapping. The police quickly discovered the body and charged the four with second-degree murder. Though Lt. Massie accepted responsibility for firing the pistol, all four were placed on trial for conspiracy to commit murder. For their defense Mrs. Fortescue hired Clarence Darrow for a $40,000 retainer raised with personal funds and a collection taken at Pearl Harbor. Darrow arrived in late March and the second, or Massie-Fortescue, trial began in early April 1932.

Darrow was an "outsider," a mainlander who came to Hawai'i to defend other mainlanders against islanders. Like many who came before him, he saw himself as a benevolent outsider—one who sincerely tried to understand, albeit imperfectly, what he experienced. Despite his good intentions he emerged baffled—sometimes enchanted, sometimes tormented—by what he found. Darrow's presence and conduct in Honolulu were in many ways symbolic of the mainland's perception of Hawai'i. His observations show how even one of the most enlightened mainland minds still found the territory inscrutable in the decade before World War II. In the opening lines of his account of the trial Darrow mused, "Many times I have been asked why I went to Honolulu. I was not sure then, and am not sure now. I had never been to that part of the Pacific." The Chicago attorney's uncertainty about his presence in Hawai'i increased as the trial began.[12]

Once in court, Darrow presented a "temporary insanity" defense for Lt. Massie with an array of psychiatric experts, not unlike his dazzling Chicago defense in the Leopold-Loeb case of 1924. The drama of the case and its connection to the mainland were heightened with the transoceanic broadcast of Darrow's summation to the jury, the first live radio transmission between Hawai'i and the West Coast. To counter Darrow, the prosecution offered its own psychiatric witnesses who claimed Massie was quite sane, even though distraught. The jury for the Massie-Fortescue trial, composed of six haoles, one Portuguese, two Chinese, and three part-Hawaiians, was considerably more "white" than the hung jury in the first trial. Nonetheless, the jury did not agree with Darrow and convicted the four Caucasian defendants of manslaughter with a recommendation of leniency. In May 1932 Judge Charles Davis, a Caucasian of New England background, sentenced the defendants to ten years at hard labor.

The territory and its court system had handled this racially explosive issue. A racially mixed jury had convicted three white men and a white woman of a crime against a young Hawaiian. A Caucasian judge had sentenced them. The mainland, however, could not handle this level of justice in Hawai'i. The navy, the mainland press, and numerous members of the U.S. Congress were outraged. Territorial Governor Lawrence Judd was barraged with telegrams demanding that he pardon the four. Fearing congressional retaliation if he did nothing, Judd decided to commute the sentences from ten years at hard labor to "one hour" to be served in his office. He did not yield to the demands of Darrow, the mainland press, and numerous congressmen for pardons. The commutation sustained the conviction of guilt.

The Massies and Mrs. Fortescue, as well as Darrow, left the islands a few days after the sentence was commuted. The earlier case against the local "boys" that had ended in a mistrial was dismissed because of the absence of the victim, Thalia Massie. Soon after his return to the mainland the Chicago lawyer tried to make sense of the happenings in Hawai'i. Darrow claimed he was quite fond of the islands and wanted to blunt the violent racial image of Hawai'i being portrayed in the mainland press as well as any continued conservative reaction from Washington. He quickly wrote a new chapter on the Massie case that was appended to his recently published autobiography, *The Story of My Life* (1932). In it Darrow tried to counter the image of Hawai'i that he thought dominated the mainland mind. "However much one may read of Hawaii," he explained, "the stranger is apt to think of these islands as a foreign and uncivilized territory; to most people in all ages the words foreign and uncivilized mean much the same thing. But, aside from the greater number of brown people that one notices, there is no striking difference between the residents of Hawaii and ourselves." Darrow went on to describe the excellent condition of Hawai'i's schools and pictured Honolulu as a modern American city.[13]

But it was that initial description of the color of the people that Darrow, a man who considered himself free of racial prejudice, could not come to terms with. During the trial he could not free himself from the equation of race and citizenship. Darrow said of the five islanders accused of attacking Mrs. Massie: "None . . . were Americans. One was a Hawaiian and the others were of mixed blood." The diverse racial mixture of the population caused him further consternation with the court and the jury. He was quick to point out the fairness of the court as well as the Caucasian background and mainland training of the judge. But he was totally perplexed by the multiracial jury that rejected his insanity plea. To explain the jury's verdict, Darrow reverted to some of the most tortured logic for a man who claimed he had no racial feelings. "Our clients were white," he reasoned, "and a white jury no doubt would have acquitted them . . . I believe the brown members wanted to be fair; there were Chinamen in the jury box, and Japanese, and Hawaiian and mixed bloods; it was not easy to guess what they were thinking about, if anything at all. Obviously, they do not think as we do, about our side of a situation." In Honolulu the Chicago lawyer saw what looked to him like an American court, but one that did not respond to him in the manner of those courts he knew. Despite his attempts at objectivity, Hawai'i remained a different and strange part of America to Clarence Darrow.[14]

Darrow's confused explanation of Hawai'i did little to assuage passions in the islands or on the mainland. Many Asians and Hawaiians were outraged at the commutation of the sentence. They compared the treatment of the Massies and Mrs. Fortescue to the earlier saga of Myles Fukunaga, a young Japanese man under emotional stress who kidnapped and killed a Caucasian boy in 1928. After being tried and convicted, Fukunaga was hanged in 1929, despite appeals to governor Judd for clemency based on Fukunaga's mental state. Many islanders claimed the haole-dominated legal system was unfair and racially biased. But it was not the territorial court that had been unfair. It was the intrusion of the mainland that forced a commutation of the sentence. And that intrusion would not stop in 1932. Soon it would be the haoles, as well as the Asians and Hawaiians, who were outraged.

If Hawai'i was still different and strange to the liberal mind of Clarence Darrow, it was totally out of bounds to the more conservative mainland mind that included the navy and substantial portions of the U.S. Congress. A territory that could convict a white woman of kidnapping and killing a Hawaiian was, in their minds, totally out of control and incapable of governing itself. While the furor over the commutation continued, the report of U.S. Assistant Attorney Seth Richardson appeared. Richardson had been sent to Hawai'i in January 1932 at the request of the U.S. Senate to investigate law enforcement procedures in Hawai'i.[15]

Richardson's report muted the hysteria of the navy and found Hawai'i a law-abiding community that was in no way under the spell of a racial crime wave. Nonetheless, Richardson criticized the police and law enforcement agencies in the territory. Though territorial governor Judd and other island leaders had already recognized this problem, Richardson downplayed territorial efforts at reform and called for greater federal intervention and appointment in island affairs. Among other suggestions, he proposed presidential appointment of the then-elected territorial attorney general, removal of the local residency requirement for the governor, and consolidation of federal and territorial courts. While he stopped short of recommending a military commission or the imposition of martial law, Richardson clearly reinforced the momentum toward greater federal control in the islands.

Richardson's recommendations as well as the more extreme measures advocated by the navy found expression in a number of bills presented in the U.S. Congress in the last months of 1932. A proposal for a military commission was presented in the Senate by Connecticut Republican Hiram Bingham, a grandson of the first missionary leader to Hawai'i and himself born and educated in Hawai'i.

It was now time for the haoles to be alarmed. They had allied with the military for years in controlling the islands. A few had even cooperated in stoking the navy's outrage over the Massie case. But their quest for control in no way included handing over the islands to mainland rule via either the military or the Congress. The congressional attack was particularly vexing because Hawai'i had been virtually immune from congressional interference since 1900. For the first time in over thirty years the "colonial" aspects of territorial status were brought home to the haoles.

The change in national administration from Republican to Democrat after the elections of 1932 did not blunt the national attack on Hawai'i. Even the election of local Democrat Lincoln McCandless as territorial delegate did little to assuage the Congress or the new president. Soon after taking office, President Franklin Roosevelt backed Richardson's recommendation to remove the residency requirement for the governor and other appointed territorial offices. These recommendations were incorporated in the Rankin Bill sponsored by Mississippi Democrat John Rankin. The bill passed the U.S. House of Representatives in 1933. A bipartisan group of islanders, soon called the Home Rule Committee, organized to oppose the Rankin Bill. Opposition in the Senate killed the legislation in the upper house. Roosevelt withdrew the bill from further consideration.

The move to change the territorial government lost ground for the moment. Even the hysteria of the navy abated somewhat in 1933 with the transfer of Admiral Yates Stirling to New York and the appointment of Admiral Henry Yarnell in Hawai'i. But Hawai'i's problems were not over. A year later Congress intruded again and reconfirmed the potential "colonial" dependency of the islands on the mainland.

The Attack on Sugar and the Move toward Statehood

As part of Roosevelt's New Deal agricultural policy Congress passed the Jones-Costigan Act in 1934. The act created quotas for sugar production throughout the United States, but placed Hawai'i in a category with foreign producers that lowered the amount of sugar it could send to the mainland by about 8 to 10 percent. Mainland discrimination against Hawaiian sugar galvanized the political posture of the haoles. Annexation had supposedly freed Hawai'i from the vagaries of import quotas and treaty restrictions by making the islands a part of the United States. Was the territory of Hawai'i not still a part of the United States in 1934?

In July 1934 President Roosevelt visited Hawai'i for the first time and called the territory an "integral part of the nation." But the chief executive's words had little impact on Secretary of Agriculture Henry A. Wallace. The territory challenged the Jones-Costigan Act in the Superior Court of the District of Columbia, but Wallace spoke against Hawai'i. The court ruled in October 1934 that Hawai'i was a part of the United States, but that a territory was totally under the power of Congress, which included the power to pass discriminatory legislation against it. Alarm bells went off in the islands. The threat of a commission government and now discrimination against Hawaiian sugar caused the ruling haoles to rethink many of their previous political assumptions. A compromise agreement with the Department of Agriculture raised Hawai'i's sugar quota and averted the immediate crisis. Nonetheless, the islands could not risk future congressional action. The harmful power of the national capital was now abundantly clear. Neither a voteless delegate in Congress, Republican or Democrat, nor elegant entertaining in Washington by the HSPA could protect Hawai'i. Something had to be done.

In a dramatic turnaround from their previous position, the sugar planters and other haole leaders suddenly advocated statehood as the only way to prevent discrimination against the islands. The change in position was indeed abrupt. As late as 1927 Lorrin A. Thurston, the leader of the 1893 overthrow of the Hawaiian monarchy and now publisher of the *Honolulu Advertiser,* announced, "Hawaii needs statehood as much as a cat needs two tails." But in the fall of 1934 Samuel Wilder King, the Republican candidate for territorial delegate to Congress, pledged to win equal rights for Hawai'i and eventual statehood. King, a part Hawaiian from an old island family, had served fourteen years as a naval officer before returning to Hawai'i to run a real estate business and sit on the Honolulu Board of Supervisors. The Republican challenger solidly beat Democrat McCandless, who was now seventy-five and at odds with a portion of his party. In 1935 King arrived in Washington with statehood legislation in hand and the public support of the HSPA.[16]

The transition from the stance of Thurston in 1927 to that of King in 1934–35 signaled the arrival of a new generation of Republican political leaders with a more outward-looking political posture who would champion statehood. The local elections of 1934 brought Joseph Farrington, the son of former territorial governor Wallace Farrington (1921–29), to the territorial legislature, where he supported statehood. He would later take the statehood cause to Washington, where he succeeded King as territorial delegate in 1943. Joseph Farrington's advocacy of statehood represented not only local desires, but also the influence of mainland political values on the islands. The new legislator's political education had been shaped outside, as well as inside, Hawai'i.

The Farringtons were not an old island family. Wallace Farrington first came to Honolulu in 1895 as editor of the pro-annexationist *Pacific Commercial Advertiser.* He and his wife returned to the mainland in 1897, and their son Joseph was born that year in Washington, D.C. The family came back to Honolulu in 1898, and Wallace became managing editor and later owner of the *Honolulu Star-Bulletin.* Farrington became active in the Republican Party, and in 1921 President Harding appointed him territorial governor. Some accounts indicate that he foresaw eventual statehood, with Hawai'i's multiracial population forming a true American community. But in the first three decades of the new century there was little ground in which the newspaper publisher/governor could plant statehood seeds.

Wallace Farrington was certainly an influence on his son, but not the only one. After finishing the local Punahou School in 1915, Joe Farrington entered the University of Wisconsin and graduated in 1919. According to his wife, Elizabeth, whom he met in Madison, it was in Wisconsin that Joe's political views were substantially molded and directed toward statehood. Farrington roomed with Philip La Follette, who became governor of Wisconsin in the 1930s. Philip was the son of Robert La Follette, Wisconsin's famous Progressive governor and U.S. senator, and the brother of Robert La Follette Jr., who succeeded his father to the Senate in 1925 and served there until 1947. Mrs. Farrington explained in a 1978 interview that her husband's awakening to statehood stemmed from the liberalism he discovered in Wisconsin, not from his father's views in Honolulu. "It was the influence of the La Follettes more than anything else, and old Senator La Follette," said Mrs. Farrington. "[I]t was the liberal idea that every citizen who paid taxes had a right to vote and all this, and be a first-class citizen and all." According to Mrs. Farrington, statehood was clearly on Joe's mind when he proposed marriage to her in 1917. He told his future wife to carefully consider his offer because "there will be many times in my life I'll have to sacrifice you and the children we hope to have for the cause of statehood, because I'm dedicating my life to it. And I want you to know that and think it over." Betty thought about it until 1920, when the two were married in Washington, where both Farringtons worked as congressional correspondents. With two children adopted on the mainland, the new family shaped by Wisconsin and the nation's capital returned to Honolulu in 1924.[17]

Back in Hawai'i, the governor's son became managing editor of the *Star-Bulletin*, a post he held at the outbreak of the Massie trial. The repercussions of the trial launched Joe Farrington's political career and his public advocacy of statehood. In 1932 Farrington became executive secretary for the Hawaii Legislative Commission, a committee appointed by the territorial legislature to oppose the recommendations in the Richardson report. When those recommendations emerged the next year in the Rankin Bill, Farrington helped organize a home rule group to oppose the legislation in Congress. His close connection to the La Follettes was no doubt helpful in securing the bill's defeat in the Senate, where Robert La Follette Jr. was one of its principal opponents. While Farrington warred against the Rankin Bill, his father died in October 1933. Joe became publisher of the *Star-Bulletin* in 1934 and decided to run for the territorial senate on the platform that "ultimately the territory will realize its ambition to become a state."[18]

With Farrington's election to the territorial senate and King's election as territorial delegate, the modern statehood movement was born.

King began his term in Congress by introducing statehood legislation. This was not the first time a Hawai'i statehood bill had entered Congress. Prince Kūhiō had introduced the first bill in 1919 and again in 1920. Victor Houston followed suit in 1931, as did Lincoln McCandless in 1934. But King's bill was the first to have the backing of Hawai'i's political and economic establishment, including the support of the HSPA. And it was the first Hawai'i statehood bill that did not vanish in congressional committee. In 1935 the House of Representatives scheduled the first hearings on statehood for Hawai'i and sent a delegation to Honolulu.

While King pursued statehood in the Congress, Farrington moved the territorial legislature to action. In 1935 the legislature created the Hawaii Equal Rights Commission to push for equal treatment of Hawai'i, oppose discriminatory federal legislation, and study "all aspects of statehood for Hawaii and the advantages of submitting the issue to a plebiscite at some future date." The 1935 legislature also passed a concurrent resolution asking Congress for statehood. The territorial impetus for statehood had thus begun. The Equal Rights Commission later became the Hawaii Statehood Commission and functioned without interruption until the eventual granting of statehood in 1959.

Progress at the national level was halting at best. President Roosevelt announced his opposition to statehood even as the first congressional hearings began. The subcommittee that visited Hawai'i in October 1935 expressed concern about the islands' Japanese population and did not recommend further congressional action. It did say the issue of statehood should continue to be studied. Reelected delegate in 1936, King pushed for statehood legislation in Congress during 1937. Later that year a joint congressional committee visited Hawai'i. The committee confirmed Hawai'i's deserving status and noted that it had "fulfilled every requirement for statehood heretofore exacted of territories." With war clouds in the Pacific becoming an increasing national concern, Hawai'i's Japanese population was still a problem for the visiting congressmen, particularly for Representative Rankin. The committee recommended no further congressional action, but suggested that a plebiscite be held to determine the true interest of islanders in statehood.[19]

The proposal for a plebiscite gained the backing of the Hawaii Equal Rights Commission in 1938. The next year Joe Farrington championed passage of a bill in the territorial legislature to authorize the plebiscite for the general election in November 1940. When the vote was in, statehood carried 46,174 to 22,428, a 2–1 margin. Hawai'i was ready to join the union, but as the polls and surveys conducted by Gallup and *Fortune* revealed, the nation was not ready for Hawai'i. Despite Hawai'i's modern economy and stable government, the alarms sounded by the military and the headlines spawned by mainlanders such as Clarence Darrow in the decade before Pearl Harbor left many Americans confused and unsure of the island territory. Hawai'i had indeed become a military Gibraltar. But mainlanders were still unsure if it was a Gibraltar worth defending, much less worth admitting as a state. It would take a global war for them to get to know Hawai'i better.

Chapter 2
Alaska: A Land without People

Alaska has always seemed like a frozen waste, a continental dead end.

—*Jean Potter, describing Alaska in 1941*

I f mainland Americans were unsure of Hawai'i in 1940–41, they had little or no basis for making any judgment at all about Alaska. The northern territory had largely escaped their notice in the decade before the war. Just before the outbreak of war in 1941 *Fortune* writer Jean Potter took the steamship *S.S. Mt. McKinley* to Alaska to see the recently deployed military installations there. She described her trip as a veritable voyage into the unknown: "Lying up at the top of North America, Alaska has always seemed like a frozen waste, a continental dead end. It led nowhere, and, to most Americans, it seemed in itself a kind of nowhere." She said she wanted to help answer the questions that people all over America were asking: "What have we got up there, anyway? What kind of country is it to fight in? to live in? What kind of people are the Alaskans? What does Alaska need from us, and how can we use it to help win the war?"[1]

When she arrived, she quickly found that Alaska was becoming as armed a fortress in the North as Hawai'i was in the mid-Pacific. In fact, most of Potter's fellow passengers on the steamship were construction workers headed north to build those fortifications. By the time Potter completed her book in July 1942 she estimated that military appropriations to Alaska had reached $200 million. Unlike Hawai'i, the northern military buildup had not taken place over the preceding four decades, but literally over the preceding two years! In 1939 there were only 524 military personnel in the territory, and the first substantial defense appropriation was not made until the spring of 1940. Potter saw this as a blatant example of federal neglect, noting, "The neglect of Alaska in the decades following World War I presents a startling contrast to the attention meted out to the island of Hawaii, which was strongly fortified in the years when Alaska, even closer to Japan, was left without means of defense."[2]

If Alaska's military fortifications had been neglected for decades, Potter found other aspects of Alaska's political and economic life in an equally underdeveloped state. She was struck with the fact that most of the people she saw were either newly arrived construction workers or soldiers. The Alaska they came to was, in her words, "a land without people," with virtually no permanent residents. In fact, the 1940 census placed the territory's population at only 72,524.

For Potter, transportation was equally stunted. Alaska could be reached only by sea or air. This fact led her to describe the territory as an "island" that was "as insular as the Philippines." Though she noted the railroad link between Fairbanks and Anchorage, the transportation system that most attracted her attention was the emerging aviation system, even if aviation facilities were still primitive in 1941. She saw Fairbanks not as a future railroad mecca but as having the potential to be "one of the leading air stations in the world." Given the weak transportation system, Potter found the territory's economic resources largely undeveloped. Prophetically, she noted that Alaska's most significant undeveloped resource was oil.[3]

Turning to government, the *Fortune* writer emphasized the dominant federal presence in contrast to the weakness of the local territorial government. She saw "imposing" federal buildings and above all the federally owned Alaska Railroad as the evidence of this commanding presence. Alaskans, she observed, detested the way some federal officials, particularly Interior Secretary Harold Ickes, had treated the territory and mismanaged the railroad. Alaskans themselves, however, were responsible for the weakness of the territorial government. The territorial legislature was small and under the influence of lobbyists for absentee-owned businesses. It had passed little legislation of benefit to the population and lacked a modern tax structure, personal or corporate. Alaska had no income tax; Hawai'i had adopted one in 1901. The light tax structure was a product of pressure from both the outside interests that wanted to keep taxes low and from the Alaskan population that did not want to tax itself at all. According to Potter, "Considering the unstable pattern of the Alaskan economic scene, it is hardly surprising that political maturity has not been achieved." She did observe that the federally appointed territorial governor, Ernest Gruening, was trying to bring a modern government and tax structure to Alaska, though the legislature and the population in general disliked him.[4]

The misunderstood "land without people" that Potter found in 1941 was certainly a contrast to the more economically and politically mature territory of Hawai'i that had just held a plebiscite endorsing statehood. Just why was Alaska so backward as both a civilian entity and a military fortification in 1941? Why had Alaska's past left so little impression on the American mind after almost seventy-five years under the U.S. flag?

An Absentee District with Golden Promises, 1867–1912

Though Alaska may well have been "misunderstood" by the vast bulk of the American population, it was not unknown. Most Americans in 1941 knew that the United States had purchased Alaska from Russia sometime after the Civil War, though they probably had been taught in school that the Alaska Purchase of 1867 was known as "Seward's Folly." The persistence of the image of folly had a basis in reality that was carefully cultivated in the first decades after the purchase.

Despite an initial public enthusiasm that Alaska would boom, the northern land quickly languished soon after the purchase. Up to a thousand boomers flocked to Sitka in the summer of 1867, but most were gone a year later. Fewer than four hundred Americans could be found there by 1869, a year when the total native population of Alaska numbered approximately thirty thousand. Given the smallness of the American population, the federal government decided not to create a territorial government but to make Alaska a customs and military district under the control of the U.S. Army.

Though American boomers and would-be settlers failed to establish a strong presence, American companies, usually San Francisco–based, did come north. A group of investors bought the old Russian-American Company that had run the Russian colony and formed the Alaska Commercial Company (ACC) in 1868. The ACC secured a twenty-year monopoly on the Pribilof Islands fur seal trade in 1870 from the federal government. It also established a series of trading sites along the Yukon River. Over the ensuing twenty years the San Francisco company earned substantial profits for its investors while developing a position on the political development of Alaska that bred a permanent tension between absentee-owned companies and local boosters. Using natives as its labor supply, the ACC had no need to stimulate Caucasian migration or to

encourage further governmental organization. The former could disrupt the fur trade, and the latter might lead to local taxation and regulation. In public reports and testimony before Congress, the company,
with the aid of U.S. Treasury agent Henry Wood Elliott, pictured Alaska
as an undeveloped area that was not in need of territorial government.
While Elliott and the ACC enhanced the iceberg image of Alaska in the
1870s and 1880s, American settlers blamed the company and the federal
government for "neglecting" Alaska, a theme that would be repeated
many times before—and after—1940.[5]

The pattern begun by the ACC in the fur trade was quickly dupli-
cated by other San Francisco companies in the salmon canning industry. Alaska's abundant fisheries attracted the first cannery to Klawock in
southeastern Alaska in 1878. The canning industry spread from the
southeast to central and western Alaska in the 1880s and 1890s. The
number of cases of canned salmon increased dramatically, from 8,977
cases in 1881 to 719,196 cases eight years later. By the mid-1890s, 90
percent of all canneries in Alaska were controlled by the San
Francisco–based Alaska Packers Association.

Alaska's small population influenced the canners in a number of
ways. The companies initially used local labor, both native and
Caucasian, as fishermen and cannery workers. But the overall labor
shortage caused them to import seasonal employees from San Francisco
and other Pacific ports who returned home after the two- to three-
month canning season. Thus the growth of the canned salmon industry, like the fur seal trade, did not lead to increased settlement and
population growth. Like the ACC, the San Francisco salmon packers
emerged as a self-sufficient operation opposed to any local political
development that might spell increased taxation or regulation. From the
1880s onward "absentee companies" came to characterize Alaska's development, much in contrast to the locally owned sugar companies in
Hawai'i. It should be noted that absentee companies did not displace
or drive out preexisting local companies. There simply were no locally
owned enterprises when Alaska was purchased from Russia. The old
Russian-American Company departed with the Russians.[6]

In the first fifteen years of American rule, economic development in
Alaska occurred without the usual accompaniment of population growth
and political organization. The 1880 census, though disputed by some,
estimated Alaska's population at only 33,426, of whom only 430 were
Caucasian. Alaska began to grow in the early 1880s with the discovery

of gold in southeastern Alaska. Two miners, Joe Juneau and Frank Harris, established a camp at a spot known as Gold Creek, which soon became the town of Juneau. The Juneau gold rush brought several hundred Caucasian settlers north, who began clamoring for governmental organization. The successful push for such organization, however, came not so much from the miners' demands as from Presbyterian missionary Sheldon Jackson. Jackson was concerned with providing protection for Alaska's native population from any potentially harmful effects the mining population might bring. He did not want Alaska natives to suffer the fatalities that befell California Indians in the gold rush of 1848–50. Jackson's work for Alaska was primarily carried on in the nation's capital, where he secured the passage of the First Organic Act in 1884.

The 1884 legislation did not create a territory. Alaska's settler population in 1883–84 was still less than two thousand. The Juneau gold strike was not the equivalent of the Comstock Lode that had propelled Nevada to territorial status twenty-five years earlier. Instead Alaska remained a district, but now a civil, judicial, and land district rather than the previous customs and military district. It would have an appointed governor, a district court with a judge and district attorney, a marshal with four deputies, and a set of four U.S. commissioners who would act as justices of the peace.

The Organic Act did not create a legislature with lawmaking powers. The general laws of Oregon formed the civil and criminal code for Alaska. Federal mining laws were extended to the district, but other American land laws were still not operative in Alaska. This situation meant that private individuals could not own land, and town sites could not be legally established. There was no power to incorporate municipalities or to levy taxes. The latter provision—or omission—was agreeable to the San Francisco companies that dominated the economy of the district. Jackson's stamp on the Organic Act was evident in the guarantee of land to native missions and the provision that natives would not be disturbed in their current occupation of land. Jackson hoped the act would attract the better sort of settler in contrast to the miner element who made up the bulk of Alaska's Caucasian population. Most miners and local politicians did not like the Organic Act. Alfred Swineford, the first federally appointed district governor, asserted that the lack of land laws and full home rule inhibited Alaska's economic development and population growth. Ernest Gruening would later call the 1884 Organic Act proof of the federal government's "flagrant neglect" of Alaska and of its lack of "curiosity or interest" in an "area one-fifth as large as the United States."[7]

Actually the federal government was quite curious about the northern land in the 1880s. Before and after the passage of the Organic Act, the army extensively mapped Alaska. In 1883 Lt. Frederick Schwatka navigated the full length of the Yukon River. His voyage was widely publicized in national magazines. In the summer of 1885 Lt. Henry Allen explored the Copper River as well as the Tanana and Koyukuk Rivers. Allen's 1887 report added to the interest in Alaska stimulated by Schwatka and was a readable guide that hastened further exploration of the interior. Tourists as well as military explorers were attracted to Alaska. In 1890 some five thousand tourists came north, more than the estimated Caucasian population of 4,298.

While Alaska's permanent population did not grow substantially in the 1880s or early 1890s, the curiosity stimulated by the Juneau gold strike and the ensuing federal explorations led to the arrival of even more miners, who ventured farther into the interior of Alaska to look for the next great strike. By 1886 over two hundred miners had entered the Yukon River Valley. In that year gold was discovered at Forty Mile on the Canadian side of the U.S./Canada border. Other mining strikes took place in Alaska along the Yukon at Circle City in 1893-94 and at Rampart in 1896. Finally the big strike that would rival California or the Comstock Lode came in mid-August 1896, when George Washington Carmack and his native companions, Skookum Jim and Tagish Charley, found gold at Bonanza Creek in the Canadian Klondike, a tributary of the Yukon. Miners from Circle City and Forty Mile flocked to the new find in the fall and winter of 1896 and founded Dawson City. In the early summer of 1897 they sailed out with their gold. In July of that year two ships, the *Portland* and the *Excelsior,* arrived respectively in Seattle and San Francisco with news and golden evidence of the Klondike. Within a few weeks of the ships' arrival, thousands of young adventurers, including novelist Jack London and gunfighter Wyatt Earp, headed north on steamers.

In the years 1897 and 1898 an estimated sixty thousand to one hundred thousand people, predominantly Caucasian males, headed for the Klondike; some forty thousand actually arrived. Though the Klondike was in Canada, it could be reached principally through Alaska. The majority of the argonauts took the steamer route up from Seattle or San Francisco to southeastern Alaska and entered the Klondike by climbing the Chilkoot or White passes. The settlements of Skagway and Dyea boomed to service, and in many cases exploit, the travelers. Other adventurers took the longer but less arduous all-water route by sailing to the western coast of Alaska and then traveling up the Yukon for 1,700 miles from St. Michael to Dawson.[8]

Most of the Klondike's riches had been claimed by the time the argonauts of 1897 and 1898 arrived. As the fortune hunters left the Klondike and sought better diggings, they provided a ready population when gold was discovered in 1898 and 1899 on the creeks and coastal beaches of Alaska's Seward Peninsula at a spot to be named Nome. In 1899 gold worth $2.8 million was found in Nome; a year later the sum rose above $4 million. By 1900 Nome's prospector population far surpassed that of Juneau, where gold mining was now a heavily industrial hard-rock operation. Nome boasted 12,488 people that year—three times the total Caucasian population of Alaska in 1890. Alaska's 1900 population rose to 63,592, of whom 30,450 were Caucasians. The total was only a little less than what Jean Potter would find in 1941.

The Klondike boom and its spillover into Alaska caught the attention of the federal government and the American people as nothing in the North had done before. The national government began to treat Alaska like other western territories. The number of judicial districts grew from one to three with courts located at Juneau, St. Michael, and Eagle City, a Yukon River settlement on the U.S./Canada border spawned by yet another gold discovery in 1898. Federal legislation allowed municipalities to incorporate, thus giving towns the power to levy property taxes. The extension of the Homestead Act to Alaska made it possible for individuals to gain title to land. A limited form of taxation to pay the expenses of the expanded government was established in the form of license fees and a four-cents-a-case tax on canned salmon. The San Francisco–based salmon industry agreed to this mild form of taxation to bring limited federal regulation and order to the expanding industry. Congress also authorized the transfer of the district capital from Sitka to Juneau in 1905, a symbolic move that signified a shift away from the old roots of Russian America and Sheldon Jackson's missionary community to a new American mining and business community. In 1906 Alaskans were allowed to elect a voteless delegate to Congress, and the old "district" was renamed a "territory," though it still lacked a legislature. Added to these congressional measures was the earlier appointment of John Green Brady as territorial governor in 1897.

Brady, a Presbyterian missionary who came to Alaska in 1878 and then became a merchant, represented the "right sort" of Alaska settler who could bring stability to the new territory and lead it forward.

Enhanced activity by the U.S. Army also increased with the spillover of the Klondike gold rush into Alaska. To bring order to the booming mining camps of the interior, the army established a set of forts along the Yukon River from St. Michael to Eagle, and near the south central and southeastern gateways to the Yukon at Valdez on Prince William Sound and at Haines near Skagway. The army's presence spurred the federally financed construction of a telegraph system to connect the forts and towns with each other and then with the outside via a submarine cable to Seattle. The Washington-Alaska Military Cable and Telegraph System (WAMCATS) was a monumental engineering feat and clearly ranked as one of the major federal projects in the American West. Between 1900 and 1903 army crews successfully completed the 1,500-mile line between St. Michael and Eagle and then down to Valdez. A year later the marine cable linked Valdez to Seattle. A young army officer who surveyed and constructed much of the route, Lt. William "Billy" Mitchell, would never forget Alaska. After a distinguished career in World War I, he became a major advocate of expanded U.S. air power and of the use of Alaska as a strategic air defense installation.

As the twentieth century progressed, it appeared that the northern boom would go on forever and usher in a permanent era of prosperity and development for Alaska. The Yukon Valley and its tributaries continued to produce new gold discoveries. In 1902 Felix Pedro found gold in the Tanana Valley near a spot on the Chena River where merchant E. T. Barnette had gotten stuck the previous winter while trying to navigate his way from St. Michael up the Yukon and Tanana Rivers. Barnette decided to start a settlement there that was soon named Fairbanks for Charles W. Fairbanks, a U.S. senator from Indiana who was elected vice president of the United States in 1904. In 1903 Fairbanks boasted a population of 1,200 and became the seat of the third district federal court, which relocated there from Eagle. By 1905 Fairbanks supplanted Nome as the largest city in Alaska. In 1906 the mineral output of these two far northern towns, along with the mines of Juneau and neighboring Douglas Island, made Alaska the second largest gold producing region of the United States after Colorado. From Nome to Fairbanks to Eagle and Circle City, the Yukon and Tanana Valleys became the new centers of Alaska's population. There was even talk in Fairbanks that agriculture could flourish and attract an ever-increasing population, with some booster estimates rising into the millions.

Outside investors found limitless opportunities in Alaska in the new century. Proposals for railway projects abounded, particularly after the successful completion in 1899–1900 of the British-financed White Pass and Yukon Railway linking Skagway and the Canadian Yukon. In 1906 New York investors led by the Morgan-Guggenheim interests formed the Alaska Syndicate. The syndicate planned to develop the copper deposits its investors had acquired in the Copper River Valley north of Prince William Sound. It would also develop a transportation system to deliver the copper ore to its smelters in Tacoma, Washington. To do this the syndicate purchased two Seattle-based steamship companies and combined them as the Alaska Steamship Company. Between 1908 and 1911 the syndicate built the Copper River and Northwestern Railroad, linking its Kennecott Copper Mine to Cordova on Prince William Sound. Mining and railroad activity seemed to bring stability to the North. By 1910 the census showed that Alaska's Caucasian population had risen to 36,400 from 30,450 a decade earlier. Because of a decline in the native population, Alaska's overall census figure was 64,356, just slightly more than in 1900.[9]

Alaska's growth clearly caught the consciousness of the nation. Novels of mining adventures in the North such as Jack London's *The Call of the Wild* (1903) and *White Fang* (1906) as well as Rex Beach's *The Spoilers* (1906) were widely read. A succession of world's fairs in western cities proudly proclaimed Alaska's future throughout the decade. The capstone of the propaganda bonanza came in 1909 when Seattle businessmen joined with their northern counterparts to sponsor the Alaska-Yukon-Pacific Exposition (A-Y-P). The A-Y-P touted Alaska's mineral production as well as its agricultural possibilities. The exposition trumpeted a coming prosperity of Pacific trade ranging out of Seattle north to Alaska and across the Pacific to Hawai'i, the Philippines, and the Asian mainland.

Alaska's continued growth from 1900 to 1910 led to further demands for a change in its governmental structure. Both local residents and the outside interests agreed that Alaska needed a more advanced political structure, but the precise nature of that new structure was up for argument. Nearly everyone conceded that the delegate to Congress authorized in 1906 was important. But the creation of a legislature with taxing and regulatory authority was opposed by many of the absentee interests.

In particular, the canned salmon packers opposed territorial control of the fisheries—a power that the territory of Hawai'i held.

Economic reform was also a federal concern in Alaska, though this reform was not always welcomed by either local residents or the outside interests. The Progressives, with their concern for "good government" and the economic consolidations of "monopolists," turned their attention to the presence of the Morgan-Guggenheim interests in Alaska. The control of Alaska's substantial coal deposits was a key ingredient to the Alaska Syndicate's railroad and mineral development plans. When it appeared that the Guggenheims might monopolize Alaska's coal lands, which were open to claim and ownership through the homestead laws, President Theodore Roosevelt withdrew any further coal lands from claim in 1906. Thus the coal-rich territory suddenly became dependent on imported coal, mainly from British Columbia, for fuel. In 1911 irate residents of coastal Cordova staged a "Coal Party" and dumped several tons of British Columbia coal in the harbor.

Economic and political reform for Alaska gained further momentum in the administration of Theodore Roosevelt's successor, William Howard Taft. However, continued controversy about Alaska's coal lands split the national Republican Party and tarnished the new president's Progressive image. In 1909 Gifford Pinchot, head of the U.S. Forest Service, accused Secretary of the Interior Richard Ballinger of aiding the Alaska Syndicate in securing patents to coal lands that had been selected by other individuals prior to Roosevelt's coal closure in 1906. The Ballinger-Pinchot Affair became a national argument that prompted a congressional investigation in 1910. Though Ballinger, whom Taft supported, was cleared by Congress, there was a bitter division in the Republican ranks. Ballinger resigned in 1911. The affair severely weakened Taft within his own party and helped lead to his defeat by Woodrow Wilson in the 1912 election.

The Ballinger-Pinchot Affair might well have soured Taft on Alaska and caused him to leave the so-called "territory" alone. But before the president left office, Alaska became a territory in function as well as name. When he assumed the presidency in 1909, Taft suggested a commission form of government for Alaska like the one he had presided over in the Philippines. Taft's suggestion outraged Alaskans and mobilized the pro-territorial forces. Finally, in 1912, Congress, with Taft's support, passed the Second Organic Act for Alaska that created a territory with an elected legislature. The new legislature reflected the influence of the "inside" and "outside" forces that had been building Alaska since 1867. It was more restricted in its lawmaking power than any other territory. It was denied the authority to regulate Alaska's natural resources, particularly the fisheries, or to alter the taxation system created by the federal government a decade earlier. A further hindrance to full self-rule was the fact that the new legislature was quite small—a Senate of eight members and a House of Representatives of sixteen. In contrast Hawai'i's territorial legislature had a Senate of fifteen and a House of thirty. Such a small body would be easy to manipulate by the absentee fishing and mining interests. While the legislature was limited, there was no territorial judiciary as in Hawai'i. The territory could not create its own territorial courts. Thus all territorial laws would be adjudicated in the existing federal courts.

Though Alaska was finally a functioning territory, the degree of home rule it enjoyed was substantially less than in Hawai'i. The more optimistic boosters could at least hope that future growth might lead to expanded home rule. What happened between 1912 and Potter's arrival in 1941 to advance or retard that dream?

Boom and Bust in a "Neglected" Territory, 1912–1939

In the years immediately following the 1912 legislation it certainly looked as if Alaska was rushing forward with a speed similar to that of the previous decade. The 1912 Organic Act contained more than just an outline for territorial government. It also included provisions for the first phase of what could be called a federal policy for the economic development of Alaska. Section 18 of the act authorized the appointment of an Alaskan Railroad Commission to investigate the possibility of a government-constructed or -financed railroad from tidewater to the interior, a dream of both private and public Alaska developers. Woodrow Wilson, who succeeded Taft as president in 1913, affirmed the plans for the railroad. Alaska featured prominently in the new president's first State of the Union Message in December 1913. "A duty faces us with regard to Alaska," Wilson announced, " which seems to me very pressing and very imperative; perhaps I should say a double duty, for it concerns both the political and the material development of the territory. . . The people of Alaska should be given the full territorial form of government, and Alaska, as a storehouse, should be unlocked. One key to it is a system of railways. These the Government should itself build and administer. . ."[10]

By February 1914 a bill authorizing the construction of a railroad or railroads connecting at least one Pacific port in Alaska to the coalfields of the interior passed both houses of Congress and was signed into law by Wilson in March. The Alaska Railroad Act provided for construction of up to one thousand miles of track and a total expenditure of $35 million, some of which could be used to buy existing private lines. The Alaska Railroad was as dynamic a project as the federally financed Panama Canal. In fact the three-man Alaska Engineering Commission (AEC) that was appointed in 1914 to oversee construction of the railroad included Lt. Frederick Mears of the U.S. Army, chief engineer for the railroad built along the Panama Canal. By the spring of 1915 the commissioners selected the "western," or Susitna, route running from the tidewater port of Seward via Ship Creek and the Matanuska coalfields to Fairbanks. The commissioners decided not to buy and extend the Alaska Syndicate's Copper River and Northwestern Railroad, which had also been considered. The commissioners made this decision to avoid potential fallout from the Ballinger-Pinchot Affair, as well as to pacify Alaska's congressional delegate James Wickersham, who was rabidly anti-syndicate. Construction on the new line began in the spring and summer of 1915.[11]

The AEC built towns as well as a railroad. In 1915 the commission built a construction camp at Ship Creek, which it named Anchorage. The government intended for the camp to become a full-fledged town and sold lots to private individuals. By 1917 Anchorage had a population of 3,928. The AEC efficiently operated Anchorage until 1920, when it became an incorporated municipality. Oddly enough, some of the first citizens of Anchorage, who had grown accustomed to federal paternalism, regretted the arrival of self-government and local taxation.

As railroad construction moved north of Anchorage from 1915 to 1917, some East Coast Americans feared a repetition of the slaughter of the buffalo that had occurred fifty years earlier in the building of the transcontinental railroad. Though buffalo did not roam along the Alaska line, caribou, moose, bears, and mountain sheep did. Hunting became so intense along the construction line that both eastern conservationists and big-game hunters feared the interior herds would soon be depleted. With urging from the members of New York's Boone and Crockett Club, the nation's most prestigious big-game hunting organization, Congress created Mt. McKinley National Park in 1917, not so much to preserve the natural beauty of the mountain area as to create a protected game park. A station at Mt. McKinley National Park became a part of the railroad route north.

The construction of the railroad was only a part of Wilson's initial plan for Alaska. One major purpose of the railroad was to open Alaska's coal lands so as to provide a ready source of fuel for the navy's Pacific Fleet. In 1914 Congress ended Roosevelt's 1906 closure with legislation that authorized the leasing of federal coalfields in tracts up to 2,560 acres. By 1920 coal production reached 61,000 tons.

While railroad construction boomed, mining output also expanded. Though the Yukon Valley mines declined after 1912, industrial gold operations in Juneau spurred Alaska's economy in the mid-1910s. In 1916 Alaska's gold mines yielded a product valued at $17 million—only slightly below the peak production of 1906. While gold production progressed, the output of copper from the Kennecott Mine sent Alaska's overall mineral production to new heights in the second decade of the century. In 1911, the first year of operation for the Kennecott Mine, copper production was 27 million pounds valued at $3 million. Rising prices during World War I propelled output to over 119 million pounds valued at $29.5 million in 1916. The combined value of gold and copper now topped the headiest years of the Klondike-Yukon boom.

In addition to minerals, the production of canned salmon also boomed during the second decade of the twentieth century. In 1912 Alaska produced four million cases of canned salmon. With the onset of World War I in 1914, canned salmon became a staple in American food relief for war-torn Europe. American entry into World War I in 1917 spurred even greater military purchases. Wartime demand thrust output to 6.6 million cases valued at $51 million in 1918 and made salmon the territory's most valuable export. To some boosters it seemed as if World War I were being fought by Alaska with canned salmon and copper shells.

In the early months of 1917 Alaska seemed poised on the takeoff of a boom that would surpass even the Klondike. The railroad would be the key to it all. Though American entry into World War I in April 1917 slowed the pace of building, most of the major construction was accomplished by 1919. Final completion of the line continued into the administration of Warren Harding. By 1921 freight service opened from Seward to Fairbanks, though several rivers still had to be forded by boat. In 1923 the last bridge spanning the Tanana River at Nenana was finished. Symbolizing Alaska's importance to the nation, President Harding came to Nenana in July of that year to drive the golden spike.

Though the golden spike ceremony in 1923 was certainly a heyday in the development of Alaska, the aftermath of the ceremony pointed to tragedy not only for the president but for the emerging territory as well. After the railroad ceremonies, Harding headed back to Seattle, where he gave a talk extolling Alaska's future. The president collapsed at the end of the speech, but continued on to San Francisco, where he died on August 2. The death of Warren Harding on his trip to hail the completion of the Alaska Railroad was symbolic of Alaska's troubled future. The railroad had been built on the hope and promise that economic development would miraculously follow its completion. Harding's death symbolized the end of the era of great expectations. Signs of trouble had in fact been on the horizon since American entry into World War I, though few saw them as such in April 1917.

Two weeks after Wilson called for a declaration of war against the Central Powers, the Treadwell Mine in Juneau caved in. The damage was so severe that Treadwell, once the world's largest gold stamp mill, ceased operation in 1922. Mining operations at Juneau, Kennecott, and elsewhere in Alaska were also impacted by the wartime loss of manpower and a general price inflation that made Alaska an even more expensive place for business than usual.

By 1920 the toll of the war years on Alaska's population was evident. The overall population dropped from 64,356 in 1910 to 55,036 in 1920, the loss entirely in the Caucasian population. Of course, the effects of the war might have been reversed after 1920 had people returned to reclaim the boom of early 1917. But there was simply not the economic energy to renew that boom in the postwar years. By 1930 the territory's population had recovered only to 59,278, an increase primarily due to growth in the native population. The American settlers who left in World War I did not return.

The population dilemma could be explained by industrial statistics. Declining gold prices and low-grade ore caused gold production to plummet in the 1920s and early 1930s. By 1933 gold output was valued at only $9 million. Help came in 1935 when the federal government mandated a price increase in gold to $35 an ounce. By 1940 the dollar value of gold reached an all-time high, though actual production in ounces was still low. The federal government did not rescue copper. Its price fell after World War I and fluctuated erratically during the 1920s and early 1930s. Declining prices and low-grade ore finally persuaded the Alaska Syndicate to close the Kennecott Mine permanently in 1938;

the Copper River and Northwestern Railroad made its last run in November of that year.

The dream that the Alaska Railroad could bring coal to tidewater for export to supply the West Coast and the Pacific Fleet collapsed even before it boomed. The opening of the Panama Canal in 1914 lowered freight rates so that eastern U.S. coal shipped through the waterway soon supplied the West Coast. Plans for northern coaling stations to fuel the Pacific Fleet soon collapsed as the burgeoning California petroleum industry of the 1920s convinced the navy to convert to oil. The imperial dream of the 1890s and early 1900s of ships plying an Alaskan route to the Orient with coaling stations at Kodiak and in the Aleutians never materialized. Though coal production did increase between 1920 and 1940, it was used primarily for local needs. With declining mineral production no one was quite sure what the trains would take out of Alaska or what they would carry in. During the 1920s and 1930s Alaskans hid from these true economic facts and simply blamed federal mismanagement of the railroad for thwarting Alaska's development.

With mineral production declining in the 1920s and 1930s, Alaska's economy depended more and more on its maritime base—the canned salmon industry. Salmon output, like mineral output, declined immediately after World War I, due in part to wartime overfishing. The federal government soon came to the aid of the salmon fishery. Harding's secretary of commerce, Herbert Hoover, mounted a personal crusade to save Alaska's fishing resource and even accompanied the president to Alaska on that fateful 1923 trip. To control overfishing, Congress passed the White Act in 1924, which required a 50 percent release of the annual catch. The salmon resource recovered and resumed its growth by 1926. Despite another setback in 1930, canned salmon production reached an all-time peak output of 8.4 million cases valued at $44.75 million in 1936. Except for the setbacks in the early 1920s and early 1930s, both the production and value of canned salmon increased steadily from 1900 to 1936.

The dominance of the absentee-owned canned salmon industry in territorial Alaska would shape the parameters and rhetoric of the post–World War II statehood movement. But we will delay a full discussion of the salmon industry until after the war. The underdeveloped, underpopulated Alaska that Jean Potter confronted in 1941 resulted primarily from the decline of mineral development. The failure of such land-based development led some Alaskans in the 1930s to look at another potential use of the territory's vast interior spaces: national defense.

Fortress Alaska and Its Tortured Political Tradition

Both civilian and military observers had long noted Alaska's strategic location. It almost touched Russia at Bering Strait and was easily accessible to Japan via the Aleutian Islands. In the earlier part of the century the navy had designated Kiska Island in the Aleutians as a naval reservation to serve as a coaling station for the Pacific Fleet. As noted earlier, the use of the Aleutian route to Asia and the use of Alaskan coal as a fuel for the naval fleet were abandoned in the 1920s. A further blow to the importance of the Aleutians came in 1922. That year the Five-Power Naval Treaty emanating from the Washington Armament Conference included the stipulation that the Aleutians would not be fortified, as part of an American concession for Japanese naval reductions.

As war clouds grew in both Europe and Asia in the 1930s, the route from the American Pacific Coast to Asia via Alaska was reinvigorated as an air route. Whether by air or sea, the shorter distances to Japan via Alaska—in comparison to the mid-Pacific route via Hawai'i—still applied. As the 1930s progressed, arguments in favor of air bases in Alaska became part of the general military argument for an increased role for air power. Alaska governor George Parks first made a plea for air defense installations in 1931, but he received no response from Congress. The sustained push for defense fortifications in Alaska was carried by Anthony J. Dimond, who was elected as the territory's delegate to Congress in 1932.

Dimond's pleas for the fortification of Alaska gained momentum in 1934 when the Japanese abrogated the Five-Power Treaty, thus reopening the issue of the fortification of the Aleutians. Dimond also looked beyond the Aleutians to Alaska's mainland and advocated air bases in Anchorage and Fairbanks with the theme "Defend the United States by defending Alaska." Dimond pointed to the level of defense installations in Hawai'i as a prime reason for fortifying Alaska. If Alaska was undefended, the fortifications in Hawai'i alone could not protect the mainland. The Japanese could use the Aleutians as the alternative route for reaching the United States. "What is the use of locking one door," explained Dimond, "and leaving the other one open?"[12]

In 1935 the discussion grew on the need to increase air protection and to fortify Alaska. General Billy Mitchell, who had helped build the WAMCATS telegraph line at the turn of the century, had long been one of the chief advocates for increased air power and for the increased use of Alaska. As assistant chief of the U.S. Army Air Service after World War I, he sponsored an air expedition from New York to Nome in 1920 to show the feasibility of an Alaskan air route. Though no longer in the army in 1935, he testified before Congress on the need to fortify Alaska as an air base. As Mitchell explained, "Japan is our dangerous enemy in the Pacific. They won't attack Panama. They will come right here to Alaska. Alaska is the most central place in the world for aircraft, and that is true either of Europe, Asia or North America. I believe in the future he who holds Alaska will hold the world, and I think it is the most important strategic place in the world."[13]

As a result of the advocacy of Dimond, Mitchell, and other members of the military, Congress named Alaska as one of six strategic areas for air bases in 1935. Bases were authorized in Anchorage and Fairbanks, but no appropriations came. To some extent Alaska was hindered by the fact that other West Coast states, such as Washington and California, wanted to get the appropriations first, not only to defend their borders but also to reinvigorate their Depression-torn economies. Dimond continued to emphasize that the best way to defend the Pacific Coast was to defend Alaska. If Alaska were occupied, Seattle would be in great danger, regardless of any fortifications built in Washington State.

National military advisers also reiterated Alaska's strategic location in naval as well as air defense. The Hepburn Report of 1938 specified the need for fifteen new naval air stations, including locations in Alaska. Congress had earlier appropriated funds to build a limited seaplane base in Sitka in 1937. As a result of the Hepburn Report, funds became available in 1939 to expand the base at Sitka and build another naval air station at Kodiak. Dimond's push for air bases in Anchorage and Fairbanks finally received modest success in the spring of 1939 when Congress appropriated $4 million for a cold-weather research facility in Fairbanks, which later became Ladd Field. At least the army could learn how to fly and maintain planes in the cold in anticipation of future bases being built in the northern territory.

Though Dimond had long emphasized the need to fortify Alaska against a Japanese attack, it took the outbreak of war in Europe to prod Congress into action. In the spring of 1940 Dimond, as well as General

George C. Marshall and Army Air Corps chief General H. H. "Hap" Arnold, requested an appropriation to fund the previously authorized air base in Anchorage. Congress responded by specifically excluding funds for Anchorage in early April 1940. However, when Hitler occupied Denmark and Norway a few weeks later, Congress quickly made an appropriation for the Anchorage base, Fort Richardson and Elmendorf Field. The logic of the sudden appropriation in Dimond's view was that Germany could now send planes from Norway to Alaska via the trans-polar route. Neither the Atlantic nor the Pacific Fleet would be able to intercept such an attack. Mitchell's 1935 statement that Alaska was the key to defending attacks from both Asia and Europe rang true. In May 1940 Congress also appropriated funds for another naval base at Dutch Harbor in the Aleutians. The tide had turned for the fortification of Alaska. By the end of 1940 almost $18 million had been appropriated for airfields alone, with another $30 million coming in 1941.

By late 1940 and early 1941 construction of the new installations had started, though none of the airfields was ready for action by the time of the bombing of Pearl Harbor. By the end of 1940 about three thousand troops, commanded by General Simon Bolivar Buckner, were in Alaska. A year later almost twenty-five thousand troops were stationed there. As Potter headed to Alaska in late 1941, it was no accident that she found herself in the midst of a great migration filled with construction workers and soldiers. On the eve of American entry into World War II, the creation of Alaska as a military outpost had just begun.

The emergence of Alaska as a major defense installation started to turn the tide of Alaska's economic underdevelopment by 1941. Would this economic surge also lead to changes in Alaska's political underdevelopment? Would Fortress Alaska, like Hawai'i, soon be ready for statehood? Jean Potter linked the territory's political immaturity to its economic status. However, there was one seminal aspect of Alaska's political immaturity that Potter did not immediately grasp. Since the dawn of the twentieth century Alaska's governors, and to a lesser degree its congressional delegates, had regularly arrived and departed without establishing a permanent political base or tradition to guide the territory. This situation was unlike that of Hawai'i, where the political establishment was so stable that it was often labeled oligarchic. Some of the political immaturity and instability of Alaska was due to the ups and downs of its economy. But a significant factor in the instability came from the vicious personal and partisan infighting of the constantly changing political figures in the territory. If Potter talked mainly to Anthony Dimond and Ernest Gruening, this was in large part because there were so few seasoned politicians in the territory. A brief background sketch should explain this forty-year dilemma.

The appointment of John Green Brady, the missionary turned merchant, as governor in 1897 was hailed as securing the "right sort" of stable figure for Alaska. Some viewed Brady as too staid and conservative. But the governor became so caught up in Alaska's post-Klondike boom that he agreed in 1903, while governor, to be listed as a director of the Reynolds-Alaska Development Corporation, a mining and railroad firm. Secretary of the Interior Ethan Hitchcock thought such an association with a private corporation created a conflict of interest. After considerable newspaper criticism Brady resigned as governor in 1906. However, he continued his association with the Reynolds Corporation after leaving office. When Reynolds went bankrupt in 1907, so did Brady. Economic necessity forced him to leave Alaska for almost a decade. Thus no Brady tradition developed in Alaska politics. Brady's successors in the governorship were drawn from the volatile mix of people who arrived during and immediately after the Klondike boom.[14]

Just as Brady resigned, Alaskans were allowed to elect a delegate to Congress. The most significant turn in Alaska politics came in the congressional election of 1908 that sent James Wickersham to Congress. Wickersham was an intriguing and irascible political figure. A former city attorney and state representative from Tacoma, Washington, Wickersham first came to Alaska in 1900 to serve as a federal judge. Twinges of a scandal in Washington State involving a young woman followed him to Alaska and were often brought out in political contests. Nonetheless, Wickersham served effectively as a judge, presiding over a number of controversial cases. As a judge, Wickersham's rulings in business cases often favored the interests of the Alaska Syndicate. By 1907 Wickersham's decisions had inevitably created political opponents to his reappointment, including territorial governor Wilfred Hoggatt and U.S. senator Knute Nelson, a Minnesotan with business interests in Alaska. To avoid continued controversy over his judicial tenure, Wickersham decided to resign that year.[15]

At first the former judge decided to apply for a job as general counsel for the Alaska Syndicate. By the time he applied for the position, the syndicate had hired another law firm. In June 1908 Wickersham decided to run as a Republican for delegate to Congress and sought the syndicate's endorsement. The syndicate responded that it had already backed a candidate and suggested that Wickersham not run at this time. Wickersham then decided to run on an anti-syndicate platform, which he thought would elicit popular support. Wickersham maintained the anti-syndicate stance with its populist, anti-monopoly rhetoric for the next dozen years. Other politicians in Alaska, including the territorial governors, were seen as either "pro-Wick" or "anti-Wick." This situation could have created an interesting political tradition if Wickersham had actually espoused a philosophy that highlighted syndicate abuses or sought to replace the syndicate with other business models. But even historians who are critical of the syndicate can find no rationale for Wickersham's political stance except that the syndicate did not hire him as general counsel or endorse his run for Congress. Wickersham did not necessarily want to change the syndicate; he just wanted to run against it. Historian Elizabeth A. Tower, who is sympathetic to the syndicate, sees Wickersham's stance as a major force in retarding the economic development of the territory. Wickersham further complicated political matters by switching his party label from time to time.[16]

Wickersham's strong position on the syndicate brought increased political instability to the territory. Though Wickersham was reelected in 1910, 1912, and 1914, the elections of 1916 and 1918 were fraught with problems. In both elections Wickersham ran against Democrat Charles Sulzer, a southeast Alaska copper mine owner and brother of New York congressman and former governor William Sulzer. Voting irregularities, particularly with the military and natives, caused the two elections to be contested. In both cases Wickersham was finally declared the delegate, but only in the last few days of each term. Thus from 1917 to 1921 Alaska had no clear and certain representation in Congress.

Wickersham's election debacles caused damage to the governorship. In 1913 Woodrow Wilson appointed Democrat J. A. Strong, a popular miner and newspaperman from Nome and Juneau, as governor. When he became governor, Strong transferred his paper, the Juneau *Alaska Daily Empire,* to John Troy, another Klondike-rush newspaperman whom Strong had brought to Juneau. In 1917 Strong, acting as a member of the canvassing board to decide the 1916 election, voted for Wickersham as the winner. Territorial Democrats then turned against the governor. Troy used the governor's former paper to launch an attack against him. He announced that Strong, whose exact past and origins had always been murky, was in fact a Canadian citizen. Strong did not stand for reappointment in 1918 and soon left the territory.

Wickersham's election disasters convinced him not to run again in 1920. He gave his support to his political ally Dan Sutherland, though they soon parted company when Sutherland did not endorse Wickersham for governor in 1921. Sutherland came to Alaska during the Klondike rush and later became a fisherman as well as a member of the territorial legislature. Winning the delegate election in 1920, Sutherland went on to serve five terms in Congress. Though a popular delegate, Sutherland decided not to run again in 1930 because he could not support himself on a delegate's salary. Once out of Congress, Sutherland did not return to Alaska but instead moved to Pennsylvania. Wickersham then succeeded Sutherland for one more term in Congress, before being defeated by Anthony Dimond in 1932.[17]

Dimond originally came to Alaska in 1905 as a copper prospector and later became a lawyer in Valdez, where he represented the Alaska Syndicate as well as other clients. Before running for Congress, he served two terms in the territorial senate (1923–25 and 1929–31). As a Democrat, Dimond was elected to Congress in the Democratic landslide of 1932. Dimond brought stability for Alaska in Congress, but the governorship could not find a similar even keel in the 1930s, despite some preceding interludes of stability.

After Governor Strong's departure in 1918, President Wilson appointed Thomas Riggs, one of the AEC engineer/commissioners, as governor. Riggs was a good choice, but he resigned in 1921 to seek economic opportunities outside of Alaska. The internal politics of Alaska with the continuing Wickersham controversy were so rancorous in 1921 that President Harding conferred the governorship on an outsider, Seattle newspaperman Scott C. Bone, who served until 1925 and then moved to California. The governorship appeared to stabilize between 1925 and 1933 with the appointment of George Parks, an engineer and long-time federal land office bureaucrat in Alaska. But the Democratic landslide that brought Dimond and Franklin Roosevelt to power in 1932 brought Alaska a new governor from the old ranks. Roosevelt appointed John Troy as a reward for his long party service. Troy, who first came to Alaska in 1897, had been a newspaper critic of John Brady in 1906, a decade before his attack on J. A. Strong. The newspaper would be his undoing as well. Unlike Strong, Troy continued to own the *Alaska Daily Empire* as governor. When it was discovered in 1939 that he gave government printing jobs to his own paper, Troy resigned rather than face federal prosecution.

This forty-year pattern of disaster with gubernatorial appointments in Alaska led Franklin Roosevelt and Interior Secretary Harold Ickes to appoint Ernest Gruening, director of the Interior Department's Division of Territories and Island Possessions, as territorial governor in late 1939. Gruening would be the first governor who was not connected to the miner/newspaper world of Alaska and Seattle that had dominated politics since Brady's resignation in 1906. Despite the "carpetbag" nature of the selection, there was a seeming logic to this appointment. Alaska had been a part of Gruening's division in Washington, and the director had visited the territory in 1936 and 1938. But that was not exactly why he was appointed. The economic and political redevelopment of Puerto Rico had been Gruening's chief concern in Washington. His policies in that regard had become unpopular. Both Roosevelt and Ickes wanted to get Gruening out of Washington. Thus the twin sagas of gubernatorial dilemmas in Alaska and political problems in Puerto Rico pulled and propelled Gruening to the North. Though Gruening at first said he did not want to be governor, Roosevelt resolved the issue by simply announcing the appointment on national radio while Gruening was on vacation. The deed was done. Gruening and his family arrived in Juneau in December 1939. He would remain an Alaskan for the rest of his life.[18]

When Jean Potter undertook her Alaskan assignment in 1941, she talked avidly with Gruening and Dimond. But just where were the others? Wickersham had died in 1939, and Sutherland was in Pennsylvania. Of the previous delegates only Frank Waskey, who had served as delegate for three months in 1906–7, was still alive and in the territory. Of the previous governors, most were either dead, out of the territory, or in the case of Troy discredited. Only George Parks was still in Alaska, now serving as district engineer.

In talking with Dimond and Gruening, Potter did not merely learn the details of a new economy and defense installation in the making. She heard the voices of a new political tradition being born. Dimond had placed Alaska on a stable path by emphasizing the territory's role as a military fortress. He would serve as delegate until 1945, when his former chief aide in Washington, Bob Bartlett, succeeded him as delegate in Congress. Bartlett would serve as delegate until 1958, when he was elected as one of Alaska's first two U.S. senators. Dimond's godson in Valdez, William Egan, who had just been elected to the territorial legislature in 1940, would chair the writing of Alaska's state constitution in 1955–56 and become the state's first elected governor in 1958–59.

Even Dimond's personal secretary, Mary Lee Council, would stay in Washington with the Alaska delegation until 1967.

Gruening, who had been born in New York and had worked for years as a journalist and federal official, brought a strain of East Coast progressivism to Alaska. The territory he found in 1939 lacked an adequate legislature and an adequate tax policy, and had no judicial system at all. Gruening would modernize the territory and put Alaska in a position to become a state. Unlike most of his gubernatorial predecessors, he would remain in political power for decades to come. He served as territorial governor until 1953, when President Dwight Eisenhower and the Republicans came to power. After that he campaigned for statehood. Along with Bob Bartlett, Ernest Gruening would become one of Alaska's first two U.S. senators.

The emerging Alaska of 1941 was quite unlike Hawai'i. The mid-Pacific territory had steadily grown into a politically and economically mature territory between 1900 and 1941. Alaska had created and recreated itself any number of times since the United States first acquired it in 1867. It was still in the process of doing so in 1941. Hawai'i was ready to become a state in 1941. Congressional hearings had been held, and the population had voted for statehood. Only the inbred suspicion and animosity of the mainland United States for Hawai'i's Asian population stood in the way. Though Wickersham had introduced the first statehood bill for Alaska in 1916, no congressional hearings on statehood had been held by 1941. Nor had the territorial legislature memorialized the U.S. Congress for statehood. In fact, it defeated a motion to do so in early 1941. No popular referendum had been held in the territory on the issue. Unlike Hawai'i, Alaska in 1941 lacked the economic, political, and population bases to become a state.

World War II would change the political, economic, and social anomalies of Alaska and Hawai'i. It would bring thousands of mainland Americans into those territories for military service. The war would recreate Alaska into a military defense territory that would emerge as a viable candidate for statehood in the decade after the war. It would also transform the way the nation perceived Hawai'i, and in the postwar years transform the internal politics of the islands. Hawai'i's Japanese and Chinese Americans would increasingly come of voting age. And their exemplary war record would challenge the suspicions once held against them. All of these changes still lay in the future. In 1941 Jean

Potter and her fellow journalists had just begun their investigations of the last two territories. A few weeks later the war came.

Hawai'i Before World War II

1. Hawai'i in the 1930s was a thoroughly modern community, as seen looking down on Honolulu. Courtesy of the Hawai'i State Archives.

2. Hawai'i's prewar sugar/pineapple economy was agricultural as seen in this field photo of workers picking pineapples. Courtesy of the Hawai'i State Archives.

3. Hawai'i's prewar economy was also industrial, as seen in this photo of the Hawaiian Pineapple Co. cannery in Honolulu. Courtesy of the Hawai'i State Archives.

4. The entrance to Hickam Field, seen here in 1938, was part of the elaborate prewar military fortifications that made Honolulu the Gibraltar of the Pacific. Courtesy of the Hawai'i State Archives.

5. *Congressional committees came to Hawai'i in the 1930s to investigate the territory's readiness for statehood and its military preparedness. This committee is touring Wheeler Field in 1937. Courtesy of the Hawai'i State Archives.*

6. *Though prewar Hawai'i was a modern American territory, it also carried the heritage of its Hawaiian past and the monarchy that was overthrown in 1893. In this 1914 photo the deposed Queen Lili'uokalani is flanked by Sanford B. Dole, a leader of the revolution that overthrew her, and Lucius Pinkham, territorial governor in 1914. Standing is Henry Berger, leader of the Royal Hawaiian Band, created during the days of the Monarchy. Courtesy of the Hawai'i State Archives.*

7. The link to the Hawaiian past was also personified by territorial senator Alice
Kamokila Campbell, pictured here in 1945 with native Hawaiian U.S. veteran
Capt. Alexander Kaheapea. Campbell entertained and supported U.S. troops
during World War II, but she spoke against statehood at the 1946 Larcade com-
mittee hearings. She asked that Hawai'i be "left alone." Standing between Senator
Campbell and Capt. Kaheapea is Charles Morris of the American Legion.
Courtesy of the U.S. Army Signal Corps. Photo no. 1396, Hawai'i War Records
Depository, Special Collections, University of Hawai'i Library.

Hawai'i in World War II

8. *General Delos Emmons assumed command of the Hawaiian Department on December 17, 1941. He served as military governor until he departed in 1943. Emmons is credited with forestalling the mass internment of Hawai'i's Japanese population. He later served as commanding general in Alaska from 1944 to 1946. Courtesy of the Hawai'i State Archives.*

9. *Under the recommendation of Emmons and others, young Japanese American males in Hawai'i were recruited to join the all-Nisei 442nd Regimental Combat Team. In this photo young AJA recruits take their oath of service in Kaua'i, 1943. Courtesy of the Hawai'i State Archives.*

10. *Ready to depart for training at Camp Shelby, Mississippi, in April 1943, over 2800 Nisei of the 442nd Regimental Combat Team assembled on the grounds of `Iolani Palace in Honolulu. Courtesy of the Hawai`i State Archives.*

11. *During World War II one of the most common memories of servicemen in Hawai`i was overcrowding. In this photo a group of sailors and soldiers on "liberty" descend on downtown Honolulu in 1944. Courtesy of the Hawai`i State Archives.*

12. *Though advertised as a "paradise," service personnel often found Waikiki beach fortified with barbed wire in case of a Japanese invasion. This photo is in front of Honolulu's fashionable Royal Hawaiian Hotel. Courtesy of the Hawai'i State Archives.*

Alaska: The Frozen Territory Prepares for War

In the years before World War II many mainland Americans had little current knowledge of Alaska and still held images from the turn of the century of Alaska as an exotic frozen wasteland punctuated by a few mining strikes.

13. In 1898 the Great Klondike Gold Rush was in full swing. In this photo prospective miners climb the "Golden Stairs" up the Chilkoot Pass in Alaska enroute to the Canadian Klondike. Courtesy of the Albert J. Johnson Collection acc#89-166n, Alaska and Polar Regions Department, Rasmuson Library, University of Alaska Fairbanks.

14. *In 1909 the wealth from the Klondike and other mining strikes in Alaska sealed a relation between the North and the port city of Seattle which staged the Alaska-Yukon-Pacific Exposition. Courtesy of the Charles Bunnell Collection, Alaska and Polar Regions Department, Rasmuson Library, University of Alaska Fairbanks.*

Alaska of Value as Defense Outpost

The Boston Globe　　　　June

First Regular Passenger Flight Moves It Within Six Hours of U. S.

The first passenger flight on a regular route between the United States and Alaska is described here by a West Coast newspaper correspondent who was born in Alaska and knows the country intimately.

By ROYAL ARCH GUNNISON

Alaska moved three days closer or within six hours of the United States this week.

The first passenger airplane to fly a regular route between Seattle, Wash., and Ketchikan, Alaska, completed its first flight in five hours and 20 minutes. It skirted the rugged Canadian coast nearly 12 miles at sea all the way north.

With Europe's war raging nearly 7000 miles away and all America's attention on it, the first reaction to this historic flight to Alaska by the pioneering Pan American Airways system might be, "so what?" But, aboard the 32-passenger, four-motored Sikorsky S-42 Alaska clipper, the 20 passengers, including Alaska's Governor Ernest Gruening, talked significantly of little else but Alaska's inestimable value as Uncle Sam's first defense outpost, definitely tying it into the World War scene.

Gov. Gruening contributed the first blitzkrieg of the flight by pointing out that a few parachuters "could take Alaska today." Alaska is wide open—the achilles heel of North America today. We have appropriated close to $45,000,000 to start the Alaska North Pacific de-

ERNEST H. GRUENING
Governor of Alaska

trip into reverse and were to take off in a bomber from Nome, Alaska, only 100 miles from the Siberian coast and a few hours flying time from Japanese bases off the tip of

15. *To publicize Alaska's potential value as a defense installation in 1940, territorial governor Ernest Gruening placed stories in the nation's newspapers such as this one in the Boston Globe in June 1940. Courtesy of the Historical Photograph Collection, Alaska and Polar Regions Department, Rasmuson Library, University of Alaska Fairbanks.*

16. By 1941, one of the most modern facilities in Alaska was the new KFAR radio station in Fairbanks. Young Augie Hiebert, pictured here at the station's controls with his dog "Sparky," received the first word of the bombing of Pearl Harbor and phoned Army headquarters at Ladd Field to convey the news. Courtesy of the Reuel Griffin Collection, acc#59-845-1052N, Alaska and Polar Regions Department, Rasmuson Library, University of Alaska Fairbanks.

17. Air fields in Fairbanks and Anchorage, built in the early 1940s, were among the major World War II military installations in Alaska. Artist Henry Varnum Poor (1888–1970) painted this rendition of Ladd Field at Fairbanks in 1943. Courtesy of the University of Alaska Museum, #81-3-177.

Part II

And the War Came:
World War II in the Territories, 1941–1945

The simple phrase "and the war came" was first used by Abraham Lincoln in his 1865 Second Inaugural Address to encapsulate the momentous changes that had engulfed the nation since he took office four years earlier. For Lincoln's generation, war, more than any other force, had been the great transformer. For the next seventy years no part of the nation feared invasion or experienced war firsthand.

With the Japanese bombing of Pearl Harbor in December 1941 and the ensuing attack at Dutch Harbor on the Alaska Peninsula in June 1942, war came to the nation's two distant territories, Hawai'i and Alaska. As in Lincoln's day, war would be the great transformer. The war put both territories on center stage of the American national consciousness and served as the catalyst that would eventually propel the two toward statehood.

Chapter 3

World War II and the
Transformation of Hawai'i

From the moment bombs fell... these isolated islands became
an integral part of the fabric of the nation at large.
—*Gwenfread Allen, on the impact of World War II on Hawai'i*

“Yesterday, December 7, 1941—a date which will live in
infamy—the United States of America was suddenly and
deliberately attacked by naval and air forces of the empire of
Japan." Such were the words used on December 8 by President Franklin
Roosevelt to describe the Japanese bombing of Pearl Harbor in the territory of Hawai'i and to ask the U.S. Congress for a declaration of war
against Japan. Congress agreed with the president and granted the declaration that day. The war had finally come.

The date was indeed one that would live in infamy, but the exact
nature of that infamy varied with different Americans—particularly
with some of those Americans who actually saw the bombs fall in
Honolulu. Young Daniel K. Inouye, a seventeen-year-old Nisei student
at Honolulu's McKinley High School, was preparing for breakfast with
his family that Sunday morning of December 7 when news of the attack
came on the radio a little after 7:55 a.m. The family rushed outside their
house and could see the planes coming over from the direction of Pearl
Harbor. Dan looked at his father, who was "caught by that special horror
instantly sensed by Americans of Japanese descent as the nightmare
began to unfold." Looking at the Japanese planes fly over, he heard his
father cry, "You fools."[1]

Within minutes the young Inouye, who had recently taken a Red
Cross course, was called to report to a nearby first aid station. Inouye
rode his bicycle to the station, fearing the casualties he might find when
he got there. What first disturbed him, however, was the emotional pain

he saw on his neighbors' faces as he rode through his Japanese American section of Honolulu. "They had worked so hard," he later wrote. "They had wanted so desperately to be accepted, to be good Americans. And now, in a few cataclysmic minutes, it was all undone, for in the marrow of my bones I knew that there was only deep trouble ahead." Inouye looked into the skies and shouted, "You dirty Japs."[2]

The "trouble" that elicited the seventeen-year-old's bitterness was the certainty of a backlash against Hawai'i's Japanese and Japanese American population. As Inouye put it, "I carried the full and bitter burden shared by every one of the 158,000 Japanese-Americans in Hawaii: not only had our country been wantonly attacked, but our loyalty was certain to be called into question, for it took no great effort of imagination to see the hatred of many Americans for the enemy turned on us, who looked so much like him. And no matter how hard we worked to defeat him, there would always be those who would look at us and think—and some would say it aloud—'Dirty Jap.'"[3]

Inouye initially believed that the "hard work" of the prewar Japanese American community had been quashed by the Japanese bombs. But in many ways December 7 was as much a beginning as an end for the territorial community that in the decade before the war had been so misunderstood by Clarence Darrow and for which the navy harbored such deep suspicions. The war would transform both the territory and its Japanese American population and invigorate the recently begun statehood movement. Within twenty years Inouye would find himself a member of the Congress that Roosevelt addressed—first in the House of Representatives and later in the Senate, where he remains with the writing of these words in the year 2003.

Before statehood could be achieved, the "trouble" that Inouye so feared indeed occurred. Though the Japanese bombing of the islands lasted only a few hours, the backlash from both the local military authorities and the national government on the mainland would continue for the next three years in the form of martial law. On December 7, the day of infamy, the military occupation of Hawai'i began—even before Roosevelt secured his declaration of war against Japan.

Hawai'i under Army Rule

Students of American political theory and practice are sure to read the Federalist Papers and the writings of Thomas Jefferson. It is unlikely that many have ever heard of a thin volume that should also be required reading: *Hawaii under Army Rule,* by J. Garner Anthony. Anthony, a prominent Honolulu lawyer who served as the territory's attorney general from October 1942 to December 1943, describes in vivid detail what may well be the most extraordinary disruption of government and civil liberties in the history of the United States.[4]

If American war ships were caught off guard in Pearl Harbor on December 7, military and civilian authorities in the territory were not found lacking in their preparedness plans for the islands. In October 1941 the territorial legislature had passed the Hawaii Defense Act, sometimes called the M-Day Act, which authorized the transfer of substantial powers, including legislative powers, to the territorial governor in the event of a military emergency. The territorial legislation was to some extent a preemptive act to prevent the federal Congress from passing other emergency legislation. The logic was to show that Hawai'i was capable of "home rule" even in emergency situations.

The territory's hope to govern itself in times of emergency was of brief duration. Territorial governor Joseph Poindexter invoked the Hawaii Defense Act at 11:30 a.m. on December 7, but retained control for only a few hours. Shortly after noon Lt. General Walter Short, commanding general of the Hawaiian Department, appeared in Poindexter's office. He demanded that the governor invoke martial law and transfer control of the islands to the military. In theory American governors invoke martial law when the civilian population is in disarray and cannot be controlled by civilian authority. Neither on December 7 nor afterward was the civilian population ever in disarray in Honolulu. However, the fear of chaos that could occur should a land invasion follow the Pearl Harbor bombing, coupled with the suspicion that Honolulu's Japanese and Japanese American population contained saboteurs, prompted Poindexter to yield to Short's request after a brief telephone conversation with President Franklin Roosevelt. Poindexter made the decision with the assumption, supported by Short, that the need for martial law would be temporary, probably not exceeding thirty days. Poindexter proclaimed martial law at 3:30 p.m. on December 7. General Short then proclaimed himself military governor of Hawaii, a title that was later assumed by Short's successors in Hawai'i—General Delos Emmons and General Robert Richardson. President Roosevelt confirmed and approved the martial law proclamation on December 9. Poindexter told his secretary, Charles Hite, that he "never hated doing anything so much in all his life."[5]

In invoking martial law Poindexter transferred most of the powers he had assumed through the Hawaii Defense Act to the military. He also transferred judicial power to the military and suspended the writ of habeas corpus. This was a particularly controversial decision because many people in Hawai'i did not think that the M-Day powers gave Poindexter the right to transfer judicial authority. Nevertheless, the army assumed jurisdiction over both civil and criminal cases and established provost courts without juries. The provost courts claimed jurisdiction over offenses ranging from traffic violations to murder. Cases having nothing whatsoever to do with military security, such as the trial of a stockbroker who embezzled from his clients, came under military sway. In addition to these judicial powers, the army also assumed the power to regulate labor affairs in the islands and required workers to remain in their current jobs at fixed wages for the duration of the war. Whether in the courts or on the job, virtually everyone in Hawai'i found their lives under military supervision. All islanders were fingerprinted; a general curfew and blackout were in force every night. All mail to and from Hawai'i was read by censors. Inter-island and trans-Pacific telephone calls were monitored. Privacy was a thing of the past.

Poindexter's assumption that martial law would be temporary proved illusive. Thirty days came and went. Not until October 1944 did President Roosevelt terminate army rule in Hawai'i, though there were intermediate stages of a return to civilian authority. Most critics of martial law in Hawai'i, including Garner Anthony, agreed that the invocation of martial law on December 7 was justified. Even though the civilian population was not in disarray, the potential for chaos in the aftermath of the bombing was clear. But when did most reasonable people say the state of military emergency ended? By early 1942 any concern that local Japanese or Japanese American saboteurs had been active in the December 7 attack was dismissed by the presidentially appointed Roberts Commission, which found that no treasonous acts whatsoever had been committed in Hawai'i. After the Battle of Midway in June 1942, the fear of a potential Japanese land invasion or even a renewed bombing of Hawai'i was removed. During the summer of 1942, however, neither the army nor the national administration showed any disposition to end marital law or return judicial and labor affairs to civilian hands. By late 1942 a local movement to end army rule began.[6]

In August 1942, Roosevelt replaced Governor Poindexter with Honolulu federal judge Ingram Stainback, a critic of martial law. The replacement did not indicate any change of heart by FDR concerning martial law. Instead it was initiated by Interior Secretary Harold Ickes, who was annoyed that he had not been consulted in the decisions to invoke martial law in 1941. Governor Stainback appointed Garner Anthony, one of the earliest critics of martial law, as territorial attorney general in October. Stainback and Anthony, both Democrats, gained a Republican ally in Joseph Farrington, who was elected territorial delegate to Congress in 1942 after delegate Samuel Wilder King decided to return to the U.S. Navy where he had previously served. In December 1942, Farrington went on record in opposition to martial law. Farrington's paper, the *Honolulu Star-Bulletin*, and its editor, Riley Allen, also opposed martial law.

There was not, however, a united front of opposition in the territory. The *Honolulu Advertiser* took a decidedly different tack and even endorsed army rule as good for the territory. The paper's publisher, Lorrin P. Thurston, was appointed public relations advisor to the military governor in November 1942. As George Chaplin, a later editor of the *Advertiser,* noted, "The Army offered to make Thurston a colonel, but he declined. As it was, he could hardly have been more an advocate of military control." The Honolulu Chamber of Commerce also shared the views of the *Honolulu Advertiser.* The local Democratic Party, though not the national Democratic Party, went on record in opposition to martial law. The local Republican Party made no mention of martial law, despite Farrington's opposition.[7]

The team of Stainback, Anthony, and Farrington went to Washington with the goal of repealing martial law or at least returning selected governmental functions to civilian control. In March 1943 a partial restoration of civilian rule occurred, though it was not always clear exactly what had been returned. The military provost courts continued to operate, and it was unclear if the territorial government had regained the right to issue writs of habeas corpus for suspects imprisoned in military jails. Anthony sought to test the extent of military rule with a series of cases centering on the writ of habeas corpus and the basic legality of the provost courts during 1943 and 1944. One of those cases, *Duncan v. Kahanamoku,* resulted in an appeal to the U.S. Supreme Court. In February 1946 the Supreme Court ruled that martial law in Hawai'i, particularly the operation of the military courts, had been unconstitutional. But by that time the war was over, and martial law itself had been repealed in October 1944.

Both the imposition of and the battle against martial law had repercussions in the transformation of Hawaiʻi and the postwar statehood movement. The group of people who opposed martial law added yet another wing to the incipient statehood movement. It was now clear that the price of freedom in Hawaiʻi, not just the price of sugar, was subject to the whim of the national government. What happened to Hawaiʻi under army rule highlighted the parameters and consequences of territorial status. Commenting after the war, federal district judge Frank McLaughlin said of the army's rule, "They did it because Hawaii is not a state." Joseph Farrington remained as Hawaiʻi's territorial delegate to Congress until his death in 1954 and sponsored several statehood bills after the war. The *Star-Bulletin* became the leading press supporter of statehood. Garner Anthony became a member of the 1950 convention that the territory convened to write a model constitution for the potential new forty-ninth state of Hawaiʻi. Stainback initially supported statehood after the war, but made a strange about-face in 1946–47 that will be discussed later.[8]

If martial law created a greater resolve for statehood in a portion of the population, possibly the more striking aspect of the situation is the fact that only a small group of people actively opposed army rule and that some actively supported it. Even after the war ended and the U.S. Supreme Court ruled the military courts unconstitutional, Lorrin Thurston editorialized in March 1946 about the army's conduct, "They did it and we liked it." Postwar critics of martial law point to other members of Hawaiʻi's Caucasian business elite, such as Walter Dillingham, as supporters of army rule. However, Garner Anthony made it clear that the older, elite haoles were not alone in their silence or open support. Labor unions, including the International Longshoremen's and Warehousemen's Union (ILWU), made little protest of the army's control of work activity. Anthony felt that the civilian population acquiesced to army rule partially because the army made sure that the islands were well stocked with food and only mildly constrained by the wartime rationing system on the mainland. "The Army," explained Anthony, "deprived the citizen of his most cherished possession—the inheritance of free men—which the founders of this country had waged bloody battles to secure, and these were supinely exchanged for meat, butter, Kleenex, and liquor."[9]

Was there really no more to the public's silence than just their liking for Kleenex and butter? Some historians have also linked the extended army rule to the military's innate suspicion of Hawai'i's Japanese population. According to historian Gary Okihiro, "The declaration of martial law on December 7, 1941, was fundamentally an anti-Japanese act." Anthony also speculated that the "military mind," trained to obedience and deference to authority, was reluctant to admit that it had made a mistake for fear that this would embarrass those who made the decisions and undermine their authority. Thus when military rule extended beyond any reasonable "emergency" period and civilian criticism emerged, the army was reluctant to relinquish its rule, as relinquishment might be an admission of error.[10]

Anthony's analysis of the military mind may also shed some light on why the civilian population acted as it did. Civilians, regardless of race, knew that the "military mind" in Hawai'i that demanded martial law was the same "mind" that had reacted so stridently to the Massie case—and to the treatment of that case by Hawai'i's courts and territorial governor—a decade before. If the navy had called for the abolition of territorial government and its replacement by military commission in peacetime, what further steps beyond martial law might it propose in wartime in the wake of strident local protest? Martial law had not abolished civilian rule; it had simply superseded it. During World War II the structure of territorial government remained in existence. But the jurisdiction and extent of its functions were curtailed for an admittedly "temporary" period. Also, the same president, Franklin Roosevelt, and the same national Democratic Party that had supported the Rankin Bill in 1933 remained in power. Neither the party nor the president chose to overrule the military before late 1944. The civilian population in Hawai'i may well have concluded, with sound reason, that a scenario much worse than "temporary" army rule could be forced on the island territory—even a scenario that could alter Hawai'i's territorial status and make it ineligible for statehood once the war ended.

If such reasoning seems too speculative, take as an example Hawai'i's reaction to mainland criticism of one totally normal and lawful aspect of political life during the war. Gwenfread Allen notes that in 1942 several Nisei, or Americans of Japanese Ancestry (AJA) as they were called in Hawai'i, continued to run for political office in the primary elections—and won. The *New York Daily News* criticized such activity and suggested that the candidates "go back where they and their ancestors came from." As a result four of the Nisei primary victors for local offices in Kaua'i withdrew from the general election. A good number of other

AJAs had already decided not to run in the 1942 elections. In 1941 the territorial legislature contained seven AJA members. In 1943 and 1945 it had none. Whether in reaction to the "military mind," to FDR, or to mainland press opinion, many people in Hawai'i may well have concluded that the parameters of political action without fear of repercussion were severely limited.[11]

Though writers and historians have speculated on the meaning of martial law and the operation of the military mind, the reasons for the seeming indifference or acquiescence of the local population remain unclear even sixty years after the event. Possibly the lack of clarity in the operation of the "military mind" and martial law in Hawai'i stems from the fact that no assessment from the three generals who served as military governor (Walter Short, Delos Emmons, or Robert Richardson) has been a part of the histories and critiques previously mentioned. A recently discovered typescript "personal history" by General Emmons offers new light on the situation.

Emmons, who would become a staunch friend of Hawai'i and its AJA population, assumed command of the Hawaiian Department on December 17, 1941. In that capacity he also assumed the role of military governor. He served as military governor longer than either his predecessor or successor. Upon his arrival in Honolulu the general noted that he "found everything in great confusion and the inhabitants very frightened." He was particularly concerned with the plight of the islands' Japanese population. "Most of those of Japanese descent, citizens or not," he explained, "had been discharged from their jobs, ships were not being unloaded and many more were arriving and en route. A very large percentage of the skilled workers, truck drivers, etc., were of Japanese descent . . . These people could not get hospital treatment or even buy food and other essentials from most stores."[12]

Moving from chaos to order, Emmons went on to say that martial law was crucial in the first year of the war:

> The results in Hawaii, for the first year at least, were spectacular. Citizens had confidence and were no longer frightened. Those of Japanese descent were put back to work, an immense amount of construction was accomplished, the economy of the Islands was protected, new hospitals were provided, food became ample in a very short time. . . . Martial law was very popular with nearly the entire civilian population up to a

certain time, with the exception of some lawyers which could be expected because their income suffered.[13]

Evidently the military could have the same contempt for the legal mind that lawyers professed for the military mind!

Emmons clearly saw martial law as a temporary arrangement and said that after "about a year" he "was prepared to relinquish some of my authority as most of our work had been done." He explained that he had worked with the civil governor (Stainback) as well as the U.S. attorney general and the secretary of the Interior to issue proclamations to that effect in the spring of 1943. On the issuance of these proclamations in February 1943, the narratives of Emmons and Anthony agree. As noted earlier, it soon became unclear exactly what level of civil authority was restored. The confusion may have resulted not from the "military mind" but from a change in that mind. Emmons explained in his memoir that by June 1943 he was "prepared to recommend to the President that martial law cease." Before he could do this, he was assigned to take over command of the Western Department in San Francisco. He told his successor in Hawai'i, General Robert Richardson, that he thought it was time to cease martial law, but left the decision up to Richardson. In Emmons's words, "he decided to keep on with it for a few months longer until he had an opportunity to learn the situation. In my opinion, he kept it on too long."[14]

Anthony and other critics of martial law put little emphasis on the changeover from Emmons to Richardson. Nor do they mention any cooperation between Emmons and Stainback in early 1943. However, it is clear from Anthony's account that most of his problems—and the court cases to test the suspension of habeas corpus—emanated from Richardson's tenure. Had Emmons remained as military governor the latter-day criticism might have assumed a different tone. Emmons noted that both houses of the territorial legislature "passed resolutions praising me for my work." Anthony did not mention this action of the legislature. By the time that Emmons wrote his short memoir he appears to have been aware of Anthony's book. But there is no indication from either Emmons or Anthony that the two men ever talked or corresponded after the war. This lack of contact is unfortunate. As we will see, General Emmons well deserved the praise the legislature gave him.[15]

The Internment Decision: A Different Path for Hawai'i's Japanese

Was the invocation of martial law in December 1941 a prelude to further reprisals against the islands' Japanese population, or did it preclude
the more drastic step of wholesale internment of Hawai'i's Japanese
population, as occurred later on the Pacific mainland? The future
course of action was not entirely clear in the early days of the war. In
the immediate aftermath of the Pearl Harbor bombing, the FBI
quickly took into custody several hundred local Japanese community
leaders that it suspected of subversive activity. Though some were
released after questioning, others remained in custody and were later
interned, in some cases for the duration of the war. The initial arrests
were not limited to Japanese or Japanese Americans, but also included
Germans and Italians. It was the German detainees whom Garner
Anthony later used in his test cases against the army to restore the writ
of habeas corpus.

How much further would the initial round of arrests go in Hawai'i?
Over the course of the war slightly fewer than fifteen hundred Japanese
and Japanese Americans were taken into custody. Of those about one
thousand were interned. For the purposes of such detention the military government established the Sand Island Detention Center and the
Honouliuli internment camp in Hawai'i. From 1942 to 1945 most of
the internees along with family members who chose to accompany
them—approximately two thousand persons—were transferred at various intervals to internment camps on the mainland. Even when count-
ing the family members who voluntarily entered the internment camps,
only 1–1.5 percent of Hawai'i's Japanese and Japanese American population was interned.[16]

Of the internees about two-thirds were Issei, first-generation immigrants, many of whom were teachers in the Japanese language schools,
Buddhist and Shinto priests, and others who had close cultural ties
to Japan. It is often noted that most of the Nisei who were interned
were the so-called Kibei, Hawai'i-born Japanese Americans who spent
a portion of their lives in Japan for education. Though a connection to
Japan, whether among the Issei or Nisei, is often emphasized, a few of
the Nisei internees were among those who seemed to be the most
"Americanized"—including two members of the Hawai'i territorial
legislature. Sanji Abe was born in Hawai'i in 1895 and served with the
U.S. Army in World War I. He later became a deputy sheriff in Hilo

and in 1940 was the first AJA elected to the territorial senate as a Republican from South Hilo. Abe was arrested and later interned in 1942, allegedly for the possession of a Japanese flag, a prop in a movie theater he owned in Hilo. Though formal charges were never brought against him, he was interned for a total of nineteen months at Sand Island and Honouliuli. With the writ of habeas corpus suspended, there was no recourse in law to preclude this retention. He resigned from the territorial senate as he was unable to serve when the 1943 legislative session began.[17]

The other legislator interned was Thomas Sakakihara, also of Hilo. By 1942 Sakakihara had been a member of the territorial house of representatives for several terms, having first been elected in 1932. In the 1941 session he was one of six AJA representatives. Immediately after Pearl Harbor, Sakakihara was made a special deputy sheriff in Hilo to serve as a liaison between the police and the military. But he was soon discharged from that position and subsequently arrested in February 1942 "on suspicion of being an alien" though he had never been outside of Hawai'i. He was detained at Honouliuli until November 1943, when he was released with the requirement that he sign a "promise that he would not bring a damage suit against the U.S. government as a result of the internment."[18]

Though the detention and internment of even 1 percent of Hawai'i's Issei and Nisei population was an insult and an infringement of civil liberties, Hawai'i, in contrast to the West Coast, escaped the total evacuation of its Japanese population. In February 1942 President Roosevelt issued Executive Order 9066 that authorized military commanders to evacuate and intern all Japanese and Japanese Americans in the area under their command. On the mainland this order led to the evacuation of virtually the entire Issei and Nisei populations of the West Coast states to a series of internment or relocation camps for the duration of the war. Families had to sell or otherwise dispose of their property and homes in the removal. Some 110,000–120,000 people were affected. Executive Order 9066 was effective in the Hawaiian Department of the Army. Why was it not implemented?

Most sources agree that military and civilian officials at the national level, particularly President Franklin Roosevelt and Secretary of the Navy Frank Knox, fully wanted and intended that the order be implemented in Hawai'i. Martial law was not a substitute for internment. Emmons noted in his memoir, "During the first six months after Pearl

Harbor, there was great pressure brought to bear to evacuate all persons of Japanese descent from the Islands, especially by the Navy because of the great importance of their Naval Base at Pearl Harbor." Even before the issuance of EO 9066, Knox called for a total evacuation of the islands' 158,000 Japanese. Emmons, however, disregarded the memoranda and recommendations from his superiors in Washington and stalled for those first six months. He usually cited the need for Japanese labor and the significant logistical problem of evacuating that many people. During the spring of 1942 Emmons's tactics and ploys led Washington to reduce its demands from total evacuation to an evacuation of fifteen thousand to twenty thousand Japanese. Emmons continued to stall even after an "infuriated" Roosevelt directed Secretary of War Stimson to tell Emmons that "the labor situation is not only a secondary matter but should not be given any consideration whatever." Emmons, at risk to his career, maintained his own course and interned only the two thousand Japanese noted earlier. Why was Emmons willing to act in this manner?[19]

Emmons had been to Hawai'i in the months before Pearl Harbor and had met with his predecessor, General Short. This early encounter with the islands did not necessarily incline him to be favorable to Hawai'i's Japanese population. Honolulu attorney and AJA war veteran Ted Tsukiyama has reported that Emmons initially asked his intelligence officer Col. Kendall Fielder, "How many Japs did you pick up today?" But within a very short time Emmons began listening to both Fielder and the local head of the FBI, Robert Shivers, who were very sympathetic to the local Japanese community and convinced of its basic loyalty.[20]

Shivers and Fielder came to this conclusion after having worked with a variety of multiracial citizen advisory groups within the Honolulu community for the previous two years—most notably the Hawaii Council of Interracial Unity. As FBI head, Shivers, working with the staffs of army and navy intelligence and the espionage unit of the Honolulu police department, began compiling lists of local Japanese leaders and investigating them for loyalty. It was those lists that were then used for the arrests on and after December 7. Once the war began, both men continued working with community leaders and the Emergency Service Committee, a group organized by the military government to work with the Japanese community. They also continued to receive information from the police department, which organized the Police Contact Group to work closely with the local Japanese.

There has been some debate as to which members of the Honolulu community were most effective in shaping the conclusions of Shivers and Fielder. Ted Tsukiyama emphasizes the role of Big Five executive Charles Hemenway, vice president of Alexander & Baldwin and a regent of the University of Hawai'i. Before the war Hemenway had testified to congressional committees on the loyalty of Hawai'i's Nisei population. In 1940 he helped organize the Council of Interracial Unity. Daniel Inouye, as well as historians Dan Boylan and Michael Holmes, suggest that it was John Burns, then a Honolulu police officer who headed the espionage unit and the Moral Contact Group, who charted Shivers's direction. Burns is noted for a letter published in the *Honolulu Star-Bulletin* on November 18, 1941, that affirmed the loyalty of the Japanese population as prewar tensions mounted. Historian Roland Kotani indicates that Shivers responded directly to requests from the Japanese Chamber of Commerce to meet with local leaders. Shivers and his wife, both from the southern United States, also employed a young Japanese woman, Shizue Kobotake, as a house servant to learn more about the local Japanese community.[21]

Rather than any one person being the most effective, further research by Ted Tsukiyama and Tom Coffman makes it clear that Hemenway, Shivers, Burns, and others including naval intelligence officer Cecil Coggins all worked together. Hemenway reached out to Shivers. Shivers contacted Burns and sought his aid through the espionage unit of the police department. Hemenway and Coggins also brought Walter Dillingham into the conversations and engaged his support. Thus the levels of interaction ran from the Big Five through the police department to the Japanese chamber of commerce. The Honolulu community was amazingly well organized in its ability to bring information to the military and the FBI. Shivers and Fielder became convinced of the loyalty of the population and conveyed that to Emmons. Dillingham, as the islands' business patriarch, was particularly close to Emmons.[22]

Coffman also suggests that by the time of the Pearl Harbor attack, military authorities in Hawai'i, in stark contrast to their mainland counterparts, had become convinced of the basic loyalty of Hawai'i's Japanese population. They were also supportive of the use of the Nisei as American soldiers. Not only the work of Shivers and Fielder, but also substantial investigations begun in the late 1930s by the Office of Naval Intelligence buttressed this view. Because the potential consequences of "disloyalty" were so great in Hawai'i, the military mounted a massive investigation of the local Japanese population. General Short was favorably impressed with Hawai'i's Japanese, even if Emmons may not have picked this up on his brief visit in the summer of 1941. The army had no problem in supporting an ROTC unit at the University of Hawai'i and in commissioning some Nisei officers before the war. Substantial numbers of Nisei had also been drafted by late 1941.[23]

The lines of communication and the scope of previous investigations in Hawai'i seem clear, but what *really* convinced Emmons to stall and thwart his superiors in Washington throughout his tenure in Hawai'i? He could easily have pleased the president and advanced his personal position by evacuating the Japanese. The answer to this question may never be known. Emmons sought and got the support of Admiral Nimitz in stalling Washington. Yet all he reported in his memoir was, "Admiral Nimitz appreciated my position and the need for them as workers." Roosevelt, however, would have sent Emmons as many workers as he needed. It is unclear whether any inner personal moral or principle guided Emmons or whether he simply agreed with the recommendations of his intelligence officers. It is clear that the local business and professional community, with a few exceptions, encouraged and supported his actions—in sharp contrast to the situation in California, where the business community demanded evacuation. Or possibly Emmons thought he had more important matters to attend to. As head of the Hawaiian Department of the Army—and former chief of the Army Air Corps—he was heavily involved in planning aerial support for the navy at the Battle of Midway. American success at Midway in mid-1942 gave him a degree of military clout that may have insulated him from reprisals for his stand on Japanese evacuation. There is also the possibility, almost never discussed, that his capacity as military governor gave him a sense of greater responsibility to the territory and its population. Suffice it to say that by the time that Emmons relinquished his command in June 1943 any further substantial evacuation of the Japanese population was no longer an issue of military concern in Washington or Honolulu.[24]

While Emmons forestalled the massive evacuation of the Japanese, the local population chafed under other restrictions. All citizens of Japanese ancestry, along with those of Italian and German descent, were ordered to give up their firearms and other suspect possessions. Dan Inouye pointed out that this order included the destruction of his family's cherished shortwave radio. In fact, some thirteen thousand shortwave sets that could be accessed by Japanese—including those in Caucasian homes with Japanese servants—were destroyed or modified. Some land held by Japanese near defense installations was taken over by the military. But property owned by non-Japanese, including the grounds and buildings of the elite haole Punahou School, was also taken over for war purposes. Possibly the greatest burden carried by the Japanese population was the constant fear that at any moment a wholesale evacuation might be ordered. At the individual household level few people were aware of General Emmons's efforts at the top to prevent a full scale internment.[25]

Despite these privations, the islands' Japanese population remained intact and in Hawai'i during and after the war. The physical integrity, rather than the dislocation, of the Japanese community, both Issei and Nisei, during and after the war would be a major factor in the political development and push toward statehood of Hawai'i after World War II. Most of the internees from Hawai'i who were sent to the mainland returned after the war. Though Sanji Abe never ran for the legislature again, Thomas Sakakihara did not let his internment thwart his career. He ran for reelection in 1946 and won along with five other AJAs who joined him in the 1947 territorial legislature. After the war the internment saga, unlike martial law, did not became an issue that was widely discussed. In fact, it was rarely mentioned and to a great extent forgotten in Hawai'i for the next three decades. Executive Order 9066 actually remained in force until it was finally repealed by President Gerald Ford in February 1976. At that time the *Honolulu Star-Bulletin* ran the front-page headline "Honouliuli: Oahu's Little-Known World War II Internment Camp." The article quoted a number of prominent Hawai'i political figures who said they were unaware that such a camp had ever existed. Seemingly for the first time, internees like Thomas Sakakihara were interviewed and finally asked to tell their story. It would be another decade after 1976 before any glimmer of General Emmons's story would be known. The many pieces to Hawai'i's wartime internment puzzle are only becoming clear almost six decades after Pearl Harbor.[26]

The AJAs Go to War—And Come Back

While stalling Washington on the evacuation of the Japanese, General Emmons constantly had to think of ploys and acts to placate his superiors and the rampant anti-Japanese hysteria on the mainland. His evacuation of two thousand internees alone was not a sufficient act. He soon authorized another form of relocation both to allay national military concerns and to influence mainland opinion about Hawai'i's AJA population, particularly about its young men of draft age.

The loyalty of the Nisei was of paramount concern to the American military after the bombing of Pearl Harbor. But a year before, in September 1940 when the national Selective Service Act was enacted, it had not seemed so crucial. As noted earlier, military commanders in Hawai'i were favorable to the use of Nisei soldiers. Between September 1940 and December 1941 some three thousand men were drafted in Hawai'i, 50 percent of whom were Nisei. The pre–Pearl Harbor draftees of all races remained in Hawai'i and were trained at Schofield Barracks. By the war's outbreak they had completed their training and were members of the Hawaii National Guard. Could they now be treated differently from any other American soldiers?

Soon after the Pearl Harbor attack the AJA soldiers were separated from the other members of the Guard and were required to give up their rifles, though they soon got them back. General Short resisted suggestions to discharge the AJA Guard members in the few days he remained in command after the bombing. After assuming command, General Emmons found that newly arriving soldiers and their commanders from the mainland were "surprised to see Japanese in uniform and guarding sensitive areas." There was concern in both Hawai'i and Washington about the continued presence of the Nisei soldiers in the islands. What if the Japanese invaded Hawai'i and disguised themselves as Nisei Guard members? Emmons also received reports that in the event of a land invasion the Japanese would fire first on the AJAs in uniform. And some people still worried about the "loyalty" of the AJAs should an invasion occur.[27]

Emmons was under constant pressure from Washington to do something about the Nisei soldiers and to relocate them out of Hawai'i. By early 1942 Emmons, like his predecessor General Short, was convinced of their loyalty. He did not want to intern them. Instead he wanted to send the men out of Hawai'i and reorganize them as a combat unit to serve in Europe or Africa. As a Japanese naval attack on Midway Island seemed imminent in the spring of 1942, the concerns about the Nisei and Emmons's desire to relocate them increased. Emmons petitioned the War Department to organize the combat unit, but was rebuffed with the reply that a service battalion was more suitable. Under increased pressure from Emmons, Washington finally granted his request in late May—just as plans for Midway were in the final stages.[28]

In June 1942 the AJA Guard members, now called the Hawaii Provisional Infantry Battalion, were told to pack their bags and report to the docks; they were being shipped out. On June 5, as the Battle of Midway raged, the *SS Maui* left Honolulu with over fourteen hundred AJA Guard members, now redesignated as the 100th Infantry Battalion, on board. But where were they going? Many of the guardsmen thought they were being taken to relocation centers on the mainland. Their suspicions were not allayed when the ship docked in Oakland. They remained on board during the day and were then taken off at night and put in a series of trains traveling on different routes with the shades drawn. Days later they arrived in Wisconsin, not at a relocation center but at Camp McCoy, where they would undergo further military training. Later, in January 1943, they reported to Camp Shelby in Hattiesburg, Mississippi. Thus began the journey and adventures of the all-Hawai'i 100th Infantry Battalion, composed solely of AJA soldiers. The two top commanders, Farrant Turner and James Lovell, were Caucasian, but fully sixteen of the twenty-four officers were Nisei who had been commissioned before the war started. The 100th was a separate, stand-alone battalion, unconnected to a larger regiment. Its battle motto was "Remember Pearl Harbor."[29]

Even in the early days of their training, the AJAs of the 100th were well aware of the many battles they were fighting. As articulated by twenty-four-year-old first lieutenant and former junior high school teacher Sakae Takahashi, "We're fighting two wars. One for American democracy, and one against the prejudice toward us in America. That's a fact even in Hawaii." Takahashi wanted to win first-class citizenship for himself and his men back in Hawai'i once the war was over, including full participation in politics. The 100th could provide a base on which to build that political future at home. But in early 1943, the 100th was still in Mississippi.[30]

Even before the 100th left for the mainland, the fate of other young Nisei men in Hawai'i who had not been drafted before December 7 was uncertain. After the Pearl Harbor bombing they could not enlist or be drafted. Instead they were classified as 4C, enemy aliens, ineligible for the draft. A group of AJA ROTC students at the University of Hawai'i who had joined the Hawaii Territorial Guard were discharged from service. The dispossessed AJAs had supporters in Robert Shivers and Kendall Fielder, as well as Charles Hemenway and Hung Wai Ching. Ching, a Chinese American who had graduated with Hiram Fong from McKinley High School in 1924, was the director of the University YMCA and had served as secretary of the Council of Interracial Unity. Many of the ROTC students had been his "boys" at the "Y." Upon the recommendation of Shivers, Fielder, and Ching, General Emmons allowed the ejected ROTC students at the University of Hawai'i to form the Varsity Victory Volunteers in February 1942. The new group could work with the Corps of Engineers on local road maintenance and other military defense projects. Would there be a further role for these "college boys" in the future? In the spring of 1942 the status of the drafted Nisei in the National Guard and plans for the Battle of Midway remained in the forefront. The Varsity Victory Volunteers would have to wait.

Allied victory at the Battle of Midway in June 1942 precluded a Japanese land invasion of Hawai'i, and hence the fear that enemy troops would disguise themselves as local Nisei soldiers. Nonetheless there was a new concern that the draft-age Nisei, both in Hawai'i and on the mainland, might well feel insulted that their loyalty was challenged by their 4C classification. Would they now become hostile and alienated? Admiral Chester Nimitz soon joined with his military and civilian colleagues who had organized the Varsity Victory Volunteers and favored a new, all-volunteer Nisei combat unit. The new unit would take the AJAs out of Hawai'i along with mainland Nisei now in internment camps.[31]

The drive for the 100th and the Varsity Victory Volunteers had been an effort that originated and gained force in Hawai'i. The drive for a new all-volunteer Japanese American combat unit of both Hawai'i and mainland Nisei appears to have had early origins in Washington as well as in Honolulu. Colonel Moses Pettigrew, who had served in Hawai'i, was by 1942 General George Marshall's Far East intelligence officer in Washington. Pettigrew began pushing for a new all-Nisei unit in early 1942. There was almost total resistance to the idea in the capital. As the year wore on—particularly after the Battle of Midway and the organization of the 100th—other national figures began to promote the idea as a way to combat Japanese propaganda that the Americans were conducting a race war at home as well as abroad. Edwin O. Reischauer, a Harvard instructor in Far Eastern languages, advocated such a unit as did Elmer Davis, the director of the Office of War Information. Secretary of War

Henry Stimson came to support the idea, as did General Marshall. Marshall wanted to improve America's image among its allies and further affirm the principles recently enunciated in the Declaration of the United Nations. The holdouts were regularly President Roosevelt and Secretary of the Navy Knox.

Crucial in cementing the final decision was Assistant Secretary of War John G. McCloy. McCloy had consistently favored an all-Nisei unit and had been a supporter of Emmons in Washington. In December 1942 McCloy visited Hawai'i and was taken to see the work of the Varsity Victory Volunteers by Hung Wai Ching. He also met with Emmons and members of the Emergency Service Committee. McCloy carried news of his favorable findings in Hawai'i back to Washington. Exactly who convinced the president is unclear. But by January the War Department was ready to authorize the new unit. In February 1943 President Roosevelt gave his approval to the formation of a new all-Nisei unit—the 442nd Regimental Combat Team to be composed of both Hawai'i and mainland Nisei soldiers, but commanded by "white American officers." Roosevelt made his announcement with the statement:

> No loyal citizen of the United States should be denied the dem-
> ocratic right to exercise the responsibilities of his citizenship,
> regardless of his ancestry. The principle on which this country
> was founded and by which it has always been governed is that
> Americanism is a matter of the mind and heart; Americanism
> is not, and never was, a matter of race or ancestry.[32]

Roosevelt's words and actions were treated with joy and celebration in the islands. Some ten thousand AJAs in Hawai'i volunteered, includ-ing Dan Inouye, who had already begun his premedical training at the University of Hawai'i. Though the army initially planned to take fifteen hundred recruits from Hawai'i and three thousand men from the main-land, the proportions were soon reversed. On March 28, 1943, some 2,686 AJA volunteers, including members of the Varsity Victory Volunteers, sailed from Hawai'i to begin their training along with the men of the 100th at Camp Shelby, Mississippi. A crowd of over fifteen thousand cheered them off at the docks. This was quite a different scene from the clandestine departure of the 100th ten months earlier. The men of the 442nd, like those of the 100th, were going to prove their loyalty and change things at home upon their return. Their motto "Go for Broke," a term from the plantation game of craps played by many of the volunteers, would later be heard around the world.

Amidst the cheers and jubilation at the docks, we should remember that the departure of the 442nd was still a part of the army's overall goal of relocating a certain portion of the Hawai'i's Japanese population to avoid what it saw as complications at home. Would it work? The Japanese in Hawai'i were prepared to hope for the best in 1943. In those hopes they transformed President Roosevelt into their hero. As author Masayo Duus explained, "Not only had Roosevelt not put them in relocation camps, but he had allowed the Japanese Americans to volunteer for military service as full-fledged Americans." Roosevelt still kept the islands under martial law and continued to intern mainland Japanese Americans. There is also evidence that the famous words "Americanism is not a matter of race" had been added to his speech at the last minute by Office of War Information director Elmer Davis. Did the president mean what he said at all? In the jubilation of March 1943 no one seemed to care. Pictures of Roosevelt now adorned the walls of the homes of the "boys" who left with the 442nd. If on the mainland "Dr. New Deal" had become "Dr. Win the War," one may well say that in Hawai'i "Dr. Martial Law and Relocation" was transformed into "Dr. Go for Broke."[33]

The 442nd arrived at Camp Shelby in April 1943 to join the 100th for training. The older unit then went to the European theater of war, landing first in North Africa and then continuing to Salerno, Italy, in September 1943. Over the next year the 100th fought at Cassino and Anzio. In June 1944 the 442nd joined the 100th in Italy, where the two units were combined as the 442nd, though the 100th always kept its separate battle insignia. The combined units fought together in Italy and then went to France in October 1944. They landed at Marseilles, but proceeded on to heavy fighting in the Vosges Mountains of northeastern France. After spending the winter of 1944–45 guarding the French/Italian border near Menton, the 442nd spent the last months of the war with General Mark Clark's forces back in Italy near Genoa in March–May 1945.

The military record of the 442nd / 100th forces became legendary. Possibly the most celebrated maneuver was the rescue of the "Lost Battalion" of the 36th Infantry Division during November 1944 in the Vosges forest. The 36th Infantry Division was originally a unit of the Texas National Guard, though by 1944 it was composed of soldiers from many states. The 1st battalion of the division's 141st Regiment, the so-called "Lost Battalion," was surrounded by German troops during a battle to liberate the town of Bruyeres. The 442nd freed the "Lost Battalion" after four days of heavy fighting. Of the 275 men in the Texas unit, 211 were rescued. In this rescue and other fighting in France, the 442nd lost 161 men with another 2,000 wounded—over two-thirds of the 2,943-man force that entered the Vosges in October. When the 442nd returned to Italy, it was reinforced with newly "drafted" and trained Nisei troops. In January 1944 the draft restriction on Japanese Americans had been removed. The only restriction was that all Nisei draftees would be assigned to the 442nd.[34]

For their fighting in France and Italy, the 442nd / 100th won more decorations than any other unit during World War II. General Mark Clark called it "the most decorated unit in the history of the United States." Some 6,000–8,000 individuals received over 18,000 decorations including 9,500 Purple Hearts, 4,000 Bronze Hearts, 52 Distinguished Service Crosses, 22 Legion of Merit medals, and 1 Congressional Medal of Honor. The combined units received seven Presidential Distinguished Unit Citations. They had certainly proven their loyalty. But the list of honors at the end of the war did not tell the entire story. Fifty-five years later, in the year 2000, the records of those decorated were reviewed, and twenty members of the 442nd/100th were upgraded to the Congressional Medal of Honor. Six of those men, including U.S. Senator Daniel Inouye, were present to receive the award from President Bill Clinton on June 21, 2000. "Their motto was 'Go for Broke'," announced the president. "They risked it all to win it all." The medals won by the 442nd/100th show their victory in Sakae Takahashi's "first war" to win American democracy. But even before the decorated AJAs returned to Hawai'i, forces were at work on the young men that prepared and transformed them to win that "second war" for "first-class" citizenship in Hawai'i.[35]

Dan Inouye's 1967 autobiography *Journey to Washington* is a classic document in tracing the transformation of a "local boy" from Honolulu, whose life ambition in 1941 was to become a surgeon, into an aspiring national politician. The transformation began the moment he enlisted. Initially Inouye was turned down for service on the grounds that his medical training made him more valuable in Hawai'i than out of Hawai'i with the 442nd. After several entreaties to the draft board and his resignation from the university, Inouye was finally allowed to enlist—

the next to last of the 2,686 volunteers. In opting for the infantry over medical school and seeking to overturn the initial draft board decision, Inouye began his transformation by rejecting his assigned or designated role in the local community.

Once Inouye and his fellow AJAs landed on the mainland the changes gained speed. For the first time Inouye and most of the other Nisei saw another part of the United States. Inouye's account tells not merely of a different landscape but of a different set of social relations. The members of the 442nd often wrote that they were amazed to see Caucasians or haoles in working-class positions. In Mississippi the Nisei confronted southern racial patterns and the anomalous position of being told to act Caucasian.

While seeing new landscapes Inouye also grew into a position of leadership among his men. Before leaving home a family friend took Dan aside and taught him how to play craps. In the training barracks he soon became a leader among his buddies with his uncanny ability to play the odds, take the sweepstakes most nights, and then serve as an informal lending bank to his friends. Once in combat the leadership training continued as Inouye advanced from squad leader to lieutenant and platoon leader.

The greatest transformation, however, took place after Inouye was wounded and lost an arm in battle. This injury occurred in Italy in April 1945, just weeks before the end of the war. To recover Inouye was taken out of his all-Nisei unit and transferred over the next two years to a series of army hospitals and rehabilitation centers in Italy, Miami, Atlantic City, and Battle Creek, Michigan. In these new locations he found himself mainly in the company of wounded haoles.

In Atlantic City Inouye and his haole friends became particularly close after the death of one of their companions. This bonding led to what Inouye describes as a true "Pygmalion project" in which his haole buddies "decided they were going to buff the jagged corners of the kid from Moiliili who pretended to know all there was to know about anything worth knowing—but still broke into pidgin-English when he got excited; who had been in some of the best restaurants in the world's most sophisticated cities—and was still more comfortable with chopsticks . . . whose idea of a stimulating evening was a high stakes crap game; and whose favorite before, during, and after-dinner beverage was 3.2 beer." His haole friends orchestrated the transformation by changing his speech patterns from the pidgin English of the islands to standard English. And he added the game of bridge to his repertoire of card games. "I'll have to admit," Inouye later noted, "that bridge never gave me the gut-tightening excitement of a good crap game, but on the other hand, these days I sometimes wonder how many people a United States Senator could round up for a crap game. But make it bridge and there's no problem."[36]

Inouye's easy interaction with the hospital haoles was quite a change from social interactions in Hawai'i, where the hierarchy was more rigid and where he might have been expected to stay in his place. The end result of such a change was not merely social polish and gentlemanly manners. "More than any single grace or amenity," explained Inouye, "they taught me to feel relaxed and at home among people of all sorts. . . . You might even say that by washing the grime from my poor boy's face and straightening my nisei necktie, they made it possible for me to think seriously about trying for political office."[37]

Inouye's transformation was not totally haole driven. There was one other Nisei in the rehabilitation ward in Atlantic City: Sakae Takahashi, the lieutenant from the 100th who had talked so often of winning that "second war" against prejudice at home. Inouye and Takahashi talked of their dreams for Hawai'i and of aspiring for political offices and positions that Japanese Americans had not previously thought could be theirs. It was here that Inouye, who could never become a surgeon with one arm, decided to give up any form of medicine and become a lawyer and budding politician.

If the political transformation of Daniel Inouye took place because of his "relocation" outside of Hawai'i, the absence of a massive relocation of the Japanese in Hawai'i also made that transformation possible. If Inouye, Takahashi, and other 442nd/100th veterans wanted to change things at home, it was crucial that there be a home to change. The Hawai'i AJAs had this "home" in contrast to many of their mainland Nisei buddies who had left their families in the relocation centers at Manzanar, California; Topaz Lake, Utah; or Jerome, Arkansas.

Not only did the AJAs have a home to change, they could also use the organization of the 100th and 442nd to bring about that change. The importance of the 100th and the 442nd clubs that emerged in Hawai'i after the war cannot be overstated. Prior to the war there were very limited venues in which the AJAs could prepare for political or civic life. Their unenfranchised parents could not train them in local political party traditions. Labor union activities, dormant since the 1920s, were just reemerging in 1941. Their prewar knowledge of, and venue for participation in, civics came mainly from their high school teachers and high school activities. It was in their army units that they finally gained their most valuable lessons in leadership and public participation. The Hawai'i AJAs brought this new knowledge honed in Europe back to the mid-Pacific. We may well wonder if such changes could ever have been "homegrown." Would the transformation of Dan Inouye and other AJAs have occurred if the war had not come, and if the 100th/442nd had not been "relocated" outside of Hawai'i?

The Mainland Comes to Hawai'i

The transformation of the AJAs was by no means the only change that the war brought to Hawai'i. While the AJAs and other islanders who served in a wide variety of different military units left Hawai'i, hordes of individuals and groups came to train and work in Hawai'i during the war. They too would alter and reshape the life of the islands.[38]

Before the mainlanders began pouring in, it took a few months to assess both the damage done to the islands and the role Hawai'i should play in the war. Possibly the most notable effect of the bombing at Pearl Harbor was how little damage actually occurred outside of the sinking of the fleet. The pictures that appear in most textbooks, as well as motion pictures, of Pearl Harbor on December 7 give an image of massive destruction. But the military capability of Honolulu, including Pearl Harbor, was effectively back to normal in a matter of weeks. In the first months of 1942 Hawai'i girded for another aerial attack and a possible land invasion by the Japanese. What was most noticeable in those months was an outflow of people. The military moved some thirty thousand women and children, about two-thirds of which were military dependents, to the mainland to protect them from the feared attack. But by late spring of 1942, and particularly after the Allied victory at the Battle of Midway, Hawai'i shifted from being a defensive installation to become, in the words of Gwenfread Allen, "a springboard for the Pacific offensive . . . as a training, staging and supply, and casualty evacuation area for all branches of the armed forces." The direction of the human flow quickly reversed into the islands.[39]

The number of military personnel who flooded the islands was staggering; nearly all of them were centered on the island of O'ahu, and most of them were male. On December 7, 1941, there were 43,000 soldiers on O'ahu; by June 1942 there were 135,000. When naval ships docked in Honolulu, as many as 35,000 sailors at a time would come on shore. By the peak year of 1944, the population of Hawai'i had doubled from its 1940 level of 427,884 to 858,945, including 406,811 members of the armed forces. Staggering as these numbers are, the total number of individuals who passed through the islands in military service from 1942 to 1945 is much greater, though difficult to calculate. At least one million men in the army alone were trained at Schofield Barracks during the war. Possibly some indication of the overall numbers can be gleaned from the statistic that sixty-six million individual visits were made to USO facilities during the war.[40]

The military personnel were only part of the inflow. Civilian workers arrived in droves, primarily as construction workers. As many as 82,000 civilian workers, almost one-quarter of the civilian labor force and mostly single men, arrived from the mainland during peak construction periods. If the men of the 442nd first saw haoles in working-class positions when they went to the mainland, the islanders who stayed at home saw working-class Caucasians for the first time with the imported war workers. In the same vein, if the AJAs were first introduced to southern racial patterns when they went to Camp Shelby, homebound islanders saw those same racial relations as thirty thousand African Americans, both civilian and military, interacted with southern whites who arrived in the islands during the war.

Such floods of new war immigrants could not simply blend into the landscape away from the prewar resident population. By 1945 the military permanently occupied twice as much land as it held in 1940. Hundreds of millions of dollars of new construction for buildings, roads, airfields, radio towers, and other defense installations were ordered by the armed forces. When there were not sufficient buildings or installations on the military bases to house all operations, the military simply took over civilian buildings, including the campus of Punahou School in Honolulu. "Practically every square mile of the Islands," explained Gwenfread Allen, "underwent some measure of physical change."[41]

Islanders and newcomers were constantly in contact with each other—not always in a mutually advantageous way. With the imposition of martial law, islanders were frozen in their jobs and wages as of December 20, 1941. They saw newcomers from the mainland take highly paid jobs that they could not obtain. Many writers suggest that the labor militancy that took place in Hawai'i after World War II was generated by this "frozen" labor policy.

If islanders at times resented the war workers, the reverse was also true. As Allen explains, "The story of the war workers and the community is not a happy one. The importees came with high expectations. They found chaotic conditions, and complained about Hawaii." Housing conditions were always overcrowded, if adequate at all. Even with their high wages, workers complained of the territory's 2 percent income tax.[42]

For many newcomers, both civilian and military, Hawai'i's racial and ethnic diversity presented a new challenge and tension, particularly as mainland males clashed with locals for the affection of island females. The dichotomy between what newcomers expected Hawai'i to be and what it actually was during the war created some of the biggest problems. Hawai'i had been advertised to mainlanders as a tropical paradise for decades before the war. But the reality of overcrowding, blackouts, and a curfew was too much for some. According to Allen, "The moonlight and the palms were there, but the beaches were crowded with humanity and strung with barbed wire." The simple fact that so many of the newcomers were preparing for war and anticipating combat caused them to associate Hawai'i with an unpleasant, if not deadly, future. For all of these reasons "complaining about Hawai'i" became a staple activity of many of the war workers and servicemen.[43]

Islanders and island institutions attempted to provide hospitality to the newcomers and to soften their sense of an uncertain future. In addition to the sixty-six million visits to the USO, individuals hosted servicemen in their homes. Sugar heiress Kamokila Campbell, in conjunction with the USO, entertained over 350,000 sailors and soldiers at her estate on Ewa Beach in O'ahu, renamed "Camp Bell." Churches, musical organizations, and even the Honolulu Academy of Fine Arts encouraged service personnel to participate in their activities. But the numbers of newcomers were overwhelming. Thus an individual serviceman or woman might well have remembered a delightful weekend at a secluded estate, regular involvement in a church or museum program, and dances at the USO. Some were even happily married in the islands. Others might only remember Hawai'i as a place where a tawdry—and overpriced—evening in a brothel on Hotel Street or a quick photo with a "hula girl" were the limits of island hospitality and charm. Someone—in fact, thousands of someones—could vouch for any or all of these experiences. The specific memory that the newcomers carried back to the mainland after the war might well influence their opinion as to whether Hawai'i should become a state. After the war state-hood leaders would debate whether they should appeal for support to the thousands of mainland voters who had recently come to know the islands. Should they gamble on what those memories might be?

Hawai'i endured enormous stress and trial during the war. Despite all the stress, the economic and civic institutions of the islands held up amazingly well. Before the war military authorities worried that the islands' food supply could never be adequate because so much food was imported from the mainland. What if an enemy blockade prevented the landing of supplies? In 1940 the military severely criticized the Big Five for their reluctance to convert pineapple and sugar fields to diversified agriculture. But once the war began, a storage system for stockpiling imported food worked so well that the islands experienced no sustained shortages of any item. In fact, it was the overall availability of food and staples that led Garner Anthony to conjecture about the islanders' acqui-escence to martial law. The plantations responded to the military's increased worldwide demand for sugar and its desire for canned pineap-ple as troop rations. Pineapple production actually rose over the course of the war.

As the war progressed, Hawai'i's utilities responded to the ever-increasing demand for more electricity and water supplies. The unceas-ing demand for labor found a local response from Hawai'i's schoolchildren, who attended school for only four extended weekdays in order to work on a lengthened weekend. Many of the social disloca-tions often associated with war zones were restrained or prevented in Hawai'i. There was no substantial increase in crime during the war, nor were there sanitation and disease problems. Inflation was not a major problem in wartime Hawai'i. Food prices were frozen in December 1941, and price controls were eventually instituted on almost all items of trade, including tattoos and photographs with hula girls. From mid-1943 to mid-1946 food prices increased only 3 percent, and overall prices 6 percent. In the last six months of 1946, when price controls were lifted, those percentages increased over sixfold. If Hawai'i was overcrowded and at times uncomfortable during the war, it was never dangerous, unsafe, or under any signs of social or economic collapse. In both its prepared-ness for the war and its execution as the center for Pacific operations, the territory brought distinction to itself as the nation's primary domes-tic window on World War II. Would statehood, which had been put on hold after the plebiscite of 1940, now be the reward for that service?

Hawai'i in 1945

In 1945 a transformed Hawai'i faced the nation. The islands were no longer what Gwenfread Allen had once called "an isolated Pacific paradise." Internally much, though by no means all, of the social order had been drastically changed, even overturned. Though the islands' Japanese population had been spared a massive dislocation, the "most Japanese" aspects of the population had been changed. The interning of scores of traditional Japanese cultural leaders—language school teachers, Buddhist priests, and selected other community leaders—undercut the previous leadership of the older Issei generation. Leadership now passed to the transformed Nisei, who would soon take an expanded leadership role not only within the Japanese community, but also in the overall political community of the territory and the nation.

The haole political order had also been rocked by the experience of martial law. Haole leaders such as Joseph Farrington and Garner Anthony now clearly saw the limitations and hazards of continued territorial status. The arguments of some of the older conservatives, such as Walter Dillingham, that the islands had done just fine under territorial status rang hollow to many postwar leaders.

If the islands themselves had been transformed, the nation's knowledge of Hawai'i had also been changed. Every American now knew where Pearl Harbor was, and millions had now been there and experienced life in Hawai'i. Those who had not been there had probably seen Hawai'i in the newsreels that preceded so many motion pictures throughout the war. The saga of wartime Hawai'i soon became a staple in postwar American literature. James Jones, an enlisted soldier at Schofield Barracks during the war, first published a series of short stories after the war that culminated in his classic novel *From Here to Eternity* (1951). Boston author John P. Marquand was stationed in Hawai'i as a naval attaché during the war. He later published a series of short stories that epitomized the tensions in wartime Hawai'i. In "Lunch at Honolulu" (1954) Marquand brilliantly juxtaposes the explosive personality of a young naval aviator just off a cruiser and "glad to be alive" with the pristine calm of a lunch at an elite kama'aina home. Historians Beth Bailey and David Farber hypothesize in *The First Strange Place* (1992) that the new cultural contacts of race, gender, ethnicity, and sex spawned in wartime Hawai'i paved the way for many of the racial and social changes that occurred throughout the nation after World War II. These changes, they claim, helped shape a new American identity.

But what would all of these transformations bring to Hawai'i in the immediate years after the war? If Americans now knew about Hawai'i, had they lost their prejudices against the islands' multiracial population that had so thwarted the territory's desire for statehood before the war? In March 1946 a Gallup poll indicated that 60 percent of mainland Americans approved of statehood for Hawai'i—up from only 48 percent in January 1941. Early in 1946 the U.S. House of Representatives dispatched a subcommittee headed by Representative Henry Larcade of Louisiana to hold statehood hearings in the islands. A year later Delegate Joseph Farrington seemed optimistic of Hawai'i's chances, particularly as the Republicans captured the congressional elections of 1946. In early 1947 Farrington, along with eleven other members of Congress, introduced another bill for Hawai'i statehood. To many of the islands' statehood promoters it looked as if a forty-ninth star might soon be added to flag. But there were other signs that not all of America's prewar attitudes toward the territory had been transformed by the war. In 1947 Dan Inouye had finished his mainland rehabilitation and was on the way back to Honolulu. Dressed in full uniform with his service medals and new captain's bars, he stopped at a barbershop in San Francisco for a haircut. The barber looked at him and said, "We don't cut Jap hair." Inouye responded, "I'm sorry for you and the likes of you." He continued on to Honolulu.[44]

Inouye's rebuff in San Francisco was merely an indication of the roadblocks that Hawai'i would face in the years immediately after the war. When Hawai'i eventually became the fiftieth, not the forty-ninth, state in 1959, its success turned out to be tied to the transformation of that other territory 2,500 miles to the north that was also changed by World War II. We will return to the postwar saga of Hawai'i's road to statehood. But to understand that saga, we must first look north to Alaska, the "land without people" that we left with Jean Potter in 1942.

Chapter 4

World War II and the Creation
of Modern Alaska

Never before, not even at the time of the gold rushes, was
the Territory so advertised. Americans, who seemed to have
forgotten the existence of the northern possession, redis-
covered Alaska.

—*U.S. Army Alaska pamphlet 360–5,*
on the impact of World War II in Alaska

T he radio was the all-important medium of communication that
announced the bombing of Pearl Harbor to residents of the two
distant territories as well as to millions of other Americans on that
fateful Sunday morning in December 1941. Daniel Inouye and his
family learned of the attack from a small home radio in Honolulu.
Twenty-five-hundred miles due north in Fairbanks, local broadcaster
Augie Hiebert heard the same news while listening to his shortwave
radio at the new KFAR station. The reactions of Inouye and Hiebert
were, however, quite different. Inouye waited a few moments for a
phone call from the local authorities to tell him what to do next.
Hiebert also picked up the phone, but to call the local authorities. He
suspected that they might not have heard. He called army headquarters
at Ladd Field in Fairbanks, which then contacted General Buckner in
Anchorage. This was the first that Buckner knew of the attack. In Juneau
a local radio station picked up the news from Seattle and called
Governor Gruening.[1]

The slipshod method of communication that Sunday morning was
indicative of the overall lack of preparedness in Alaska as late as
December 1941. Over the next four years a vastly different territory
would emerge. World War II did not so much transform and change an
old Alaska as it created a new modern Alaska with very few remnants

from the past. There were, of course, some elements from the old prewar sourdough Alaska that survived until 1945. But compared to Hawai'i, there was less continuity from 1941 to 1945 in Alaska and more change. The very swarm of newcomers to the land without people that Jean Potter chronicled was indicative of that coming change. When fighting reached its peak in the Aleutian Islands in 1943, soldiers and civilians swelled the territory's population to a high of 233,000. When the fighting ended, these numbers subsided. But in 1946 the territory's population was still 99,000, almost a 33 percent increase over its 1940 base of 75,000.

Population was not the only change. Alaska's economy was effectively turned upside down. Hawai'i's sugar-pineapple economy survived and even thrived during the war. Not so Alaska's extractive/mining economy. We have already noted that the Kennecott Copper Mine closed in 1938. Coal never fulfilled its prewar promise. Only gold survived by 1941. In 1942 that link to the sourdough past came to a sudden end when the National War Production Board ordered all gold mines in the nation closed as a war/labor emergency measure. Juneau's A-J Mine was granted an exemption but closed of its own accord in 1944. Though gold would have a brief revival after the war, it would never fully recover. From the old economy only salmon fishing and canning remained. As in Hawai'i, Alaska's economy shifted to military defense. By 1945 over $1 billion had been spent on military construction and operating expenses within the territory. So dramatic was the change that economist George W. Rogers labeled the 1940–58 period "Military Alaska."[2]

Military impact on the economy was only a part of that new creation. Political life in the territory was affected as much as the economy. We have already noted that the prewar, sourdough miner/newspaperman political tradition provided little in the way of continuity for the future. The newly appointed territorial governor, Ernest Gruening, seized on the expanded level of war activity in the territory to change the political life of Alaska. He pushed the territory, kicking and screaming at times, toward a modern system of government. By 1945 this modernized Alaska could at last seriously contemplate statehood.

Social changes, particularly in regard to the territory's native population, would also be a legacy of the war. Native groups, who had been effectively marginalized in Alaska's political and economic life before the war, were brought into the mainstream of territorial life and affairs. In

1945 the territorial legislature enacted the first law banning discrimination against natives in public places—a forerunner of postwar civil rights legislation in the mainland United States.

In World War I Alaska had served America's fighting men in far-off lands with its vast production of copper for shells and canned salmon for food. In World War II it was less Alaska's products that served the fighting men and more the territory itself. Alaska was now the far-off land where men were fighting and building a permanent defense force. The old sourdough Alaska was giving way to the new military Alaska that would become the forty-ninth state.

The legacy of the war would only be realized after four years of travail and dramatic change. Let us return to December 7, 1941, and follow the events that took place after Hiebert told Buckner that the war had come.

The Aleutians—Buildup and War

The attack at Pearl Harbor gave a more focused direction to the military buildup of Alaska. A year earlier it had not been clear whether the principal bastion of defense should be interior Alaska and the Arctic Coast where a German air attack might come or the Aleutians where the Japanese might strike. During 1941 construction progressed throughout the territory at Anchorage and Fairbanks, at Dutch Harbor, and at Sitka and Kodiak. None of these bases, however, was completed or prepared to combat an enemy attack when the war came in December 1941. It was now clear that the primary line of defense should be the Aleutians.

The Aleutians had great importance both as a line of defense against Japanese attack and as a line of potential offense for an Allied attack on Japan. Defense advocates pointed to the need to arm the Aleutians to prevent the Japanese from taking the islands and then threatening important defense installations on the Pacific Coast, particularly the Boeing bomber plant near Seattle or the naval base at Bremerton, Washington. Dutch Harbor must be defended because it controlled the principal sea passage, Unimak Pass, through the Aleutians to the Bering Sea and the Russian Far East.[3]

The American military never fully embraced the use of the Aleutians for offense, but this decision was not clear to the Japanese. For the duration of the war they believed that the Americans would use the islands as a path to bomb or invade Japan. Thus the Japanese had a desire to establish bases in the Aleutians to prevent an anticipated American attack, just as the Americans wanted similar bases to defend against an anticipated Japanese attack. In the winter and spring of 1941–42 the American buildup of the Aleutians gained force with construction of both navy and army bases at Dutch Harbor. To protect the crucial Dutch Harbor stronghold with air power, bases at Otter Point (Fort Glenn) on nearby Umnak Island and at Cold Bay (Fort Randall) on the Alaska Peninsula were hurried to completion. Their construction was carried on in secret with supplies en route to the islands labeled for the "Blair Fish and Packing Company" or "Saxton and Company," two fictitious canneries. Planes were able to land at these bases by March 1942. The successful construction of the airfields, as well as all other army construction in Alaska, was led by Captain, later Colonel, Benjamin Talley, an able and congenial army engineer who oversaw the completion of a $300 million military infrastructure in the territory.

While the Aleutian air bases were readying for an attack, the first American action against the Japanese actually took place in the established towns of the territory. Alaska's land operations, though not its naval operations, were under the Western Defense Command, headquartered in San Francisco. When the internment of all Japanese and Japanese Americans was implemented in California through Executive Order 9066, General DeWitt extended it to Alaska. Beginning in April 1942, some 230 Japanese and Japanese Americans were removed from the territory and placed in relocation and internment camps in various western states. While the relocation of the resident Japanese took place, American intelligence gradually pieced together Japan's intentions for the Aleutians as military cryptographers broke the Japanese codes.

By May 1942 the Japanese had decided to establish a defense perimeter from the Western Aleutians to Midway Island, and further south to Wake and the Gilbert Islands. The defense perimeter would guard against American attack and draw out the Pacific Fleet from Honolulu to places where the Japanese could engage it. Colonel Jimmy Doolittle's raid on Tokyo in April 1942 highlighted this need. Japanese intelligence ascertained that the raid had been launched from an aircraft carrier that slipped through the perimeter. But some Japanese commanders may still have believed that the attack was launched from Midway or from secret bases in the Aleutians. Whether Doolittle's attack came from land bases or from the carrier, the Japanese need for the Midway-Aleutian defense perimeter was crucial.[4]

The Japanese had two major objectives in the Aleutians for their defense perimeter. They first planned a diversionary raid on Dutch Harbor before the attack on Midway. By striking first in the Aleutians, the Japanese hoped to divert a part of the U.S. Pacific Fleet sailing from Honolulu. If this feint worked, a victory at Midway would come more easily. After the Dutch Harbor attack, the Japanese intended to occupy the islands of Kiska, Attu, and possibly Adak—all seven hundred to eight hundred miles west of Dutch Harbor. The Japanese plan intercepted by American military intelligence indicated that Attu and Kiska would be used for defensive purposes. There was no initial intent to occupy Dutch Harbor or to stage offensive operations against the Alaska mainland.

The Aleutian campaign was a naval operation and hence run by the Pacific commander, Admiral Chester Nimitz, from Honolulu. Nimitz dispatched Admiral Robert Theobald to Alaska navy headquarters on Kodiak Island in May. Buckner's land-based role was to provide support for Theobald. Though knowledge of the Japanese codes alerted the Americans to a coming attack at Dutch Harbor, the impenetrable fog along the islands prevented the Americans from actually seeing the approach of the aircraft carriers and Japanese planes. The Japanese launched their first attack on Dutch Harbor on June 3, 1942, and then again on June 4. The fighting war had come to Alaska.[5]

The Japanese caused some damage on Dutch Harbor, but the fog thwarted them as well. They were totally surprised to find that the airbases were not at Dutch Harbor but on Umnak Island and Cold Bay. The feint to divert the American fleet did not work, and Japanese fortunes soon fell at Midway. The American victory there on June 6 stopped the major Japanese advance in the Pacific. But what about their plan to occupy Kiska and Attu? Some in the Japanese command argued to abandon the Aleutian campaign. But a decision was quickly made to take the islands in order to assuage the sting of defeat at Midway. The Japanese successfully occupied Kiska and Attu on June 7. The Japanese may have been thwarted in their ambition to dominate the Pacific, but they now occupied American territory for the first time.[6]

With Attu and Kiska occupied, Alaska became a central war zone for the next fourteen months. Almost 150,000 troops along with the materiel to support them were massed to rid some 8,500 Japanese from two small, distant, fog-shrouded islands. At the time of capture, Kiska and Attu had a total population of slightly more than fifty people. These two islands, unlike Dutch Harbor, had little strategic importance in and of themselves. They would become important only if the Japanese fortified them, built airfields, and then advanced toward the Alaska mainland. Their greatest importance was symbolic—as occupied American soil. This created tremendous propaganda value for the Japanese. For the Americans it created the absolute need to free them.[7]

As a factor in the creation of modern Alaska, the Aleutian campaign of 1942–43 was all at once of seminal importance and of little importance at all. Its seminal importance was that it made Alaska central to the overall war effort. Yet once Attu and Kiska were freed in 1943, the Aleutians were quickly forgotten both by the nation and by many Alaskans. The Aleutian campaign came to be called "The Forgotten War" by many historians of World War II. The long-lasting changes that the military buildup brought would be more pronounced and important in other parts of Alaska. To understand this dual importance, let us see how the Aleutians were "freed" before we "forget" them.

Kiska and Attu were a long way from Dutch Harbor and the military installations at Otter Point and Cold Bay. A series of connecting airfields and naval bases were quickly constructed, again by Colonel Talley, on islands between Dutch Harbor and Kiska/Attu—specifically at Atka, Amchitka, and most importantly Adak. These bases and fields, hundreds of miles nearer to the occupied islands than Dutch Harbor, made it possible to stage air raids and then land troops to retake the islands. By September 1942 the airfield at Adak was complete. Throughout the summer and autumn of 1942 Attu and Kiska were subjected to continual bombing by American fliers.

While the bombing of Attu and Kiska progressed, a basic problem in command developed. Buckner and Theobald did not get along. Anchorage publisher Bob Atwood said the two argued openly at social occasions in his home. Theobald had blundered early in the campaign. He did not believe the original intelligence reports that the Japanese only intended to "occupy" Kiska and Attu. He assumed they must be planning to take Dutch Harbor and then stage further raids on the Alaska mainland. As a result, he positioned his ships east of Dutch Harbor and failed to engage the enemy. Buckner thought Theobald was too cautious and even distributed a poem that seemed to mock the admiral's bravery. There were rumors that Buckner might be removed, but in January 1943 Nimitz replaced Theobald with Admiral Thomas Kinkaid, who had performed heroic duty at the Battle of

Guadalcanal. Kinkaid and Buckner worked well together, and their joint effort progressed.

After the Americans occupied Adak, the Japanese assumed that this marked an American offensive along the Aleutians to invade Japan. They responded by reinforcing the garrisons at Kiska and Attu. Kinkaid countered by establishing a naval blockade at the rear of the islands. In March 1943 Japanese ships attempted to challenge the blockade. On March 26 near the Russian Komandorski Islands a grueling three-and-one-half-hour gunnery battle, the longest in American naval history, ensued and the Japanese fleet retreated. After the Battle of the Komandorskis, Kiska and Attu were effectively isolated from further Japanese reinforcement.

By May 1943 U.S. troops were massed, principally at the Adak naval base, for an assault on the more distant Attu, chosen as the first island to invade because it was considered to be less heavily occupied and fortified than Kiska. The Attu invasion, one of the first major amphibious landings of World War II, began on May 11, 1943 with some sixteen thousand troops. At the outset American commanders anticipated a three-day battle. The weather and the terrain, coupled with the fact that the Japanese were entrenched in the central mountains of the island, turned it into a grueling affair. As the Japanese intended to leave no survivors, the fighting continued for nineteen days. On May 30, 1943, Attu was back under the American flag. As a proportion of casualties to troop strength, the battle of Attu was the second bloodiest of World War II, surpassed only by the capture of Iwo Jima. American deaths numbered 549 with another 3,200 wounded or incapacitated. Of the 2,600 Japanese on the island, only 28 were taken prisoner.

Even while the battle of Attu wore on, Colonel Talley established airfields on Attu and neighboring Shemya Island to be used for an aerial and land assault on Kiska, where 6,000 Japanese were entrenched. In June and July American planes bombed Kiska over and over again. Given the high casualty rate at Attu, a much larger force of 34,000 troops and thirty-four ships was readied for the Kiska invasion. By early August, American surveillance planes reported that they could not see any enemy troops. This time it was Admiral Kinkaid's turn to doubt intelligence reports. He assumed that the Japanese had entrenched themselves in the central hills as they had done at Attu. The intelligence reports were correct again. The Japanese had decided to evacuate Kiska to avoid another Attu. In late July under cover of fog a Japanese fleet of fourteen ships evaded the American blockade. Though two Japanese vessels collided and sank, nine destroyers slipped into Kiska Harbor and evacuated the remaining troops by August 1. When the Americans finally landed on August 15, 1943, they found an empty island. Despite the absence of the enemy, about one hundred Americans were killed by friendly fire, by Japanese booby traps, and from the sinking of a ship that hit a Japanese mine. With the successful occupation of unoccupied Kiska, the Aleutian Campaign came to an end. In the minds of many it would soon be "forgotten." Why?[8]

As noted earlier, the occupation of Kiska and Attu posed a threat only if the Japanese decided to advance forward from those strongholds. The islands themselves were not of great strategic importance. Thus regaining them was not of great consequence. Though the new naval bases and airfields built on the Aleutians might have been used for an assault on Japan, this did not happen except for a series of raids on the Kurile Islands in the last year of the war. The impenetrable weather of the Aleutians, which had so confounded both sides in the Aleutian campaign, made the islands a less than optimal staging ground for aerial assaults. As Samuel Eliot Morison, the earliest and most noted historian of the Aleutian Campaign, explained, "flying weather was the exception rather than the rule." Instead the mid-Pacific islands far to the south of the Aleutians became the "island-hopping" route for the assault on Japan. It was to those other locations in the Pacific that the troops amassed in Alaska moved.[9]

Those later raids on the Kuriles were actually more important than most observers on the local scene realized at the time. In a later chapter we will see how the Pentagon secretly planned an expanded role for Alaska and the Aleutians. However, what seemed most visible to those in Alaska in 1944 was an ever-growing demobilization. Troop strength dropped from its 1943 peak of 152,000 to 104,000 by 1944 and to 50,000 by 1945. As the troops left, so did their leaders. Colonel Talley departed for Europe to prepare for Normandy. General Buckner, now wearing three stars, was transferred to Honolulu and finally to Okinawa. Admiral Kinkaid moved to the Southwest Pacific where he supported General Douglas MacArthur. One of the few legacies or written memories of the Aleutians after these major departures was Gore Vidal's first novel, *Williwaw* (1946). The teenage Vidal was stationed in Anchorage and Dutch Harbor from late 1943 to 1945. He wrote a fictional account, based on his own experience, of life on a transport ship servicing the Aleutians. Rather than a story of heroism and war, it was more a story of boredom and what one critic has called an "obsessive and compulsive concern with the weather." In the absence of the Japanese enemy, the major action in the novel concerns the fate of the men in a "williwaw" or Aleutian windstorm.[10]

The fact that the Aleutian Campaign did not appear to be a turning point in the war or pave the way for a future offensive has led many historians to downplay or dismiss it. Morison calls the campaign a "Theater of Military Frustration" and concludes, "Both sides would have done well to have left the Aleutians to the Aleuts." Air force historian John Cloe goes further and claims that both the troops and the dollars spent on the Aleutian campaign could have been better used elsewhere. "In the end," he concludes, "the price of pride was paid for by the young men, American, Canadian and Japanese, who fought with great bravery and then were forgotten by history." The "price of pride" to which Cloe refers was the symbolic freeing of occupied American soil. Possibly that symbolism did not advance the overall cause of the war, but it had a dramatic effect on the future development of Alaska as the forty-ninth state. For fourteen months that symbolic piece of occupied soil was in Alaska. The American public was well aware of this. Popular magazines such as *Reader's Digest* ran articles about the Aleutians. Well-known journalists rushed books to the public after the Aleutian victory in late 1943 and early 1944 including Joseph Driscoll's *War Discovers Alaska* (1943), Corey Ford's *Short Cut to Tokyo: The Battle for the Aleutians* (1943), and William Gilman's *Our Hidden Front* (1944). Filmmaker John Huston came north and produced *Report from the Aleutians* (1943) to boost American morale once the islands were liberated. Symbolically, when Alaska was freed, America was freed. Though the specific campaign in the Aleutians might soon become forgotten, Alaska had been fixed in the public mind as never before. It was no longer the strange and unknown land to which Jean Potter had come in 1941.[11]

Repercussions and Legacies from the Aleutians—Far and Near

Far—The Alaska Highway, ALSIB, and CANOL

The total military effort to support the Aleutian campaign was not geographically limited to the island chain. The island war elicited reactions and repercussions in other areas of the territory and in western Canada that had a great bearing on the creation of the modern Alaska that emerged from World War II. The 1,500-mile Alaska Highway—

stretching from Fairbanks to Dawson Creek, British Columbia, and then connecting to Edmonton, Alberta—may seem as far away from the Aleutian Islands as possible. But the extensive land buffer that separated the two created the very rationale to build the route. That is why the highway and the Aleutians are connected as a legacy of World War II.[12]

If ever there was a prewar project for the economic development of Alaska that stood little chance of success, but which was made possible by the advent of the war, it was the Alaska Highway. Since the late 1920s and well into the 1930s Alaska developers, as well as those in British Columbia, had proposed building a highway to connect Fairbanks with Seattle and the Pacific Northwest via western Canada. The plan had the backing of the province of British Columbia as well as the state of Washington and the territory of Alaska. There were two proposed routes, "A" and "B," that basically ran inward from the Pacific Coast. "A" skirted the Coast Range of mountains while "B" was some two hundred miles inland along the Rockies. Enthusiasm continued throughout the 1930s, and in 1938 Congress created the International Highway Commission to make further recommendations. Ernest Gruening was a member of the committee as well as Senator Warren Magnuson of Washington.[13]

Despite such enthusiasm, there were considerable complications that thwarted a decision to build either of the routes. First was the expense of construction during a national depression. Who would pay for it—the United States alone or the United States and Canada? Though British Columbia heartily supported the project, the Canadian federal government in Ottawa, headed by Prime Minister McKenzie King, was leery of any project that more closely tied British Columbia to a north/south commercial route between two parts of the United States. After all, it had been only seventy years since the Canadian government effectively bribed American-leaning British Columbia to join the Confederation with the promise and construction of the east-west Canadian Pacific Railroad. To further complicate matters, midwestern states and prairie provinces proposed additional routes that would turn the highway eastward from northern British Columbia and head it toward the Canadian and American plains. As a result of these proposals, there were four potential routes, "A," "B," "C," and "D," by the onset of World War II in Europe.

By the spring and summer of 1940 the military buildup of Alaska had begun. Highway advocates pushed their cause as part of that buildup.

However, in April 1940 Secretary of War Stimson announced that the potential highway had "negligible" value for national defense. The army was more interested in developing air routes to Alaska. One such route had been pioneered in the 1930s by Alaskan and Canadian bush pilots from Edmonton to Fairbanks via Whitehorse, Yukon Territory. In 1940 and 1941 the U.S./Canadian Permanent Joint Board on Defense placed much more importance on the development of this air route than on any of the proposed highway routes. By late 1941 the so-called Northwest Staging Route (NSR) from Edmonton to Fairbanks—via Dawson Creek, Fort St. John, and Fort Nelson, British Columbia; Watson Lake and Whitehorse, Yukon Territory; and Big Delta, Alaska—was near readiness. The bases from Fort Nelson north had one striking common denominator: they could only be reached by air. No service road connected them.

Just as the NSR neared completion, the Japanese bombed Pearl Harbor. If the Aleutians suddenly achieved new prominence after December 7, so did the NSR. The military now feared that Japanese ships could disrupt sea routes from Seattle to Alaska. In Anchorage a military officer was reported as saying: "Here we are perched in a hard country where civilians can't feed themselves. The Japs don't even have to attack. They need only use subs to cut our umbilical cord from Seattle, and we'll be starved to death."[14]

Even after the Pearl Harbor attack, the need for a highway was still secondary to the need for air routes. But when twelve of thirty-eight planes flying the NSR went down in January 1942, the need for a highway to supply and support the airfields gained credence. The U.S. Army and its engineers concluded that none of the previously suggested routes should be used. Instead the army proposed a route that directly connected the airfields. In early February 1942, President Roosevelt gave his approval for the building of the highway along the army's plan—even before securing Canadian approval. The Canadians were as usual reluctant, but concluded they could not balk at the defense of Alaska. What if the Japanese captured the Aleutians and then advanced on the Pacific Coast? Would the Canadians be accused of leaving the Northwest defenseless? Since the United States agreed to pay for the entire cost of construction and hand it over to Canada at the end of the war, Ottawa and McKenzie King agreed.

Even after Roosevelt's February decision the proponents of the original routes, including Gruening and Magnuson, objected. They noted that no full survey of a highway route connecting the airfields existed. The army did not technically know if there was an accessible route through the Northern Rockies. Despite the criticism, Roosevelt and Secretary of War Stimson held fast to the army's plan.

The construction of the Alaska Highway from February to November 1942 is often heralded as one of the legendary engineering feats of World War II, not to mention of the development of Alaska. The army surveyed and constructed a rough pioneer road to be used by military convoys. The civilian Public Roads Administration (PRA) then followed and upgraded the pioneer road to full highway standards. Construction was divided into a southern sector from Dawson Creek, British Columbia (where the Northern Alberta Railroad ended) to Whitehorse, Yukon Territory; and a northern sector from Whitehorse to Fairbanks, or more specifically to Big Delta, Alaska, where the Alaska Highway could connect to the existing Richardson Highway to Fairbanks. The southern sector was the more problematic and uncertain as this was the portion that had not been surveyed. The northern sector was closely linked to the original Route "A."

Initially work on the southern sector went slowly. By using local guides with their knowledge of mountain passes and by conducting aerial surveys, army engineers found a pass through the Northern Rockies. The road could go ahead. The bombing of Dutch Harbor and the capture of Kiska and Attu in June 1942 heightened the urgency to complete the highway by winter. With renewed effort the work went ahead. The southern sector was completed by September 24, 1942, and the first truck made the run from Dawson Creek to Whitehorse a few days later. The northern sector was finished by October 25, 1942. On November 20 the pioneer highway was officially opened and dedicated at Soldier's Summit near Kluane Lake in the Yukon Territory.

While the engineering achievements of the highway were formidable, the human achievements in the highway's construction were equally notable. The role of three regiments of African American troops led to a gradual chipping away at the thick layers of racial prejudice that encompassed not just American society but the American military before and during World War II. Army officer and historian Heath Twichell provides a dramatic story of their role in building the Alaska Highway in his highway history *Northwest Epic* (1992).

The urgency to finish the road before the onset of the winter of 1942–43 led to the simple need for more construction troops. Where would they come from with so many being deployed to the Aleutians and other theaters of war? In 1942 the U.S. Army was segregated with all-black soldier regiments, usually commanded by white officers. As Twichell describes the state of race relations in this segregated army, most white officers and commanders shunned the black troops and did not want them involved in their operations. Whatever the reservations of the officers in Alaska, they needed the men. Commanders elsewhere were happy to see the blacks go north. Some four thousand black troops in the 93rd, 95th, and 97th Engineer Regiments joined approximately six thousand white troops in 1942. This did not necessarily mean that the white officers in Alaska, including General Buckner, welcomed the blacks. Preconceived ideas abounded as to whether the blacks could survive the Arctic cold or whether the quality of their work would contribute to the overall construction effort.[15]

The three regiments not only survived but also achieved exemplary work standards. On parts of the highway there was a competition between the black and white regiments to work from different ends and join at the middle. The blacks often beat the whites, including the linking of the northern sector in October 1942. The wire-service photo of the event sent to newspapers around the nation showed a black soldier and a white soldier shaking hands, each atop his bulldozer. As to the problems of surviving the Arctic cold, who knows which man had the tougher time? The black was from Philadelphia, the white from Texas! It would be an exaggeration to say that the performance of the African American regiments on the Alaska Highway ended racial prejudice in the army, much less in the nation. But it is also clear that the attitudes of many white officers, including Heath Twichell's father, began to change. Suffice it to say that during the summer, fall, and winter of 1942 in the remote wilderness of northwestern Canada, a step forward was made toward the eventual desegregation of the army in 1948 and the ensuing postwar civil rights movement.[16]

The pioneer road and the upgraded PRA highway that followed now provided the land supply route. As the Japanese never disrupted sea transport lanes to Alaska, neither the highway nor the NSR became a crucial or indispensable domestic supply line for Fairbanks. But the road/air inland route soon assumed great importance as part of the Lend-Lease program. In 1942 the United States agreed to supply the Soviet Union with aircraft. What was the best and safest route to send the planes from the United States to Russia? The NSR, particularly with its support highway, was an appealing choice for an air ferry system that came to be known as the Alaskan/ Siberian Ferry Route (ALSIB). Beginning in September 1942 aircraft were delivered from factories throughout the United States to Great Falls, Montana. From there ALSIB followed the NSR to Ladd Field in Fairbanks. In Fairbanks the American pilots turned over the planes to Russian pilots who flew them to Nome and then across Bering Strait to Siberia—first to Uel'kal' on the coast and then hundreds of miles inland to Novosibirsk. From September 1942 to September 1945, 7,926 planes—fighters, bombers, and cargo— were ferried along ALSIB. The old gold rush town of Fairbanks became an international mercantile center where Russian pilots stocked up on candy, perfume, and lingerie to take home. More important than its role as an emporium for luxury goods, Fairbanks's role as a major air center was confirmed by the Lend-Lease air ferry. This role, in both its military and civilian capacities, was one of the major legacies of World War II. Billy Mitchell had been right.[17]

ALSIB saved the highway from being "forgotten" after the Aleutian campaign. But another engineering feat, even grander in scope, that was designed to complement the highway and ALSIB was not only "forgotten" but also marked with a disgrace that ruined the careers of some of its supporters. This was the CANOL project.

A few months after deciding to build the highway, military planners led by the army's logistical czar, Lt. General Behron B. Somervell, concluded that any Japanese disruption of sea transport would also curtail the shipment of oil north to Alaska and the NSR. An inland oil supply was needed as much, if not more so, than the highway. In 1920 oil had been discovered at Norman Wells, Northwest Territory, a location about four hundred miles northeast of Whitehorse on the MacKenzie River. Wells had been drilled there, and a small refinery was established. In its current state the Norman Wells field and distribution system could not supply Alaska or the NSR. Somervell proposed a grand scheme to construct a pipeline from Norman Wells to Whitehorse, where a new refinery would be built. From there a new distribution system would connect with Fairbanks and the NSR. Also, a four-hundred-mile service road would be constructed from Whitehorse to Norman Wells. The whole system, which would be built by the United States and handed over to Canada at the end war, was called CANOL (Canadian Oil).[18]

The cost and construction of CANOL were even more problematic than the Alaska Highway. The terrain was more difficult, and there was not an existing surveyed route for the road or the pipeline. Even backers of the Alaska Highway, such as Interior Secretary Ickes and Alaska's Tony Dimond, would not give their support to CANOL. Somervell prevailed, and by early May 1942 the War Department approved the project. The bombing of Dutch Harbor in June accentuated the need for both the highway and CANOL.

By November 1942 the Alaska Highway was complete and functioning. But the construction of CANOL seemed to go on forever. By the autumn of 1943 Attu and Kiska had been reclaimed. There was no longer a concern about the disruption of sea routes to Alaska by the Japanese, and ALSIB had been functioning quite well for almost a year. CANOL now appeared to be a huge drain of money and troops for a project that was not needed.

Such an expensive project, seemingly in the middle of nowhere and serving little defense purpose, soon attracted the scrutiny of U.S. Senator Harry Truman and his Special Committee Investigating the National Defense Program. Truman's committee had achieved a fine reputation as a government watchdog on expensive defense projects since its creation in 1941. In November 1943 Truman conducted hearings on CANOL. The project appeared to be wasteful and excessively costly. Nonetheless General Somervell staunchly defended it. In December 1943 the committee submitted a report highly critical of CANOL.[19]

By the time of Truman's final report it was cheaper to finish CANOL than to scrap it. CANOL was completed in April 1944, when the first oil arrived at Whitehorse. The project's permanent fate, however, had been sealed not only by the Truman Committee but also by the cost for continued operation. The army abandoned CANOL in April 1945 and soon dismantled much of what had been constructed. Though the $134 million CANOL project was soon forgotten, the repercussions of the CANOL hearings led to both advancement and oblivion for its participants. According to Heath Twichell, Somervell's defense was so embarrassing to the army that talk of his possible choice to become chairman of the Joint Chiefs of Staff was effectively over. He retired in 1946. On the other hand, Truman's conduct of the CANOL hearings enhanced his public and political image and helped elevate him as the Democratic candidate for vice president in 1944. Political controversy in the Far North clearly had far-sweeping national ramifications.[20]

The Alaska Highway and CANOL should be seen as a joint reaction to the Japanese threat to Alaska. In 1942 both the highway and

CANOL were considered expensive, and both had their critics. The highway's rapid completion gave it a purpose while the Aleutian war still raged. Once the Aleutians were freed, ALSIB sustained the need for the Alaska Highway to the war's end and protected it from the fallout from CANOL. Even during the CANOL investigations some of the highway's detractors still criticized the inland route as a "great blunder." Had the highway not been completed in such record time, it might well have shared the same fate as CANOL.

With the end of the war, ALSIB also came to an end. The highway alone survived. Once Canada took over its section of the highway in 1946, there was an added imperative to its survival. As important as supporting Alaska and ALSIB, the highway had opened the Canadian Northwest. Before 1940 the Canadian Northwest of northern British Columbia, the Yukon Territory, and the Northwest Territories was truly the "last frontier," as Ken Coates and Bill Morrison have ably shown in their book *The Alaska Highway in World War II: The U.S. Army of Occupation in Canada's Northwest* (1992). The area's population was scarcely over five thousand and predominantly native. Transportation routes were mainly by river, and the economy was based on fur trapping. Even more, the Canadian federal government in Ottawa had consistently neglected the area, much to the ire of western Canadians. The highway changed all of this. It opened the region, gave it a long-needed transportation system, and introduced it to many aspects of twentieth-century life. It made Whitehorse, rather than gold rush Dawson City, the capital of the region. After it was opened by the Americans, the Canadians could hardly close the highway and send the Northwest back to the status quo of 1940.

The road from Fairbanks to Edmonton opened the Canadian Northwest, but it did not redirect Alaska's commercial orientation to western Canada. Edmonton did not become the new emporium for the American territory. Alaska's commercial links still remained along the potential Route "A" to Seattle. Possibly the most advantageous feature of the highway built during the war was the so-called Haines Cutoff that linked the highway north of Whitehorse to the southeastern Alaska port of Haines. The Haines Cutoff allowed sea traffic up from Seattle to join the highway into Fairbanks. In effect a land/sea Route "A" was completed. If the east-west Alaska Highway did not revolutionize commercial routes after the war, it had a symbolic effect in preparing Alaska for eventual statehood. The remote territory had drawn national attention because of the war. The highway created an important and symbolic land link to the continental United States. Once in Edmonton, north-south roads connected the Alaska Highway to the United States. Though opponents of statehood for Alaska after the war would insist that Alaska was "non-contiguous" to the lower forty-eight states, it was now non-contiguous with a long umbilical cord, albeit a cord going through another nation. The Alaska Highway ended a great part of the mental picture of isolation that many Americans held of the distant territory. It was no longer the "island" that Jean Potter had found in 1941.

Near—The Aleut Evacuation

The wartime saga of the Aleutian campaign brought 150,000 U.S. troops to Alaska. The inland supply route involved over 10,000 military and civilian personnel. In contrast to such numbers, the fate of less than 1,000 native Aleuts in the war zone from Attu to Dutch Harbor may seem to pale in significance. To some extent it has. The evacuation and plight of the native inhabitants of the Aleutians in World War II has come to be known as the "Untold Story." Only in the 1980s and 1990s has it reached a wide audience through a variety of sources including Dean Kohlhoff's excellent book *When the Wind Was a River* (1995). Though the story has been late in its telling, the fate of the Aleuts in the 1940s is important to our understanding of the changes that took place in Alaska during World War II.[21]

Prior to 1940 the Aleuts were an isolated people with little connection to the emerging political structure of the territory. Living on the windswept island chain, they were effectively wards of U.S. Department of the Interior agencies, either the Bureau of Indian Affairs or the Fish and Wildlife Service, which administered the harvesting of fur seals by the Aleuts on the Pribilof Islands. By most accounts the Aleuts were a happy people in their isolation. Only in the community of Unalaska was there a substantial mixing of Aleuts with Caucasians. On the smaller islands the Aleuts lived by themselves with only a few government agents, such as BIA schoolteachers. Few Aleuts had ever left their islands. There were no clusters of Aleut migrants in other parts of Alaska. As a result there were no other places in Alaska or in the lower forty-eight states that were similar to the Aleutian Islands in either their geographic or demographic makeup. The war would upset the isolation in which the Aleut world existed.

The first impact of the war buildup was at the Dutch Harbor naval base located on the same island with the Aleut community of Unalaska.

The sudden infusion of civilian war workers and troops in 1941 had a debilitating effect on the Aleuts. Secretary of the Interior Ickes dispatched his special assistant Ruth Gruber, who would later become known for her work in the resettlement of European refugees, to report on all aspects of Alaska's preparedness, including the condition of the Aleuts. Even before the attack on Pearl Harbor, Gruber noted that the Aleut community at Unalaska was quickly deteriorating under the influence of money, liquor, and prostitution. Something needed to be done to protect the Aleuts, but who should do it? The Interior Department decided that military authorities should handle the deteriorating social situation—the first of many instances of shifting responsibility and authority over the Aleuts.[22]

After the bombing of Pearl Harbor, fear of an attack on the Aleutians mounted. Should the Aleuts on the more isolated islands as well as those on Unalaska be evacuated from a potential war zone? There was no clear answer, nor there was there a clear agency or authority in command to execute that answer. Neither Governor Gruening nor General Buckner wanted to evacuate the Aleuts. They thought that the Aleuts could not survive—or certainly not thrive—if separated from their island homes. Somehow they thought the Aleuts would survive better at home, even in case of combat. There was no place like the Aleutians, nor any Aleut communities outside of the Aleutians, for relocation. Unless the Aleuts asked to be relocated—which they did not—military and civilian authorities chose to leave them where they were.[23]

With the bombing of Dutch Harbor and the occupation of Attu and Kiska all of this changed. The forty-two Aleuts on Attu were taken prisoner by the Japanese and eventually removed to Japan. Could the United States allow this to happen on the other islands? In the midst of confusion, the military decided to act—though not together. First the navy acted on its own and on June 12 evacuated Atka, the island nearest to Kiska. As the natives left their village, the navy burned it to prevent a Japanese takeover. The army then evacuated the Pribilof Islands a few days later. Unalaska was the last to be evacuated, in late July. There is no question that the forced evacuation was done for the safety of the Aleuts, though it can be questioned whether the military was genuinely concerned for the Aleuts or for the political fallout that would occur if other islands were attacked. Thus in a haphazard action in the months of June and July 1942, a total of 881 Aleuts from the islands of Atka, Unalaska, Akutan, Umnak, and the Pribilofs were evacuated. The Aleuts had no advance warning of their evacuation and often left their most valuable possessions, particularly Russian Orthodox religious icons, behind. Nor did the military have any advance planning for where they would take the Aleuts. Even as the evacuation ships took the Aleuts from their islands, military authorities did not know where they were bound.[24]

Facilities for relocation were finally found and established in southeastern Alaska at a collection of deteriorating sites that included an abandoned fish cannery and a former gold mining camp, both on Admiralty Island near Juneau, and a former Civilian Conservation Corps camp near Ketchikan. The physical and sanitary conditions at the relocation camps were deplorable. Ruth Gruber came again in October 1942 and reported serious conditions of overcrowding. Some few Aleuts in the camps near Ketchikan and Juneau found wage work away from camp. But most of the evacuees detested their new situation. Forested southeast Alaska was a totally different environment from the windswept, treeless Aleutians. The death rate was high. Over the two- to three-year period of evacuation approximately 10 percent of the 881 Aleuts died, preponderantly older people who contracted pneumonia. This death rate was estimated at three times the previous mortality rate of the Aleuts on their home islands. What was most distressing about the camp conditions was the fact that little was done by any agency—civilian or military—to improve conditions over the years. About the best thing that can be said of the evacuation is that the Aleuts in southeastern Alaska suffered less death than the Attuans who were captured and taken to Japan, where 40 percent died.[25]

Once the Aleutian War ended in 1943, plans were formulated to repatriate the Aleuts. Some of the Pribilovians returned home in 1943 and 1944 to work the seal harvest. But the full repatriation of the other islands did not occur until 1945. Upon their return the Aleuts found many of their villages ransacked, not by enemy forces but by the U.S. military. Some restitution was made at the time, but not until 1988 were substantial reparations made by the United States to the Aleuts. With the push for reparations—done in conjunction with reparations for Japanese American internees—the full story of the evacuation became more widely known. Aleut leaders pushed for publication of the "untold story" as successive generations of their children said they did not believe that the United States could have treated their people so poorly.[26]

In the 1980s and 1990s the federal reparations settlement and the "telling" of the "untold" story of Aleut suffering have attracted wide attention. Though less publicized, there were changes soon after World War II that led to the transformation of the Aleut world and the territory itself. The war ended the splendid isolation that the Aleuts had known, much in the way that the building of the Alaska Highway ended the isolation of Northwest Canada. Never again could the Aleuts live apart. To some extent their helplessness in southeastern Alaska resulted from the fact that they had no political voice. That would change. In the Pribilofs where government control was the most paternal, evacuated Aleuts began filing lawsuits in the early 1950s to redress long-standing grievances. Though much of the legal action saw no progress until after statehood, the genesis of Aleut self-determination can clearly be found in the evacuation experience. As Aleut leader Alice Petrivelli has noted, "One positive effect that the evacuation had on the Aleut people as a whole was exposure to the political process. This helped the Aleut people to become more self-determined about making decisions that affected their lives."[27]

If the Aleuts became exposed to the need for inclusion in the political process, such could also be said for the territory at large. Part of the Aleut problem resulted from the overlapping jurisdictions of so many federal agencies. As a result no single entity was really in charge. Decision-making as well as responsibility was haphazard at best. Such governmental indecisiveness and confusion were not limited to the Aleut evacuation. The overall territory was plagued with this problem in both peace and war. One of the goals of the statehood movement would be to end such federal chaos with a strong, coordinated state government. The evacuation of the Aleuts highlighted the overall situation that the territory had to change politically and had to become more culturally unified if it were to survive.

Ernest Gruening and the Creation of Modern Alaska

Reactions to the war cut a wide swath of change from Attu to Fairbanks to Whitehorse, Yukon Territory. Neither Alaska nor northwestern Canada could return to the way things had been before the war. No one saw this better than Alaska's territorial governor, Ernest Gruening, who had set out to revolutionize the territory during the war. A journalist and government administrator before being appointed governor of Alaska in 1939, Gruening had never been elected to any public office. He owed all of his positions in the government and newspaper worlds to appointments made through connections with powerful people. To understand what Gruening did for Alaska, we need to know more about the political ideas and traditions that he, at age fifty-two, brought to the territory in 1939. To a great extent the ideas of government that the territory acquired during the war were those that Gruening brought with him. In fact, by 1945 Alaska's political alliances were effectively formed around those people who followed Gruening and those who opposed him—though, of course, no one actually voted for or against him! They voted for or against candidates for territorial office whom he supported.

Born in 1887 to a well-to-do New York City medical family, Gruening was educated in private schools and graduated from Harvard in 1907. He then went to Harvard Medical School, not out of any sincere devotion to medicine but to please his father. By the time he finished medical school in 1912, his true interest was in journalism, particularly in covering the political events and programs of the day. He thus went to work not as a physician but as a reporter for the *Boston Herald,* where his first assignment was to cover the election of Woodrow Wilson as president in 1912. Gruening's political coming of age from his time at Harvard through his early reporting days was steeped in the Progressive tradition of Theodore Roosevelt and Woodrow Wilson. He was suspicious of big business and early developed a strong anti-monopoly philosophy. As his journalistic career progressed, he edited other newspapers in Boston and New York, where he became the managing editor of the reform magazine *The Nation* in 1920. In 1927 Gruening moved on to be the first editor of the *Portland* (Maine) *Evening News,* where he was a virulent critic of the electric utility monopoly of Samuel Insull.[28]

Early in his journalistic career Gruening professed a strong sense of civil rights and racial justice that came from his family tradition. His sister Martha was an early supporter of the National Association for the Advancement of Colored People (NAACP). Though Ernest was offered a position with the NAACP, he chose to remain in journalism and work for civil rights. He initiated a policy at his papers not to mention a person's race in news stories, particularly in criminal court cases. In addition to civil rights, Gruening was also a crusader for civil liberties. During World War I he criticized the wartime curtailment of civil liberties by the federal government.[29]

After World War I Gruening developed an interest in Latin American affairs and helped found the Spanish-language newspaper *La Prensa* in New York. During his time at *The Nation* he opposed U.S. intervention—

military and financial—in Haiti, Mexico, and other Latin American countries. Gruening pursued a strong anti-imperialist, anti-colonialist stance that was evident in his editorials and articles. In 1928 he published *Mexico and Its Heritage,* a well-received book on the political and social traditions of the United States's southern neighbor. Gruening advocated economic and social reform as a way to build stable governments. By the 1930s he was considered a prominent expert in Latin American affairs. In 1934 this reputation led him into government service with an appointment as director of the Division of Territories and Insular Possessions of the U.S. Department of the Interior. His principal role in that appointment was to bring about economic reform in Puerto Rico. As noted earlier, complications in his handling of Puerto Rican affairs led to his transfer to Alaska.

Throughout his pre-Alaska journalist/government career, Gruening espoused and wrote about reform. But in practical terms Gruening's opponents at the local level, whether in Maine or in Puerto Rico, often proved more politically adept than the reformer. As a result, Gruening could point to his well-written editorials and books more than to his practical political reforms. In this vein one of his most recent biographers, Robert David Johnson, has noted that the reforming Gruening became better known as a critic or an apostle of the "dissenting tradition." In 1939 the dissenting Gruening arrived in the North carrying his anti-monopoly, pro-civil-rights, anti-colonial philosophy. By the time he accepted the Alaska governorship, some of Gruening's ideas were becoming outdated by "Lower 48" standards. But if Gruening was a little behind the times, he had come to the right place. The Progressive era had largely bypassed the northern territory. Reforms and governmental practices that had become standard in Hawai'i during the first decade of the century, particularly local taxation, had yet to see the light of day in the North. For Gruening it was as if the unreformed America of 1900–1910 lay fresh before him. He immediately set out to analyze, criticize, and re-create Alaska.[30]

The new governor had some previous experience with Alaska in his role as director of the Division of Territories and Insular Possessions. He had made two brief visits to the territory in 1936 and 1938. He was aware of Alaska's economic underdevelopment and of the antiquated tax system at both the territorial and the local level. Basically most businesses and property escaped taxation—either in the form of income or property taxes. The territory's main source of revenue was a per-case tax on canned salmon and assorted license fees that secured negligible amounts of revenue. Gruening noted on one of his trips that the A-J Mine in Juneau was exempt from any property tax. He was also aware that the small territorial legislature was under the influence of lobbyists—and certain legislators under their control—who opposed any form of new taxation. While still in Washington, he had also been appointed in 1938 to the International Highway Commission that was to study plans for an Alaska Highway.

With this background Gruening arrived in Alaska in late 1939, just as construction was beginning for the naval installations in Kodiak, Sitka, and Dutch Harbor. He would have to wait until 1941 to deal with the legislature, as its biennial session in 1939 had already ended. From his arrival Gruening changed the concept of the territorial governor from that of a representative of the federal government to a local reformer/state builder. In the two years he waited for the legislature to convene, Gruening turned his attention to Alaska's municipalities and helped them create better systems of local taxation. The new governor also took on several issues that would become hallmarks for nearly all of his successors in the executive office. One such issue has been called "Alaska Hire." Gruening discovered that contractors for the new defense installations were hiring laborers from Seattle-based union halls to the exclusion of local Alaskans. When the contractors and local naval officials refused to accede to his request to hire Alaskans, the governor went to the secretary of the navy in Washington and won his "Alaska Hire" demands.[31]

Gruening's tiff with the military over "Alaska hire" should not be confused with any opposition to the military buildup of Alaska. His earlier anti-imperialist stand in Latin America had an anti-militarist component. But the new governor placed this position aside in Alaska. Gruening clearly saw that support for the military was possibly the only way to secure federal appropriations for economic development in the North. Initially Gruening proved quite friendly with General Buckner, who arrived in Alaska a few months after the governor. While staying on cordial terms with the military, Gruening's principal concern at the end of 1940 was how he would fare with the new territorial legislature.

When the territorial lawmakers met in 1941, Gruening exhorted them to adopt his progressive taxation measures including a comprehensive property tax as well as business and personal income taxes. Gruening emphasized that out-of-state—or out-of-territory—businesses, particularly defense contractors, would pay a substantial share of any new taxes. The legislature rejected all of his proposals. They did not want to tax themselves at all, no matter how much of the overall tax bill out-of-state businesses paid. The territorial house of representatives showed its opinion of the new governor with a resolution asking the U.S. Congress to limit the gubernatorial appointment to Alaska residents. Of course, such a resolution had no force; it was mainly intended as a slap to Gruening. The governor could respond in kind. At the end of the 1941 legislative session he chastised the legislators for their ties to absentee economic interests, particularly the fish packing industry. He even asked the FBI to conduct an investigation of some of the legislators. That initiative was as abortive as the lawmakers' resolution against the governor. Such was Gruening's first tempestuous year with the legislature. Before he could test another legislature, the war came.[32]

In Hawai'i the war led to the immediate imposition of martial law. Would this happen in Alaska? Would Gruening's power be taken away even before he had established it? After the attack at Pearl Harbor, it appears that General DeWitt in San Francisco sought to impose martial law on Alaska. Such did not happen because General Buckner advised against it. Buckner had little fear of any subversive elements in Alaska's population. And there was little in the manner of territorial rule that needed to be suspended. Unlike Hawai'i, Alaska had no territorial courts to be taken over by the military. The only courts in the territory were federal courts. There was such a small resident labor force that there was little practical need to freeze wages. As far as preparing Alaska for war, there was little that Buckner was not already empowered to do. President Roosevelt did propose to lessen Gruening's power by placing him under the direction of the secretary of war. Secretary of the Interior Ickes, though no fan of Gruening, intervened to dissuade the president in order to maintain *his* control over the territorial governor. Instead the president established by executive order the Alaska War Council, with Gruening as chair, to coordinate territorial and military affairs. Gruening actually welcomed the War Council and saw it as a way to build alliances with the military to maintain his independence and his ability to reform the territory.[33]

Not every aspect of the war and military conduct pleased Gruening. His long-standing battle with the suppression of civil liberties in wartime surfaced when he learned that the censorship of civilian mail, as was practiced in Hawai'i, had been extended to Alaska. Groups of censors in Seattle opened all mail coming or going to the territory, including magazines, and at times removed seemingly harmless material. When Gruening asked under what authority this was being done, military authorities told him that Congress was in the process of enacting a law that allowed such censorship in territories. Gruening rushed to Washington, where he used his congressional contacts to call for a "reconsideration" of the bill. He was successful. Censorship of civilian mail in Alaska came to an end.[34]

Gruening's championship of civil rights, as well as civil liberties, also found room for expression once the war came. Alaska's initial lack of preparedness caused Gruening and others to fear that Japanese land invasions might occur at many points in the territory. He wanted to organize a territorial guard of local citizens in every community to be prepared for such incursions. Such a guard in Gruening's mind required the inclusion of Alaska's natives. While Gruening formulated his plans for a civilian guard, the same thought came to Major Marvin R. Marston.

A western American who spent much of his career in the mining industry of northern Canada, Marston joined the army and was commissioned because of his knowledge of the Arctic. When Marston arrived in Alaska in March 1941, he was not sure of his exact assignment. From the outset Marston chafed at the professional military mind and constantly complained about "red tape" and slow decision-making. By early 1942 he had become the "morale officer" at Elmendorf Field in Anchorage. In March Marston brought the well-known comedian Joe E. Brown to Alaska to entertain the troops. After visiting most of the bases in the territory, Brown said he wanted to see "some real Eskimos." Marston took him to the remote St. Lawrence Island, located off the coast of Northwest Alaska. While visiting the island Marston became convinced of two things. The Eskimos were left unprotected from Japanese attack. But their knowledge of the coast and their survival skills in the Arctic made them the best possible group to form a reconnaissance defense force that could alert the military to any Japanese threat. Like Gruening, he wanted to organize a civilian guard. According to Marston, "the idea of organizing the natives into defense units came to me out of the clear. From that moment to this it has been the driving force of my life."[35]

Once back in Anchorage Marston presented his plan to the military authorities, but got no positive response. In the meantime Gruening pushed General Buckner for help in organizing a territorial guard. Buckner assigned Marston to Gruening as an aide. Some accounts say

that Buckner did not like Marston and tried to get rid of him by sending him to Gruening. But Gruening and Marston got along well.
Gruening found that Marston did not have the prejudices against natives
that many Caucasians held. Marston found that Gruening shared some
of his frustration with the regular army. Marston and Gruening toured
the Arctic during the summer of 1942 and organized guard units. There
was no doubt in Marston's mind that this tour had a civil rights objective. As he explained, "This was the first time a Governor had ever
toured the Eskimo empire. Indeed it was the first time in history that
these natives were regarded as bona fide citizens."[36]

Some 2,700 Eskimos in northwestern and southwestern Alaska—
100 percent of the able-bodied men between the ages of sixteen and
sixty-five—joined the Alaska Territorial Guard. They were also called
the "Eskimo Scouts" or "Gruening's Guerrillas." As a civilian force their
principal function was to work as a reconnaissance group. But they
were also trained in guerrilla tactics should the enemy come ashore.
Marston armed the men with Enfield rifles and gave them basic military drill as well as rifle instruction. In the latter regard he was aided
by Captain Magnus Colcord "Rusty" Heurlin, a noted Alaskan artist
as well as a rifleman. He taught the Eskimos how to shoot, and he left
behind a portfolio of paintings that superbly illustrated the activities
of the Scouts.[37]

Marston's account of the territorial guard, *Men of the Tundra: Eskimos
at War* (1969), is required reading for anyone who wants to understand the
impact of the war in creating modern Alaska. If Garner Anthony's *Hawaii
under Army Rule* highlights the perils to democracy that came from the
war, *Men of the Tundra* highlights the possibilities for democracy that came
from the war. The Alaska Territorial Guard pulled natives into the overall
war effort and gave them a claim to national recognition. It also served as
an inclusive organization that brought the Eskimos together from many
isolated villages. Marston encouraged the Eskimos to use their newfound
organization to combat the discrimination they often faced from whites.
And he encouraged them to vote. Self-determination for natives came
much more quickly to the Eskimos than to the Aleuts. In 1948 Percy
Ipalook, an Alaska Territorial Guard member, and William Beltz of Nome
were elected to the territorial legislature. Marston's experience also turned
him into a lifelong Alaskan, now with the added nickname of "Muktuk."
Muktuk Marston would become a member of the 1955–56 Alaska
Constitutional Convention and a constant champion of native rights.[38]

While Marston continued to organize the guard in the fall of 1942, Gruening's attention turned once again to the upcoming session of the biennial legislature and his hopes for taxation reform. The 1943 session proved no more promising than in 1941. To make matters worse, Gruening's taxation foes controlled both the presidency of the Senate and the speakership of the House. Much to the governor's regret the millions of dollars in profits being made by defense contractors from the mainland states remained untaxed. Convinced that his taxation initiatives could go nowhere, Gruening tried to persuade the legislature to pass what would be revolutionary civil rights legislation. Despite the success of the Alaska Territorial Guard, natives were still widely discriminated against in public places. Effectively, a southern style Jim Crow segregation could be found in "No Natives" signs at restaurants and movie theaters. Even the military banned young native women from attending USO parties in such places as Nome, where the ALSIB planes coming from Fairbanks were flown to Siberia.[39]

Initially Gruening tried to persuade restaurant owners to take down their discriminatory signs on a voluntary basis. When this approach brought little success, he persuaded members of the 1943 territorial legislature to introduce bills banning discrimination in public places. Gruening emphasized to the legislators that natives were serving in the military but discriminated against at home. Though the bill failed to pass the entire body, it did succeed in the senate. Possibly the next legislative session in 1945 might make more progress. In the meantime Gruening persuaded President Roosevelt to ban discrimination against natives at USO functions.[40]

As Gruening contemplated the future, he realized that the structure of the territorial legislature itself was a major part of his problem. There were people in Alaska, including members of the legislature, who supported his plans for reform. Those plans, however, required the passage of new legislation. The passage of a bill requires a majority vote in both houses. The defeat of a bill requires only a tie vote in one house. Four people in the eight-member senate could thus block any new legislation. The lobbyists could easily control four votes. How could things be changed?

There is no evidence that Gruening was influenced by Franklin Roosevelt's New Deal plan to overcome a recalcitrant Supreme Court by enlarging it. But the governor concluded that the best way to handle the legislature was to increase its size. The opposition would then have to garner more votes. And an expanded legislature would bring in new members who might not yet be under the lobbyists' control. A change in the territorial legislature required an act of Congress. Congressional Delegate Tony Dimond had advocated this plan earlier but had not succeeded. Working together, Gruening and Dimond secured passage of a bill that increased the size of the senate from eight to sixteen members and the house from sixteen to twenty-four members. While members of the senate would still be equally divided among Alaska's four judicial districts, members of the house would be elected on the basis of population.[41]

The election of 1944 attracted the first candidates for the expanded territorial legislature. Gruening encouraged his friends to run for office, particularly natives. When the ballots were counted, Gruening supporters gained seats in both houses. Two natives, Frank Peratrovich and Andrew Hope, both Tlingits from southeastern Alaska, were elected to the house of representatives. Hope and Peratrovich were not the first natives elected to the legislature. William Paul, also a Tlingit from southeastern Alaska, had served in the house from 1925 to 1929. But there had been an interim of fifteen years with no native representation. The election of Peratrovich and Hope marked the beginning of an uninterrupted line of native lawmakers to the present day.[42]

The 1944 election also opened the seat for the congressional delegate. Tony Dimond wanted to retire and accept a federal judgeship in Alaska. Gruening urged Bob Bartlett to run for the office. Bartlett, a former newspaperman in Fairbanks, had been Dimond's aide in Washington from 1933 to 1934. Roosevelt appointed him secretary of the territory in 1939. Though the secretary's office had little power or function, Gruening had augmented Bartlett's role as a result of his many trips to Washington. In Gruening's absence Bartlett was "acting governor." It was Bartlett, not Gruening, who represented the governor's office at the opening of the Alaska Highway in November 1942. In working with Gruening, Bartlett came to share many of the governor's goals for reform.

Despite Gruening's urging, Bartlett was reluctant and ambivalent about running. He just could not make up his mind. Gruening asked Dimond to endorse Bartlett, but Dimond would not do so until Bartlett filed for the office. Frustrated, Gruening simply told Dimond that Bartlett had filed. Dimond then publicly offered his support. Dimond was furious when he learned that this was all a Gruening ruse. Bartlett was now backed into a corner. He could not embarrass Dimond. Though it took substantial pressure from his friends, Bartlett filed, ran, and won. Gruening played the same trick on Dimond and Bartlett that Roosevelt had played on him in 1939 when he was reluctant to accept the governorship! Bartlett would stay in Washington for the rest of his life as territorial delegate and then as U.S. Senator. As he grew in stature and standing in the Capitol, he later resented some of Gruening's meddling in his affairs. Nonetheless he owed his office to Gruening's meddling support![43]

In 1945 Gruening had solid support in both Washington and Juneau. He hoped for the best as the 1945 legislative session began. Even the reformed territorial legislature was not quite ready to adopt Gruening's taxation measures. The house backed Gruening's plan, but the senate defeated it. The legislature did enact the governor's proposal for an Alaska Development Board that would aggressively plan and coordinate economic growth. The crowning achievement of the 1945 legislature was the successful passage of the bill to ban discrimination against natives in public places. The presence of native legislators and the impassioned appeal to the assembly by a native woman, Mrs. Elizabeth Peratrovich, secured the winning vote. This was one of the first such bills passed by a state or territorial legislature. It predated the passage of such an act in the U.S. Congress by twenty years. As a portent of things to come, the new legislature passed for the first time a resolution supporting statehood. It also passed a bill calling for a referendum on statehood in the 1946 general election.

Soon after the 1945 legislative session closed in March, victory in Europe was celebrated. A few months later victory in Japan came. With the enlarged legislature, native representation, progressive civil rights legislation, and a resolution for statehood, it may also be said that there was no small degree of victory in Alaska for the development of a territory that would become the forty-ninth state.

Alaska and Hawai'i in 1945

By September 1945 the war was over. The Alaska of that autumn seemed a world away from Jean Potter's 1941 "land without people." We have already traced much of the change that the war brought to Alaska. At times I have argued that the war created a new Alaska rather than merely transformed the old Alaska. This may seem like quibbling with words, but it is instructive to look at the degree of change in Alaska when compared to Hawai'i.

In 1945, as in 1941, Hawai'i was dominated by one large city, Honolulu. The war confirmed Honolulu's dominance not only as the largest city but also as the military defense headquarters. Alaska's population centers were turned on their head. In 1941 it would have been difficult to say that there was an urban Alaska. The territory had contained larger cities in 1900–1910 than in 1940. Its 1940 population was centered in southeastern Alaska where fishing and gold mining were king. The two largest towns were Juneau (5,729) and Ketchikan (4,695). By 1945 the territory's population center had left southeastern Alaska and was centered along the so-called "rail belt" from Anchorage to Fairbanks, where the army had established its headquarters and major airfields. Anchorage, now the largest town, could even be called a city. In 1945 it served a substantially different function than in 1941. Civic leader Evangeline Atwood said it concisely: "Anchorage went into World War II with a population of 3,500. Railroading was its chief industry. It came out of the war a city of 12,000 with aviation its chief industry." Evangeline Atwood's husband, Bob, was the publisher of the *Anchorage Daily Times*. Bob Atwood told me on more than one occasion that when he came to Anchorage in 1935 there was barely enough news for a weekly paper, but he insisted upon publishing daily. The war had given him the news he needed for his "daily" *Times*.[44]

Though both Alaska and Hawai'i had been inundated with service personnel and civilian workers, the role of the newcomers in the development of the two territories was different. In Hawai'i servicemen and civilian workers often came looking for paradise and found barbed wire. "Complaining about Hawaii" became a staple of war life. Most of the veterans who participated in the building of postwar Hawai'i had been local citizens before the war, particularly Japanese Americans, who served abroad and came back to the territory.

In Alaska many of the service personnel and civilian workers who came *during* the war became part of the force who built the territory *after* the war. No doubt a substantial number of men and women who came to the Aleutians complained about the weather, but they were not expecting paradise. More typical of the assumptions and warnings that people brought north was the advertisement of the Bechtel Company for workers on CANOL: "This is No Picnic . . . If you are not prepared to work under these conditions Do Not Apply." Picnic or not, a sizable number of newcomers liked the territory and stayed or returned after the war. We have already noted the decision of Muktuk Marston to stay.

General Simon Buckner planned to make Alaska his home after the war and selected property near Anchorage. Unfortunately the general would never return. He was killed in Okinawa in 1945, one of only two lieutenant generals to die in the war. For many Alaskans the most beloved of the wartime leaders was Colonel Benjamin Talley. After the war Talley continued to serve in the army outside Alaska until his retirement in 1956. He remained "outside" as a civilian engineer until 1964, when he returned north. Talley made his home at Anchor Point on the Kenai Peninsula until his death in 1998 at age ninety-five. Though Talley was not a direct participant in the immediate postwar buildup of Alaska, the $300 million infrastructure he created during the war, sometimes known as "Talley's Alaska," surely makes him one of Alaska's greatest builders.[45]

Newcomers to Alaska were not the only people changed or transformed by the war. Of all the social changes and transformations that took place in Alaska during the war, none was greater than the organization of the Eskimo Scouts by Muktuk Marston. Would this change survive the war and produce leaders for the new postwar Alaska? Marston hoped so, but he knew that some people in the territory did not want a united Eskimo population. Near the close of the war the army's local inspector general told Marston to pick up the Enfield rifles given to the Eskimos and dissolve the Tundra Army. Arming the Eskimos had empowered them as citizens. Disarming them would make them, in Marston's words, "low man on the totem pole, hewer of wood, trapper, fisherman, and second class citizen." What could he do? He asked the inspector general if he could have a day to draft a letter with a countering argument. The inspector granted the wish, but told him "it won't do any good." Overnight Marston's subconscious mind found an answer best described in Muktuk's own words:

> It was now midnight and I dozed for a time. On awakening, I had the answer. I addressed my letter to the Colonel, adding the paragraph. "My dear Colonel: I think I should advise you of something you might not have thought of. There just might be some Eskimo germs on this equipment that the Eskimo has become immune to, which might spread throughout the entire United States Army, upon re-issuing the equipment." I knew I had won by sprinkling non-existing Eskimo germs on their equipment. I was very happy and elated. I signed the letter and delivered it to the Inspector General's office at eight

o'clock the next morning. At ten o'clock, I was called in and told to forget the whole thing.[46]

With subconscious dreams of Arctic bioterrorism, Muktuk made the world, or at least his corner of it, a little safer for democracy.

Whether Alaska had been newly created or merely transformed, the citizens of the northern territory, like those in Hawai'i, now faced the future. They shared the legacy of being the two places in America where the war had come. Having fought the foreign foe, both prepared for what Sakae Takahashi had described in 1942 as "the second war" to win first-class citizenship at home. In 1945, with populations seasoned by the winds and williwaws of war, Alaska and Hawai'i faced the future to win the new battle for the inclusion of two multiracial territories in the union of states.

Muktuk Marston and the Eskimo Scounts

One of the most memorable aspects of World War II in Alaska was the organization of the Alaska Territorial Guard. Major Marvin R. "Muktuk" Marston organized the guard's western division, sometimes called the Eskimo Scouts.

18. *Artist Magnus Colcord "Rusty" Heurlin (1895–1986), who was also a rifle instructor for the ATG, drew this poster for the Guard, depicting both the northern or western sector with the Eskimo rifleman and the southeastern sector with the Indian (Tlingit) rifleman. Courtesy of the University of Alaska Museum, #69-7-1.*

19. *Artist Joseph John Jones (1909–63) drew this sketch of "Muktuk Marston Signing Eskimos into the Alaska Territorial Guard" in 1943. Courtesy of the University of Alaska Museum, #82-3-27.*

20. *Joe Jones drew this memorable charcoal sketch of Muktuk Marston. Marston remained after the war in Alaska, championed native rights, and became a delegate to the 1955–56 Alaska Constitutional Convention. Marston's strong facial features, so evident in this sketch, were often considered his trademark. Courtesy of the University of Alaska Museum, #82-3-47.*

The Bulldozer and the Alaska Highway

The bulldozer was the chosen weapon of both the African American and the white engineer regiments that built the Alaska Highway in record time between February and November 1942.

21. Lt. Walter Mason, one of the white officers commanding the African American 97th Regiment, stands in front of his "dozer" in 1943. Courtesy of Walter Mason.

22. The bulldozer could also serve as an ambulance in this photo of the transport of an injured soldier. Courtesy of Walter Mason.

23. The African American 97th Regiment poses after the completion of a "corduroy" bridge. Courtesy of Walter Mason.

24. In one of the classic photos of the building of the Alaska Highway, two soldiers shake hands. The soldier on the left is Corporal Refines Sims, Jr. of the African American 97th Regiment, and the one on the right is Private Alfred Jalufka of the white 18th Regiment. The men stand atop their "dozers" upon the link-up of two sections of the highway at Beaver Creek, Yukon Territory, in October 1942. Courtesy of the U.S. Army Corps of Engineers, Office of History.

Part III

And the War Came Again: Statehood and the Cold War in Alaska and Hawai'i, 1946–1956

World War II transformed the territories of Alaska and Hawai'i. Neither the nation nor the territories could simply return to the status quo of 1940. At the beginning of 1946 it appeared as if statehood would be the reward for the territories' valiant military service. Hawai'i was confident that it would soon become the forty-ninth state. More than likely Alaska would follow as the fiftieth state, if the residents of the northern territory signified their resolve for statehood in the plebiscite authorized for the November elections.

Yet no sooner was the war over than war came again—this time the Cold War. Former British prime minister Winston Churchill first sounded the alarm in March 1946 with his famous "Iron Curtain" speech signifying that a Russian Communist menace was now present in Eastern Europe. Over the next few years the first embers of fear implanted in Europe spread to Asia and the Pacific. The mounting tempo of the new Cold War affected the two distant territories and made them as central to the new conflict as they had been to World War II.

Alaska soon reemerged as an air defense center. Military strategists quickly saw that the shortest air route for a Soviet attack on the United States would be via Alaska. Over the next decade the territory would reclaim the defense strength it had reached at the peak of the Aleutian campaign. This time the defense buildup would be permanent.

The Cold War also reinvigorated Hawai'i as a defense center. But before the renewed troop buildup began, sudden fears surfaced that Communists had already arrived in the islands as part of an extraordinary civilian labor movement. Communist labor leaders, it was feared, planned to take over the territorial government. Hawai'i's postwar surge to become the forty-ninth state was soon stymied.

The Cold War caused the quick road to statehood to become elusive in the first decade after World War II. But that war and the ensuing military buildup in Alaska and Hawai'i kept the two territories firmly placed in the consciousness of the nation. It transformed the two once again and shaped their path to eventual statehood as much, if not more so, than World War II.

Chapter Five

The Cold War Stymies Hawai'i as the Forty-ninth State, 1946–1950

> The Kremlin in Moscow . . . regards Hawaii as one of its principal operating bases
> —*Senator Hugh Butler, after visiting Hawai'i in 1948*

Nineteen forty-six opened triumphantly for Hawai'i's statehooders. No sooner had the revelry of the New Year's celebrations ended than a subcommittee of the U.S. House Committee on Territories, chaired by Representative Henry Larcade of Louisiana, began hearings on statehood for Hawai'i on January 7. Delegate Farrington, a member of the subcommittee, proudly introduced his fellow congressmen to the islands. The timing for the hearings could not have been better. A few weeks earlier, on December 22, 1945, Secretary of the Interior Ickes had publicly endorsed statehood for Hawai'i as the official position of the Department of the Interior.

The Larcade committee hearings, as they were called, were the first statehood hearings held since 1937. Though the 1937 committee found that Hawai'i had "fulfilled every requirement for statehood heretofore exacted of territories," it had called for a plebiscite of the people of Hawai'i and had also shown concern about the potential loyalty of Hawai'i's Japanese and Japanese American population. In 1946 statehooders emphasized that both of those 1937 concerns had been laid to rest. In 1940 the people of Hawai'i had voted 2–1 in favor of statehood. And the record of the 100th and 442nd certainly put to rest any qualms about the islands' Japanese American population.

The statehooders also made note of another new improvement in the islands—labor legislation. In 1937 the committee had noted that Hawai'i seemed backward in its lack of positive legislation for unemployment or workmen's compensation. Statehood supporters, led in early 1946 by Governor Ingram Stainback, pointed to territorial laws that now made Hawai'i a leader in labor legislation. In addition to laws for general worker welfare, the 1945 Republican-dominated territorial legislature passed the Hawaii Employment Relations Act (HERA), often called the "Little Wagner Act," which allowed unionization and collective bargaining for agricultural workers. The federal National Labor Relations Act of 1935 (the Wagner Act) extended such rights only to industrial workers. Among the forty-eight states, only Wisconsin had passed similar legislation for farm workers. Hawai'i's economy was no longer grounded and mired in the paternalistic plantations. It was now a thoroughly modern display in the statehooders' showcase of progress. As further evidence of the territory's economic maturity, Governor Stainback pointed to the fact that a higher percentage of island residents filed federal income tax returns than in twenty-six mainland states.[1]

Speakers at the hearings emphasized the territory's exemplary role in World War II and proclaimed that Hawai'i deserved statehood because it needed a "voice" in the Congress with a "vote." "Twenty-five thousand young men of these islands were drafted during World War II. Yet they had no voice in the passage of the draft law, no vote in the declaration of war that sent them into battle," explained Stainback. "It is an inferior status repugnant to the spirit of America." Representative Homer Angell of Oregon agreed and replied to the governor, "That characteristic that you have just mentioned really is the fundamental of American government, isn't it?"[2]

The statehooders definitely held the platform while the Larcade committee was in Honolulu. But on the last day of the hearings one dissident note from within the islands was sounded. The testimony of prominent island resident and state legislator Alice Kamokila Campbell seemed at times almost comic. But there was a prophetic quality to her words that deserves attention before we return to the beat of the statehooders' drum.

Kamokila's Plea

Born in 1884, Kamokila Campbell was reputedly one of the wealthiest women in Hawai'i, and certainly one of the most colorful. Her father, Scots-Irishman James Campbell, came to the islands in the midnineteenth century and became one of the islands' wealthiest sugar planters and financiers. Her mother, Abigail Maipinepine Campbell, was descended from Hawai'i's ruling chiefs. Her family knew Queen Lili'uokalani well and remained royalists at the time of the 1893 Revolution. By ancestry she was part of the exclusive worlds of both Caucasian (though not American-descended) wealth and Hawaiian nobility. After her father's death she became a beneficiary of the Campbell Estate, one of the largest landed estates in the islands. Some placed her annual income in the 1940s at $200,000 a year.[3]

During the 1920s and 1930s she married three times, had five children, and moved to San Francisco. Shortly before World War II she returned to Hawai'i. During the war she was a staunch supporter of America's war effort and, as noted earlier, entertained several hundred thousand troops at her Ewa Beach estate in conjunction with the USO. She entered local politics and served as a territorial senator from Maui-Molokai from 1942 to 1946, the position she held at the time of the Larcade committee hearings. Though she had originally favored statehood at the time of the 1940 plebiscite, she claimed she grew concerned with Hawai'i's AJAs during the war. She supported martial law and in 1945 was the only member of the legislature to vote against a resolution favoring statehood. On the last day of the Larcade hearings, Friday, January 17, Kamokila was the only person scheduled to speak. She testified for two hours before a crowd of six hundred in 'Iolani Palace. Such was her appeal. Those looking for drama that day were well rewarded.

Senator Campbell identified herself as an "American," but one who was "neither missionary nor Big Five." She never specifically said that she represented the native Hawaiian community, but that is how she was received. Possibly she implied this affiliation when she said she spoke "from the heart and soul of Hawaii."

Kamokila told the visiting committee that she opposed statehood because it would increase the economic power of the Big Five and the rising political domination of AJAs. This position was somewhat ironic. She owed her election as a territorial senator to the AJA vote on Maui from the Big Five plantations owned by the Baldwin family. She claimed that the war record of the AJAs had given them an inflated ego. She opposed statehood because the people she distrusted, the Big Five and the AJAs, were for it.

She did not explain why remaining a territory would be preferable to statehood. She did not necessarily favor territorial status, but called for some form of independent government in which "the Congress of the United States would have a slight hold on us, so that we could not go absolutely haywire." The local senator implored the committee, "Please take this message back to Congress: Hawaii and Kamokila ask nothing else but to be left alone." Delegate Farrington politely tried to refute most of her positions. Nonetheless, at the end of her testimony Kamokila rose and presented the delegate with a lei and a big kiss on the cheek to the applause of the crowd and the cameras of the press.

Kamokila Campbell made good copy in the newspapers the next morning. "Kamokila Pulls No Punches" announced the *Advertiser.* Publisher Lorrin P. Thurston refuted her arguments in the paper's editorial column, but noted that her presentation was "the high spot of the entire hearings" and an "event none of our visiting Congressmen will ever forget."

Campbell's 1946 testimony had little effect on the visiting congressmen other than as an interlude of Hawaiian pageantry. Nonetheless, Kamokila's words were prophetic and would have even greater meaning in the years after the territory entered the union as the fiftieth state. The statehood story is often presented as one of "progress" toward first-class citizenship, particularly for Asian Americans, and of equal treatment for all residents of the islands. But there was another aspect to statehood coming from the native Hawaiian community. In 1946 there were still many native Hawaiians, like Kamokila, who had lived through the 1893 Revolution and ensuing annexation in 1898. An even larger number had heard about these events directly from their parents. Many, if not most, native Hawaiians had opposed the revolution and the annexation. At the time they wanted to retain their own nation, one that had earlier been recognized by the government of the United States. By the end of World War II there was little hope that the Hawaiian nation would ever be restored, but there were continued fears that the essence of Hawaiian culture within the territory was gradually eroding. Some Hawaiians feared the new groups of people coming to power—particularly the AJAs. To all groups in Hawai'i statehood signified *finality.* For the AJAs the finality would be first-class citizenship. But the finality for native Hawaiians might well be a final severing of any ties to their once different world and their culture.

Did Kamokila speak for the native Hawaiian community or only for herself? In 1946 no one knew whom Kamokila Campbell represented. No others echoed her testimony at the hearings. Though

Kamokila's testimony indeed raised questions about the future of the native Hawaiian community, statehood remained the principal concern of the Larcade committee and the nation at large. On January 21 President Truman endorsed statehood for Hawai'i in his State of the Union address to Congress. The Larcade committee favored immediate consideration of statehood, but the full Committee on Territories decided to defer consideration until the next session of Congress in 1947. Progress still seemed imminent in the fall elections of 1946 that returned a Republican majority to Congress. This outcome boded well for Hawai'i, as the territory had long been Republican. During the elections the Republican National Committee adopted a resolution favoring statehood.

Delegate Farrington introduced the necessary legislation in the new Eightieth Congress as HR 49. In March 1947 the House Lands Committee reported favorably on the Hawai'i statehood bill. In testimony before the committee the new Secretary of the Interior, Julius Krug, enthusiastically endorsed statehood for Hawai'i. Victory seemed close at hand in June when the full House of Representatives concurred with a vote of 197 to 133. Though the vote was bipartisan, there was more Republican support than Democratic. Southern Democrats then and in the future would form a major bloc of opposition because of the racial implications of statehood for Hawai'i. In their minds any congressional delegation from Hawai'i would provide votes in favor of civil rights legislation.[4]

The next step was to send the bill to the Senate. In the summer of 1947 there was every reason to believe that statehood was imminent. Hawai'i, the long expected forty-ninth state, was ready to join the union. Could anything block the way?

Stainback's Lament and the Rise of the ILWU

In the fall of 1947 the first block came not from southern Democrats in the U.S. Senate, but from the territory's own governor, Ingram Stainback. As part of an Armistice Day talk in November Stainback announced that Communism was rampant in the islands and that there was a Communist plot to take over the territory. From late 1947 on, Stainback emerged as one of the leading opponents of statehood. In January 1946 Stainback, the governor who had defeated marital law, had been a supporter of statehood. What happened to change his mind?

Stainback's conversion to the anti-Communist cause marks the first inroad of the Cold War to Hawai'i, though exactly why Stainback became such a convert is difficult to trace even in the present day. In early 1947 President Truman initiated a loyalty program by which federal employees would be screened for any present or prior Communist affiliation. In Hawai'i the main federal employer was the military. In March 1947 the army commander in Hawai'i, General John Hull, informed Stainback that there were significant numbers of Communists in Hawai'i. Over the course of 1947 Stainback's interest in the anti-Communist cause increased. He began his own loyalty checks among territorial employees. At the time of his November announcement the alleged "Communist plot" concerned the writings of a Honolulu high school teacher, John Reinecke, who had first published a pamphlet entitled "What We Must Do" in 1934. John and his wife, Aiko, both allegedly Communists, were soon suspended from their teaching positions. The suspension was sustained after a lengthy hearing a year later that became an anti-Communist spectacle in the territory.[5]

The real thrust of Stainback's anti-Communist concern, however, was not against the Reineckes or any other Honolulu schoolteachers. In 1947 the governor's attention fell more directly on the International Longshoremen's and Warehousemen's Union (ILWU) and its local head, Jack Hall. In January 1946 Stainback bragged to the Larcade committee about Hawai'i's improved labor image. The ILWU, representing 33,000 members, was a firm supporter of statehood and endorsed Stainback's reappointment as governor in May 1946. To understand why Stainback turned against the union that supported him, a background to labor's rapid rise to power is in order.

As noted earlier, labor activity and strikes on Hawai'i's plantations had been part of the early twentieth-century history of the islands. After the Sugar Strike of 1920, labor activity waned in the islands. While the local unions were subdued, the national labor movement as characterized by the American Federation of Labor (AFL) took little interest in the islands. The national unions had long been noted for their anti-Asian position. Much of the anti-Japanese position of the national Democratic Party emanated from the demands of West Coast labor unions. In the early 1930s visiting representatives of the U.S. Department of Labor noted that labor activity and union membership were virtually nonexistent in the islands. The Big Five firms that controlled both the plantations and the docks remained hostile to labor. They were backed by territorial legislation that provided anti-picket laws and gave police full power to disperse "riotous" crowds. If a labor movement were to develop in the islands, either a locally based union would have to arise against management pressure or a national union that was willing to buck the West Coast anti-Asian tide would have to enter the islands. The latter scenario emerged. The Hawai'i labor movement that began in the 1930s and 1940s was exported and directed from the West Coast.[6]

The docks of the territory, rather than the plantations, were the most fertile grounds for new union activity. Because of the ebb and flow of maritime activity, waterfront workers knew more about labor movements on the West Coast than did their isolated plantation counterparts. In the mid-1930s local men, particularly Jack Kawano and Harry Kamoku, tried to organize a longshoremen's union to bring wages in Hawai'i up to West Coast levels. The potential for labor activity increased after the San Francisco Dock Strike of 1934, when growing numbers of West Coast dock workers and seamen migrated to Hawai'i. Among the new arrivals in 1935 was Jack Hall, a twenty-year-old California sailor with a assignment from the Sailors' Union of the Pacific to investigate the possibilities for union organization in Hawai'i. Hall found the Honolulu and Hilo waterfronts ripe for organization and made contact with local dockfront leaders. Hall's arrival coincided with the passage of the National Labor Relations Act that guaranteed industrial workers the right to union organization and collective bargaining. Hall's efforts attracted the interest of Harry Bridges, head of the San Francisco–based ILWU, a well-known radical union whose predecessor, the International Longshoremen's Association (ILA), was responsible for the 1934 San Francisco dock strike.[7]

From 1937 on the ILWU aggressively recruited members in Hawai'i. The union supported strikes in Hilo in 1938 and on the Kaua'i dockfront at Akuhini in 1940. Though both strikes were violent and ended in defeat for the workers, they brought the various racial groups, (Japanese, Hawaiian, Filipino) together in united action. Union activity soon moved from the docks to the plantations. In 1938 Jack Hall began working for the United Cannery, Agricultural, Packing and Allied Workers of America (UCAPAWA)—a newly organized Congress of Industrial Organizations (CIO) union. In 1940 the union successfully organized industrial workers on the McBryde sugar plantation on Kaua'i and became the collective bargaining agent. By late 1941 union membership among waterfront and plantation workers stood at ten thousand.

While mounting such impressive gains in organization, the ILWU and UCAPAWA also showed a desire to influence local politics by backing particular candidates for the territorial legislature who would sponsor legislation friendly to the unions. As early as 1938, union-backed candidates won election on Kauaʻi. Jack Hall worked for those members in the territorial legislature by drafting pro-labor legislation. The early political activity of the ILWU was directed primarily, though not exclusively, through the Democratic Party. The party was a logical choice for the union. It was the weaker and more malleable party in Hawaiʻi and presented the possibility of becoming a union-controlled entity.

As the ILWU flexed its political arm, the specter of radicalism emerged. There was no doubt that the union had a radical reputation—at least in the league with the old International Workers of the World (IWW). Its West Coast leader, Harry Bridges, was alleged to be a member of the Communist Party, which he was. Jack Hall also joined the Communist Party in 1936, though he never publicly acknowledged this. What did this Communist link mean, and who knew about it? John Burns told writer Lawrence Fuchs in 1958 that he knew Hall was a Communist, along with others in the union. Through his work in the police department, he was well aware of the background of union leaders. Burns insisted, however, that Hall joined the Party not because of any devotion to Marxism but because the Communist Party was one of the few organizations willing to give organizational support to union activity among Hawaiʻi's multiethnic population. Writing in the 1970s Sanford Zalburg, the leading chronicler of the ILWU, confirmed Hall's early membership in the Communist Party and basically agreed with Burns about the parameters of Hall's commitment to Communism. Hall used the Communist Party for his purposes rather than the reverse. Before the war, however, any potential Communist tinge to the ILWU in Hawaiʻi was little known to those outside union, police, or FBI circles. In the wider public eye the ILWU was simply a militant labor union. That was sufficient cause for concern to the territory's traditional business leadership.[8]

With its ten thousand members the union certainly posed a challenge to the territory's economy. But before this challenge could fully develop, World War II came. Under the provisions of martial law the wages of resident workers were frozen, a resident worker could not leave one job for another, and collective bargaining agreements were suspended. Union membership plummeted from ten thousand in December 1941 to four thousand by late 1942, with some estimates putting membership at a low of nine hundred by 1944. While the war undermined union growth, it may well have created the conditions for explosive union growth after 1944. The wartime "wage freeze" of resident workers caused much resentment. But resentment against whom? It was a federal/military regulation to freeze wages. Much of the worker dissatisfaction, however, was directed toward plantation management. The federal government subcontracted plantation laborers for war work and paid the plantations a premium over the wage paid the workers (sixty-two cents an hour versus forty-one cents) to cover the cost of plantation perquisites such as housing and medical care. The wage freeze prohibited the plantations from passing on this premium. The Hawaiian Sugar Planters' Association (HSPA) claimed that the premium did not fully compensate them for the displaced manpower. The HSPA also insisted it had been ordered against its wishes to subcontract the workers. Regardless of these technicalities, workers felt that the plantations were in league with the government to exploit them. It should come as no surprise that plantation workers wanted a greater say in the direction of their livelihood, regardless of the true source of their wartime frustrations.[9]

With the partial lifting of martial law in late 1943, the ILWU resumed its prewar organizing activity. While reestablishing its position on the waterfront, it moved to control the sugar plantations and took over the organizing work of its sister CIO union, UCAPAWA. During 1944 Hall became the local head of the ILWU in Hawai'i. Active recruiting proceeded with help from a cadre of ILWU organizers sent from San Francisco. Organizing the plantations was still complicated by the division between workers classified as "industrial" (for example, mill workers, equipment operators) and "agricultural" (for example, field workers). The "agricultural-industrial" complication was eliminated in 1945 when the territorial legislature passed the HERA and extended the right of collective bargaining to agricultural workers. This was a step virtually unprecedented in American labor history. How did it come about?

Labor historians emphasize that Jack Hall and the ILWU sponsored the HERA in the 1945 legislature through newly elected pro-labor candidates. In the elections of 1944 twenty-one candidates backed by the union were elected. Nonetheless the 1945 legislature still retained a Republican majority with a management orientation. Why did such a legislature agree to a union-initiated bill? Labor economist Thomas Hitch contends that during the war management "saw the handwriting on the wall" and assumed that union activity would surge after the war, particularly given the very visible wartime frustrations with the wage freeze on the plantations. The major employers, long noted in Hawai'i for concerted action, reacted with a plan to protect themselves from a "tsunami" of inevitable unionization.

In 1943 they created the Hawaii Employers Council (HEC), which included the Big Five and most other major employers in the territory. The HEC imported labor lawyer James Blaisdell from San Francisco to create a plan for postwar industrial relations. Management agreed not to oppose union organization with the proviso that the unions nego-tiate through only one channel—as opposed to separate strikes and sep-arate negotiations on each plantation. According to Hitch, Republicans were willing to support the HERA in 1945 because they still had the power to influence the precise writing of the bill. Better to support a management-influenced bill in 1945 than one dictated in the future by greater ILWU strength in the legislature. After the passage of the HERA, membership in the ILWU swelled to a total of thirty-three thousand by early 1946. On the sugar plantations the ILWU won elec-tions at all but one of Hawai'i's thirty-four plantations. In late 1945 the ILWU concluded its first contract with the sugar industry. It was now the recognized bargaining agent for sugar workers.[10]

Such joint union-management cooperation provided the background for Stainback's glowing testimony to the Larcade committee. But the har-mony started to unravel later that year when the ILWU and the sugar plantations entered into contract negotiations again. The union now looked for a more substantial victory to assert its role as a major player in the territory's economy. The ILWU wanted to raise wages and end the perquisite system of plantation housing and medical care, which its mem-bers saw as a paternalistic method of social control. Management also wel-comed an end to the perquisite system, as the concept of a company town or company plantation was outmoded by 1946. When the ILWU and the plantations could not reach an initial agreement, the first of the major postwar strikes ensued—the seventy-nine-day sugar strike of 1946 last-ing from September 1 to November 8. As the strike dragged into the third month the ILWU dispatched negotiators from San Francisco. The U.S. Department of Labor also sent a team of negotiators to Hawai'i from Washington. The final contract raised basic wages and ended the perquisite system. Both sides claimed victory, but the "victory" for the ILWU was probably greater as it represented the first time labor in

Hawai'i had emerged from a prolonged strike with a favorable agreement. The victory for both sides, however, was tinged by the fact that "outside" negotiators had been needed to settle the strike. This left the impression that both local management and union leaders needed more time and negotiating experience to work effectively with each other.[11]

The 1946 sugar strike itself did not cause a reaction from Stainback. Rather it was the continued political activity of the ILWU in the elections of 1946, which coincided with the strike, that caused the governor concern. Through its political action committee (PAC), the ILWU retained its influence on the legislature with the election of twenty union-backed candidates. Most, though not all, of the candidates were Democrats. This brought the legislature as close as it had ever been to Democrat/Republican parity. The House was evenly divided and the Republicans controlled the Senate by only one seat. Despite such dramatic support for the Democrats, the ILWU endorsed Republican Joseph Farrington for congressional delegate over little-known Democratic territorial tax commissioner William Borthwick. ILWU regional director Robert McElrath later explained why Farrington was the better candidate from a union perspective: "You could talk to Joe Farrington. He certainly wasn't pro-union, but he wasn't anti-union, either. He had a union contract at his newspaper, the *Star-Bulletin*. He had a contract with the typographical union." At the time some union critics alleged that the ILWU made a "deal" with Farrington to gain favorable treatment of the ongoing sugar strike from the *Star-Bulletin*. Both Farrington and the *Star-Bulletin* denied that any "deal" was ever made. Regardless of the reasons for the endorsement, Stainback was furious with the ILWU because Borthwick had been his handpicked choice for delegate. The governor had expected ILWU endorsement of his candidate, particularly as he had appointed Jack Hall to the Honolulu Police Commission in 1945.[12]

Stainback was not the only person upset in the 1946 election. Republican Lorrin P. Thurston, publisher of the *Honolulu Advertiser*, turned against Farrington because the delegate did not *reject* the ILWU's endorsement. Farrington did not formally accept or embrace the ILWU, but reasoned that anyone or any organization could endorse him. He said he would not *reject* the organization's support in the same fashion that he would not reject anyone's vote for him. Thurston and the *Advertiser* endorsed Borthwick. Republican criticism of Farrington spread beyond the pages of the rival newspaper. Betty Farrington noted that when she and her husband were in Hawai'i during the 1946 elections, many Republicans shunned them and would not come to social/political occasions at their home. As expected, Farrington was reelected in November. But the territory now presented the unseemly spectacle of some Republicans opposing their strongest flag bearer and of the Democratic governor turning against the union that had almost secured a Democratic victory in the legislature.[13]

The 1946 election set the governor and the ILWU at odds. Stainback's immediate reaction was to ask Jack Hall to resign from the Police Commission, allegedly because Hall had criticized a judge on Kaua'i for issuing an injunction during the sugar strike. Hall resigned but with the retort that Stainback's real reason was to avenge the ILWU's failure to back Borthwick. Despite this quick act of political retribution, Stainback did not yet have a serious charge to make against the union or its leader. Only after Truman initiated the loyalty program in early 1947 did anti-Communism come into play.[14]

After the army contacted Stainback in March, the governor made hints and innuendoes about the Communist threat in Hawai'i and its connection to the ILWU. As the year 1947 wore on, the ILWU staged a strike against the pineapple industry in the summer. The strike was not as well organized or successful as the earlier sugar strike. Though a contract was finally reached, the ILWU did not emerge with the same victorious aura as in 1946. The pineapple strike also led to internal dissension within the union as some of its Hawai'i-born organizers began to rankle under Hall's leadership. This dissatisfaction may have given Stainback a sense that the union was more vulnerable than it had been a year earlier. His Armistice Day speech in November was his most open accusation against the growing power of Communists within Hawai'i and the ILWU. His statement gained added emphasis a few days later days later when Ichiro Izuka, one of the disgruntled ILWU members, published a pamphlet, "The Truth about Communism in Hawaii," which lambasted the union. "Stainback's Crusade," as Sanford Zalburg called it, was now in full force and attracted new followers every day.

At this point we may well wonder what was on Stainback's mind. Hall and the radicalism of the ILWU were certainly known in Hawai'i before 1947. Had the governor just become aware of Hall's alleged Communist affiliation? Did he truly fear that Hall and the ILWU were tools of Moscow? Or was he just worried about the growing power of the ILWU within the Democratic Party, and how that might affect him?

The answers are not at all clear. As late as 1953 Stainback told a visiting committee of Congress that he had known nothing about the connection of Hall or other union members to the Communist Party until the army contacted him in 1947. He claimed that no one else knew either; it was only the 1947 Communist revelation that turned him against the union, not the 1946 election or the power of the union within the Democratic Party.[15]

Regardless of his motives, the governor quickly translated his concerns with Communism and the ILWU to an opposition to statehood. He reasoned that statehood would then give the Communists control of an elected governorship. The governor's changing stance on statehood became well known inside and outside of Hawai'i. Both Stainback and Ernest Gruening of Alaska attended the June 1947 meeting of the U.S. Conference of Governors. Gruening noted that he had "difficulty" enlisting Stainback's support for a resolution endorsing statehood for both Alaska and Hawai'i. A year later at the 1948 meeting Gruening reported that Stainback had become a virtual opponent of such a resolution and told the other governors that "Communism was rampant in Hawaii." By 1948 Stainback publicly opposed granting statehood any time soon. He retained this stance for the duration of the statehood battle. In 1954 he openly testified against statehood before a congressional committee, saying that Communism had become worse since 1948 and 1950 when he had been in a mood of deferral for statehood rather than total opposition. When Edward R. Murrow interviewed Stainback for his *See It Now* program in 1958, the former governor, now a member of the territorial supreme court, had not changed his mind.[16]

Not unexpectedly, Lorrin Thurston became as livid an anti-Communist in 1947 as Stainback. He continued to lambaste the ILWU and Delegate Farrington in the *Advertiser*. This position was particularly embarrassing to the statehood cause because the legislature had just appointed Thurston to the new Hawaii Statehood Commission that it created and funded to lobby for statehood. Though the *Advertiser* and Thurston claimed they still supported statehood, both paper and publisher devoted much more energy to their attacks on Communism, the ILWU, and Delegate Farrington. The *Advertiser* also lent support to national politicians who called for further investigations of Hawai'i's Communist problem. What Hawai'i needed most in 1947 was a united front. Instead, Stainback and Thurston were at cross-purposes with Farrington and the territorial legislature.

Senator Butler and the Derailing of Statehood

The emerging anti-Communist hysteria of late 1947 could not have come at a worse time. The victorious 1947 statehood bill introduced by Farrington and passed by the House was on its way to the Senate. The chairman of the Senate Committee on Public Lands (later Interior and Insular Affairs) that would oversee the bill was Republican Hugh Butler of Nebraska. Butler was emerging as one of the leading anti-Communists in the Congress. In November Stainback—either directly or through James Coke, a Democrat and retired chief justice of the Hawaii Supreme Court—informed Butler of the increasing Communist threat to the islands and the need to delay statehood.[17]

A year earlier Butler had shown his opposition to both Hawai'i and Alaska by suggesting that Alaska become a county of Montana and Hawai'i a county of California. He had also shown his aversion to potential Japanese American members of Congress from Hawai'i. Despite these prior inclinations, Butler dispatched Senator Guy Cordon of Oregon, chairman of the subcommittee on territories, to Honolulu in January 1948 to conduct statehood hearings. Cordon, who went to the islands alone, concluded that Hawai'i had passed every test ever demanded of a territory to become a state. If there were a Communist menace, it was not one of sufficient size to defer the granting of statehood. Cordon found fewer than one hundred Communists in the territory and no Communist penetration of the legislature. The senator also heard from Kamokila Campbell. Now a Republican and no longer in the legislature, Kamokila asserted that Communism was a problem in the islands and linked to the territory's Japanese population. Anti-Japanese sentiment was not new in Campbell's testimony. In 1948 she simply added Communism to her earlier list of objections to the Japanese. Campbell made no more impact on Cordon in 1948 than she had on the Larcade committee in 1946, but her testimony was indicative of a linkage between anti-Japanese sentiment and anti-Communism in the rhetoric of local conservatives. James Coke had made the same connection in his communications to Butler.[18]

Back in Washington, Cordon's subcommittee recommended that the full committee report the bill positively to the Senate for consideration. Butler would have none of it. He first called for additional hearings in Washington that he would chair. When those hearings, held in April, were positive for statehood, he balked again. He wanted to defer the bill indefinitely until he and other members of the committee had an opportunity to visit Hawai'i and to assess the Communist threat. Eugene Millikin of Colorado proposed a resolution to keep the bill in committee until Butler could go to Hawai'i. By a committee vote of seven to five the resolution passed. There was virtually no hope that a Hawai'i statehood bill would reach the floor of the Senate during the Eightieth Congress.

Republican William Knowland of California, a strong statehood supporter, tried to override Butler with the support of Guy Cordon. Knowland proposed a resolution in the full Senate to discharge the bill from the committee and bring it directly to the floor for consideration. Such a move was within Senate rules, but to bypass a committee and its chairman was a step rarely taken except for legislation of *compelling* national concern. In 1948 statehood for Hawai'i was not such an issue. It was not a first priority for most members of Congress, even for those who favored statehood. The Knowland Resolution was defeated 51 to 20, not because those who voted *No* were opposed to statehood for Hawai'i, but because there were not compelling reasons *for* Hawai'i that warranted an extraordinary process. What the Senate vote on the Hawai'i statehood bill would have been had it reached the floor in the Eightieth Congress will forever remain a mystery.[19]

Butler finally arrived in Hawai'i, alone and without other members of his committee, in late October 1948. He conducted seventy-seven formal interviews and claimed he talked with an additional one hundred people. During his time in the islands he became particularly alarmed with charges that the ILWU had taken over the territorial Democratic Party at its May 1948 convention. The union had definitely tried, but had not succeeded—a fact Butler did not understand. Upon his return to Washington, Butler delayed issuing his final report until June 1949. The report, entitled *Communist Penetration of the Hawaiian Islands,* proclaimed that "international revolutionary communism at present has a firm grip on the economic, political, and social life of the Territory of Hawaii." He listed as "identified" communists, Harry Bridges, Jack Hall, and other leaders in the ILWU. Bridges, he claimed, was the "unseen Communist dictator of the Territory of Hawaii." Communist influence was not merely local but "directed from Moscow.""The Kremlin in Moscow..." asserted Butler,"regards Hawaii as one of its principal operating bases.""Statehood for Hawaii," the senator explained, "is a primary objective of Communist policy in the territory." If Moscow was for statehood, Butler was predictably against it. Though the senator affirmed that the bulk of the islands' population were loyal Americans (making no anti-Japanese references), he recommended that "statehood for Hawaii be deferred indefinitely, until communism in the Territory may be brought under effective control." Technically Butler's 1949 report concerned a bill in the now expired Eightieth Congress. It was not Butler's report but his delaying tactic that had killed statehood in the Eightieth Congress. Had one man stopped statehood for Hawai'i or was he a proxy for wider and deeper forces in the Congress?[20]

Though it is tempting to look for a deeper or broader meaning to Butler's tactic, the overall lesson to be gleaned relates more to the nature of the U.S. Congress than to broader forces at work for or against statehood for Hawai'i. No southern Democrats were on Butler's committee nor did the Republican from Nebraska seem to have a more substantial following among congressional anti-Communists. Butler wrote James Coke in June 1949 that he had been conducting his campaign over the last two years "almost single handed." In 1950 other well-known anti-Communists in Congress would go to Hawai'i and find much less a menace than did Butler. Rather than an indicator of broader opposition, Butler's actions supported the reality that one member of Congress, particularly one who controlled a committee through which statehood legislation must pass, could single-handedly stymie action. In the course of future legislation on statehood for both Hawai'i and Alaska, the power of one man on a key committee would reoccur. It was only when there was a substantial tide of committed support *for* statehood that such one-man power could be overcome, as would be the case in 1958 when the Alaska statehood bill was discharged from the House Rules committee and its obstructionist chairman, Howard Smith of Virginia. But that action lay a decade ahead. Butler's actions in 1948–49 tell us much more about the "power of seniority" in the U.S. Congress than about the forces against Hawai'i.[21]

Butler's action broke the bubble of postwar euphoria that in 1946 appeared to be propelling Hawai'i into the union. Whether Butler or his report would have any influence in the Eighty-first Congress was still questionable. Hawai'i had cause for hope in the new Congress. The 1948 elections gave the Democrats control of both houses of Congress. Though Butler remained a member of the Interior and Insular Affairs committee, he was no longer the chair.

Statehooders were particularly energized by the endorsement of "immediate" statehood for Hawai'i at the 1948 Democratic National Convention. Local Democrat and Chinese American lawyer Chuck Mau, who sponsored the plank in the platform, told me that the 1948 convention was the most exciting experience of his life. Mau recounted how he sat through three days of committee meetings without leaving the room for fear he would be absent when called to speak. One can well understand Mau's excitement. Franklin Roosevelt's Democratic Party had been a threat to the islands. It brought martial law to Hawai'i and would have interned the islands' Japanese population, alien as well as citizen, had it not been for General Emmons. Roosevelt's successor, Harry Truman, was a true friend of the islands who tried to lead the party toward Hawai'i. He first endorsed statehood for Hawai'i in January 1946. Now the party was behind its presidential candidate as they both rode to victory in 1948. Mau, who was trying to reshape the Democratic Party in Hawai'i, could well draw comfort from this support at the national level that had been lacking in the past. As the Democratic order began to change nationally and locally, James Coke lamented that he just did not "understand President Truman."[22]

In a strange reversal of fortune, the Democrats in Hawai'i lost strength as the national party rose to power in 1948. The year of turmoil over the Communist connection to the ILWU and the ILWU's attempt to control the local May 1948 Democratic convention left the party seriously divided and weakened. Though the Democrats had almost taken control of the legislature in 1946, the Republicans came back with massive strength in 1948 and secured their prewar hold on both the territorial house of representatives and the senate. AJAs substantially increased their participation in the legislative races and won *as Republicans.* After their wartime hiatus AJAs had returned to the legislature in 1947 with six seats. In the new 1949 legislature their numbers doubled to twelve—four of whom were Democrats and eight of whom were Republicans.

The Republican resurgence that swept the legislature also reelected Joseph Farrington as delegate. Farrington's foes, particularly Lorrin Thurston and the Honolulu *Advertiser,* continued to lambaste the delegate in 1948 for his failure to reject the ILWU's endorsement in 1946. Nonetheless, Farrington won by even greater margins than in 1946 over his new Democratic challenger, John Burns, who had resigned from the police department to help rebuild the local Democratic Party. Farrington approached the new Eighty-first Congress with confidence. On the first day of the new session he introduced HR 49 once again. By March 1949 the House Lands Committee reported the bill favorably and sent it to the Rules Committee to be scheduled for floor debate and a vote. At this time statehood for Hawai'i became joined with statehood for Alaska as the Lands Committee also reported an Alaska statehood bill and sent it to the Rules Committee. That committee quickly became enmeshed in a partisan debate over which territory to schedule first—Democratic Alaska, the less mature territory, or Republican Hawai'i, the more mature territory. While the wrangling and delaying tactics in the Rules Committee progressed, Butler's report appeared. New events in Hawai'i added even more fervor to his charges.

The ILWU Strikes Again

Senator Hugh Butler may have been a "single-handed" loose cannon who was out of power in 1949, but the timing of his various anti-Communist shots at Hawai'i was brilliant. His need to visit Hawai'i and his delay in making that visit had stalled statehood legislation in 1947 and 1948. He arrived in Hawai'i just in time to witness the turmoil of the 1948 elections. He could have issued his report early in the first session of the Eighty-first Congress but delayed doing so until June 1949. During the first part of that year the ever-increasing Red Scare of the Cold War intensified nationally with the Alger Hiss trial and the first Smith Act trial. This made Congress even more sensitive to any accusations of Communist penetration in Hawai'i. The islands themselves provided the perfect backdrop for Butler's anti-Communist crusade. The ILWU Dock Strike, the most tumultuous labor action in Hawai'i's history, began just a month before Butler released his report.

The Dock Strike of 1949, like other ILWU actions in Hawai'i, had both "local" and "imported" mainland origins. In 1948 the ILWU had staged a dock strike in San Francisco that resulted in a substantial wage increase. In 1949 the union wanted to secure a new contract in Hawai'i that brought island dockworkers nearer to West Coast wage standards. In Hawai'i the last ILWU dock strike in 1940 at Akuhini on Kaua'i had resulted in disaster for the union and its members. A victorious strike on the waterfront, not just a reasonable contract, was clearly a prime issue for the union's survival—particularly after its setback as a political force in the 1948 elections.

Negotiations between the ILWU and the stevedoring companies, as represented by the HEC, began in early 1949 with the union initially wanting to increase wages by thirty-two cents an hour. Management offered eight cents. By late April the negotiating gap had narrowed to a twenty-one-cent demand by the ILWU and a twelve-cent offer by the HEC. Officially this gap created the impasse that led to the strike that began May 1. Unofficially, both union and management sources report that in the last minutes before the strike deadline the gap narrowed to a fifteen-cent offer versus a sixteen-cent demand. Thus historians and critics ask, "Did the union throw the islands into turmoil over a penny?" or conversely, "Did the Big Five throw the islands into turmoil over a penny?" Regardless of who held out for a penny, turmoil was the result of the strike, which lasted for 177 days until late October.[23] Obviously the effects of a general dock strike in Hawai'i would be much greater than in California because of the islands' dependence on maritime transportation. With no labor to unload or load ships, commerce into and out of the islands steadily deteriorated. Most sources confirm that there was never a serious food shortage and that the ILWU agreed to unload emergency supplies. Nonetheless there was a substantial impact that spread beyond the union and the dock companies to the general public, particularly to small businesses that did not see themselves as part of the struggle between Big Labor and the Big Five. Food prices rose, a number of small merchants went out of business, tourism declined, and unemployment rose. The generally accepted figure for the strike's impact on Hawai'i's economy was $100 million. Though the $100 million impact would not begin to be felt until later in the summer, Lorrin Thurston early set the hysterical tone that marked public reaction to the strike. Thurston hit a new high of anti-Communist fervor with a series of "Dear Joe" letters in the *Advertiser*, written as dialogue with Joseph Stalin about his plans for a Communist takeover of Hawai'i. Other local critics of the strike echoed Thurston's line as Congress read Butler's report.

As the strike wore on, Hawai'i's political establishment from Governor Stainback to Delegate Farrington implored President Truman to invoke the new Taft-Hartley Act, which would send strikers back to work for a "cooling off" period. Residents of Hawai'i made a massive effort to reach out to their mainland friends for support. Some congressmen received far more constituent correspondence on the Dock Strike than on statehood. For example, the correspondence of Florida Senator Spessard Holland, who became a supporter of statehood for both Hawai'i and Alaska, contained considerably more letters on the Dock Strike. The senator received letters from several Florida chambers of commerce and Jaycee groups urging him to support any kind of legislation that would end the strike. The letters from Florida businessmen usually included copies of statements from their counterparts in Hawai'i deploring the ILWU's tactics and its Communist connection.[24]

Neither Truman nor the Congress responded with a Taft-Hartley injunction or other legislation. Though he had invoked a Taft-Hartley injunction during the 1948 dock strike in San Francisco, the president did not like the legislation. He had originally vetoed the act in 1946 and called for its repeal in his 1949 State of the Union address. In the absence of any national remedy, the territorial legislature with its solid Republican majority passed the Dock Seizure Act in August, which allowed the territory to take control of the docks and hire non-union labor to unload the ships in Hawai'i's ports.

The Dock Seizure Act only partially restored maritime commerce. While ships could now be loaded and unloaded in Honolulu, the ILWU staged a countermeasure on the West Coast and refused to load ships bound for Hawai'i or unload those coming in from the islands. Thus the sugar companies could not unload at their California refinery. Finally, in October 1949, the strike was settled in San Francisco, where a major stockholder in the Matson Line, Hawai'i's principal shipping company, brought the ILWU and the HEC together to negotiate an agreement. The union got its twenty-one-cents-an-hour increase, though in increments of fourteen cents and seven cents over two years. As in the sugar strike, both sides claimed victory. Management had averted federal arbitration, which was one of its greatest fears. Though the employers welcomed federal intervention with a Taft-Hartley injunction, they did not want federal or "outside" intervention in the form of an arbitration panel. The ILWU claimed victory for the simple fact that it had held out for 177 days and negotiated a favorable contract for its members. This was a first in a Hawai'i dock strike.

The ILWU was now a recognized force in the fields and on the waterfront. Whatever the severity of the strike or the Communist allegations against its leaders, the union's members remained loyal. The ILWU was now clearly the major voice of labor with which management must deal. And deal they did. The union successfully negotiated a new sugar contract in 1950 without a strike. No further strikes occurred in the fields or on the docks until the sugar strike, or "Aloha strike," of

1958, which was lengthy but relatively mild in its impact on the general public. Ultimately cooperation between management and labor became the modern pattern of labor relations in Hawai'i. But it took five years, from 1945 to 1950, for both sides to learn their parts in the scenario that had been envisioned in 1943–45 when the Hawaii Employers Council supported the HERA and in effect gave the ILWU the go-ahead to organize the plantations and negotiate within certain guidelines. There were also considerable political repercussions for both the ILWU and the territory in that "learning period."

Despite the contract victory, the general public blamed the ILWU, not the Big Five, for the power it exerted in disrupting the territory's economy. Many people now wondered just what the ILWU's plans for Hawai'i were. Whatever those plans and wherever their origins, many people wanted to limit them. Most commentators agree that the 1949 strike ended the ILWU's momentum as a dominant *political* force in Hawai'i—or at least that it marked the beginning of the end. Jack Hall resigned from the Democratic Party in November 1949, and the union severed its official ties with the party.

There were political ramifications in Washington as well as Honolulu. The Dock Strike and Senator Butler's report postponed any further action by the Rules Committee on Delegate Farrington's statehood bill during the first session of the Eighty-first Congress. Was there reason for hope in the second session that would begin in 1950?

Even as the strike wore on in the summer and autumn of 1949, Farrington and other statehood leaders were still hopeful that the statehood bill could reach the floor of Congress in the second session of the Eighty-first Congress. They needed a way, however, to dispel the negative connotations of the strike. As a tactic to build support for the bill and to demonstrate Hawai'i's fitness for statehood, the 1949 territorial legislature called a constitutional convention for April 1950. There the residents of Hawai'i would show the Congress that they were perfectly capable of designing a sound government. In March 1950 sixty-three delegates were chosen in nonpartisan elections for the convention. To minimize the Communist specter, the 1949 legislature also suggested that the House un-American Activities Committee (HUAC) hold hearings in Hawai'i concurrently with the constitutional convention. Supposedly Congress would see that the people writing the constitution were certainly not those being questioned by the HUAC about their Communist activities. Or so it was hoped.

As the year 1950 opened, these hopes and anticipations appeared to bear fruit. President Truman implored Congress to grant statehood for both Hawai'i and Alaska. He personally asked the chairman of the Rules Committee to report the two statehood bills. When the Rules Committee continued to delay, the Lands Committee used a recently approved tactic to discharge both bills from Rules and bring them to the floor of the House. In early March the House approved the Alaska bill by a vote of 186–146. A few days later the Hawai'i statehood bill received an even greater victory of 262–110. Both bills were soon on their way to the Senate. Hawai'i's supporters now saw the upcoming constitutional convention as the perfect way to draw attention to Hawai'i and gain a favorable Senate vote. With approval by Congress there was no doubt that President Truman would sign the statehood bill and add a forty-ninth star to the flag.[25]

The 1950 Constitutional Convention and the Second Defeat of Statehood

The 1950 Hawaii Constitutional Convention was one of the true milestones in the statehood battle of Hawai'i—and later of Alaska. The constitution it produced was a model of modern statecraft that would later serve without revision as the constitution for the new state of Hawai'i. If the convention's only function had been to produce a constitution, it would probably be remembered today as one of the great events in the territory's history. But more baggage than the simple creation of a constitution was attached to it. The convention was supposed to shine as a showcase of Americanism against the "Red attack" of Senator Butler. Statehooders hoped the convention would prompt the U.S. Senate to grant admission in a matter of months. With so many demands placed upon it, the 1950 Convention would eventually be forgotten for what it did not accomplish rather than remembered for the remarkable product in statecraft that it produced.[26]

The legislature's call for the convention was a ploy to energize the stalled statehood movement. In Hawai'i, and later in Alaska, various statehood research and study groups searched for tactics that had been used by other territories to gain admission after a frustrating wait. The researchers discovered that fifteen territories had called constitutional conventions prior to the passage of statehood legislation—as opposed to waiting for Congress to pass enabling legislation that would authorize a constitutional convention. In all fifteen cases the territory was admitted to the union in a relatively short period of time. Hence the purpose of the constitutional convention was not to produce a document that was a particular reflection of local priorities, but one that would be seen on the mainland as a "model" document that would elicit praise from constitutional experts. Such a constitution should not contain innovative or radical features like a unicameral legislature. To understand the document the convention produced, we do not need to understand the subtleties of island life. Rather we need to understand the guidelines prepared by the National Municipal League for a model state constitution. The major principles of those guidelines were:[27]

1. The constitution should provide a concise, basic framework of government. It should not include items that were legislative in nature. State constitutions, in contrast to the federal constitution, had long been criticized by political scientists for their excessive length and detail. In a modern state the people should control their lawmakers by holding them accountable at the ballot box, not by hamstringing them with a constitution that limited their ability to pass laws. The legislature in a modern state should be large enough so that legislation could not be stalled by a few members. In Hawai'i and Alaska both houses of the legislature were increased in size. The experts also wanted to free the legislature from interference by the old Progressive measures of initiative and referendum. If the people did not like the legislature, they should change the members, not the laws the legislature passed or failed to pass.

2. The constitution should establish a strong executive branch with only the governor and lieutenant governor being elected officers. In a modern state the governor must have the power to govern. To do this, the governor must appoint his/her cabinet and hold the members responsible. Political scientists found that too many governors were weakened because cabinet members were elected and owed their allegiance to the voters, not to the governor. Again constitutional experts thought the people should exert their influence by electing one person to govern and then giving him/her the authority to do so. The states, the experts believed, should try to emulate the federal president and cabinet.

3. The constitution should create a state court system with appointed, not elected, judges. Elected judges were anathema to the modern state as envisioned by the experts. How could a judge fairly interpret laws, if

his/her job were subject to the emotional whims of the electorate? The proper role for the people was to elect legislators who could change the laws, not to remove judges who tried to enforce them.

Hawai'i, and later Alaska, produced such model constitutions. These constitutions were basic frameworks of government containing 12,000–14,000 words—a far cry from California's 75,000-word constitution or Louisiana's 201,000 words. Of those 12,000–14,000 words about a third spelled out a new system for apportioning the legislature. There were a few exceptions to the proviso against items of a legislative nature. The 1950 constitution prescribed that the centralized administration of territorial schools—Hawai'i had no local school districts—would be maintained. Constitutional status was also given to the existing state university. Such educational matters were handled by statute in many states. The Hawai'i constitution also sanctioned the continuation of the Hawaiian Homes Commission (HHC), a territorial agency that provided homesteads and other land privileges to native Hawaiians. Again, land provisions were considered by some to be a legislative action. Marguerite Ashford, the one delegate who refused to sign the Hawai'i constitution, did so because she protested the protection of the HHC within the constitution. The convention was more influenced, however, by the native Hawaiian community, which vowed to oppose the constitution and statehood if the HHC did not receive constitutional protection.

The Hawai'i constitution, and later the Alaska constitution, were hailed by the National Municipal League as models for reform in other states. Though the constitutions did not contain radical new features, they did step forward with modernizing innovations. Both constitutions contained guarantees against racial discrimination and lowered the voting age. In Hawai'i the new voting age would be twenty; only Georgia had a lower voting age at eighteen. To catch up with other states, Hawai'i's constitution eliminated a territorial restriction that disqualified women from sitting on juries.

If the "product" of the convention was effectively preordained by the National Municipal League, the "process" at the convention reflected the 1946–50 turmoil in Hawai'i politics. The delegates were elected in early 1950 on a nonpartisan basis, supposedly as good citizens. Still there were cries of partisan domination. A plurality of the delegates were Republicans, who also held the major leadership positions. The president of the convention was Samuel Wilder King, the

Republican delegate to Congress from 1935 to 1943. The secretary, Hebden Porteus, was a Republican member of the legislature. The delegates did represent a broad ethnic and gender diversity, including twenty-seven Caucasians, eleven native Hawaiians, five Chinese Americans, and twenty Japanese Americans. This diversity, for the most part, represented the older established order of both parties. The AJA chosen as one of four vice presidents of the convention was Republican Thomas Sakakihara, the prewar legislator who had been interned and then reelected after the war. Chinese American Hiram Fong, first elected as a Republican in 1938, was another vice president. The one Democrat who served as a vice president, Charles Rice, represented the Old Guard in the party.

The new order in Hawai'i politics tried to advance its cause at the convention but did not succeed. The ILWU ran fourteen candidates, of whom only two were elected. Chuck Mau and Nelson Doi, who represented the new reform faction in the Democratic Party, were elected. But others in the reform group, such as William Richardson, Sakae Takahashi, and John Burns, ran for the convention and lost. Though men like Mau and Doi were proud of the constitution, they did not remember the convention as one of the more important events in their political lives. Chuck Mau told me that his experience at the 1948 Democratic Convention was much more important to him. "Not only was it more important to me," he said, "but perhaps more important to the people of the then territory of Hawaii." The convention has thus been seen as one of the best and final hours of the Old Guard rather than as a new chapter in the evolving political order.[28]

The "process" of the convention extended far beyond the dynamics of who ran and who was elected as a delegate. The showcase aspects of the convention were supposed to shine brightly in full view of the HUAC hearings. Those hearings were to begin a week after the opening ceremonies of the convention. In the early months of 1950 most islanders welcomed the "Red probe" because they thought it would put Senator Butler's charges to rest. The initial plan was to have both the convention and HUAC meet in 'Iolani Palace, the seat of the territorial legislature. This plan caused some logistical concern, and the Star-Bulletin mused:

If, as is proposed, the meetings of the visiting committee of Congress on Un-americanism are to be held in the senate

chamber, Iolani Palace will be in colloquial language, a cross
between a mad house and a rat race.[29]

This unsavory possibility was averted when the convention moved
across the street to the Honolulu Armory to hold its main sessions after
the opening ceremony of April 4. During that ceremony the delegates
took an oath that they were not now nor had been in the last five years
a member of the Communist Party.

The HUAC hearings, chaired by Representative Francis Walter of
Pennsylvania, began on April 10. The committee's spotlight quickly fell
on the convention when it called two delegates—Richard Kageyama,
a Honolulu insurance agent, and Frank G. Silva, an ILWU agent on
Kaua'i—to testify. On the first day of the hearings, Kageyama stated that
he had been a Communist Party member for nine months in 1947. He
told the committee that he became "disillusioned" and left the party
when he found out what it stood for. The day following his testimony
Kageyama tendered his resignation as a delegate to the convention. The
newspapers and the congressional committee complimented Kageyama
for testifying so honestly. The convention itself voted down a resolution commending him for this "courageous act" but decided on a
divided vote that his cooperation with the committee "has been a distinct service to his country." Kageyama had acted in a manner approved
by the convention.[30] The case of Frank Silva was another story.

On the second day of the hearings, Ichiro Izuka, the former union
organizer who had first laid Communist charges against the ILWU in
1947, accused Silva of being a Communist. Silva refused to answer a
number of questions before the committee including whether or not
he had ever been a Communist Party member. Silva maintained that
he had a constitutional right to remain silent, but HUAC recommended
that he be cited for contempt. Constitutional or not, Silva's actions upset
the convention, which appointed a select committee to "investigate the
qualifications of Frank G. Silva to retain his seat as a delegate." Silva,
who had been involved in controversy for over a decade for his union
activities, protested the investigation. He took it personally and declared
that the convention was filled with people "who have blacklisted me
since my youth." "This is no bipartisan convention," Silva announced.
"This is a Republican-dominated Big Five Convention. I know . . . that
this convention is determined to expel me. The Convention is not concerned with me as an individual."[31]

The convention took offense at Silva's language and continued with its investigation. It concluded that Silva could not be disqualified for contempt, as this was still only a recommendation by HUAC. Instead the members decided that he should be disqualified because of his "contumacious conduct," whatever that was. By this time the convention had turned itself into a committee of the whole to discuss Silva's conduct. Just what was "contumacious conduct"? As the debate went on, the charge became clear. Silva's offense was that he had not been a model of cooperation in the presence of the convention or the congressional committee. The model convention writing a model constitution in full view of the eyes of Congress wanted model, not contemptuous, or "contumacious," members. Delegate Nils Larsen left no doubt of the convention's concern:

> We are only interested in one thing here, and that is the success of statehood, the success of this conference. The only fear that I've seen in anybody's mind here is the fear that we might not succeed. We have the right to decide whether any one of our members possibly will block that success.

Delegate Garner Anthony, who had led the attack against martial law during the war, announced that Silva's failure to testify "casts a shadow over this convention." Anthony feared that Senator Butler would use Silva's conduct as proof that Hawai'i was infested with Communists. "In other words," Anthony concluded, "his very conduct in failing to appear before that UnAmerican Activities Committee is bringing us in disrepute. It is jeopardizing the thing we are set out to do here, and I say that alone is sufficient for us to hold him guilty of contumacious conduct."[32]

Silva's individual rights were not at issue; the image of the convention was. Though one might be critical of this stand after years of hindsight, it is clear from the convention's proceedings that the delegates were sincere. Statehood, the cause that would bring full governmental rights to everyone, was more important than the technicalities or legalities of one young man's performance before a congressional hearing. The committee of the whole reported the resolution to disqualify Silva on "contumacious conduct" to the convention, where it passed 53–7. The *Star-Bulletin* editorialized that nearly all the delegates liked Frank Silva personally and added, "They regarded him as a young man of sincerity and good character, but terribly led astray." The paper reminded its readers that his offense was failing "to render due and proper assistance to a duly constituted body of the United States." Silva was out of the convention, and his case thus came to an end.[33]

By the end of April, the Communist flap seemed to be over. HUAC adjourned its hearings on April 20. In Washington the Senate Interior and Insular Affairs Committee began hearings on the Hawai'i statehood bill. In early May Representative Walter told the Senate committee that Communism was on the decline in Hawai'i. To underscore Representative Walter, sixteen convention delegates, including convention president King and all four convention vice presidents, left Hawai'i for Washington to testify before the statehood hearings. In June 1950 the Interior and Insular Affairs Committee issued a favorable report on both the Hawai'i statehood bill and the Alaska statehood bill. Senator Butler was the lone dissenting vote on the committee. Representative Walter, rather than Senator Butler, now seemed to represent the mood of Congress. What more could statehood supporters have wanted as the Hawai'i constitutional convention adjourned in July?

Actually what statehood supporters needed was more time. The Eighty-first Congress would adjourn shortly—possibly as early as mid-August—so that its members could prepare for the off-year elections. By July statehood was not the only affair on the mind of Congress. In late June 1950 the Korean War began. With a new war commanding the attention of Congress, neither the Hawai'i nor the Alaska statehood bills was a top priority before the election adjournment. To further complicate matters, Southern Democrats threatened a filibuster if either statehood bill came to the floor. No floor action ensued before the November elections. Though it appeared that Senator Butler had been trounced in the favorable vote of the Senate Interior and Insular Affairs Committee, he had actually "won the war" against Hawai'i in the Eighty-first Congress. His 1949 report delayed congressional action until the 1950 second session. When the statehood bill finally came to the floor, Butler had exhausted so much time that it was too difficult to rally support against the perennial southern opposition. Butler remained the most effective opponent of statehood whether his party was in the majority or the minority!

Hawai'i's statehood supporters still did not despair. After signing the constitution in July, statehood leaders pushed to convene a special session of the legislature in September to approve the constitution and send it to the voters for a ratification vote in the November general election. Thus a constitution approved by the people could be presented to the Senate after the election recess when a floor vote was again possible. The voters complied in November and ratified the constitution by a 3–1 margin, despite the public opposition of the ILWU, which claimed that the document created too much centralized power.[34]

The statehooders' carefully planned scenario failed to secure the needed Senate vote once again. In late November President Truman indeed encouraged the Senate to act favorably on both the Hawai'i and Alaska statehood bills. But Truman's influence had been weakened by the success of his opponents in the 1950 elections, who campaigned against the liberal bent of pending legislation backed by the president. Almost on cue Southern Democrats threatened yet another filibuster once Congress reconvened. Statehood for Hawai'i and Alaska, along with other Truman-backed civil rights legislation such as the Fair Employment Act, failed to come to a vote in the last days of the Eighty-first Congress. Had Southern Democrats and a handful of red-baiters defeated statehood once again? In one sense they did. Their threatened filibuster prevented a floor vote, which might well have been favorable in the Eighty-first Congress. Still, the Southerners did not really block statehood. They placed a block in the path of statehood that statehood supporters did not yet have the strength or time to go around. In a senator's mind, voting for statehood was one thing. Making statehood such a priority that a senator was willing to defeat a threatened filibuster was another matter. Obstructions are a part of the congressional process. The same Southern Democrats who threatened a filibuster in 1950 would be there when statehood passed in 1959 and after both Hawai'i and Alaska entered the union. In later chapters we will examine the more important dynamic in which statehooders garnered sufficient support to overcome the perennial Southern opposition.[35]

The defeat of statehood for Hawai'i in 1950 cast a legend of oblivion on the 1950 Constitutional Convention. That carefully orchestrated showcase of Americanism directed to the attention of a Congress in session had not brought about the main hope of its organizers. The excellent constitution it produced almost served as a consolation prize. Had the convention succeeded in bringing about statehood, its leaders would likely have become the elected governor and congressional delegation of the new state. By the time statehood eventually came in 1959, many of the convention's leaders were no longer in the positions of influence they had enjoyed a decade earlier. A newer and younger generation of leaders, many of whom had not participated in the convention, were in power. In 1959 few people looked back or remembered the decade-old convention. In 1959 the *Honolulu Advertiser* ran a three-hundred-page edition on statehood. The convention received only a two-paragraph mention. There were no pictures of the delegates or their ceremonies. If the process of the convention was forgotten, at least its product, the 1950 constitution, survived and was heralded in a two-page spread.[36]

In 1950 statehood had failed again. The high hopes of 1946 and the acclaim Hawai'i earned from World War II had been stymied by the linkage of the Cold War Red Scare to the islands. That anti-Communist scare, however, was also linked to an unresolved agenda from the war on what the internal, as well as the external, future of the islands would be. If Hawai'i had simply emerged from the war unchanged since 1941, admission to the union as the forty-ninth state might easily have been its reward. But as has been noted repeatedly, Hawai'i was transformed by the war. Many in its population now sought a wider political, economic, and social democracy. Statehood was a part of that democratic quest, but so was the Communist-tinged union movement that moved with such lightning speed to change both the economic and political order of the territory. The quest for statehood, as signified by the passage of a specific piece of legislation in Congress, progressed hand in hand with the internal transformation of the islands. At times the two came in conflict with each other—certainly in the perspective of the Congress.

Over the next six years from 1950 to 1956 those twin drives for congressional legislation and for internal transformation continued to march together—again with repeating frustrations. These two drives would also become entwined with yet a third force—Hawai'i's expanding role in global affairs. All three drives would fall under the umbrella of the growing Cold War. The outbreak of the Korean War may well have stalled congressional action on statehood in late 1950. But it also hurried the transformation of the territory as Hawai'i took on a new role as a Pacific Cold War beachhead and as a decisive player in America's emerging global role in Asia. It would become clearer to some in Congress that the United States actually needed Hawai'i to be a state.

Congressional admission would not come by 1956. But those interconnected drives in the transformation of Hawai'i continued to revolutionize the territory that would eventually enter the union not as the postwar forty-ninth state, but as a new fiftieth state.

Chapter 6

The Continuing Transformation
of Hawai'i, 1950–1956

He died at his post of duty as surely, as devotedly, as stead-
fastly, as any man in uniform who sacrificed his life at the call
of his country.
—Honolulu Advertiser, *on the death of Joseph Farrington, 1954*

During the January 1946 Larcade committee statehood hearings
in Honolulu, the *Christian Science Monitor* ran a major national
feature that analyzed the connection between statehood for
Hawai'i and America's emerging role in the Pacific. "World Policy
Tied to Islands' Status" was one of several headlines in the feature. The
newspaper explained: "The present is a transitional period. The pattern of American peacetime policy is just beginning to emerge. By
deciding the Hawaiian issue, Congress will take an important step in
deciding the character and extent of United States policy and
influence in the Pacific."[1]

The paper predicted that if Congress rejected statehood for Hawai'i,
"this step . . . well might be interpreted in foreign capitals as presaging
an equivocal or weak-kneed American policy in the Pacific." The paper
hoped this would not be the decision of Congress and went on to say:

> If, on the other hand, Congress should decisively grant state-
> hood to Hawaii, American hegemony in the Pacific would
> be confirmed. Such a vote would move the domestic fron-
> tiers of the United States proper 2,200 miles westward, estab-
> lish the first overseas American state, and establish an
> American lake between San Francisco and Honolulu, secure
> beyond reach of any vicissitudes of policy. It would serve
> notice on the world that the Central and Western Pacific con-
> stitute a defense zone of the United States.

Possibly no greater prophecy of the importance of Hawai'i in the post-war world had ever been made. The paper's ability to see the future was indeed great, as it went on to say that "If Congress should grant state-hood to Hawaii, the precedent undoubtedly would provoke new inter-est in the question of admitting Alaska as a state."

But in January 1946 the *Christian Science Monitor* seemed to be a voice ahead of its time. Congress did not see exactly what the *Monitor* saw. U.S. Senator Lyndon Johnson later admitted that he had been "one of the majority of Americans who thought of our destiny largely in terms of relations with Europe . . . We therefore looked away from the Pacific, away from its hopes . . . One consequence of that blindness was that Hawaii was denied its rightful part in our union of states for many, many years. Frankly for two decades I opposed its admission as a state."[2]

In the last half-decade of the 1940s the nation followed the vision of Johnson rather than of the *Christian Science Monitor*. The first embers of the Cold War were indeed European in origin. As a result, Hawai'i's postwar military role in terms of both personnel and spending steadily declined from 1945 to 1950—when there were actually fewer troops in Hawai'i than in Alaska. Even if America turned its back on the Pacific during those first years of the Cold War, Hawai'i still suffered from the Red Scare as some politicians linked the islands to that European cold war as an outpost of Moscow.

Some military leaders, however, never had any doubt about Hawai'i's strategic role and the benefit that statehood could bring. A steady stream of generals and admirals consistently spoke in favor of statehood for Hawai'i at the various hearings from 1946 to 1950. With the fall of China to the Communists in 1949 and the outbreak of the Korean War in 1950, both congressional and military leaders increasingly linked Hawai'i to the developing Asian cold war. Troops and dollars returned quickly to the islands in the first half-decade of the 1950s. Military strength rose from 20,000 uniformed personnel in 1950 to 57,000 by 1956. Including dependents, the military population reached 107,000—almost one-fifth of the territory's total population—that year. Military spending rose from $147 million in 1950 to $284 million by 1956, eclips-ing agriculture as the mainstay of the islands' economy. Even as the ILWU came to dominate the fields and docks of the territory, those same fields and docks were becoming less and less important as the islands' economy underwent yet another transformation.[3]

As war came again, Hawai'i became a central part of it. After 1950 it would become an outpost to combat Communism, rather than merely a location infected by it. Hawai'i's importance, as the *Monitor* predicted, was linked to American policy toward Asia and the Pacific. A part of that Cold War policy had ramifications that dramatically altered the status of Hawai'i's "different" population. Even before the end of World War II, there was a clear recognition both in Washington and abroad that the treatment of the nation's Asian population—which was so dominantly represented in Hawai'i—affected U.S. foreign affairs. In 1943, when the United States was still a military ally of China, the 150-year-old prohibition against the naturalization of Chinese immigrants was eliminated. This change was done in part to combat Japanese propaganda that America was waging a race war against all Asians at home. It was also evident that postwar alliances with the emerging nations of the Philippines and India would require legislation. In July 1946 the prohibition of naturalization for Filipino and Asian Indian immigrants was also lifted, even before India freed itself from British rule. By 1950 Japanese and Korean immigrants, as well as some Pacific Islanders, were still denied a chance for citizenship. While modernizing and transforming mainland Japan after World War II, General Douglas MacArthur recommended that this stigma also be removed. Efforts begun in Hawai'i after the war would finally persuade Congress to lift that ban in the early 1950s.

If Hawai'i's global role underwent change from 1950 to 1956, the local agenda of who would rule at home continued in the tumultuous fashion that had marked the immediate postwar period. Possibly no single development highlighted that agenda more than the evolution of the local Democratic Party. The surging power of the ILWU with its Communist tinge as well as the hopes and aspirations of Hawai'i's AJAs seemed to converge on the twists and turn of the Democrats. This perennial minority party in 1950 would become the majority party by 1956.

To understand how certain people in the islands came to lead those local changes, we will need to look at an aftermath of World War II that we have not previously touched on: death. While death from war is often attributed to those who died on the battlefield or from wounds sustained there, many who stayed at home worked so hard that death also came to them in the years soon after the war. As in England where King George VI exhausted himself from his wartime pace and died in 1952, the war bore a similar fruit in Hawai'i. One of the most celebrated deaths would be that of territorial delegate Joseph Farrington, who died at his desk in Washington in 1954.

While the saga of global change, local tumult, and death progressed, Hawai'i's hope to become the forty-ninth state still lay with the passage of one piece of legislation in the U.S. Congress. Though the Senate and House would both vote in favor of statehood in 1954, the intricacies of the congressional process would once again withhold the new star from the flag. Let us first look at the local political saga and then at the renewed congressional battle to pass the statehood bill.

The Evolution of the Democrats

The Republican Party had been the dominant party in the territory since annexation. It controlled the legislature and, with the exception of the years 1923–27 and 1933–35, elected the territorial delegate. The Democrats were perennially the minority party. But what or whom did the parties represent? Hawai'i political writer Tom Coffman has pointed out that Hawai'i's political parties did not necessarily reflect the same origins and values as their mainland counterparts. The local Republican Party had its origins as the party of the haole revolutionaries and annexationists of the 1890s because the national Republican Party backed their efforts. The Republicans were, for the most part, the party of the sugar interests and had as their major national goal the protection of Hawaiian sugar against tariffs and other discriminatory legislation. The Republicans were often identified as the party of the Caucasian business community or the "oligarchy" party. However, to capture the native Hawaiian vote representing the majority of local voters, the Republicans had agreed in 1902 to support Prince Jonah Kūhiō Kalaniana'ole for territorial delegate and to provide a substantial number of government jobs for Hawaiians. So whom did the Democrats represent? Were they the party of labor and the working classes? Not exactly.[4]

As the working classes were predominantly immigrant Asian, most were ineligible for citizenship in the early 1900s. As the Hawai'i-born Asian generation came of voting age in the 1920s and 1930s, those few who entered politics, both Japanese and Chinese, found a home in the dominant Republican Party. Of the twelve AJAs elected to the legislature before World War II, only one was Democrat. The Democrats thus emerged as a fragmented and feuding coalition of some Hawaiians who could not reconcile themselves with the annexationists and of assorted Caucasians who were dissatisfied with the Republicans. The Rice family of Kaua'i, sugar barons of that island, were Democrats. Of the Hawaiians connected to the party, the best known was John H. "Johnny" Wilson. Born in 1871, Wilson grew up before the 1893 Revolution and spent much of his early youth in the court of Queen Lili'uokalani. Trained as a civil engineer at Stanford University in the 1890s, Wilson worked as a private contractor and then as county engineer in Honolulu. In 1920 he was first elected mayor, a post he held at varying intervals until 1954. He was the most "electable" of the Democrats. The party also attracted some mainland Caucasian migrants to the islands in the twentieth century who had been Democrats at home, such as Ingram Stainback, who came to Hawai'i from Tennessee in 1912. The Democrats had no specific "issue" with which to distinguish themselves from the Republicans. They seemed to be simply the "opposition" or "anti-oligarchy" party.

In a state, even a minority party would have to elect a governor from time to time to gain political patronage for party members. Given the factional weakness of Hawai'i's Democrats, they might well have collapsed as a party. But Hawai'i was not a *state;* it was a *territory.* The governorship and related patronage were matters of appointment by the dominant national party. The local Democratic Party, regardless of its influence at home, could gain the governorship simply by waiting for the Democrats to win in Washington. Thus from 1934 on, a succession of Democrats held the governorship based on nothing more than the fact that a Democrat resided in the White House. This did not require popular support at home or even a particularly effective party organization. In fact, party members, as well as political commentators, have called the Hawai'i Democratic Party immediately before and after World War II a "shambles."[5]

Such a derelict party in executive power certainly presented an interesting vehicle for takeover by any new or emerging group in the islands. The ILWU spotted the opportunity and did just this. Though it initially supported both Democrats and Republicans, it clearly had the greatest political opportunity in the party of the feuding factions rather than the party of the Big Five—regardless of any ideological distinction between a union party and a management party. The ILWU breathed new life into the party beginning in 1938 by electing candidates that it backed. After a wartime hiatus the union resumed its political march in the election of 1944. Much to the surprise of the Old

Guard in the party, there was a chance that the Democrats might actually become a party with elected power. This opportunity clearly became evident in 1946 when the party was only one or two seats away from controlling the legislature.

If the ILWU breathed life into the local Democrats, it was not just Senator Butler who wondered what that new life would be. Exactly what did the ILWU want to do once a few pieces of positive labor legislation were passed—or anti-labor legislation repealed? What would a union/labor party be like, particularly a radical union/labor party? There was no national norm. Roosevelt's Democratic Party had embraced labor, but labor was only a part of the party. It is not clear that the ILWU had an exact agenda behind its political drive. No ILWU statements or subsequent interviews with union leaders indicate any goals beyond basic labor legislation. The ILWU's 1946 resolution in favor of statehood noted that the union had supported the extension of minimum-wage legislation and collective bargaining to agricultural workers. If the ILWU had further plans, it did not state them publicly.[6]

Such wondering about the intent of the ILWU attracted the attention of a group of men who had been important in the liaison groups between Hawai'i's Japanese population and the military during World War II, particularly the Emergency Service Committee (ESC) and the Police Contact Group under John Burns. As the men in these groups had worked with each other during the war, it was not unusual that they decided to continue informal meetings to discuss Hawai'i's postwar future, particularly the role of AJAs in that new society. By 1944 a group known as "The Five"—including Burns; Dr. Ernest Murai, an AJA dentist who chaired the ESC; Mitsuyuki Kido, a high school teacher who had been executive secretary of the ESC; Jack Kawano, an early ILWU organizer; and Chuck Mau, the Chinese American lawyer who would place the plank for Hawai'i statehood in the 1948 Democratic National Platform—were meeting regularly.

Though Kawano and Mau were active in the Democratic Party by 1944, it was not a foregone conclusion that all of the Five would place their future hope in the Democratic Party. As noted earlier, many AJAs and Chinese Americans had found a niche in the Republican Party. Burns had worked well with Republican Party boss Roy Vitousek during the war. Burns left the police department in 1945, and Vitousek encouraged him to join the party. Burns's own brother, Edward, who had also been a Honolulu policeman, joined the Republicans. But John

Burns told Vitousek that he could not join the Republicans because the Democrats were the natural "party of the people."[7]

There is no reason to doubt Burns's commitment to a "party of the people," but his commitment to and concern for the Hawai'i Democratic Party may have also come from the growing role of the radical-tainted ILWU. Burns downplayed the importance of the Communist affiliation of ILWU leaders in his 1958 interview with Lawrence Fuchs. But Fuchs noted that Burns admitted "he was sufficiently worried about the growth of communism in strength and power during the '40s and the building of the ILWU, that he began to think that the second major political party in Hawaii, would be a labor party, which could be infiltrated by Communists." Fuchs went on to add that Burns "claims this was one of his motivations in setting out to build a democratic party."[8]

Burns's concerns about the ILWU, Communism, and the Democratic Party may also have been influenced by his devout Catholicism. It is unclear whether Burns felt a specific Catholic mission to combat Communism within the ILWU and the Democratic Party. But he said on numerous occasions that his Catholic faith was stronger than any Communist ideology he might have to confront. Burns and his group noted repeatedly that the Democratic Party could not survive with a pronounced ILWU/Communist taint. "The Five" were well connected to the ILWU, particularly through Kawano. They worked to ensure that the ILWU remained a part of the party—but not the dominant part.[9]

By 1945 "The Five" were definitely committed to the Democrats. In 1946 Mits Kido was the first of the group to be elected to the legislature, one of two AJA Democrats in the body. In 1948 Burns was elected chairman of the O'ahu Democratic Party. His group, soon to be called the Burns faction, succeeded in keeping the ILWU and Jack Hall from taking over the Democrats at the May 1948 party convention. Later that year Burns ran as the party's candidate for territorial delegate, not because he was seen as the party flag bearer but because William Borthwick did not run. Burns lost to Farrington, but the 1948 delegate race attracted the interest and support of several returning AJA veterans. Daniel Inouye, who returned to Hawai'i and joined the Democrats in 1947, campaigned for the candidate because he remembered Burns's 1941 newspaper letter affirming the loyalty of Hawai'i's Japanese.[10]

The efforts of Burns's group in 1948 to limit the influence of the ILWU within the Democratic Party were reinforced a year later by the political repercussions we have noted in chapter 5 from the 1949 Dock

Strike. Though the strike weakened the Democrats as a whole, by late 1949 leadership and momentum within the party were forming behind the Burns faction that was in touch with, but not dominated by, the ILWU. Exactly what the Democratic Party would become was still in question, but at least the party's radical tint had been diluted.

The spring of 1950 brought all sorts of opportunities and possibilities for the Burns group. Initially they had hoped to establish a position at the constitutional convention. Though many in the Burns faction did not win the place they had hoped for there, they soon took center stage at another convention held concurrently, the 1950 Democratic Party Convention. Elections to that convention in early April gave the Burns group a commanding slate of delegates; Burns was likely to be elected convention chair when the body opened on April 30, 1950. However, complications from the HUAC hearings, which had adjourned only a few days earlier, led to an early imbroglio with the anti-ILWU Old Guard in the party, including Governor Stainback.

HUAC had cited thirty-nine people for contempt because of their refusal to testify and answer questions about their Communist Party affiliation. They were quickly called the "Reluctant 39." Of the thirty-nine, sixteen had been elected delegates or alternates to the Democratic convention. When the convention opened, the Old Guard in the party demanded that fifteen of the sixteen should not be seated. When the Burns group along with others refused to accede to the request, about one-fifth of the delegates left the convention and were called the "walk-outs." Those who stayed were known as the "standpats." While much has been written on the continued tumult at the convention, suffice it to say for our purposes that the "standpats," usually though not exclusively connected to the Burns group, held the convention and gained control of the Democratic Party through its central committee. As expected, Burns was elected convention chair. Chuck Mau became party chairman, and Dan Inouye replaced Wilfred Oka, one of the Reluctant 39, as secretary of the central committee.[11]

The immediate effect of the "walkout/standpat" saga was to divide and weaken the Democrats. For the rest of the year the "walk-outs" tried to reorganize the party without success. In the November 1950 general elections the Republicans increased their hold on the legislature and easily reelected Joseph Farrington as delegate. Democrat Johnny Wilson, who sided with Burns and the "standpats," was reelected mayor of Honolulu, thus retaining that important position within the "standpat" group. Another important position held by the Democrats was also up for reconsideration. The new dominance of the Burns group within the Democratic Party presented the opportunity to remove Governor Stainback and recommend a more amenable candidate to President Truman for appointment in 1951. Who would that be?

Within Hawai'i political culture the position of governor had to belong to someone with rank, position, and respectability. This generally meant that the person would be a haole or Hawaiian. The Burns group obviously wanted to nominate someone sympathetic to their aspirations. "The Five" themselves, including Burns, did not have the important qualifications of rank and position. Johnny Wilson had long hoped to become governor, but by 1951 Wilson was considered too old by many. The person to whom the Burns group first turned did have rank and position; he had also been one of the prime World War II contacts with the Police Contact Group and the Emergency Service Committee—former FBI director Robert Shivers.

Shivers had remained in Honolulu after the war, but moved from the FBI to become collector of customs in 1944. The Democrats had mentioned his name for governor in 1947 when Jack Hall proposed that Shivers replace Ingram Stainback. Shivers did not welcome the ILWU endorsement and waited out the ensuing years with his customs position. In the summer of 1950 the Burns group returned to Shivers and proposed him once again to replace Stainback. Before his name could be presented to President Truman, the fifty-six-year-old Shivers died of a heart attack. Tom Coffman suggests that the years of wartime stress had taken their toll upon him. Had he lived, what role would Shivers have played in the new Hawai'i? Of course, we will never know. President Truman had not even appointed him before he died. Death quickly brought oblivion to Shivers. The man who had been one of the keys in saving the Japanese community in World War II gets barely a footnote or even an index reference in most postwar histories of Hawai'i. But when Shivers's brother visited John Burns, who was then governor of Hawai'i, in 1968, Burns greeted him by saying, "If Bob had lived, he would be sitting where I sit."[12]

Shivers's death prepared the way for others. The Burns group now searched for another candidate. After some discussion they turned to the seemingly logical choice of Oren Long, territorial secretary since 1946 and former territorial superintendent of schools. Long moved to Hawai'i in 1917 from Tennessee, where he had been a schoolteacher.

After doing social settlement work, he became vice principal of McKinley High School in 1919. He was appointed deputy superintendent of schools in 1925 and then superintendent in 1934. In that year his name had been submitted as a possible choice for governor to President Roosevelt, but Joseph Poindexter was chosen instead. By 1951 Long had established friendships within many factions of the party. He had served with Stainback and was acting governor in his absence. Former teacher Mits Kido had good memories of him as school superintendent. Kido's wife also remembered the Longs fondly as she had once served as housemaid for them. It is important to understand that in the midst of radical labor strikes, social change, and political takeovers, kindly relations between employers and servants as well as deference to rank and position were still among the bonds that held the postwar Hawai'i community together.[13]

President Truman appointed Long governor of the territory in 1951 and put Stainback on the territorial supreme court. Long was a firm supporter of statehood. No one could have been more pleased with the appointment than Ernest Gruening of Alaska, who reported that it was much easier to work with Long at the U.S. Conference of Governors than with Ingram Stainback. With Long as governor, the "standpat" Democrats finally freed themselves of the millstone that Ingram Stainback had become. Burns and his group still had to resolve the issue of the ILWU's connection to the party and the continuing stigma that the union's Communist reputation raised.[14]

Even before Long's appointment, matters improved for the party in January 1951 when federal judge Delbert Metzger, an active member of the Democratic Party, acquitted all of the Reluctant 39 of contempt charges. There was still, however, the question of how to handle one of "The Five" who was also one of the Reluctant 39, ILWU leader Jack Kawano.

We have encountered Kawano's name before. He had organized waterfront workers in Honolulu during the 1930s. At the end of World War II he was instrumental in bringing the ILWU and the Democratic Party together. Chuck Mau stated emphatically that Kawano was the key member of "The Five" who brought life to the Democrats at the end of the war, much more so than Burns. After the war the ILWU under San Francisco direction gradually pushed Kawano aside in favor of Jack Hall. By 1949 Kawano had become bitter about the way the union and Hall had treated him. Unbeknownst to many of his friends in the Democratic Party, he had been a member of the Communist Party, like the ILWU leaders from California who displaced him. Mau stated that neither he nor other non-union Democrats knew of this affiliation until shortly before Kawano was called to testify at the 1950 HUAC hearings. Kawano told Mau that he had been a member of the Communist Party, but was no longer involved. At the hearings Kawano said that he was not now a Communist, but refused to answer other questions about his past. For those refusals he was cited for contempt and became one of the Reluctant 39.[15]

Even after Judge Metzger dismissed the contempt citation, Kawano continued to discuss what he should do with the others in "The Five." The group encouraged Kawano to make public what he knew about the ILWU and its Communist affiliation, particularly as the CIO had severed its affiliation with the ILWU in late 1950 because of the Communist link. "The Five" hoped that further testimony from Kawano would show the Democratic Party's determination to rid itself of the ILWU-induced radical tinge—while still retaining ILWU members as a major group within the party.

In February 1951 Kawano made a public statement in Hawai'i that connected the ILWU to the Communist Party. Accompanied by Chuck Mau, he then went to Washington in July and testified once again before HUAC. Kawano explained the development of the Communist Party in Hawai'i and its connection to the ILWU. He indicated that the party controlled the union. He said that Hall and other union leaders were members of the Communist Party, as he had been. What would come of Kawano's testimony?

Nothing might have happened had it not been for further intervention by Chuck Mau. Mau had recently been appointed a federal judge by President Truman. By the time he accompanied Kawano to Washington, confirmation of that appointment was being stalled by staunch anti-Communist Senator Pat McCarran. Mau needed to complete the task of distancing both the Democratic Party and himself from Communism. He had a definite strategy in mind.

One of the major anti-Communist purges launched by the federal government in the late 1940s and early 1950s was a series of Smith Act trials held in various cities around the country. The Alien Registration Act of 1940, called the Smith Act for its author, Representative Howard Smith of Virginia, made it illegal to advocate the overthrow of the U.S. government. By implication anyone who was a member of the

Communist Party violated the Smith Act. As strengthened in 1948, the Smith Act exacted high penalties for anyone convicted. The first of the postwar trials was held in 1949 in New York City. Others were planned around the country. While in Washington Mau went to the attorney general's office and asked when a Smith Act trial would be held in Hawai'i, particularly given the revelations in Kawano's testimony. He was first told that a trial was not likely to happen as the Communists in Hawai'i were not very important. Mau then emphasized Hawai'i's new centrality in the growing Asian cold war and the danger of any Communist presence there. Honolulu quickly became a priority for the next round of Smith Act trials. In August 1951, Jack Hall and six other Communist leaders cited by Kawano were arrested in Honolulu for violating the Smith Act. The ensuing trial of the "Hawaii Seven," as they were called, lasted until June 1953 when a jury convicted all of them. Though the group was released on bond pending appeal, the saga dragged out until 1958, when Hall and the others were finally acquitted.

The Hawai'i Smith Act trial lasted for over half a decade. Interested readers may well want to consult the sources noted below for details. We should focus our attention on how the trial affected the Democratic Party in its evolving stages. By 1952 the party had effectively taken a stand against Communism and limited the influence of the ILWU. Though ILWU members would continue to be a strong part of the party, the outside charges that the ILWU could take over the party were substantially abated. As Dan Inouye put it, there was an end to "the union tail wagging the party dog." However, Kawano's testimony and the Smith Act trial effected a change in the leadership of the Democratic Party among The Five. Mau's aggressive actions against the ILWU, combined with his federal judgeship, gradually removed him from a leadership position in the party. Kawano's life within both the party and the union quickly came to an end. By 1953 he had moved to California, where he spent the rest of his life. Dr. Ernest Murai took a back seat in party affairs. This left Mits Kido and John Burns.[16]

Kido had been the most "electable" of The Five, serving three terms in the legislature from 1947 to 1953 and then becoming a delegate to the Democratic National Convention in 1952 along with Burns and Oren Long. But there was hesitancy within the party to pass leadership to an AJA. When asked in 1975 why the AJAs did not champion Kido ahead of Burns, Daniel Inouye offered an interesting analysis of postwar AJA culture:

It's very difficult to describe this.... It's a strange attitude the Japanese have, that they would like to have men who rise to great heights become humbled. The higher you go, the greater your humility must be. And once in a while you have some strange mental gyrations, they'll say, "I think this guy is getting a little too big for his britches and I think maybe the time has come to teach him a lesson."[17]

Kido's very success was thus a mark against him! Burns with his expanding circle of AJA veteran supporters became the frontrunner. He was not called to testify at the Smith Act trial, thus retaining his cordial links with both Hall and the ILWU constituency of the Democratic Party. In 1952 John Burns succeeded Chuck Mau as chairman of the Hawai'i Democratic Party.

Much of the evolution of the Hawai'i Democratic Party was complete by 1952. This did not, however, translate to victory at the polls. Nationally the 1952 elections brought the Republicans back into power in the Executive Branch and gave them a slim majority in both houses of Congress. In Hawai'i Republican Joseph Farrington was reelected delegate to Congress. As was often said locally, the Democrats gave Judge Delbert Metzger the "privilege of losing to Farrington."[18]

The Republicans also retained control of the legislature. No small part of that Republican strength came from the invigorated participation of AJAs in the 1952 elections. An all-time high of sixteen AJAs were elected to the legislature, up from twelve in the 1948 and 1950 elections. Of the sixteen, eleven were Republicans and five were Democrats. Even more significant, it was the Republican AJAs who increased their lead in 1952 by gaining three more seats than in 1950. The Democrats elected only one additional legislator in 1952. The strength of the Republicans among AJAs cannot be overemphasized—if for no other reason than the fact that it has been so underemphasized, if not totally ignored, in virtually all postwar histories of Hawai'i. The Democrats *would* come to power in 1954 with a substantial number of AJAs winning seats in the legislature as Democrats. By 1958 the Democratic hold on AJAs would seem so complete that historians would somehow look back and claim that the Democrats and the AJAs had been together all along. Even as respected a commentator as Lawrence Fuchs, who conducted extensive interviews in Hawai'i in 1958 and 1959, wrote in *Hawaii Pono* that the

Democrats and AJAs had been growing in power steadily since the end of World War II. He reported that the 1952 elections brought to the legislature "seventeen haoles and the same number of AJA representatives, and nearly all of the latter were Democrats." Actually two-thirds of the AJA legislators were Republicans. Rather than a reflection on Fuchs's ability, his errors were probably more attributable to the fact that by 1958 the Democrats and the AJAs seemed so entwined that no one bothered to check the records of only a half-decade before.[19]

Local Republicans also regained the governorship as a result of the national election. The new president, Dwight Eisenhower, appointed Samuel Wilder King as governor in February 1953 to replace Democrat Oren Long.

Thus, for all the twists and turns of the Democratic Party, the Republicans remained in power with substantial support from Japanese Americans. As late as 1952 the aspirations of Hawai'i's AJAs were still linked to the Republican Party, and most of all to the benevolent efforts of the party's flag bearer and delegate to Congress, Joseph Farrington. In 1953 Farrington returned to Washington to begin his sixth term as delegate. Unbeknownst to him or anyone else, this would be his last term in office. Let us leave the evolving Democrats and turn to Farrington.

Joseph Farrington and the Last Days of Patrician Rule

Daniel Inouye decided to join with John Burns and the Democrats as soon as he returned from the war, but he was quick to point out in a 1975 interview that for most of his buddies in the 442nd during those immediate postwar days, "Farrington was the favorite. We would give him birthday parties and special luncheons and all of this." There was a good basis for that popularity. Farrington had spoken consistently for the loyalty of the Issei and Nisei before and during the war. He sought to end martial law and to prevent the internment of Hawai'i's Japanese. He supported the formation of the 442nd and visited the AJA warriors in Italy. After the war he became a champion for the naturalization of the Issei. Today Farrington is mentioned only in passing in Hawai'i and is virtually unknown and unsung outside of the islands. We need to look more carefully at the man and his goals.[20]

Joseph Farrington was a champion of the underdog, but he had never been an underdog himself. As noted earlier, he was the son of Wallace Farrington, territorial governor and publisher of the *Star-Bulletin*. Later he too became publisher of the newspaper. After serving in the legislature, he agreed in 1942 to run for territorial delegate at the request of Sam King. Even in that first election, a specter haunted him. Farrington had a heart condition. Both he and Betty feared he might not survive the first campaign.

Farrington survived and won in 1942—and in five more elections. In his campaigns for office and his demeanor in Washington, there was a certain patrician "noblesse oblige" to Farrington's politics. He did not hold fundraisers and personally financed his own campaigns. Thus when the controversial ILWU endorsement came in 1946, there was no money involved that tied him to the union. Farrington's personal wealth made it possible for him and his wife to obtain a large house on Washington's fashionable Kalorama Circle. The Farringtons entertained extensively to "convert" both Republicans and Democrats to statehood. "During the war," Betty Farrington explained, "there were very few parties and our house was the center of all this activity and to this day they talk about what a marvelous time we had." At one of those marvelous times in April 1945, Vice President Harry Truman was a guest. While Truman played the piano that night, another guest left a burning cigar on the piano case. The Farringtons decided to let the cigar scar remain as a testament to their bipartisan popularity and a vivid memory of "the night Truman played the piano," particularly as he became president a few days later![21]

During Farrington's time in Washington, statehood had no greater friend than Harry Truman. It could probably be said that no two occupants of the White House and the Congress ever jointly shared a broader view of an America with civil and equal rights than the often beleaguered Democratic president Truman and the always voteless Republican territorial delegate Farrington. The president and the delegate were truly saddened by statehood's defeat in both 1948 and then again in late 1950. Success proved even more elusive in the narrowly Democratic Eighty-second Congress that convened in 1951.

When the Democratic Congress convened in January 1951, bills for both Hawai'i and Alaska were introduced first in the Senate. Given the repeated success in passing statehood bills through the House, supporters thought it was best to get a vote in the Senate and then proceed to the more reliable chamber. Both bills were reported favorably by the Interior and Insular Affairs Committee early in the first session, though Alaska received less support than Hawai'i.[22]

The overriding issues of concern to the Congress continued to be the Korean War and anti-Communism. In the battle to root out domestic Communism, Republican Hugh Butler was aided by a Democratic newcomer, George Smathers of Florida. Smathers, who had been a member of the House, unseated Senator Claude Pepper in the 1950 election. Smathers charged that Pepper was soft on Communism and labeled the incumbent "Red" Pepper. Butler and Smathers would be the principal obstructions in the Senate. Butler initially tried to sidetrack the Hawai'i bill by issuing a dissenting report to the Interior and Insular Affairs recommendation that raised the "Red" specter once again. Though Butler's report received little support, floor debate and a vote were postponed for the remainder of the session while more immediate Cold War concerns loomed. It is unclear whether Kawano's testimony in the summer of 1951 and the ensuing Smith Act arrests of the Hawaii Seven influenced that first-session delay. Most sources place more emphasis on a threatened Southern filibuster than on the continuing Communist taint in the islands.

In preparing for the eventual floor debate and vote, statehood supporters thought it would be best to debate and pass Hawai'i first, as Hawai'i had long been considered the stronger candidate. Some northern and western Democrats had another fear. If Hawai'i passed first, a coalition of Republicans and southern Democrats might let Alaska die. So there was also talk that Alaska should go first. If the weaker Alaska passed, how then could the stronger Hawai'i be denied? The entwinement of the Alaska and Hawai'i statehood bills presented problems for both territories. There was the partisan split between supporters of Democratic Alaska and Republican Hawai'i. The Communist issue drew attacks on Hawai'i from both parties. Alaska received bipartisan criticism because there was a serious question as to whether Alaska was mature enough—economically and politically—to become a state. It seemed clear, however, that either both territories would be admitted or neither would. Senators often combined and entangled the weaknesses of each territory as a justification to defeat both.

When the second session convened in 1952, the Democrats successfully ruled that Alaska, not Hawai'i, be the first statehood bill for floor debate. As the debate began, further confusion surrounded the admission of Alaska and Hawai'i because of Puerto Rico. In 1952 Puerto Rico was granted "commonwealth" status. Under this new creation of Congress, Puerto Rico did not have representation in Congress but its residents were exempted from paying federal taxes. Some members of Congress, principally George Smathers, now advocated that Alaska and Hawai'i be considered for commonwealth status. This diversion also attracted some interest within both territories. Statehood supporters were quick to point out that Alaska and Hawai'i were in no way similar to Puerto Rico. In a series of U.S. Supreme Court cases tried in 1901, known as the Insular Cases, the court ruled that Alaska and Hawai'i were "incorporated" territories eligible for statehood while Puerto Rico was an "unincorporated" territory ineligible for statehood.

While confusion reigned, Smathers—with the backing of Hugh Butler, Russell Long of Louisiana, and John Stennis of Mississippi—moved to recommit the Alaska statehood bill to the Interior and Insular Affairs Committee. Smathers also recommended that the committee consider commonwealth status for both Alaska and Hawai'i. The debate on recommittal was fierce. The vote to recommit tied three times until it finally passed, 45–44. Though technically the motion was merely to recommit the Alaska bill, it effectively ended any debate on Hawai'i. Statehood for the island territory floundered once again.

Though statehood failed in the Eighty-second Congress, Farrington achieved success with another measure that may well be considered an even more important victory for democracy and equality—the naturalization of the Issei. On the spirit of this legislation both Farrington and President Truman agreed. But the actual wording of the new act caused Truman to veto it repeatedly. Farrington and his supporters then had to override Truman's veto to pass the 1952 McCarran-Walter Act. Why the split between Truman and Farrington?

As noted earlier, the 150-year-old ban on Asian naturalization changed during World War II with the need for strategic Asian alliances with India and China. The ban remained for Japanese, Koreans, and certain Pacific Islanders. With the end of the war Japan was no longer the enemy and was soon placed under the wardship of General MacArthur for modernization. Korea, which in the short span of fifty years had been colonized by Japan, liberated by the Allies, and then divided again, was also in the process of reorganization. Was there a U.S. imperative in Asia that argued for removing the prohibition against the Japanese and Koreans? The ban was humiliating both for the immigrants in the United States and for the countries of their national origin.

The first move for naturalization of the Issei came from the Hawai'i territorial legislature. In 1945 it passed a resolution to naturalize the parents of Nisei servicemen. Naturalization would thus be a reward to the Issei for the war service of their children. The momentum soon passed to Washington, where Farrington introduced the first bill in July 1946 to eliminate any form of racial discrimination on naturalization. This bill did not gain sufficient support to pass, nor did a similar bill introduced by Representative Walter Judd of Minnesota in 1947. When the Eighty-first Congress convened in 1949, Representative Francis Walter of Pennsylvania introduced yet another bill to end any racial ban on naturalization. Possibly Walter's long standing as a member of HUAC added momentum to the bill. It passed the House in the summer of 1949. The Walter Resolution, as it was called, would affect approximately 88,000 Asians who had legally immigrated to the United States before 1924, when further Asian immigration was banned. The numbers could be divided as approximately 85,000 Japanese, of whom about 38,000 were in Hawai'i, and 3,000 Koreans, of whom about 2,300 were in Hawai'i.[23]

The Senate began discussion of the Walter Resolution in the spring of 1950—the same time in which it also considered the Hawai'i Statehood Bill and in which Representative Walter conducted the HUAC hearings in Honolulu. The Resolution fared better than the statehood bill, but with a number of changes and revisions. At first Senator Richard Russell of Georgia wanted to exclude Koreans. Farrington prevailed upon Russell to withdraw his objection to Koreans. Under the influence of Senator Pat McCarran of Nevada a number of anti-Communist amendments were added to the bill. Among these was a ban on naturalization to an immigrant of any race who belonged to a subversive organization. There was also a provision to rescind the naturalization of any immigrant who joined a subversive organization within five years of being naturalized. With such security amendments, the bill passed the Senate and was accepted in its amended form by the House. President Truman, who truly believed in the naturalization of the Issei, would not tolerate the anti-Communist amendments and vetoed the bill in 1950. The Congress failed to override Truman's veto.

Neither Farrington, Walter, nor McCarran abandoned their issues when the Eighty-second Congress convened in 1951. Over the next two years the Congress debated and passed the McCarran–Walter Act (the Immigration and Nationality Act of 1952). This bill was much broader than the earlier amended 1950 Walter Resolution. As in the previous bill, race could no longer be a basis to ban naturalization. The new bill codified for the first time the many separate immigration bills that had been passed for over 150 years. In adopting a coordinated immigration policy, the new bill retained the quota provisions that marked the 1924 Immigration Bill. Unlike the 1924 legislation that barred Asian immigration entirely, the new law did create a quota for Asians, but a very small one. The McCarran-Walter Act also retained the anti-Communist provisions of the amended Walter Resolution. Truman once again balked at the anti-subversive measures and at the retention of the quota system. In June 1952 the president vetoed the McCarran-Walter Act. Within a week the Congress successfully overrode the veto. The naturalization provisions for the Issei would go into effect on Christmas Day 1952. Farrington did not bring home statehood in 1952, but at least no part of Hawai'i's population was banned from becoming a citizen of the state that was yet to be.

What effect did the McCarran-Walter Act have in Hawai'i, where some 38,000–40,000 people were eligible for citizenship? The "Christmas Present" law, as it was called in Hawai'i, drew great public praise. It is not clear how many Issei or Koreans wanted to apply for citizenship. The new law required that the naturalization test be taken in English. This requirement presented a problem to some of the older Issei. However by 1957 the Immigration and Naturalization Service in Honolulu noted that almost five thousand people had become citizens since 1952 based on the McCarran-Walter Act. Others who did not become citizens were able to gain legal resident alien status. Though the actual numbers may not have been great, the removal of the ban against Japanese naturalization convinced many Issei and Nisei that the path to first-class citizenship was much wider than before. Speaking as a U.S. congressman in 1967, AJA veteran Spark Matsunaga explained his reaction to the 1952 act:

> One fact that bothered me while I was a soldier was the fact that my parents were barred by the laws of the greatest nation on earth from becoming naturalized citizens purely on account of their Oriental birth... For me it fulfilled my fondest hopes of witnessing my 82-year old father take the oath of American citizenship after having been a permanent resident of Hawaii for 63 long years.[24]

Joseph Farrington had been one of principal architects of this new path for the AJAs and their parents in the Eighty-second Congress. When the Eighty-third Congress opened in January 1953, he hoped he could widen that path further with the ultimate prize—statehood. He almost did.

Republican victories in the 1952 elections made it look as if 1953 would be the best of times for Farrington. The Republican platform pledged immediate statehood for Hawai'i. The new president, Dwight Eisenhower, was a staunch supporter as was Senator Robert Taft of Ohio, who had been the other contender for the Republican presidential nomination. Both the Eisenhower and the Taft Republicans were for Hawai'i. Unlike Truman, Eisenhower did not bundle his support for Hawai'i with other causes such as civil rights. The Congress was Republican, though their majority in the Senate was a narrow 48–47. Senator Hugh Butler was once again the chairman of the Interior and Insular Affairs Committee. But the Nebraska senator made a sudden about-face and supported statehood for Hawai'i. As a Taft Republican, he agreed to follow the party line. Though there were indications that he privately harbored his old reservations, he nonetheless reported the Hawai'i statehood bill favorably when it came to his committee in 1953–54.[25]

If it was the best of times, it was also in true Dickensian fashion the worst of times. Though the Republicans were solidly in support of Hawai'i, President Eisenhower turned on Alaska and refused to support the northern territory. Before he became president, Eisenhower had made several statements in support of Alaska, and the Republican platform endorsed statehood for Alaska. Some commentators claim the president acted for purely partisan reasons because he wanted to bring in only the Republican territory. But Republicans in Alaska had captured the traditionally Democratic territorial legislature in the 1952 elections. It was evident to most members of Congress that either both territories would come in or neither would. So Eisenhower's reluctance to support Alaska was in effect a negative for Hawai'i. Whether Eisenhower was playing partisan politics or whether he had serious reservations about Alaska's fitness for statehood is unclear. A later chapter on Alaska will discuss the various Cold War considerations that may have influenced Eisenhower. This presidential conundrum would eventually thwart both territories, but let us first follow the "best of times" scenario.

As it had done several times in the past, the House Interior and Insular Affairs Committee reported the Hawai'i statehood bill favorably, and the Rules Committee scheduled it for debate. During the debate on Hawai'i attempts were made to join the bill with an Alaska statehood bill. Such maneuvers failed and on March 10, 1953, the Hawai'i bill passed the House 274–138. This was the third time a Hawai'i statehood bill had received a favorable House vote. A separate Alaska statehood bill was reported favorably by the Interior and Insular Affairs Committee, but failed to make it out of the Rules Committee.[26]

The Senate Interior and Insular Affairs Committee wanted to combine the Alaska and Hawai'i bills and began hearings on the two territories in July 1953. To some extent Hawai'i continued to be its own worst enemy. A group of local Democrats including former governor Stainback, James Coke, and William Borthwick testified against statehood on the grounds that the Communist menace in the territory was worse than ever. They emphasized the conviction of the "Hawaii Seven" in June 1953. Even Senator Butler was no longer an ally in this outmoded attack.

Butler's committee was not ready to make a final report until after the second congressional session convened in January 1954. Eisenhower once again urged Congress to admit Hawai'i but demurred on Alaska. The Interior and Insular Affairs Committee was prepared to report a combined bill until Eisenhower finally agreed that Alaska could be debated separately after Hawai'i. In March 1954 the committee reported a separate Hawai'i bill. When floor debate began, a move to combine Alaska with Hawai'i gained forced once again. Alaska supporters feared that separate bills would not work. They felt that Eisenhower would sign the Hawai'i bill into law and later veto an Alaska bill. So they wanted the president to have only one choice. He would have to accept or reject one bill that granted statehood to both territories. If supporters of Alaska and Hawai'i favored a joint bill, some opponents of either or both territories also favored a combined bill. They were convinced that a combined bill could not get a favorable vote when it was returned to the House where the Republican majority was larger. Thus a strange coalition of supporters and opponents of statehood successfully passed a joint Alaska-Hawai'i statehood bill on April 1, 1954, by a vote of 57–28. This was the first time a Senate vote had been taken on either territory. In all of the commotion we may well ask if anyone actually knew what was going on? No senator who voted for the bill actually said he was opposed to it. Some statehood supporters truly believed that the only hope of success in the Senate lay in a combined bill. It would be only after the failure of the combined bill in the House that supporters saw the ultimate perils of a combined bill.

The combined bill from the Senate was sent to the House in April. There the bill could either be brought to the floor for debate or it could go to a House/Senate conference committee, where a compromise might be arranged between the House-passed Hawai'i bill and the Senate-passed Alaska/Hawai'i bill. The House Rules Committee was not inclined to schedule the combined bill for floor debate or to call for a conference committee. The Eisenhower administration did not support any further action on the combined bill. Supporters continued to push for House action into the summer. Though elated that a Hawai'i statehood bill had finally passed both the House and the Senate, Joseph Farrington was weary after all the years of wrangling. The delegate visited several members of the Rules Committee on Saturday morning, June 19, hoping to gain their support. After lunch he returned to his office and a short time later died at his desk of a heart attack.[27]

There could be no greater testament to the affection that islanders, as well as members of Congress, held for the delegate than the manner in which he was buried and praised. When Congress reconvened on Monday, June 21, members of both parties eulogized Farrington on the floor of the House. Some suggested that statehood should be granted as a memorial to the delegate. Delegate Bob Bartlett of Alaska said of his colleague in the quest for statehood, Farrington "worked for it. He fought for it. He pleaded for it—in season and out of season ... A leader has fallen in the heat of battle and at the threshold of victory."[28]

Two days later a memorial service was held for the delegate at National City Christian Church, with four hundred friends present, including sixty members of Congress. Philip La Follette, the former governor of Wisconsin who had been Farrington's college roommate, accompanied Mrs. Farrington there. Joined by eleven congressmen, Mrs. Farrington and her family returned to Honolulu with the delegate's ashes. He was first given a traditional Hawaiian service at 'Iolani Palace on June 26. This was the first time such a service, usually reserved for those of royal blood, was held for a haole. The next day a funeral service took place in Central Union Church, one of the bastions of Hawai'i's haole elite, where Garner Anthony gave the eulogy. The delegate's body was finally laid to rest at the family plot in Nu'uanu Memorial Park.[29]

Farrington's death was a watershed in many ways for Hawai'i politics. The Republicans had now lost their standard-bearer. Who could take his place? Farrington's death, along with the deaths in earlier years of party chairman Roy Vitousek and Charles Hemenway, severed the vital link that connected the Republicans to the wartime effort to save Hawai'i's Japanese population from internment. Even though some AJAs were suspicious of the Republican Party, they had been loyal to Farrington. That link to the past was now gone.

Another watershed would be the effective end of the old paternal, patrician rule of the haoles. Never again would a candidate be above money in the way that Farrington was. For this the delegate paid another price in addition to his life. He spent virtually all of his own fortune. Mrs. Farrington noted that her husband spent over $1 million as a delegate and left the family $200,000 in debt. Eventually the *Star-Bulletin* would have to be sold.[30]

If Farrington's death brought an end to patrician rule, the delegate's legacy was nonetheless one that looked to a more democratic future. His commitment to statehood was unflinching. Years later some Democratic detractors would claim that Farrington was not for statehood. The ridiculousness of such a statement has been effectively challenged by historian Roger Bell, who noted, "This claim . . . was as inaccurate as it was partisan." Later we will examine why such statements were made. Though he did not win statehood, his commitment to democracy and equality for Americans of all races bore a rich harvest. Farrington consistently spoke in favor of Asian Americans in the U.S. Congress at a time when most congressmen were anti-Asian or looked the other way. The end of martial law, the diversion of internment, the creation of the 442nd, and the ban on race as a criterion for naturalization were all battles fought and won by Farrington. The delegate deserves an honored place in the history of civil rights in the United States. The civil rights movement is often seen in terms of the American South and African Americans. In the South local custom sought to thwart national policy. But in terms of Asian Americans and Hawai'i, it was national policy that sought to thwart the rights that were being affirmed at the local level. Farrington helped to change that national policy in the Congress. As Garner Anthony said in his eulogy, "to his colleagues in Congress he was the living symbol of Hawaii." Joseph Farrington, the haole patrician who imported La Follette Progressivism to the islands and then helped change the attitude of the

Congress toward Asian Americans, deserves much greater attention by historians than he has yet received.[31]

Farrington was dead at age fifty-six. Who could replace him? The mantle immediately shifted to his widow, Elizabeth, who had been with him all those years from Wisconsin to Hawai'i to Washington. Governor King wanted to appoint Mrs. Farrington as delegate so that Hawai'i could quickly regain representation in Washington while there was still time to bring the statehood bill out of the House Rules Committee. An appointment required special congressional legislation. King's initiative to appoint gathered little support in the islands or in Washington. Without such new legislation, a delegate could not be replaced by gubernatorial appointment. A special election must be held. In late July Mrs. Farrington was elected by a 2–1 margin over Judge Delbert Metzger to fill the remaining months of her husband's term.[32]

Upon her return to Washington the new delegate lobbied members of Congress to bring the combined statehood bill out of the Rules Committee. She visited President Eisenhower and implored him to ask the House to bring the bill to the floor or to call for a House/Senate conference committee. Mrs. Farrington was well aware that both Alaska and Hawai'i must be admitted. She explained this to the president, who remained intransigent in his opposition to Alaska. Mrs. Farrington also visited House Speaker Joe Martin and former speaker Sam Rayburn. But the House was set in its ways. It would not bring the combined bill to the floor or call for a conference committee. Statehood floundered yet again in the summer of 1954.[33]

The emotional outpouring of feeling for the late delegate and the 2–1 majority that Betty Farrington received in July gave little indication of what lay in store for Hawai'i in the coming fall elections. As Betty Farrington prepared to return to Hawai'i and seek a full term as delegate, neither she nor many others in the islands predicted the revolution at the polls that would come in November.

The Revolution of 1954

For many people in Hawai'i the territorial elections of 1954, the so-called "Revolution of 1954," are even more important than statehood. Some see the "Revolution" as the ultimate result of the Democrats' steady rise to power since World War II. Others claim that the "Revolution" gave legislative representation to Japanese Americans and other non-Caucasians in proportion to their numbers for the first time. Those who emphasize such changes assert that a "party of the people" finally replaced a "party of privilege and property." What actually happened—in contrast to what the "revolutionists" say happened—may well be two different things.

If some kind of inexorable rise of the Democrats approached a peak in 1954, it was not immediately obvious to members of either party in the months before the November elections. In July Republican Betty Farrington defeated Democrat Delbert Metzger by a substantially greater margin than her husband had defeated Metzger in 1952. In the 1953–54 legislature Japanese Americans were already well represented with sixteen of the forty-five seats—about 36 percent, a figure almost identical with the Japanese share of Hawai'i's overall population. The majority of the AJA legislators were Republicans. One of the best descriptions of the "reality" of the months preceding November 1954 comes from Democrat George Ariyoshi, later governor of Hawai'i from 1974 to 1986, who ran in his first race for the legislature in 1954. "In the making of modern Hawaii," Ariyoshi explains, "the year 1954 is always described as a great turning point, but that description is the result of hindsight and the writing of history. As the election season approached, there was—to my knowledge—no great sense of change in the making."[34]

Once the polls closed in November, the results were clear. Democrats took control of the territorial legislature for the first time. The number of AJAs elected to the legislature rose from sixteen in 1952 to twenty-one in 1954. Even more striking than the actual rise in numbers was their party affiliation. In 1952, ten of the sixteen AJAs were Republicans; in 1954, sixteen of the twenty-one AJAs were Democrats. What did this change in numbers really signify? Had Hawai'i's AJA voters shifted overnight from being Republicans to Democrats, or had the Democrats simply produced a more attractive slate of AJA candidates?

The evidence that would suggest a massive shift of political sympathy among AJAs from Republican to Democrat is simply not there. In fact, polls taken in the mid-1950s show no appreciable shift in party affiliation in Hawai'i since World War II. Pollsters Daniel Bergman and Kunio Nagoshi reported in 1956 that the percentage of voters who identified themselves as Democrats rose slightly from 27 percent in 1948 to 29 percent in 1955. For Republicans the percentages changed from 19 percent in 1948 to 14 percent in 1955. Nearly a majority of voters consistently called themselves Independent: 48 percent in 1948 and 48 percent in 1955. Significantly, voters who claimed they had no affiliation rose from 6 percent in 1948 to 9 percent in 1955. Why then did so many people who still considered themselves "independent" before and after the "Revolution" vote for Democrats in 1954?[35]

Some commentators insist that the AJA voters were influenced by the "dream" of the Democrats. It is more likely that they were charmed by the attractive array of young AJA veterans who were ready to run for the first time in 1954. Tom Brokaw's "greatest generation" had finally returned to the islands—particularly those who had decided to train themselves as lawyers using the GI Bill. The University of Hawai'i had no law school in the years after World War II. Both those veterans who graduated from the university before the war (for example, Spark Matsunaga), and those who graduated after the war (for example, Daniel Inouye) had to leave Hawai'i for several years to attend various law schools on the mainland. By 1952 most had returned to Hawai'i. Their first priority was to find a job. The Honolulu municipal administration of Democrat Johnny Wilson reached out and employed a number of these young lawyers, such as Daniel Inouye. In contrast Republican law firms representing the Big Five extended few job offers to the returning AJA veterans.[36]

The Democratic employment opportunities were not the only party force at work. Burns proved to be a focal point for a number of the young veteran lawyers. Inouye had been attracted to Burns before he left for law school in 1950. Upon his return to the islands in 1952, he and other veteran lawyers, like his hospital mate Sakae Takahashi, renewed their attachment. Burns and this core of 442nd veterans talked constantly about the future of Hawai'i and extended their reach to other veterans who could be candidates for office.

Burns could not really teach the Nisei how to get elected, how to give speeches, or how to mingle in the throng from successful personal experience. These were not his strong points. But he talked and talked with the "boys," as he called them, and encouraged them to believe in themselves and their role in shaping Hawai'i's future. Historian Gavan Daws has skillfully explained the charismatic appeal that emanated from Burns's very weakness:

> There was nothing facile or even ordinarily fluent about his speechmaking: the best he could manage was a strained,

earnest, faintly brooding kind of utterance. And yet this somber awkwardness was a source of strength as much as a limitation. Because he knew no other way to speak, he spoke simply and plainly, and no one could mistake his meaning, or miss the fact that he meant what he said.[37]

In his plain talking Burns encouraged the young lawyers to run for office—long before some thought of doing it themselves. Through a friend, twenty-eight-year-old George Ariyoshi, an AJA veteran of the Military Intelligence Service (MIS), met John Burns only three days before the filing deadline for the 1954 elections. After some preliminary conversation about their hopes and dreams for Hawai'i, Burns said to Ariyoshi, "You should run for office." Ariyoshi's reaction is best conveyed in his own words:

> My response was, "I'm too young. Nobody knows who I am."
> He said, "It's not the age. It's the heart. It's how you feel."
> He was insistent. "Run for office this year, and there'll be some other people running with you." He was clear about not waiting.

Ariyoshi ran, campaigned vigorously, and won a seat in the territorial house of representatives in 1954.[38]

The Burns group did not so much sway the ideology of Japanese voters as it produced a superb roster of young candidates from the "greatest generation" who could appeal to voters, particularly AJA voters, of any political affiliation. As Inouye put it, "Unlike past years when a sort of Democratic suicide squad—loyal workers but something less than inspiring candidates—ventured forth to have their brains beaten in by Republican opponents, 1954 was the year of the eager young hopefuls, better-educated, thanks to the GI Bill, unscarred by past election defeats, and all a-brim with vigorous, forward looking ideas about the management of the Territorial government." The list of those AJAs elected for the first time to the legislature in 1954 reads like a "Who's Who of Hawai'i Politics" and a "Who's Who of AJA World War II Veterans"—Sakae Takahashi, the lieutenant in the 100th who dreamed of the "second battle" for democracy at home; Daniel Inouye of the 442nd, who would become a U.S. Representative and a U.S. Senator;

Spark Matsunaga of the 100th, who would become a U.S. Representative and a U.S. Senator; and George Ariyoshi, the veteran of the MIS, who would be the first AJA governor of Hawai'i.[39]

The appeal of the young AJA veterans becomes even more evident when we look at whom they defeated to take power. They defeated Republicans, but not necessarily or exclusively haoles or representatives of "The Big Five" order. They defeated older Asian Americans. Among those who were vanquished by the Revolution of 1954 were AJA Thomas Sakakihara and Chinese American Hiram Fong. Sakakihara was a true pioneer of democracy for the AJAs. He first ran for office in 1926, when he was twenty-four years old, and was first elected in 1932. Like the AJA veterans a quarter-century later, he too was a lawyer, educated not through the privilege of the GI Bill or the agency of Harvard Law School, but by "reading the law" in the office of a local lawyer in the nineteenth-century fashion of Abraham Lincoln. Elected to four terms in office before World War II, he was arrested and interned by the government of the United States in 1942. He rose to run another day and was reelected four times after the war, only to suffer defeat in the Revolution of 1954. Hiram Fong had also led the way to a multiethnic democracy in Hawai'i. The son of poor immigrant laborers, he graduated from McKinley High School in 1924. He did go to Harvard Law School after finishing the University of Hawai'i in the 1930s. He returned to Honolulu and worked as an attorney for the city/county government. First elected to the legislature in 1938, he rose to become Speaker of the House, the position he held when he too was defeated in 1954.[40]

Exactly what were the voters saying in 1954? Had they been swayed by the "dream" of the younger candidates? Or as Thomas Sakakihara insisted, had Jack Hall and leaders of the ILWU exerted their power to defeat certain candidates, including him? According to Sakakihara, Jack Hall had a plan to "take over the government of the territory." On the other hand Daniel Inouye emphasized the vigorous campaigning of the new Democratic candidates and their attention to the "issues." In his 1967 autobiography he scoffed at Republican "red baiting" attempts during the 1954 election to tie the Democrats to the ILWU. Of course, Inouye had been trying to distance the party from the ILWU since the early 1950s. Still, the influence of the ILWU within the Democratic Party was clearly noticed in 1954. In his 1997 autobiography George Ariyoshi expressed concern over the level of control that the ILWU exerted in the 1954 elections, particularly the union's insistence that

Democratic candidates run as a team and not as individuals. Summing up the power of the ILWU in 1954, the former governor stated:"While I would eventually come to work constructively with various out-standing and responsible leaders from the union, I have to say that the ILWU leadership in the early days harbored a distrust of candidates it did not control. They had a reputation for being dictatorial."[41]

A half-century later the message of the Revolution of 1954 is still unclear. It was *not,* as some of the mythmakers have insisted, the first time significant numbers of non-Caucasians were elected to office. The march for equal rights and democracy by AJAs and other non-Caucasians had long and deep roots in Hawai'i. It began with Sakakihara, Fong, and other Japanese Americans and Chinese Americans long before bombs fell on Pearl Harbor. The Republicans had nurtured the march as much as the Democrats had. Local studies have not yet been researched and written that tell us the difference between the AJA Democrats and the AJA Republicans, or that explain exactly what influenced the voters in 1954. Was it idealism or the ILWU? Though the picture is still murky, it seems clear that in 1954 the real victory was a victory of the "greatest generation."

The "boys" of the greatest generation did come to power in 1954. But their mentor did not. John Burns ran for delegate against Betty Farrington. He had lost to Joe in 1948, and he lost to Betty in 1954—though his 1954 loss was only by 960 votes. What did Burns's defeat in the midst of the Democratic Revolution mean? Was there still a sympathy vote for Joe Farrington, as most historians insist? Or did the territory still vote Republican when neither candidate was a young veteran? Regardless of the message of the voters, the outcome of the Democratic Revolution of 1954 gave a Republican Farrington one more chance to put the forty-ninth star in the flag.

The Last Hurrah for the Would-Be Forty-ninth State

When Betty Farrington entered the Eighty-third Congress in its last days and then was elected to a full term in the Eighty-fourth Congress as a delegate, she became the first and last woman ever to serve as a territorial delegate. She was an interesting person in her own right, not just as the wife of Joseph Farrington. Born in Tokyo in 1898, she was the daughter of missionary parents. Her parents' travels took her to schools in Tokyo and then back to the United States in Tennessee, Texas, and

California. In 1916 she entered the University of Wisconsin to major in journalism. After her marriage to Farrington she maintained her status as a newspaper correspondent even during their years in Washington. After a dozen years as the wife of the delegate from Hawai'i, she was well known in Washington by 1954. Nonetheless, Betty was not Joe. Neither her uniqueness as the first female delegate nor her insider knowledge of Washington gave her the clout to push statehood legislation, particularly not in the Eighty-fourth Congress.

In the 1954 elections the national Democrats regained the Congress, but by only the narrowest of margins in both the Senate and the House. The congressional Democrats would consider only a combined statehood for Alaska and Hawai'i, though in reality they were not enthusiastic about either. Both the House and the Senate were now run by Texans—Sam Rayburn and Lyndon Johnson, neither of whom favored statehood. The Eisenhower administration was still for Hawai'i but adamantly opposed to Alaska. Some congressional Republicans were now uneasy about Hawai'i. The Revolution of 1954 posed the possibility that the island territory might well send Democrats to the Congress as a state. Some commentators, such as historian Roger Bell, highlight the civil rights issue as the great obstruction to statehood in the 1955–56 Congress. Though statehood was no longer tied to civil rights as in Truman's day, some members of Congress may still have equated the admission of Alaska and Hawai'i as a step that would bring in two pro–civil rights states. Other members of Congress simply did not want to bring in two new states of any stripe. New representatives from Alaska and Hawai'i would eventually force some other state(s) to lose representatives. Simply put, there was no momentum for statehood for either territory in early 1955.[42]

Action on statehood in the Eighty-fourth Congress is easily told. The House Interior and Insular Affairs Committee favorably reported a combined statehood bill early in 1955. The House Rules Committee scheduled it for debate, but with a rule that forbade the separation of the two on the floor. When the combined bill reached the floor, a motion to recommit was made by Representative John Pillion (R-NY), a livid anti-Communist foe of Hawai'i. By a vote of 218–70, the combined bill was returned to the Interior and Insular Affairs Committee. No further House action took place.[43]

The Senate was not inclined to move beyond the House. No statehood bill—combined or separate—was reported to the floor of the

Senate. Majority leader Johnson had no propensity to push for it. Instead, in late 1956 a subcommittee of the Senate Judiciary Committee held hearings in Honolulu, chaired by Senator James Eastland of Mississippi. The hearings probed the remaining extent of Communist infiltration in the islands. It seemed that when the Congress was incapable of action, it dusted off the Red Scare for lack of anything else to do.

Mrs. Farrington's maiden voyage as delegate brought forth an empty harvest. As in the summer of 1954, she visited members of Congress and the administration during 1955–56, hoping to get the statehood bill out of the House committee and back on the floor. Her efforts were to no avail. Statehood was dead. When she announced her intent to run for yet another term in 1956, she had no statehood success to hold before the voters. She had secured legislation to expand the size of the territorial legislature and to found a Geophysical Institute at the University of Hawai'i. This was not the kind of legislation on which to base a victory. And the memory of her husband was fading.

Islanders were dissatisfied with the Republicans in Washington and the Republicans at home. Republican governor Samuel Wilder King had vetoed virtually all the legislation passed by the new 1955–56 Democratic legislature. Even Mrs. Farrington found that King's actions complicated her life in Washington. In the 1956 elections the Democrats retained control of the territorial legislature—substantially increasing their hold on the territorial senate while losing a little of their majority in the house. The "action" was really within the camp of the AJAs. Though there were now twenty-two AJAs in the legislature, some of the Republican AJAs who were defeated in 1954 regained their seats in 1956.[44]

The big change was not in the legislature, but in the delegateship. John Burns ran once again. Having lost to both Joe and Betty, he finally won in 1956 by a substantial majority. Burns owed his victory to many reasons. Mrs. Farrington was a weaker candidate after her failure to bring statehood progress. Burns was also strengthened by the fact that his "boys" who had firmly secured their seats in the legislature could actively campaign for their mentor. In the fall of 1956 the "boys" help elect their "father" to office. When asked about the election years later, Mrs. Farrington analyzed her defeat from a number of angles. Carrying on the patrician ways of her husband, she held no fundraisers, though she claimed she turned down $250,000 from the ILWU. She also said that she remained in Washington too long while the campaign was underway in Hawai'i. "That's always true of anybody who's in there in

Washington," she explained. "We couldn't come home every other week, it's too far, you couldn't do that." Though some of her reasons sounded like "sour grapes," there was a prophetic quality to her comment about staying in Washington too long. A few years later John Burns would suffer the same fate. In Hawai'i the voters expected their candidates to campaign, regardless of what they had done in the nation's capital.[45]

Mrs. Farrington did not take her defeat well. There was no gracious handing over of the office; there were no introductions of the new delegate to Hawai'i's friends in Washington. Even a quarter-century later she continued to make disparaging remarks about Burns. The animosity between Mrs. Farrington and the Burns camp would seriously distort the historical record of the Hawai'i statehood movement. Despite the tension in the changing of the guard, Hawai'i had a new advocate in the fall of 1956: John A. Burns, who would try once again to put the star in the flag.

Hawai'i 1946–56: Global Storm or Congressional Frustration and Local Politics?

As the first decade after World War II drew to a close, Hawai'i was no closer to becoming a state than it had been in 1946—at least in terms of the passing of a statehood bill in the U.S. Congress. To some extent the statehood story has been one frustrating lament about a deadlocked Congress and obstructionist maneuvers. What could be less interesting? Or so I learned in the years in which I tried to attract the attention of other historians to the statehood story. Why not study any number of other bills that failed to pass the Congress, most replied?

If the legislative saga was dull, what about the saga of local politics that occurred concurrently? Was this any more than local precinct bickering in a small isolated territory that had been coincidentally the center of Pacific operations in World War II? Many of Hawai'i's Democrats admitted that much of their history had been little more than constant, local squabbling? Outside of Hawai'i, who had really heard of Joseph Farrington or John Burns—or cared? Even FBI director J. Edgar Hoover noted that by 1951 there were only thirty-six Communists in Hawai'i compared to 4,500 in California and 22,000 in New York. Even subversion in the territory was second-rate![46]

It is certainly possible to interpret this decade of discontent in Hawai'i in purely local terms. But I would suggest to readers both inside and outside of Hawai'i that much more than a local story transpired in the islands after World War II. Many of the major themes in postwar American, even world, history occurred in a heightened and important form in the territory. Hawai'i's very location in the mid-Pacific set a global stage for the local acts. Chuck Mau used Hawai'i's strategic location in the Cold War to force the Smith Act trial in Honolulu. The passage of the McCarran-Walter Act was influenced by the need for alliances with Asian countries. Both before and after World War II, the treatment of Asian Americans in Hawai'i was a gauge for the nation's overall Asian policy.

One of the major themes in postwar America, Europe, and Asia was the fear of advancing Communism. In what other political community in the nation did that fear become so enmeshed in the burgeoning of a major labor movement that sought to take over a territorial branch of the national Democratic Party? Maybe Hawai'i's Communists were "second-rate," as Hoover insisted, but they pervaded local life in a way unseen in the rest of the nation. The responses of the local community—whether from Burns and Inouye to control the influence of the ILWU within the Democratic Party or from "The Big Five" to come to terms with the radical union and preserve the local economy—were without precedent. Turbulent political forces, evident in small doses in the rest of the nation, converged in Hawai'i to create the perfect political storm.

If Communism and anti-Communism were national, even global, themes in the postwar era, so too was the civil rights movement. In national terms this was often seen as an issue with African Americans. In global terms it emerged as a movement against colonialism. In Hawai'i that movement had its finest hour with Asian Americans. Gradually but surely, Hawai'i-born Asian Americans had been entering local politics for a decade before World War II. After the war they gained increasing force. With the aid of Hawai'i's congressional delegate they changed a national policy that withheld citizenship from their elders. President Truman understood that Hawai'i's local politics had a national and global significance. That is why statehood for Hawai'i was part of his vision of civil and equal rights for the nation.

Hawai'i endured a decade of congressional frustration and stagnation after World War II. But in that decade the territory became a focal point for many of the trends and movements that shaped the nation and the world. In what we have called the "transformation of Hawai'i," a paternalistic plantation economy changed into one of the most unionized economies in the nation. Labor strikes with an intensity rarely seen in other parts of the nation burst forth. Nonetheless, a business community steeped in the traditions of deference and paternalism skillfully learned how to deal with one of the nation's most radical unions—and vice versa. A political system long dominated by one party changed to a two-party system with the most ethnically diverse set of voters and candidates in the nation. An isolated mid-Pacific community gradually emerged as a central control point of the nation's global Asian policy. Hawai'i's turbulent, local saga from 1946 to 1956 took on global dimensions.

While Hawai'i emerged in the center of this global storm, the quest for statehood continued. John Burns now carried the torch to Washington. The new Eighty-fifth Congress that he faced in 1957 had a more substantial Democratic majority than in 1955. But his approach and action in the Eighty-fifth Congress would not or could not be quite the same as the Farringtons had enjoyed since 1943. Hawai'i had always been the more mature and prepared territory. It seemed certain to be the forty-ninth state, with Alaska trailing in on its coattails as the fiftieth. But when Burns arrived in the nation's capital in late 1956, he encountered a new stance on the part of Alaska's supporters. Substantial changes had taken place in the northern territory that invigorated its statehooders to take the lead in pushing for admission. In Washington even the resistance of Eisenhower to Alaska would change. Burns soon found that Hawai'i would have to prepare to become the fiftieth state behind Alaska as the forty-ninth.

Before joining Burns in Washington, we must return to the northern territory, which we left in 1946 in what might be called a political prenatal condition.

Chapter 7
The Cold War Activates Alaska, 1946–1954

> The people who came with military Alaska were not inde-
> pendent, self-sufficient agricultural pioneers of past centuries
> . . . They required and expected the same standards of com-
> munity living and services available elsewhere.
>
> —*George Rogers, on the impact of the*
> *postwar military population in Alaska*

In early 1946 Hawai'i was ready to become a state as a reward for its wartime service. It was as mature, economically and politically, as many of the existing forty-eight states. Such could not really be said for its northern neighbor. Though Alaska served proudly in World War II, it did not have the requisite population, much less a developed econ-omy and political structure, to exist as a civilian state. The territorial legislature had endorsed statehood in 1945, but the popular referendum would not be held until October 1946. In his January 1946 State of the Union Address President Truman urged Congress to admit Hawai'i, but suggested the body wait on Alaska until "it is certain that this is the desire of the people of that great territory."[1]

Truman was not alone in wondering what the future of Alaska might be. Many of the territory's residents were also unsure. The territory's mines had closed during the war, and its fishing resource was substan-tially depleted by early 1946. During the war Alaska had become a pow-erful military defense installation. But would the future hold a continued military role for the territory? We have noted that many his-torians downplay Alaska's military importance after the Aleutian War and even refer to that campaign as "the forgotten war." By mid-1944 most of the leaders of the Aleutian campaign—Buckner, Kinkaid, and Talley—had departed the territory for seemingly more important the-aters of war. Troop strength was declining rapidly. There was, however, a signal in 1944 that Washington did not intend to forget Alaska and envisioned an expanded military role for the territory. That signal, which few Alaskans interpreted at the time, was occasioned by the appointment of Buckner's successor in June 1944: General Delos Emmons, the former military governor of Hawai'i.

General Emmons's Alaska

In 1940 Buckner had reported to Alaska as a colonel and subsequently advanced to lieutenant general. Emmons arrived as a three-star general, a rank indicative of the importance that Washington continued to place on Alaska. Emmons was no stranger to Alaska. He first came to the territory as a young lieutenant in 1912 and was stationed at Fort Gibbon on the Yukon River. While there, he volunteered to climb Mt. McKinley with Archbishop Hudson Stuck but was not given army permission. He left Alaska in 1914 and followed an ever-advancing career that led him eventually to Hawai'i in 1941. In June 1943 Emmons left Hawai'i with orders to take a three-month tour of the war's global fighting fronts before replacing General John DeWitt as head of the Western Defense Command in San Francisco.[2]

As part of that tour, Emmons first came to Alaska to gain information on the planned invasion of Kiska. He departed the northern territory in advance of the Kiska action and continued to Washington, where he recommended that Alaska be organized as a separate department, not a subordinate unit of the Western Command. He then flew to England to familiarize himself with plans for the invasion of Europe. After proceeding to Cairo and Malta, he returned to Washington. In September 1943 he finally assumed his new post in San Francisco.

While in California, Emmons tried to reverse the actions of General DeWitt in interning the Japanese population of the West Coast. His success in Hawai'i was not repeated on the mainland. He recommended that the Japanese internees be allowed to return to their homes, but noted that the "Attorney General of the United States and the Secretary of the Interior . . . recommended against it purely on political grounds." Possibly as a result of the strenuous round of activities since leaving Hawai'i, Emmons suffered his first heart attack in the spring of 1944.[3]

After recovering from his heart problems, Emmons was ordered in June 1944 to take command of the new Alaskan Department, created in November 1943, that he had earlier recommended. The army created a separate Alaskan Department and appointed one of its senior generals to its command. This action would certainly seem to indicate that Washington had something more in mind than "forgetting" about Alaska in mid-1944. Emmons's appointment was significant for another reason. Emmons was one of the earliest advocates of unity of command. He had practiced what he preached in Hawai'i, where he readily subordinated himself to Admiral Nimitz. One of the grave problems in Alaska during the Aleutian campaign had been the inter-service rivalry and friction between General Buckner and Admiral Theobald. The appointment of Emmons would clearly preclude such a recurrence if wartime action resumed in Alaska. Just what action did Washington and Emmons anticipate in mid-1944?[4]

In his hitherto unpublished "brief personal history" Emmons made it clear that both he and Washington anticipated a future role for Alaska. He noted the following four objectives for his new command:

(a) To defend the area.
(b) When the Navy and troops were available, to launch an attack on Northern Japan. This was the Keelblocks plan.
(c) To make frequent air attacks on the Kuriles to draw Japanese aircraft there for defense and away from the Central Pacific area. This had excellent results at critical times.
(d) To utilize our radio equipment to deceive the enemy into believing that we were preparing for an attacking force from the Aleutians. This deception proved to be of substantial assistance to our advance in the Central and Southwest Pacific areas.

Though Gore Vidal and other enlisted men may have been bored in Alaska in 1944–45, clearly General Emmons was not.

An expanded role for Alaska in the last year of the war was heavily dependent on Russian entry into the war against Japan. Both Emmons and Washington anticipated and planned for this event. According to the general, a plan emerged late in the war to capture a "secure sea way" through the Kurile Islands "in order that the U.S. could construct a railroad across part of Eastern Siberia to enable over a million tons of supplies to be delivered to the Russians who were to advance against the Japanese to the South." The general went on to say that orders were actually given to begin the construction, though they were abandoned toward the end of the war. Engineers waited in Alaska in 1945 for Russian permission to enter Siberia, but "the permission never came." In April 1945 Emmons met in Fairbanks with Russian Foreign Secretary V. I. Molotov, who was en route to the San Francisco conference on the organization of the United Nations. This meeting took place just weeks after Russia pledged at the Yalta Conference to enter the war against Japan. Unfortunately, Emmons made no mention of what they discussed.

With Emmons in command, it appears that Washington had primed Alaska for an important role in the final conquest of Japan in conjunction with the Soviet Union. The eventual decision by President Truman to conquer Japan by bombing rather than by a land attack precluded that role. Still Alaska's *potential* was there, and that ever-present *potential* certainly provides a clue to its Cold War role. Russia, whether as a World War II ally or a Cold War adversary, was the key to Alaska's future role.

Even without the land invasion of Japan, the activities that Emmons directed sustained the military economy of the territory, and particularly the economy of Anchorage. Bob Atwood noted decades later in his posthumous autobiography, "Anchorage was saved by a decision in the Pentagon to make Alaska the staging area for a new phase of the war." He explained that the air raids on the Kuriles from both the Aleutians and air bases in Anchorage diverted Japanese forces from the central Pacific islands. "All of this was done," he claimed, "under the heavy shroud of military secrecy . . . Keeping Japan in the dark was part of the American strategy. They hoped the enemy didn't know where the bombers came from so it would be hard for him to plan for a defense." Atwood explained that he suspected the bombing raids because so many bombers returned to Anchorage with damage indicative of counter attacks by the Japanese. Atwood did not indicate if he knew the rest of Emmons's plan. In fact, he did not mention General Emmons at all, in contrast to his extensive discussion of his four-year friendship with General Buckner.[5]

Emmons retained his command in Alaska until June 1946, when he was transferred to Washington to organize the first Armed Forces Staff College. This would be his final act in preparing the nation for the unified military command he had advocated since the beginning of the war. The school opened in February 1947. Under Emmons's tutelage almost five hundred officers were trained in the joint operation of the three services. On January 1, 1947, a new Alaskan Command (ALCOM) was created, the first unified command in the United States. Though

Emmons made no direct mention that he recommended this, it stands to reason that Emmons's influence was there. Like Billy Mitchell, Delos Emmons was well aware of Alaska's crucial strategic location. The creation of ALCOM was sure evidence that Washington continued to see a substantial role for Alaska in the nation's postwar defense. By 1948 troop strength in Alaska, which had reached a low of nineteen thousand in 1946, rose to twenty-seven thousand. It continued to increase each year until the mid-1950s.

In 1948 Delos Emmons retired from the army, almost forty years after he graduated from West Point in 1909. He had been a leader in the development of the Army Air Corps, and he pioneered the concept of unity of command. Despite these achievements, his name is not widely known. He has gained some recognition in Hawai'i, but virtually none in Alaska, where the attention of World War II historians and buffs falls almost exclusively on Buckner and Talley. Yet in our story of the effect of World War II on Alaska and Hawai'i, no single person was more involved in the development of both territories than Delos Emmons. Replacing General Short a few days after the Pearl Harbor debacle, he served as military governor of Hawai'i and personally stalled President Roosevelt's desire to intern the territory's Japanese population. In Alaska he emphasized the territory's strategic position by recommending an autonomous military department, separate from San Francisco. He then assumed command of that department and positioned Alaska for an important future role. This able general left both territories in a more favorable position to become states than when he found either of them. He subordinated his own ego to his belief in a unified military command, an objective he saw realized in July 1947 with the creation of the Department of Defense. Delos Emmons served Alaska, Hawai'i, and the United States well. He deserves more attention than he has yet received.[6]

The Invasion of the Veterans and the 1946 Plebiscite

While General Emmons prepared Alaska for a postwar role, another war-related phenomenon began to shape the northern territory. For a host of seemingly uncoordinated reasons, an influx of veterans, some who had served in Alaska and many who had not, began to invade the territory. As Evangeline Atwood explained, "With the fighting at an end, soldiers came to Alaska by the thousands to make their future homes . . . Alaska offered them an economic and social freedom which they could not see, if they returned to their old jobs in the states."[7]

Exactly what freedoms or opportunities Alaska offered seemed to vary with every veteran. Some were drawn by special federal homestead legislation passed in 1945 that allowed veterans with nineteen months of service to claim a 160-acre homestead with only seven months' residence, instead of the usual three years. Initially the veterans were not even required to cultivate the land. In 1946 a special session of the Alaska legislature passed the Alaska World War II Veterans Act that made loans for education, housing, and business opportunities. Governor Gruening was particularly proud of this legislation, which he claimed "gave Alaska's population the beginnings of a permanence which it had lacked."[8]

Sales of military property were also a lure. In 1947 a group of five veterans bought the "surplused" Chilkoot Barracks near Haines and turned it into a residential community. Even chances for improved health were a draw. Clem Tillion, who had served in the navy and would later become a member of the new state legislature, was advised to come to Alaska in 1945 because the climate might be good for a case of malaria he had contracted.

Postwar Alaska was a great lure to aviation veterans. A number of pilots who had flown the Alaskan/Siberian Ferry Route (ALSIB) during the war decided to return. As women, Celia Hunter and Virginia Hill Wood, both WASPs (Women Airforce Service Pilots), had not been allowed to fly beyond Great Falls, Montana. In 1946 they decided to see the "end of the line" and moved to Fairbanks, where they became leaders of the Alaska environmental movement for the rest of the century. Joe Fejes had been an interpreter of Russian in the flight control tower at Ladd Field in Fairbanks. After the war he returned to New York and told his artist wife, Claire, the bride he had left behind four years earlier, to pack her bags for Alaska. Jay Hammond, a marine corps pilot who had served mainly in the South Pacific, decided that he wanted a cooler climate. He arrived with some drama in 1946 in a 1929 Loeing Amphibian biplane that he flew from New York to Alaska. He landed successfully on the Chena River in Fairbanks, but a month later the plane's engine blew up. Hammond had no choice but to stay in Alaska. A quarter-century later he would become a governor of the new state. Aviation was not the only transportation lure. The opening of the Alaska Highway to the public in 1948 brought its own set of adventurers—

some of whom commented that the pioneer highway reminded them of school lessons about the overland routes to the West a century before.[9]

There appeared to be as many reasons to come North as there were veterans. One common thread seemed to unite them. Few had any knowledge of Alaska before the war. Jay Hammond said his only knowledge of Alaska came from stories by the artist Rockwell Kent, who lived near his family home in upstate New York. Either by serving in Alaska during the war or simply by hearing about Alaska during the war, the veterans saw postwar Alaska as a land providing new opportunities. The war had broken what they expected to be their life routine. Once that routine was gone and they were displaced from their earlier homes, many thought the time had come to try something entirely different. Any number of the veterans would assume leadership roles in the emerging territory and state. When the Alaska Constitutional Convention met in 1955–56 almost one quarter of its fifty-five members had arrived in Alaska since 1940.

As both veteran settlers and new military personnel arrived in the territory after World War II, Alaska experienced a population boom. By 1950 the territory's population reached almost 130,000—30 percent more than in 1946 and 75 percent more than the 72,000 present in 1940. The growing postwar defense role for the territory, particularly air defense, brought increased military spending to the North. By 1949–50 annual defense expenditures reached $449 million. Much of this money went to turning some of the old World War II installations into permanent defense locations. The two principal sites were Anchorage (Elmendorf Air Force Base and a new Fort Richardson) and Fairbanks (Ladd Field, renamed Fort Wainwright in 1961, and Eielson Air Force Base). The Kodiak Naval Air Station was reinvigorated, and Fort Greely, a training center for cold-weather combat, was established ninety miles south of Fairbanks at Big Delta. The Aleutians were not totally abandoned. Major defense installations were reestablished at Adak Naval Air Station and Shemya Air Base, a remote eight-square-mile island that lay halfway between Anchorage and Tokyo—and 280 miles from Russia. The loser in the new defense buildup was southeastern Alaska, where no new or reinvigorated bases were established.

By 1950 the "center" of the state had clearly shifted from the southeast to the railbelt, and principally to Anchorage, the headquarters of the new Alaskan Command. Evangeline Atwood proudly announced that Greater Anchorage had a population of 31,000 in 1950—an 800 percent increase over 1940! In addition to direct military spending, civilian activities swelled to provide the infrastructure for the expanding communities of Fairbanks and Anchorage. Rising to prominence in the civilian construction boom in postwar Anchorage was young Walter Hickel. Hickel first came to Anchorage in 1940, supposedly with only thirty-seven cents in his pocket, and later worked as a flight and maintenance inspector during the war at Fort Richardson. In 1947 he put on a carpenter's belt and led the boom in housing construction, thinking that the newly opened Alaska Highway was going to bring a rush of people north. Hickel soon got involved in the statehood movement and would later become a governor of the new state.[10]

The northern territory, like Hawai'i, was indeed a magnet for the "greatest generation." Unlike Hawai'i, the veterans were not *coming back* to change prewar conditions but *just arriving* to create a new society. The newly arrived veterans quickly blended with many prewar Alaskans like Hickel, the Atwoods, Bill Egan of Valdez, and delegate Bob Bartlett to build the postwar territory.

Did this mix of service personnel, veterans, and old timers want the postwar territory to become a state? This was President Truman's question in early 1946. The first solid evidence in that direction came in the October 1946 statehood referendum. In preparation for that vote Bob and Evangeline Atwood organized the Alaska Statehood Association to disseminate information about the advantages of statehood and to build up enthusiasm among the electorate. The Atwoods noted that they were in fact wartime converts to statehood. Their conversion came after Ernest Gruening persuaded them that statehood was the *only way* to build a permanent community and economy in the North. To persuade others they hired Gruening's friend George Sundborg to prepare a study of statehood for their new association.[11]

After the ballots were counted, the score was 9,630 *for* the broadly worded question "Are you in favor of statehood for Alaska?" and 6,822 *against*. Though this was a 3–2 majority, the victory for statehood was at best inconclusive. Two of Alaska's four judicial districts voted against statehood, though the major towns in each district voted for it. And there was a question of what a "yes" vote meant. Austin E. "Cap" Lathrop—Fairbanks's leading businessman, publisher of the *News-Miner,* and an ardent *anti*-statehooder—later wrote to a congressional committee, "Many people voted 'yes' who didn't believe that Alaska is ready for statehood now." The anti-statehood *Juneau Daily Alaska Empire* explained that many people who did not desire statehood voted "yes" to keep the issue from dying altogether. Among the state's major newspapers only the *Anchorage Daily Times* and the *Ketchikan Chronicle* supported statehood.[12]

To a great extent the opposition to statehood emanated from the fact that Alaska, unlike Hawai'i, was not yet a fully developed economic and political body. Some feared, with reason, that Alaska would not be able to generate sufficient revenue to support a state government, particularly since the territory lacked a viable tax system. "Cap" Lathrop opposed statehood simply because he thought any change would disrupt his established pattern of business. In the same vein Lathrop opposed the introduction of air mail service to Alaska. He claimed that checks written by local merchants to outside suppliers would now clear through the banking system much faster than those sent by surface mail, thus ending the relatively long period of "float" or interest-free loans that the surface mail journey allowed. Other opponents of statehood believed that federal management of certain wildlife resources would be better than state management.[13]

The 1946 vote revealed no clear pattern about the stance of Alaska natives on statehood. The vote was quite erratic among different native villages, with some being decidedly pro-statehood and others decidedly against. Native Alaskans were concerned about their unsettled land claims dating back to the 1867 Purchase treaty. Some of these claims were being pursued in federal courts at the time of the referendum. As long as statehood bills did not threaten these concerns, politically active natives supported statehood. Unlike their counterparts in Hawai'i, Alaska natives did not necessarily view statehood as a threat to their lifestyle or traditions.

Supporters of statehood, in general, believed that statehood would lead to economic development and free the territory from overlapping federal bureaucracies that stymied such growth. Bob Atwood, always an unabashed booster of Anchorage, said it was difficult for the emerging city to build sewers without the approval of several federal agencies. Municipal bonded indebtedness required congressional sanction. Others who supported statehood wanted state control of Alaska's natural resources—particularly the fisheries. The Seattle-based salmon canning interests strongly opposed statehood to prevent such state or local control. The most positive vote for statehood was registered in southeastern Alaska, where the majority of the territory's resident fishermen lived.[14]

The conventional wisdom at the time assumed the newly arriving veterans supported statehood as a logical extension of "fighting for freedom" in World War II. Such an assumption was by no means absolute. Some veterans, like Jay Hammond, enjoyed the territory's undeveloped wildness and opposed statehood to limit development. How much impact the veterans had in the October 1946 plebiscite is uncertain, as many had literally just arrived.[15]

The 1946 plebiscite was a victory for the statehood forces and the essential first step in any path to eventual admission. But it was not a cause for unbridled optimism. The 3–2 majority was substantially weaker than the 2–1 majority in Hawai'i's first plebiscite held in 1940. As late as 1958 supporters still feared the potential anti-statehood opposition. Statehood leaders, particularly Governor Ernest Gruening, constantly looked for causes around which statehood could rally and continued to build Alaska into a more mature political body that could join the union.

Trapped Salmon

In looking for such a rallying cause, Gruening and others turned their attention away from the emerging military defense economy and focused on the ailing fishing industry, which in 1946 was all at once the source of greatest opposition to and support for statehood. The potency of that cause became evident two years later in a general election referendum calling for the abolition of fish traps. The electorate grew substantially, from fifteen thousand voting in 1946 to twenty-three thousand voting in 1948. The 1948 fish trap referendum passed with an overwhelming 8–1 majority. Just what were fish traps and why were so many voters so adamant about them? To understand the issue in 1948, we must first augment the brief history of the commercial fishing industry in Alaska given in chapter 2.

As noted in chapter 2, the commercial fishing industry in Alaska was the canned salmon industry. From its onset in the late nineteenth century, the industry was forced to adapt to an overall resident labor shortage. To meet the ever-rising demand for fish in the late nineteenth and early twentieth centuries, the packers imported seasonal workers, both fishermen and cannery workers, from the Pacific Coast states. In addition the packers relied on a labor-saving device to catch fish known as the fish trap, a large wood and net barrier placed on coastal locations at the entry to the rivers and streams where the salmon returned to spawn. The fish trap was a very efficient device for catching fish without fishermen. It had been introduced to Alaska by the outside packers, not to replace local fishermen but to function in lieu of them.

The initial absence of resident commercial fishermen began to change in the first two decades of the twentieth century. Though there is no recorded north migration of fishermen, the Klondike and Alaska gold rushes of the late 1890s and early 1900s brought a cadre of men to Alaska from coastal areas of both the United States and Northern Europe who had a fishing or maritime background. These men came to mine, but readily turned to water-borne activities as the mines played out in the middle of the second decade of the twentieth century. Though I know of no detailed study that substantiates this assertion, there were well-known individuals who fit this pattern, particularly Dan Sutherland, Alaska's territorial delegate to Congress from 1921 to 1931. Sutherland came north from Massachusetts in 1898 to participate in the gold rushes. He first worked out of Nome for a steamship company and then mined in various locations from Nome to Ruby for over a decade. While serving in the territorial legislature in Juneau, he decided to pursue his early dream to fish by becoming a halibut fisherman in 1918. Exactly how many others followed Sutherland's career pattern is unclear, but by 1918 the total number of fishermen in Alaska, resident and non resident, had risen to eight thousand from three thousand in 1900.[16]

The burgeoning rise of resident and nonresident fishermen was spurred by a unique attribute of the fishing resource. Unlike other natural resources that were owned publicly and then leased to operators, the fish resource was considered a natural "commons" that was free and open to all. No one—not the canneries, not the fishermen, not the territory, and not the federal government—owned it. The fishermen claimed that the right to a "free and open fishery" was a part of their Anglo/American heritage that dated back to the signing of the Magna Carta in England. That right transferred through English common law to North America. No government, they claimed, had the right to create any "exclusive use of the fishery" for any reason. No permits and no fees should ever be enacted to limit that use or entry.

The right to a free and open fishery obviously created problems for any management of the natural resource. If any and every one could fish, what could be done by a governmental agency in the Progressive era to preserve the renewable resource and prevent it from being overfished to extinction? Management of the Alaska fishery was under the control of the U.S. Bureau of Fisheries, an agency of the U.S. Department of Commerce, from 1905 until 1939. After 1939 it became a part of the newly created U.S. Fish and Wildlife Service in the Department of the Interior. The Alaska Organic Act of 1912, which created the territorial legislature, specifically left management of the fisheries under federal control. In Hawai'i the fisheries were under the control of the territorial legislature. To conserve the fish resource without violating the ancient right of the open fishery, Washington could only enact regulations that limited the length of the fishing season and the type of gear and nets that fishermen used. Within the parameters of those season and gear regulations, anyone and everyone had a "right" to fish.

Though the fishery was open to all, the resident fishermen criticized the canneries' use of imported fishermen and particularly of the fish trap. The traps were taking fish that the fishermen could otherwise catch. Though anyone could own a trap, the traps were more elaborate and expensive than other fishing gear. As a result they were owned mainly by the canneries. Rough numbers indicate that traps garnered about 40 percent of all fish caught, and upward to 75 percent of the salmon caught in western Alaska. As the traps operated near the coast, they forced the individual fishermen to go to more difficult offshore fishing locations. As time went on, the traps came to represent the interests of the *outside* packers versus the *resident* fishermen. The resident fishermen accused the packers of unfair competition. But one must remember that commercial salmon fishing by whatever means—traps, resident, or nonresident fishermen—served one major purpose: to supply the very canneries that the resident fishermen so readily criticized. In some situations, it appears that traps limited the catch of fish in interior rivers by native Alaskans for subsistence purposes. Nonetheless, the force of the protest over fish traps was not the canneries versus subsistence users, but the canneries versus individual commercial fishermen.

Despite the inherent antagonism of the resident fishermen to the packers, a relative peace existed as long as the demand for salmon rose. The voice of the residents became shrill in those first years after World War I when the catch dropped dramatically. Fishermen, newly elected delegate Sutherland, and the territorial legislature all proclaimed that someone must be to blame. Had the federal government failed in its obligation to manage the resource? Had the canneries overfished with their fish traps? Rarely did the fishermen admit that their unlimited entry might also be a problem.

U.S. Secretary of Commerce Herbert Hoover first tried to manage and conserve the fishery in 1922 by creating through executive order a "reserve" system with permits for entry into specific fishing areas. The canneries quickly garnered the lion's share of the permits, thus provoking the cry of Alaska fishermen and delegate Sutherland that the "ancient right of the open fishery" had been abridged. Sutherland tried to link Hoover to other Harding-era scandals and accused him of giving exclusive rights to the packers. In 1924 Congress responded to these charges by eliminating Hoover's "reserves" and enacting the White Act, named for its prime sponsor, Representative Wallace White of Maine. This legislation attempted to conserve the fishery by requiring that 50 percent of the annual fish run be allowed to escape into the streams for spawning.[17]

For the duration of the 1920s and 1930s the White Act seemed to solve the problem of the depletion of the fishery. Catches grew annually and reached that all-time peak production of 8.4 million cases in 1936. Even if there were seemingly enough fish for everyone, Alaska's fishermen continued to protest the use of fish traps. In their minds fish traps limited the number of fishermen who could thrive and settle permanently in the territory. Even after he left Congress, Delegate Sutherland continued to emphasize this correlation. In 1936 he told Congress that 2,793 Alaska fishermen had produced 2.3 million cases of canned salmon in 1930. In neighboring British Columbia, where the fish trap was outlawed, 9,322 fishermen produced 1.47 million cases of salmon. Rather than a testament to the labor efficiency of the Alaska salmon industry, Sutherland presented these figures as proof that the Alaska packers and their traps were denying needed employment to thousands of Alaska residents, thus thwarting the settlement of the territory. His solution was to abolish fish traps, following the pattern in all Pacific Coast states and British Columbia by 1935. Sutherland and his successor, Anthony Dimond, were unable to secure federal legislation against fish traps, even with the added impetus of a 1935 resolution against fish traps passed by the Alaska territorial legislature.[18]

The action of the legislature in 1935 highlighted the strange and strained relation between the territorial legislature and the salmon industry. The territory's prime source of revenue was a series of taxes on the salmon industry. Among these were a four-cent tax on every case of salmon, license taxes, and taxes on various kinds of fishing gear, including fish traps. Though the packers had early challenged the right of the territorial legislature to tax them, they lost their appeals in court. The White Act of 1924 formally upheld the territory's right to tax the industry. By the 1930s the salmon canneries, though not the salmon fishermen, were the primary source of revenue for the territory. Territorial treasurer Walstein Smith testified before Congress in 1936 that fish taxes averaged 74 percent of all territorial revenues from 1929 to 1934. The tax on the hated fish traps contributed an average 14 percent of all taxes for the same period.[19]

In addition to challenging the territory in court, the canneries placed lobbyists in the territorial legislature to resist further taxation. Before the 1930s they were represented by the San Francisco–based Alaska Packers Association. Under the provisions of the New Deal's National Recovery Act one dominant trade association and lobby, the Canned Salmon Industry, Inc., emerged to speak for 90 percent of the Alaska industry. In 1937 Ketchikan lawyer Winton C. Arnold became the lobbyist for this trade group, a position he held for more than two decades. As Arnold had once been a magistrate, he was often referred to as "Judge" Arnold.

The methods used by the canning lobbyists, as well as their mining counterparts, appeared to be crude bribery. The gift of a case of liquor was often the only inducement needed to gain a vote. If the lobbyists were crude, the legislators were equally crude in their willingness to accept the bribes. The packers also contributed to the campaigns of legislators in the southeastern districts where so many of their canneries were located. There was always a legislator or two rumored to be under the thumb of the canners. In the small pre–World War II legislature of eight senators and sixteen representatives, control of only a few legislators was all that was necessary to prevent further legislation or taxes on the salmon industry. The packers were reviled by many Alaskans for using undue influence on the legislature to prevent taxation—even though the canneries paid virtually all the taxes in the territory. The 1935 resolution on fish traps seemed to be an outburst by the legislature against the undue influence of the packers, though some critics noted that the cannery lobbyists had been able to prevent such a resolution from being passed since 1912. It would be another thirteen years until the expanded postwar legislature had the votes to place a fish trap referendum on the ballot.

So matters stood at the onset of World War II. For decades resident fishermen had been protesting the canneries' use of fish traps. The canneries were criticized for exploiting the territory and controlling the legislature—even though they had created the industry that gave the resident fishermen a market and the territory its primary source of revenue. But at least in the late 1930s there seemed to be enough fish—or were there?

When Gruening took office in 1939, the annual salmon catch dropped to 5.2 million cases—down over 3 million cases from the 1936 peak. Cries of depletion could be heard once again. The onset of World War II brought some relief, and the pack was up to almost 7 million cases in 1941. With the end of the war things grew progressively worse. By 1946 the salmon pack was under 3 million cases. Two years later there was no improvement. The Alaska salmon fishery seemed hopelessly depleted. And who was to blame? Alaskans, with Governor Gruening in the lead, claimed that the canneries and the federal government were responsible for the collapse of the fishery. If there was any overfishing, it was not due to the unlimited entry of fishermen but to the fish trap. The fish trap was the symbol of everything that was wrong in the fishery and for that matter in Alaska—absentee exploitation, corruption of the legislature, and inept regulation by the federal government. In a word, critics called it "colonialism." All of this appealed to Gruening's Progressive tradition. In true Rooseveltian (Theodore, not Franklin) fashion, the governor had a "bully" time "muckraking" the evils of absentee packers and vowing to free the trapped salmon.

How could the fish trap and its attendant colonial trappings be eliminated? Statehood was the answer. With statehood, Alaska could regulate its own fishery and ban the fish trap. In the eyes of many Alaskans this would restore the fishery and place residents in control. With the war's end in 1945 the expanded territorial legislature had more freedom to act. It could not be as easily bought and manipulated as before. Its first ballot proposition to the people had been statehood. As we have seen, the results were inconclusive. There were so many attendant worries attached to the word "statehood." Two years later the legislature put the fish trap referendum on the ballot. There seemed to be no attendant worries when the vote was counted. Statehooders and Governor Gruening now saw an opportunity to use the 8–1 majority for the abolition of fish traps to bolster the meager 3–2 majority for statehood. Tie statehood to the abolition of the fish trap and all it stood for. Over the next decade this would be the consistent strategy of the statehooders—even those who lived far remote from any cannery.

If the emotional issue for statehood in Hawai'i was first-class citizenship for Japanese Americans, the salvation of the fishery and the fishermen was the emotional issue in Alaska. Of course, emotion is not always the same thing as reality. Let us not forget that the future of Alaska after World War II was not based on fishing. If the ever-declining fishery had been the economic bedrock of the territory, statehood might never have been achieved. Alaska's future was based on its growing military defense role. Future prosperity was emerging along that rail belt from Anchorage to Fairbanks—not in the fishing regions of southeastern and western Alaska where the military presence was thin. But for some inexplicable reason Alaskans in every region of the territory responded with vigor to the 1948 fish trap referendum. The vote was actually stronger in Anchorage and Fairbanks than in Juneau and Ketchikan. Even in those districts that symbolized the emergence of the military defense territory the vote was overwhelmingly against fish traps—23–1 in the Ladd Field district of Fairbanks and a staggering 41–1 in the Fort Richardson district of Anchorage. Had any of those voters ever seen a fish trap?[20]

This background to the fishing industry has led us back in time from 1948. Without understanding how embedded the issue of the fish trap was in the territory's history, it is difficult to understand why it created such an emotional fervor in 1948. The statehooders had their emotional issue after the 1948 fish trap referendum. But there was still much work to be done if Alaska were to achieve a level of modernization that could convince Congress to admit the territory as a state. Let us now turn to Gruening's postwar efforts to complete the modernization program he had begun during World War II.

Gruening's Modern Alaska

Just before the end of the war, Gruening had high hopes for the expanded legislature that he and Dimond persuaded Congress to create in 1944. The 1945 legislature gave the governor anti-discrimination legislation, the statehood referendum, and the creation of the Alaska Development Board to stimulate economic growth. It defeated, though narrowly, Gruening's plans for a modern tax and revenue system. The governor placed the blame for that defeat squarely on the "outside economic interests," particularly the canned salmon industry.

From 1945 on Gruening's muckraking rhetoric about the outsiders reached a shriller pitch because the governor thought the salmon industry should share some of the profits it reaped during World War II. Gruening's postwar rhetoric now had a more focused geographic point of attack. In the preceding quarter-century cannery ownership had gradually shifted from San Francisco to Seattle. In 1944 the Skinner and Eddy Company, a major Seattle shipbuilding firm that also owned salmon canneries, purchased the Alaska Steamship Company, previously under the aegis of the New York–based Alaska Syndicate. Seattle was now the principal home of the "absentee interests" and the colonial exploitation of Alaska. Gruening's rhetoric could be directed to one particular place and to just a few families.

Ned Skinner, grandson of the founder of Skinner and Eddy, related in 1986 that Gruening constantly criticized his father for both his canning and transportation operations. Skinner thought the company had served Alaska well by shipping to many small, unprofitable ports in the territory. He noted that Gruening "thoroughly enjoyed" taking "pot-shots at the Seattle interest, suggesting that we were delaying the development of the State of Alaska or then territory." The Seattle shipper also resented Gruening's attacks on fish traps, which he claimed offered a superb way to hold and keep fish fresh until the canneries could process them. The fish trap, he explained, lowered the price of canned salmon to the housewife. Though Skinner may have been correct in citing the efficiency of the fish trap and the transportation service of the Alaska Steamship Company, such views—still held a quarter-century after statehood—clearly made the Seattle interests an easy target for Gruening.[21]

The Skinner family, however, was not Gruening's principal target. He reserved his strongest muckraking arrows for salmon industry lobbyist Winton C. Arnold. Called by some the "most powerful man in Alaska," Arnold was the most visible symbol of the packing industry. Statehooders reviled him as much as the detested fish trap. Statehooder Herb Hilscher told me that he once took a photo of Judge Arnold as he leaned over the balcony of the territorial legislature and told legislators how to vote. In 1945 the governor singled out Arnold, along with a group of legislators he had supposedly bought, for the defeat of his revenue and tax package.

Gruening attacked again in 1947 when the territorial house of representatives, now in the hands of the Republicans for the first time since the 1920s, turned on him. The Republicans had long been considered the party most connected to the Seattle interests—and most in opposition to Gruening. All of Gruening's attempts at new taxation, particularly an income tax and increased taxes on the fisheries, were soundly defeated. Basic appropriations for existing agencies went unfunded, including the veterans loan fund enacted a year earlier. The University of Alaska was left without a budget and had to borrow from private sources to continue operation. Several bills, though unsuccessful, tried to reduce the governor's powers. Gruening denounced the irresponsible acts of the legislators in a "Message to the People." Though the 1947 legislature seemingly defeated all of Gruening's measures, it made one strategic mistake. It authorized the referendum on fish traps for the 1948 ballot. Having stopped an increased tax on fish traps, this referendum may have seemed a consolation prize. The legislature did have the right to tax fish traps, but it had no right to abolish them. Any outcome of the referendum would effectively be moot. The legislators miscalculated. The voter enthusiasm generated by the referendum brought other results.

When the voters went to the polls in 1948 they gave Gruening much more than an 8–1 victory on the fish trap referendum. They elected a solidly Democratic, pro-Gruening legislature and one that contained more natives, including the first Eskimos—Percy Ipalook of Wales and William Beltz of Nome. The national return of Harry Truman to the presidency also augured well for Gruening's continued tenure as governor. Though Truman had renominated Gruening for a third term in 1947, the Congress had not confirmed his appointment in anticipation of a Republican presidential victory in 1948.

When the 1949 legislature convened, Gruening was ready to address his own choir. When the session ended a few months later, Alaska finally had a progressive income tax—both personal and corporate—that was based on a percentage of the federal return. The legislature also passed a property tax as well as increased taxes on the fisheries. The new revenues allowed appropriations for the agencies that had languished over the last two years. Gruening noted that during the legislative session Arnold came to his office. The lobbyist threatened to fight the new taxes in court and insisted that the industry would never pay. As in earlier decades, the courts upheld the taxes on the canneries.[22]

Though Gruening achieved a new victory in the 1949 territorial legislature, he faced major obstacles in the U.S. Congress. By 1949 Gruening had been governor for a decade. In that time Gruening had developed both devoted followers and confirmed opponents in both the territory and the national capital. His followers were devoted to the policies he articulated and brought to Alaska. Anchorage publisher Bob Atwood said that his devotion to Gruening came as somewhat of a surprise. "He had the potential of becoming an enemy," Atwood explained. "A liberal with a Harvard background . . . Gruening had all the qualities I had been accustomed to hate. He was an outsider, opinionated and sovereign. When I got to know him, he became my leader, my main inspiration and my mentor."[23]

Unlike Atwood, many Alaskans never changed their initial impression. Some of Gruening's opponents disagreed with the governor's policies and programs. Others simply did not like him. His Eastern intellectual demeanor often annoyed them. The energetic governor talked constantly about his policies and programs and worked actively to persuade legislators. He rarely acknowledged the validity of viewpoints other than his own. When legislators failed to enact his programs, he scolded them publicly. In many ways Gruening set the entire tone for politics in the territory. Both the Republican and Democratic parties had their pro-Gruening and anti-Gruening wings. Some Republicans supported him in the legislature, while some Democrats opposed him.

The play of the pro and anti Gruening forces at both the local and national level reached a head with the governor's renomination for a third term. With Truman's victory and a return of the Democrats to the Senate, the nomination went forward. But minority Republicans on the Senate Interior and Insular Affairs Committee forced chairman Joseph O'Mahoney to hold hearings before taking the final vote. They hoped to derail the governor with testimony from disgruntled locals in both parties.

For the hearings an anti-Gruening faction led by Cap Lathrop that included four members of the legislature (two Democrats and two Republicans) went to Washington. Gruening's opponents on the Senate committee had hoped for tales of corruption and other political abuses on the part of the governor. However, the locals delivered a rambling and inept testimony. They claimed that Gruening was "politically ambitious" and often tried to influence legislators through conversation over cocktails. When the territorial legislators also noted that their testimony had been written for them by Lathrop's secretary, it became a foregone conclusion that the ineptness of Gruening's foes had effectively secured his renomination. A much larger planeful of Gruening supporters also appeared in Washington, but they needed to add little to secure Gruening's third term. The committee confirmed his appointment unanimously.[24]

The standoff between Gruening's supporters and opponents in 1949 highlighted a trend that had followed Gruening throughout his career to reform colonialism in different parts of the Americas. He had first attempted to bring reform to Mexico and Puerto Rico. In those places, as in Alaska, he relied on his own views of what was right and often acted with a political naïveté toward the opposition. Since he tended to discount the views of the opposition, he tended to discount their power. In both Mexico and Puerto Rico the strength of the opposition brought him down and stymied his reforms. Only in Alaska, where political development was so weak and the opposition so inept, did Gruening finally succeed in opposing colonialism and creating a modern state.[25]

Secure in his third term by mid-1949, Ernest Gruening could look with some pride on his modernization of Alaska. The legislature had been expanded and included native as well as Caucasian members. The territory now had a modern tax structure. The maturing process, however, was not yet complete. Alaska still had no territorial court system, and it had no counties or territory-wide system of local government. But the territory could now assert that it had the means to support such new branches of government when it became a state. To make those assertions forcefully to the Congress, the 1949 legislature created the Alaska Statehood Committee and appointed Gruening's friend Bob Atwood as chairman.

With the triumphs of 1949 legislature, the governor could turn his attention to the economy. Behind the smokescreen of trapped salmon and the Seattle interests, Gruening and others knew that the future of Alaska did not really lie in fishing or in a revival of the mining industry. It was the development of the military defense structure that would be the salvation of the territory's economy and the stimulus to permanent economic growth. This is what would attract the attention and the concern of any Congress reviewing the pending statehood bills. To understand the Cold War military defense territory that would become a state, we must leave the fish and return to the soldiers.

Top-Secret Alaska

The "Seattle interests" had always been Gruening's nemesis and his prime target of attack. Thus it might have appeared odd in mid-1949

that the governor rushed to protect Seattle and in the process enhance
Alaska's role as guardian of the North and the nation. The "interest" of
concern was not the fish canneries but the Boeing Aircraft Company.
During World War II protection of the Boeing bomber plant in Seattle
had been one of the prime reasons for building up Alaska's air defenses.
In 1949 the air force suggested that Boeing close its bomber plant in
Seattle and produce such aircraft at its facility in Wichita, Kansas. The
move would shield the production of military aircraft from Soviet air
attack. Gruening flew to Seattle and in conjunction with the Seattle
Chamber of Commerce proposed what he thought would be a wiser
strategy: build a string of radar stations across the Arctic Coast of Alaska
to warn of any Soviet air intrusion. There would then be time for the
air force to respond before enemy planes could threaten Seattle—particularly if air bases in Alaska were enlarged. According to Gruening,
the plan to move Boeing was dropped; three years later preparations to
construct the radar line, known as the Distant Early Warning Line, or
DEW Line, began.[26]

By defending the Boeing plant, the governor made clear his own
realization that the military buildup of Alaska was the key to ensuring
the territory's economic development and to attracting national attention. In assessing the territory's future, Gruening bluntly admitted that
"in our favor was Alaska's strategic importance in the post-war antagonism between the United States and Soviet Russia." In his biography
of Gruening, historian Robert Johnson points out that the governor
may well have compromised some of his earlier—and later—"interna-
tionalist" views to win federal defense support for Alaska. "Gruening
recognized," Johnson explains, "that stressing the Soviet military threat
to Alaska offered the surest path to obtaining the desired federal aid,
and thus embraced a variety of Cold War policies that he would come
to oppose later on in his life." Whether Gruening convinced Washington
of Alaska's continued strategic importance or whether Washington came
to that conclusion on its own, an enhanced Cold War military buildup
gained force after 1949 that dwarfed the military growth in the preceding four years.[27]

The overall financial and human scope of increased military activity after 1949 was staggering. Total annual Department of Defense
expenditures (including construction and operations), which had
climbed to $449 million by 1949–50, hit a peak of $512 million in
1952–53. By contrast the total annual value of the salmon catch that

attracted so much public attention varied between $30 and $40 million in the same period. Armed forces personnel grew to 50,000 in the 1952–55 period and pushed Alaska's total population to 220,000. Including civilian workers, the Department of Defense employed 51.5 percent of Alaska's work force in 1952. The Cold War was clearly the dominant economic force in the territory.[28]

National defense strategy now included the DEW Line. Planning for the radar shield began in the summer of 1952 with a military/scientific study group convened at the Massachusetts Institute of Technology. The three-thousand-mile line would stretch along the Arctic coast from Point Barrow, Alaska, to Baffin Island, Canada, with some fifty separate installations. The first test site was constructed at Barter Island, Alaska, in 1953, and the project, whose final cost totaled almost $500 million, was completed in 1957. Alaska natives in the region were recruited to help in the location and construction of the line. Their role also included a pre-radar scouting function. The air force supplied binoculars to many native families to scan the skies for Soviet aircraft before the line was completed. In addition to the DEW Line, the military constructed the Aircraft Control and Warning System (AC&W), as well as an internal communication system linking Alaska with the lower forty-eight states called "White Alice." The White Alice system later became the civilian communication system known as Alascom.[29]

The sheer number of newly arriving military personnel was staggering. The total was much greater than the fifty thousand uniformed members (plus dependents) who were there at any one time. Military families often left within a year to be replaced by others. The experience of being in Alaska in the 1950s reverberated throughout the nation. For example, Charlayne Hunter-Gault, the African American woman who was the first to integrate the University of Georgia in 1961 and later became a commentator for the Public Broadcasting System, spent nine months as a young teenager in Alaska in 1954–55. Her father was an army chaplain at Fort Richardson in Anchorage. Her year in the eighth grade at Ursa Major school was her first in an "integrated" school, though she was the only African American there. The next year she returned to a segregated high school in Atlanta. Exactly what impact Alaska made on her is unclear. But forty years later she devoted a chapter to Alaska in her autobiography *In My Place* (1993) and noted without further elaboration that her nine months there "would affect my life profoundly."[30]

The impact of Alaska on Hunter-Gault and many others in the military population did appear to be both profound and positive. Statehooders organized massive letter-writing campaigns by the military to their "hometown" congressmen asking that Alaska be admitted to the union. Soldiers often asked their parents "back home" to join in the letter-writing campaign. This provided a reach to voting members of Congress that territorial residents could not have achieved on their own.

The impact of the new military population on Alaska was quite visible to those who came to observe the Cold War territory. The continued military buildup dramatically enhanced the emergence of an "urban" Alaska that began in World War II. Anchorage and Fairbanks doubled in size during the 1950s. By 1960 Evangeline Atwood's "Greater Anchorage" was over sixty thousand, and Greater Fairbanks approached twenty thousand. The ethnic makeup of the new military population also changed Alaska. Prior to World War II, Alaska's population was roughly 50 percent Alaska native and 50 percent non-native. By 1950 the proportions were roughly 25 percent native and 75 percent non-native; a decade later the figures were 20 percent native and 80 percent non-native. In addition to a greater influx of Caucasians, significant numbers of African Americans, like Charlayne Hunter-Gault's family, became a part of the population. Transcending race, there was also a noticeably new kind of non-native Alaskan. The old-time "pioneers," or "sourdoughs," were quickly outnumbered by the new military arrivals, who had a decidedly different value system. As Alaskan economist George Rogers has noted, "The people who came with military Alaska were not the independent, self-sufficient pioneers of past centuries, but members of mid-twentieth-century America's urban-industrial society. They required and expected the same standards of community living and services available elsewhere, and the economic prosperity which accompanied their coming made it possible to meet these demands." Though there was tension at times between the "sourdough" Caucasian community and the new military population, there was hardly a standoff. Many of the sourdoughs readily left mining or fishing to work as civilians on the expanding military posts.[31]

Military Alaska was clearly *visible*. But in the planning and dreaming for a new state, there was at times an *invisible* quality to all this growth. The transiency of the service personnel caused the permanent residents to see military Alaska as a silent backdrop to their plans— albeit one they constantly cited as proof of the territory's growing population and economic viability. Some of the military operations, like the DEW Line construction, were "top secret." Though Fairbanksans could see the coming and going of supplies to the north, the exact nature of the venture was not a subject of widespread public knowledge. That "secrecy" that Bob Atwood attributed to military operations in Anchorage at the end of World War II continued to set the tone during the Cold War. "Military Alaska" also carried the aura of "top-secret Alaska." As such it seemed to exist within, but above and beyond, the Alaska of the statehooders who were so concerned with "the Seattle interests" and nonmilitary federal mismanagement. During the Cold War Gruening and his friends might attack the Interior Department, but not the Defense Department.

This invisibility had a strange effect—or lack of effect—on territorial politics. Unlike the prewar mining and fishing industries, military Alaska did not entwine itself in territorial politics or seek special favors from the legislature. As noted earlier, statehooders at a 1996 reunion first told me that the Cold War military buildup was not on their minds in the 1950s. Later in the conversation the issue of the military impact kept recurring. Finally Jack Coghill, one of the writers of the 1955–56 constitution and twice a lieutenant governor of Alaska, explained that the military buildup "freed the population." For the first time, people came up from the "Lower 48" who were "not under the thumb of the mining and fishing industries." In Coghill's mind, the military buildup provided the precondition for statehood by "producing a free people." So all at once military or top-secret Alaska was the most important thing that ever happened to the territory and something that many people did not notice at all.[32]

If there was at times an invisible quality to the impact of the military within Alaska, lawmakers in the national capital were very aware of that impact. They reacted to and shaped statehood legislation with the military in mind. As noted when tracing the course of Hawai'i statehood legislation through the Congress, President Eisenhower often balked at admitting Alaska along with Hawai'i. While serving as army chief of staff, Eisenhower visited Alaska in 1947 and assured the residents of a continued and growing military presence. He well knew that the booming Alaska of the 1950s was the product of military spending and expansion. However, as president, Eisenhower wondered what sort of permanent community, absent the military, existed in Alaska that could become a viable state. One of his staff members noted that Eisenhower "thought statehood for such a territory ridiculous."[33]

If the president worried about Alaska's permanent viability as a state, he and members of Congress were equally concerned about the military importance of certain areas of the territory. Could sensitive military installations, particularly "top-secret" ones, be under the control and sovereignty of a state government? The president and some congressmen demanded that certain military areas be excluded from state authority in both Alaska and Hawai'i. Such military exclusions or withdrawals began to appear in the various statehood bills for Alaska and Hawai'i that emerged during the Eisenhower administration. Secretary of the Interior Douglas McKay first proposed the exclusion of a wide swath of northern and western Alaska that served as a buffer for the DEW Line and other radar installations. The final statehood bill passed in 1958 included the so-called "McKay Line" that bounded this area and a provision to reassert federal sovereignty over the excluded area in case of a national emergency. The Congress was very aware that it would be admitting a "top-secret" military state in Alaska, and to a lesser degree Hawai'i.

Keeping in mind the congressional recognition of military Alaska, let us see how the various statehood bills for admitting the Cold War territory fared in the Congress during the Truman and first Eisenhower administrations.

The Statehood Bills Falter but Strengthen the Potential New State of Alaska

Statehood for the northern territory, as for Hawai'i, was dependent on the passage of one bill through the Congress. We have already discussed the various tactics used to delay, recommit, or kill the Hawai'i bill. In the process it became clear that Alaska was entwined with Hawai'i. One territory would not be admitted without the other, if for no other reason than the partisan view that Hawai'i was a Republican territory and Alaska a Democratic territory. In the decade after World War II party strength in the Congress was closely matched, and the majority party switched from Republican to Democrat regularly. The presidency changed from Democrat to Republican in 1953. There was not an extended period of time when any one party was fully in control of the nation as had been the case before 1945. Hawai'i was generally considered to be the stronger candidate for statehood as it was more mature politically and economically. Except under the most drastic partisan scenario, it would be difficult for the Congress to admit the less mature

Alaska over Hawai'i. Alaska effectively followed on the coattails of Hawai'i from 1946 to 1954. If Hawai'i's hopes were regularly rebuffed, as they were, then there was little chance for Alaska.

While we might easily say that the early course of the Alaska statehood bill through Congress was merely an echo of Hawai'i's, there was an important difference to Alaska's legislative history that requires attention. Debates over the various Hawai'i statehood bills rarely focused on what the new state should be. The bills would simply admit the territory with its existing economic and political structure as the new state of Hawai'i. Though opponents of Hawai'i showed concern with the strength of the ILWU within the Hawai'i Democratic Party, the statehood bills demanded no fundamental changes for the new state. The Communist problem or radical unionism would be handled within the framework of existing federal law, such as the Smith Act or the Taft-Hartley Act.

In Alaska there was a different overtone to the statehood bills. There was concern over the territory's political and economic maturity. Thus the various statehood bills focused on Alaska's developmental needs—particularly on the size of the public land grant the new state would need to jump-start its economy. In 1946 less than 1 percent of Alaska's 365 million acres of land was in private ownership. The remaining 99 percent was federal land, largely unsurveyed. Traditionally, Congress granted new states two sections of public land in each surveyed township of thirty-six sections—or approximately 5.5 percent of the available public lands. This process dated to precedents first set in the Land Act of 1785 that created the township system and the 1787 Northwest Ordinance. Would that be enough for the chronically underdeveloped territory? And how would land be granted in Alaska where so few "townships" had actually been surveyed? Other nagging questions included aboriginal land claims and the management of fish and wildlife resources in the new state. As the statehood bills evolved in succeeding Congresses, the question was not simply to accept or reject statehood. An added goal was to fashion a bill that addressed these developmental issues and questions.

Like Hawai'i, Alaska had a staunch supporter in President Harry Truman and his administration. After the 1946 statehood plebiscite, members of the Truman administration consistently testified in favor of statehood for Alaska. The first bill to receive serious committee attention was introduced in the House in 1947 during the first session of the

Eightieth Congress. The size of the land grant quickly emerged as an issue. Though delegates Bartlett and Dimond had previously proposed land grants of up to all the vacant lands in the territory, the Interior Department had always insisted on using the traditional process of granting two sections of each surveyed township. By 1948 Bartlett had reconciled himself to the township formula, but he now wanted four sections in each township (a total of about forty-two million acres). The Interior Department still held to two sections (about twenty-one million acres), though it suggested that it might allow those acres to be selected from any lands in the territory. Selections concentrated in a specific area would thus be allowed.[34]

During the hearings held by the Eightieth Congress, some of the most interesting testimony came from Winton Arnold, the canned salmon lobbyist. Arnold said that statehood must be delayed until aboriginal land claims were settled. Hopeless controversy might arise, he explained, if native claims and state claims conflicted. It is uncertain whether Judge Arnold believed this or was just looking for a stalling tactic. Arnold's testimony on the lands issue would recur with great effect in ensuing hearings.

Despite the controversy on lands, the House Public Lands Committee (predecessor to the Interior and Insular Affairs Committee) finally reported the bill favorably in 1948 with the four sections per township grant favored by Bartlett. Unlike the Hawai'i bill, the Alaska bill did not make it out of the Rules Committee. Technically, it died for that reason. But there was clearly concern among many members of Congress in both the House and Senate that Alaska's hopelessly inadequate tax system was an impediment to passage of any statehood bill. Senator Hugh Butler, as staunch a foe of Alaska as of Hawai'i, made it clear that Alaska's tax structure and its dependence on military spending were major problems for him.[35]

To gain congressional favor, Alaska could address its tax structure. When the 1949 legislature passed Gruening's tax measures, Alaska quieted some of the fears about its ability to support a state government. In that year statehood bills for both Alaska and Hawai'i were reported favorably by the House Public Lands Committee. Once again the House Rules Committee attempted to withhold the bills from the floor. As noted earlier in our discussion of Hawai'i, the Eighty-first Congress had agreed to a procedure whereby a bill reported by a standing committee could bypass the Rules Committee after twenty-one days. The bypass procedure was proposed and used during the second session in 1950. Both bills passed the House, but the majority for Alaska (186–146) was considerably less than that for Hawai'i (262–110).

In the ensuing Senate hearings, Winton Arnold brought up the nature of the Alaska land grant once again. He did this with such effect that it changed the very nature of the proposed statehood land grant. After reiterating the need to settle aboriginal claims, Arnold turned to the bill's proviso to grant four sections per township. He pointed out that less than 1 percent of Alaska's land had been surveyed since 1867. Thus there was little possibility of actually conveying the township sections. In Arnold's view the land provisions of the statehood bill were flawed and needed changing. As a result of his testimony, the Senate Interior and Insular Affairs Committee revised the bill to grant twenty million acres, but twenty million acres selected as the new state saw fit from any "vacant, unappropriated, and unreserved" public lands. The township grant system that had prevailed since the 1780s was discarded for the first time in U.S. history. Equally important was a new proviso that the state would receive subsurface mineral rights to the lands it selected. This new method of selection set the tone for future Alaska statehood bills. Many statehooders at the time claimed that Arnold had no real interest in lands, only in stopping statehood. But clearly the Senate committee listened. As historian Claus-M. Naske points out, "It matters little what motivated Judge Arnold. The fact is that he made a significant contribution to Alaska statehood . . . his arguments stimulated positive discussion and action." Naske has also noted that Arnold, the great opponent of statehood, was ironically one of its greatest architects! The principle of selecting and concentrating state lands in one area—rather than receiving land scattered among many townships— became a lifeline for the new state. It eventually led to the selection of the Prudhoe Bay oilfield that gave the state its financial independence from military spending.[36]

Arnold may have transformed the Senate bill, but the Senate let it die there. As Hawai'i went, so went Alaska in the summer and fall of 1950. The Senate Interior and Insular Affairs Committee reported both statehood bills favorably. But the Senate leadership, diverted by the outbreak of the Korean War, never brought the bill to the floor for a vote. Statehood for Alaska and Hawai'i was postponed for yet another Congress.

Statehood bills for Hawai'i and Alaska met the same fate in the Eighty-second Congress. The Senate Interior and Insular Affairs Committee again reported both bills favorably in 1951. Concern with the Korean War postponed floor debate until 1952. As noted in the chapter on the Hawai'i statehood bill, the narrowly divided Senate (D49–R47) became engulfed in a partisan quarrel over which statehood bill to debate first. When the Democratic leadership insisted on bringing the Alaska bill first, a move to recommit the bill to committee ensued. During that recommittal debate a strange twist occurred among Alaska statehooders over the land grant issue.

The 1952 bill retained the twenty-million-acre "selection any-where" principle of the 1950 bill. With several additional grants the total acreage came to about twenty-three million acres. However, to some Alaskans in 1952 the question was not the method of selection, but the size of the selection. Many statehooders, including Bartlett, Gruening, and Bob Atwood, would have liked a larger land grant but were will-ing to accept a smaller grant to get the bill passed. This compromise did not please Walter Hickel, now an active statehooder in the territorial Republican Party. Hickel believed that a much larger land grant was needed if the new state were to have a viable economic future—par-ticularly since the state would gain subsurface rights to any mining or oil deposits. On his own, Hickel decided to fly to Washington and meet with the Senate's leading Republican, Robert Taft of Ohio. Hickel wanted to persuade Taft to recommit or amend the bill with a larger land grant. When Taft asked him how much land he required, Hickel was taken off guard, but asserted one hundred million acres. Hickel later noted that he actually had no idea at the meeting how many acres there were in Alaska. Upon finding out afterward that there were 365 million acres, he said he should have asked for more![37]

Whether Taft was specifically influenced by Hickel or not, he voted to recommit in the tense 45–44 vote that sent the bill back to com-mittee. As no new statehood bill was written in 1952, we do not know if he would have supported a larger land grant. But Hickel's insistence paid off. Though he was immediately reviled by some statehooders for supporting the move to recommit, Hickel asserted the principle that a proper statehood bill with a larger land grant was more important than statehood at any price. His push for a larger grant eventually influenced others. The final bill that passed in 1958 contained a grant of roughly 103.5 million acres.[38]

In addition to Hickel's push for a bigger land grant, the 1952 Senate debate contained another silver lining—actually a silver voice—that would help lead to victory for Alaska in later years. Statehood was not a burning issue for many senators or for their constituents. They often voted "no" simply because they knew nothing about it, or because a "no" vote might easily win the favor of a powerful opponent of statehood like Hugh Butler. With equal ease they could vote "yes" with little worry about fallout in their district or state. In 1952 the positive vote of Senator Fred Seaton of Nebraska became a beacon for the eventual passage of the Alaska statehood bill.

Seaton was something of an anomaly in the Senate, though not as rare an anomaly as one might think. Seaton was never elected to the Senate; he was appointed in December 1951 to fill the seat of Senator Kenneth Wherry, who had died a few weeks earlier. Death in office was not—and still is not—that rare in the Senate. In the years from 1947 to 1959 (Eightieth–Eighty-sixth Congresses), when the Alaska and Hawai'i statehood bills were debated in the Congress, approximately thirty appointed Senators took their seats. Seaton was one of four appointed senators in the Eighty-second Congress. The Nebraskan differed from some appointed senators in that he announced he had no intention of running to retain his seat in 1952. He could vote exactly as he pleased in the recommittal debate without concern for his reelection. He was, however, filling the seat of Wherry, who had opposed statehood. Seaton was also the junior colleague of Hugh Butler, statehood's most ardent opponent. Ernest Gruening might well have wondered if a call on the new senator in early 1952 was worth the time. Based on the fact that the Republican Seaton was a fellow newspaperman, the Democrat Gruening decided to make the call.[39]

Gruening reported that Seaton told him at their first meeting, "I am wholly uninformed on the subject [Alaska statehood]. But I'd be glad to be informed." After Gruening talked with Seaton for two hours, the Nebraskan said he wanted to consult with delegate Joseph Farrington of Hawai'i, a fellow Republican. He told Gruening to come back in a few days. When Gruening returned, he was pleasantly surprised to hear Seaton say, "I've made up my mind. I'm for statehood now—for both Alaska and Hawaii."[40]

Seaton was not shy in his support for Alaska. On February 20, 1952, just weeks after his visit from Gruening, he delivered his one and only speech in the Senate in favor of Alaska statehood. Gruening explained to Seaton that Nebraska's admission to the Union had been opposed by members of Congress between 1864 and 1867 because of low population and fears that it could not bear the expense of state government. Gruening wrapped all of this into a speech that became the text Seaton used.

True to his word, Seaton voted against recommittal of the Alaska bill. His colleague Hugh Butler voted for it. Butler's side prevailed in the 45–44 vote to recommit. The battle for Alaska statehood was lost in 1952, but Seaton's support was not. Though he would never again vote on the Alaska statehood bill in the Senate, he became assistant secretary of defense under President Eisenhower in 1953. Later he would become personal administrative assistant to the president and in 1956 Secretary of the Interior. The time would come when Seaton would play *the* crucial role in winning the president for statehood.

Seaton's crucial influence still lay in the future. The 1952 elections that put Dwight Eisenhower in the White House and moved Seaton from the Senate to the executive branch did not augur well for Alaska. Though the new president had offered support for Alaska in 1950 when he was president of Columbia University, he made no mention of the northern territory in his first message to Congress in 1953. As he specifically advocated the admission of Hawai'i, his omission of Alaska seemed to be no mere oversight. His first Secretary of the Interior, former Oregon governor Douglas McKay, and the newly appointed Republican territorial governor of Alaska, Frank Heintzleman, reinforced Eisenhower's hesitancy over statehood for Alaska. Bob Atwood saw all of this as a "calamity" for Alaska.

The appointment of Heintzleman in early 1953 was particularly problematic. Eisenhower's election spelled the end of Ernest Gruening's remarkable fourteen-year reign as territorial governor. Eisenhower could have appointed a dynamic pro-statehood Republican such as Walter Hickel or banker Elmer Rasmuson. But the choice of federal bureaucrat Heintzleman, then the regional forester for Alaska, harkened back to the lackluster, pre-Gruening days of Alaska politics. Heintzleman was certainly not in favor of statehood, and many thought he was actually opposed. Unlike Gruening, he was a bachelor with no particular social charm or political initiative. He was an able bureaucrat who was expected to follow the official Department of the Interior stance on statehood.

As the new Eighty-third Congress convened, it looked like the absolute worst of times for Alaska, though possibly the best of times for Hawai'i. As noted earlier, a statehood bill for the island territory quickly passed with a resounding victory in the House. The Hawai'i bill went to the Senate, where the Republican majority was only 48–47 with one independent senator. Meanwhile committee hearings were held for Alaska in the House. The most significant development in those hearings was the decision by the Public Lands Committee to increase Alaska's land grant to one hundred million acres with several specific additions that made the total close to 103 million acres. The committee favorably reported the bill, after which the Rules Committee promptly held it captive. The bypass procedure of the Eighty-first Congress had been repealed and was no longer an option to bring the bill to the floor.

When the Senate took up consideration of the Hawai'i bill in 1953, Alaska's chances seemed to grow. Alaska advocates in the Senate proposed that the Hawai'i bill be combined with Alaska. They feared that if a separate Hawai'i bill succeeded, Alaska's hopes might be permanently dashed as its cause could no longer be linked with the island territory. The Interior and Insular Affairs Committee, chaired once again by Hugh Butler, proposed that hearings be held in Alaska before considering a combined bill. Butler's move would dramatically energize Alaska's statehooders for the future. In the words of Claus-M. Naske, "Butler's hearings in Alaska were the catalyst which started the 'populist' phase of the Alaska statehood movement."[41]

Statehood opponents in the Congress often said that they heard only from the top echelons in Alaska for statehood. To some extent they were trying to categorize statehood as the desire of the "Gruening Party" that included the governor, the legislature, the Alaska Statehood Committee, a few newspapers like the *Anchorage Times,* and, of course, delegate Bartlett. With Gruening out of the governor's office, opponents wanted to show that momentum for statehood was lost—despite Bartlett's reelection in 1952 for a fifth term. Butler announced that he wanted to hear from the "little people" as he toured the territory in the fall of 1953.

The "little people" showed up in droves for hearings held in Fairbanks, Anchorage, Juneau, and Ketchikan. By late 1953 the "invasion of the veterans" along with other newcomers had swelled the ranks of statehood supporters. One group in Anchorage formed an organization called "Little Men for Statehood." Statehood supporters outnumbered opponents by a wide margin in the 1953 hearings. Cap Lathrop had died in 1950 and no longer led the opposition.

As in years past, much of the testimony against territorial status and for statehood centered on the stimulus statehood would give to economic development. However, some of the most poignant testimony came from those who described the indignities they now faced from the recently passed McCarran–Walter Act. In our discussion of Hawai'i, the McCarran–Walter Act of 1952 was a beacon of hope as it provided for the naturalization of the Issei. As noted earlier, the act was a strange blend of revised immigration policies and new internal security and anti–Communist policies. The latter included a provision for security screening of anyone entering the United States from "outside" the forty-eight states. This provision meant that Alaskans who went to Seattle were required to undergo security clearance and prove their citizenship and loyalty to the United States. Various speakers, including Republican committeewoman Margaret Rutledge, testified to the utter indignity of this new provision. When I interviewed statehooders in 1981, the humiliation occasioned by the McCarran–Walter Act was mentioned more than any other single reason as proof that territorial status was unacceptable.

Despite the testimony of the "little men" in Alaska, Butler dragged his feet in Washington. The action, or lack thereof, of the Republicans in Washington and of Governor Heintzleman at home led pro-statehood Republicans in Alaska to push for change. The territorial Republican party had long held the reputation for being anti-statehood and under the control of the" Seattle interests." Republican boss Al White, a Juneau merchant and realtor, was seen as a proxy for those interests. In late 1953 pro-statehood Republicans led a revolt within the party and elected Walter Hickel as head of the Anchorage Republican Club, and then as Republican National Committeeman in 1954. Hickel and other Republicans also wrote a letter to Heintzleman in 1953 demanding greater support for statehood. The governor reluctantly urged the Secretary of the Interior to push for an Alaska statehood bill.

In early 1954 Eisenhower once again supported statehood for Hawai'i and omitted mention of Alaska. However, it became evident to Butler that his committee could not report a Hawai'i bill without a companion Alaska bill. The bill it finally fashioned for Alaska now included a general land grant of one hundred million acres to be chosen from the unreserved lands of the territory, plus several smaller grants for specific purposes. Butler's Interior and Insular Affairs Committee then reported separate statehood bills for Alaska and Hawai'i in the spring of 1954. The Senate wanted to avoid another partisan squabble and potential recommittal fiasco over which bill should be debated first. The upper house first voted 46–43 to combine the separate bills into one omnibus bill for statehood. It then approved the combined statehood bill by an even greater margin of 57–28. As noted earlier, some senators thought they were aiding Alaska in combining the bills while others thought they were setting up the two territories for eventual defeat in the House.

The combined Senate bill returned to the House. It could be sent to a conference committee and reconciled with the 1953 Hawai'i statehood bill passed by the House. Or it could go to the Rules Committee and be scheduled for floor debate and a vote as a new bill. While the combined bill was awaiting its fate in the House, the question of land withdrawals for military defense purposes gained force within the executive branch. Governor Heintzleman and later Secretary McKay suggested a partition of the territory with the southeastern and south-central areas admitted as a state and the northern and western areas excluded. The partition movement was not acceptable to any statehooders because the partitioned area would be permanently alienated from the rest of Alaska. Though a partition was not included in any bill in 1954, the issue of special treatment for sensitive defense areas had now been raised and would recur.

For the remainder of 1954, Alaskans, like their counterparts in Hawai'i, lobbied the House of Representatives to consider the combined Senate bill. They also lobbied Eisenhower to prevail upon the House. The "little men" in Alaska, organized in 1954 as "Operation Statehood," flew to Washington. A bipartisan group including delegate Bartlett, Bill Egan, Walter Hickel, and Fairbanks Republican John Butrovich secured a meeting with the president. The meeting was heated, particularly after Eisenhower insisted upon partition and military withdrawals. Butrovich made statements that seemed to question the president's "Americanism." Hickel then made additional comments. One observer declared that the young contractor announced, "Mr. President, you're nuts." Hickel told me he did not remember exactly what he said, but he remembered that Eisenhower responded, "Well, at least you think I'm an American."[42]

Neither the strident lobbying by the "little men" of Alaska nor the gentle stroking by Hawai'i statehooders who sent tropical orchids to the capital prompted action in the House. The House leadership under Republican Joseph Martin was inclined neither to prod the Rules Committee nor to form a conference committee with the Senate. No action whatsoever took place in the House. Once again statehood for Alaska and Hawai'i died in the Congress of the United States.

For Hawai'i the 1954 debacle was yet another defeat made all the more sorrowful by the death of Joseph Farrington. It was particularly cruel as both the House and the Senate had approved statehood for Hawai'i in some fashion. Alaska, too, was defeated, but the statehood bill had changed for the better. The defeated 1954 bill now contained the 103-plus million-acre land grant in both the House and Senate versions. At home even more changes had taken place. The local Republican party was now firmly in the hands of the statehooders. Throughout the territory an enlarged group of statehooders, including the "little men," were raising their voices. In Alaska the 1954 defeat was more an energizing than a demoralizing event. As Walter Hickel said, "No longer were we asking for statehood. Now we were demanding it, right to the President's face, and demanding it on our terms."[43]

In the fall elections of 1954 Alaska voters elected a solidly Democratic territorial legislature. Despite the changes in the local Republican party, the Democrats pointed to the lackluster performance of the previous Republican legislature that had come to power in the 1952 elections. Alaskans also considered it an insult when Secretary McKay visited the territory during the summer of 1954 and scolded them for their conduct with the president. McKay told Alaskans that they could not demand statehood. Instead, they needed to "act like ladies and gentlemen" and come to Washington "with hat in hand." Former Governor Gruening was not at all inclined to take McKay's advice. Within months of the secretary's scolding visit, Gruening published his classic *State of Alaska* (1954), a statistical-laden volume of quasi-muckraking prose that portrayed the federal government with its attitudes of "neglect," "flagrant neglect," and "indifference" as the source of Alaska's major problems.

Nationally the Congress tipped Democratic in the 1954 elections, though again with only a one-vote majority in the Senate. Little would happen for statehood in Washington during the next two years. Combined bills were recommitted in the first half of 1955. But at home Alaskans were determined to do something new that would eventually force the Congress to act.

Alaska, the Cold War Territory, in the Winter of 1954

Before turning to the legislative actions of 1955, it would be well to reflect on the rapid transformation of Alaska between 1945 and 1954.

The "forgotten" territory in 1945–46 with its demobilized population of 100,000 was now the Cold War military territory of 220,000 in the winter of 1954. The arrival of General Emmons in 1944 had been a precursor to that transformation. He came in anticipation of Russian intervention in World War II. It was not until Russia became the nation's Cold War adversary that Alaska's permanent transformation took place. From Vitus Bering's arrival in 1741 to the 1867 Purchase Treaty to the World War II ALSIB and finally to the threat of Cold War air strikes across the top of the continent, Russia was *a* dominant, if not *the* dominant, player in the growth and development of Alaska.

In many ways the Cold War development of Alaska appeared tame compared with its counterpart in Hawai'i. Both experienced a military buildup, but Hawai'i also dealt with radical unionism, militant strikes, flirtations with Communism, and constant mainland suspicion of its Asian American population. To some extent Alaska profited from its very lack of development and maturity in its quest for statehood. It was always behind Hawai'i. There was not enough industry to bring unionization nor a large enough population to arouse suspicion. Anti-Communism and the Soviet threat in the northern territory were used by Gruening and others as a justification to increase military spending.

As the postwar statehood bills for the two territories journeyed through Congress from 1947 to 1954, Hawai'i continually waited for statehood. Alaska, on the other hand, continually prepared for statehood. By 1954 Hawai'i had tried every conceivable political stunt to force the issue. Alaska had not. It continually lagged behind the island territory and often borrowed from Hawai'i. Alaska scheduled its first statehood plebiscite in 1946, six years after a similar vote in the islands. In the winter of 1954 statehood supporters in Alaska thought they might repeat the trick of following Hawai'i. The northern territory could stage a constitutional convention like the one Hawai'i held in 1950. The process of creating the new state of Alaska could continue to proceed. Despite defeat after defeat in the Congress, there was still something exciting and energetic that could be done in Alaska. In contrast, Hawai'i was left to sort out the debris from its ongoing radical taint and the unstable delegate situation occasioned by the death of Joseph Farrington. Over the next two years Alaska would gradually take the lead to become the forty-ninth state while still working in tandem with Hawai'i to bring the islands in as the fiftieth state. The new scenario would begin with the first act of the Alaska territorial legislature in 1955.

Chapter 8

The Alaska Legends:
The Constitutional Convention and the
Alaska-Tennessee Plan, 1955–1956

> If Marston is crying, I've seen everything.
> —*Ernest Patty, on the emotional adjournment*
> *of the Alaska Constitutional Convention, 1956*

A State upon a Hill

When the Alaska territorial legislature convened in January 1955, the first bill filed, House Bill 1, proposed calling a constitutional convention. The idea was not new in 1955 but had been discussed ever since the Hawai'i legislature authorized such a meeting in 1949. The Alaska Statehood Committee, also formed in 1949, was given the authority to make plans for a convention, and the legislature had even discussed the possibility in 1953. However, both the legislature and the Statehood Committee decided not to follow Hawai'i's lead for various reasons—not the least of which was the fact that the Hawai'i had failed to secure statehood.[1]

The stillborn discussions of the previous five years gained energy and momentum in 1954 as part of that "populist" phase in which "little" men and women all over the territory became involved in the statehood movement. Study groups abounded as Operation Statehood in Anchorage and the Constitutional Study League in Fairbanks investigated the methods used by other territories to secure statehood. The groups found the same facts—some fifteen territories had called constitutional conventions as a method for prodding the Congress into action on statehood. Newspaper support for statehood and a convention also increased as the *Fairbanks Daily News-Miner* converted to the cause. C. W. Snedden, who took over the paper after Cap Lathrop's death in 1950, created his own study group in late 1953 and assigned one of his editors to weigh the pros and cons of statehood and to make a report. The young editor, John J. Ryan, reported that there were no "cons" to statehood, only "pros." By early 1954 Snedden renounced the anti-statehood heritage of Lathrop and joined the statehood camp. With the demise of the 1954 joint statehood bill, Alaskans were motivated to do something. Calling a constitutional convention was their answer.

There was also a partisan sting to the motivation. Local Democrats were angered when they lost the territorial legislature to the Republicans in 1952. Their ire increased over the next two years as they claimed the Republican legislature did nothing and was dissolute and corrupt. Tom Stewart of Juneau, an assistant attorney general who ran for the legislature in 1954, told me that the wastebaskets in the legislative chambers were filled with liquor bottles during the Republican interlude. The Democrats, including Stewart, dramatically regained the statehouse—or territory house—in the 1954 elections with the resounding edge of 12–4 in the Senate and 21–3 in the House. Their anger was not merely local, but also directed at the national Republicans, including the Congress and the president who had wavered on statehood. They wanted to show that they could do something that the Republicans had not done. In late 1954 the newly elected Democrats met and decided that a constitutional convention would be their first priority in the new legislature. Unlike Hawai'i with its well-honed legislative research bureaucracy, the Alaska statehooders were not exactly sure how to begin. The Democrats dispatched Stewart to visit Hawai'i and states that had recently held conventions. When the legislature convened, Stewart became the chair of a joint House/Senate committee to craft the convention bill.

Though Stewart visited Hawai'i, he did not find the islands his source of inspiration. He met with delegates to the 1950 convention as well as with Betty Farrington, now elected to a full term as territorial delegate. Mrs. Farrington's major concern was not to applaud and support Alaska's constitutional initiative, but to secure Stewart's assurance that Alaska's efforts would not derail her strategy to push Hawai'i first as the 49th state. Stewart found more inspiration talking with state leaders in New Jersey where a constitutional convention had been held on the campus of Rutgers University in 1947.[2]

By March 1955 Stewart and his committee crafted and secured final passage of a constitutional convention bill filled with more "symbols" than a biblical proverb. There would be fifty-five delegates to the convention—chosen specifically as a symbol of the fifty-five delegates who attended the 1787 Philadelphia Constitutional Convention. They would be elected in a manner that provided broad and even representation throughout the territory. Some would run and be chosen from the territory at large. Others would be elected from specific single-member districts, while a third group would be elected at large within the territory's four judicial districts. The single-member districts were particularly important, as they would ensure representation from rural areas. Members of the territorial legislature were all elected at large from the judicial districts. The urban areas of each district controlled the legislature. For example, the rural area of Palmer in the Matanuska Valley would be represented at the convention in a single-member district. It was routinely excluded from the legislature as Anchorage dominated the seats elected at large from the third judicial district.

The nonpartisan elections for delegates would be held in September; the convention would open in November and run for seventy-five days. The reason for the delay in starting the convention was twofold. Time was needed to prepare materials to guide the delegates at the convention. In Hawai'i the Statehood Commission and the Legislative Reference Bureau prepared a draft constitution as well as various manuals in advance of the 1950 convention. Alaska lacked the local expertise to do this and would have to find "outside" consultants. The winter meeting time also ensured that a broad spectrum of Alaskans could participate. Many Alaskans made their living during the summer months with fishing, mining, lumber, construction, and tourism. Winter was a more amenable time for state building—if for no other reason than the fact that many had nothing else to do.

The final symbol was the convention's meeting place. Hawai'i's convention not only met in the capital city of Honolulu but in the capitol itself, 'Iolani Palace. Though Stewart first considered Juneau as the site of the convention, he rejected the capital city in favor of the campus of the University of Alaska, set on a hill outside Fairbanks. New Jersey state leaders told him that the experience of holding their 1947 convention on the campus of Rutgers University was particularly beneficial. Fairbanks would be a break from Juneau, which had a reputation for deals made with lobbyists in bars and pool halls. Stewart said he received considerable resistance from fellow Juneau residents for this suggestion—including a swift kick in the shins by a disgruntled local legislator. Stewart hoped that the university setting would elevate the tone of the constitutional discussion and that the far north winter would deter lobbyists from attending and attempting to influence the delegates. The university offered its newly built student center as the meeting site for the convention

From the designation of the fifty-five delegates representing all areas of the territory to the snowy hilltop setting of the university, the different symbols all combined to spell a decided and conscious break from the territory's often inept political past. The convention would project a more mature and ordered future. This was the ultimate symbol and message that the territory wanted to convey to the Congress.

Unlike Hawai'i, Alaska did not purposely plan its convention to coincide with the passage of a specific statehood bill in the Congress. By May 1955 any thought that the convention would influence particular legislation in the Congress was quelled. The U.S. House of Representatives recommitted yet another tandem Alaska-Hawai'i statehood bill. It was, as baseball philosopher Yogi Berra once said, "déjà vu all over again." By the time of the September elections, there was no sense of urgency that the elected delegates must speed the convention to win a vote in the Congress.

When the ballots for delegates were tallied, a broadly representative group of Alaskans emerged. Many established political leaders like Bill Egan of Valdez and Ralph Rivers of Fairbanks won seats. The delegates represented all ages and levels of political experience from eighty-two-year-old E. B. Collins, who had served in the first 1913 territorial legislature, to twenty-nine-year-old Tommy Harris, who was running for his first elected position. The delegates included six women and one native, Frank Peratrovich, who had led the late World War II native entry into the legislature. As noted earlier, about a quarter of the delegates had arrived in Alaska since 1940. The colorful Muktuk Marston was among them. Though elected from Anchorage, he made it clear that he was there to represent the cause of Alaska natives. The "little men" also won seats. Barrie White and Victor Fischer, the president and vice president of Operation Statehood, were elected. Tom Stewart was busy organizing the convention and did not run, but Ben Stewart, his seventy-seven-year-old father and the former territorial commissioner of mines, ran and won.

As the fifty-five delegates prepared for their winter stay in Fairbanks, they had no idea if the constitution they planned to write would ever come into force. Many delegates told me that they wondered if state-hood would ever be achieved. Instead, the process of writing the con-stitution became a bonding and uniting experience for the delegates and the territory. They took their mission seriously, and with increas-ing seriousness as the winter wore on. In 1630 John Winthrop and his Massachusetts Bay Puritan followers announced on the deck of the *Arbella* that they would "be as a city upon a hill, the eyes of all people are upon us." One could say without undue exaggeration that the fifty-five delegates leaving for Fairbanks shared a similar seriousness of pur-pose in a distant and far-off land. The Alaskans did not set out to build a city, but to plan a state, upon a hill that the eyes of Congress would see and admit to the union. Theirs was certainly a modern-day "errand into the wilderness."

Seventy-five Days—And Then They Cried

As preparations for the convention reached their final days in November 1955, the frontier quality of Alaska life was in full evidence, despite what-ever modernization had been wrought by the advent of "military Alaska." As the story goes, Bill Egan, who would soon be elected pres-ident of the convention, "hitched a ride" on a freight truck from Valdez to Fairbanks. His wife, Neva, later explained to me that the story was true and that there was nothing unusual about this. Once covered with snow, the treacherous Thompson Pass that led out of Valdez could not be crossed in a passenger car. The only way out was by truck. Everyone "hitched a ride" out of snowbound Valdez.

Bill Snedden prepared to cover the convention for the *News-Miner* and to send reports on the Associated Press wire to other newspapers. To connect his reporter Florence Douthit on the university campus with the *News-Miner* building in downtown Fairbanks, Snedden bought a reel of telephone wire and strung it "through the brush and snow" on the four-mile College Road that connected the campus with the newspaper office. The delegates were housed downtown in the Northward Building and the Nordale Hotel with a bus to carry them each day to the university. Seventy-seven-year-old Ben Stewart, known to his friends as "Ben the Walker," thought this a little too modern and decided to walk the four-mile distance each way, each day![3]

When the convention opened on November 8, two delegates were still unable to get there because of illness (flu) and weather/travel conditions (minus 15 degrees Fahrenheit). Fairbanks in November was not Honolulu in April! Nonetheless fifty-three delegates assembled in the gymnasium of the university for the opening ceremonies. After welcoming remarks from Governor Heintzleman and university president Ernest Patty, the delegates heard a keynote speech from Bob Bartlett on the importance of their duties. Bartlett emphasized the need for a strong constitutional section on natural resources. Alaska's history had been one of resource exploitation by outsiders, he explained. That must now be reversed with a plan to utilize the future state's resources for the benefit of all Alaskans. Bob Atwood, chairman of the Statehood Committee, spoke to the delegates, as did Ernest Gruening. Gruening said only a few words on November 8, but returned the next day to give a rousing speech on the need for Alaskans to "end colonialism." Based on themes Gruening had developed in his recent book *The State of Alaska,* the former governor now emphasized that the federal government was Alaska's biggest problem. He compared the federal government's treatment of the territory to that of King George III toward the thirteen Atlantic colonies. To some extent Gruening was shifting his emphasis from the "Seattle, Washington, interests" to the "Washington, D.C., interests." There was also a new emotion to Gruening's commitment. Only two weeks before, his son Peter had committed suicide. Biographer Robert Johnson suggests that Gruening turned to the statehood movement with even greater vigor as a way to assuage his personal grief. By the time the convention ended, Gruening thought of running for office for the first time.[4]

Once the speeches were over, the delegates approached their business. They elected Bill Egan as president of the convention. They also organized themselves into various committees and elected chairpersons. Tom Stewart, who was not a delegate, was elected secretary of the convention and continued his role in organizing and administering the body. In that capacity he soon brought another dimension and another group of people to Fairbanks to work with the delegates. Over the course of the previous summer Bob Atwood's Statehood Committee had engaged Tom Stewart as executive officer to prepare pre-convention studies. Stewart and Atwood contracted with the Public Administration Service of Chicago for briefing papers and copies of recent state constitutions for the delegates. The briefing papers were written by various outside consultants, often political science professors at major universities. At first Stewart thought that "outsiders" could not understand Alaska's peculiar problems. By the fall he had become impressed with both their work and their enthusiasm for Alaska. He asked several of the consultants if they would be willing to come to Fairbanks and work with the delegates. He received many positive replies. But would the delegates be willing to work with the consultants in person, not just with their briefing papers? At first the delegates balked. They had come to Fairbanks to write their own constitution. All America would be watching. Like their counterparts in Hawai'i, they wanted to prove themselves equal to the task.

Stewart was persistent. A few delegates had found certain textbooks helpful. Stewart suggested that they might wish to talk with the authors. This suggestion seemed fair to the reluctant Alaskans. Stewart then arranged a meeting between one such author and a convention committee chairman. It took only a short while for the delegates to become absolutely convinced of the value of outside advice. During the course of the convention nine outside experts and one Alaskan, George Rogers, served as convention consultants. It was in this capacity that John Bebout and Emil Sady had their "religious experience" in Fairbanks, noted earlier in the introduction, that they shared with their colleagues across the nation. Ernest Bartley of the University of Florida, who advised the delegates on subsurface mineral rights, was well connected with Florida's congressional delegation and would use his influence on future statehood legislation in Congress. The use of the outside experts would prove to be a boon not only in writing the constitution, but also in creating nationwide interest in Alaska. In this way the Alaska convention differed from the "inside" job of constitution writing in Hawai'i.

The Alaskans were definitely on an emotional high in 1955 compared to Hawai'i as they embarked on their constitution-writing errand. Nonetheless, they were still successors to the work done five years earlier in Honolulu. Like their island counterparts, their goal was to produce a model constitution that would show their fitness to govern a new state. Thus their constitution followed the same model set out by the National Municipal League in Hawai'i. The constitution should be brief and specify only the organization and framework of government. The legislature should be large enough to insulate itself from the special-interest tampering that had plagued smaller legislatures. Though the Alaskans toyed for a while with the idea of a unicameral legislature, this plan was quickly abandoned with the suggestion that their new state needed to look "normal," not experimental or innovative. The model constitution in Alaska, as in Hawai'i, specified a "strong" executive or governor who would appoint his/her cabinet. Similarly, judges should be appointed, not elected. Like Hawai'i, the Alaskans also prescribed the state university as a constitutional, not a legislative, creation. Differing from Hawai'i in one respect, the Alaskans included initiative and referendum in their constitution.

Though the Alaskans borrowed heavily from Hawai'i, they never felt the need to bring in an "expert" from the islands to guide their discussions. Hebden Porteus, the secretary of the Hawaii Constitutional Convention, told me that he was invited to Fairbanks and was prepared to come. He decided not to go because neither the Alaska Statehood Committee nor the Hawaii Statehood Commission was willing to pay for his airplane ticket. Inspiration, but not cooperation, characterized the constitution-writing efforts of the two territories.

Alaska's "model" constitution was not just a copy of Hawai'i's. The Alaskans did debate and create a number of constitutional issues that were unique or peculiar to the northern territory. As Bartlett suggested, the natural resources article (article 8) was crucial. Though the "outside" interests and lobbyists were not present in Fairbanks, the delegates themselves represented the "inside" or resident interests, particularly the resident fishery interests. Thus it should come as no surprise that the "ancient right of the open fishery" was affirmed with the constitutional clause "No exclusive right or special privilege of fishery shall be created or authorized in the natural waters of the State"(article 8, section 15). This was one of the few sections of the constitution that would be revised after statehood. In order to conserve the fishery a 1972 amendment created a limited entry permit system not unlike the one Herbert Hoover had suggested in 1922.

To manage resources on land, the delegates chose a "conservationist/developmental" model using the principle of "sustained yield." "It is the policy of the State," the article began, "to encourage the settlement of its land and the development of its resources by making them available for maximum use consistent with the public interest" (article 8, section 1). There was mention of the "preservationist" ethic with an emphasis on wilderness protection and non–utilitarian use. Article 8, section 7 allowed the new state to "reserve" from the public domain "areas of natural beauty or of historic, cultural, recreational or scientific value." Though both "conservation" and "preservation" received constitutional mention, it had long been the intent of the statehooders to utilize Alaska's land resources for economic development, but in a manner that would prevent the exploitation and depletion of the past. Twenty-five years later, passage of the federal Alaska National Interest Lands Conservation Act of 1980 (ANILCA), which withdrew over one hundred million acres of land for wilderness and scenic protection, tended to reverse the "conservation/preservation" priorities of the statehooders.

Native issues also received attention at the convention. As noted earlier, the issue of native land claims had been left unsettled since the 1867 Purchase treaty. Though the convention clearly acknowledged that land claims were a federal issue, Muktuk Marston tried to advance the cause by creating a state land grant to natives. The issue was hotly debated, but the delegates decided to leave the matter in federal hands. Marston and Frank Peratrovich did succeed in limiting the English language requirement for voting to the ability to read or speak English as opposed to read and speak English. Both argued that many older natives were fully knowledgeable of voting rights. They could speak English but might not be able to pass a written test. The convention agreed. The delegates' goal was to eliminate discrimination against natives and create a state that included all people on terms on equality. The issue of aboriginal rights and prior native land claims would eventually be settled in the federal Alaska Native Claims Settlement Act of 1971 (ANCSA) that awarded forty-four million acres of land and nearly $1 billion to a series of native regional and village corporations.[5]

Of particular concern to the Alaska constitution writers was the need to create certain governmental structures that had not existed in territorial days—particularly a state court system and a system of local government. The two were interconnected, as court systems in most states began at the county level. Would there be counties and county courts in the new state of Alaska? The delegates decided to create one unified state court system. The court system would be based on a series of state superior courts with a supreme court over them. Without the need for county courts, there was no particular need for counties. Instead the delegates chose, under advice and guidance from the expert consultants, to create the "borough." This would be an intermediate level of government with taxing authority between the state and the city or municipality. Exactly what a "borough" is and does has remained a question in the half-century since the delegates created it. In a few localities, including Anchorage, the borough and municipality have been merged into one local unit. In my 1981 interviews with delegates many told me they were not sure exactly what a borough was but accepted it on the advice of the experts. Though it was the intent of the constitution to divide all of the state into boroughs, there were still in 2003 vast areas of Alaska that were not organized at this intermediate level and that still depended on a wider range of state supervision. Whatever the "borough" was, one thing was clear. The new state would lack those twin local symbols of its western counterparts—the county courthouse and the county sheriff.

One further aspect of governmental creation should be noted along with the new state court system and the boroughs: public education. Alaska had a territorial university, which was given constitutional status as the state university. In Alaska's towns there were local tax-supported public schools. But in remote rural and native areas there were multiple school systems, including schools sponsored by church organizations and Bureau of Indian Affairs (BIA) schools. The constitution specified that there would be one state school system and that it would be the responsibility of the new state to provide schooling for all Alaskans, regardless of where they lived.[6]

Whether it was the new state court system or the new commitment to public education, the state of Alaska that the delegates created would be a commanding presence in the eyes of the citizens—possibly more so than in most "lower forty-eight states." In both urban and rural areas of Alaska the dominant local symbols are the "state" court building, the "state" office building, and the "state" police or troopers. Territorial Alaska lacked local government and local courts, and in some cases local schools. The new state constitution answered those needs by making the state the primary governmental presence in the lives of Alaskans. This was one of the most important legacies that the delegates left to future generations.[7]

The winter of 1955–56 was an extraordinary experience for the delegates and the consultants. Delegate after delegate expressed this viewpoint to me in the 1981 interviews. Barrie White told me that it was not only an extraordinary and rare experience in hindsight, but one that everyone knew was extraordinary as they participated in the convention. Some delegates said that they were only "interested" in statehood before the convention. They became "passionate" about it as a result of the convention. Only one delegate, R. E. Robertson, a lawyer and former mayor of Juneau, refused to sign the constitution. Robertson claimed he objected to the constitution's inclusion of initiative and referendum and to the convention's stand against fish traps.[8]

The delegates met for the specified seventy-five days plus a fifteen-day recess for Christmas and local hearings. As the deadline drew near, the document was complete. The day for the signing came on February 5, 1956. That ceremony, held once again in the university gymnasium, still lives in the memory of everyone who attended it. Almost one thousand people crowded the basketball court as the college band played. Each delegate then walked forward to sign the constitution at a small table brightened by the glow of a jade lamp commissioned specifically for the occasion by Muktuk Marston. Marston had discovered a huge deposit of jade in northern Alaska while working with the Eskimo Scouts in World War II. He later explained the reason for creating the lamp:

> The thought I had back of this was that this jade had been here when the world was created. It was here when the mastodons roamed this country, when the first man appeared in Alaska and in the light of the ages past we could project the dream of the future and so the constitutional jade lamp has come in to existence.[9]

Tears stained the faces of many people that day, but the emotional finale came the next morning when the delegates met to adjourn and moved to honor president William Egan with a token of their appreciation. Convention delegate Victor Fischer later described the event in these terms:

> The convention ended in a state of highly charged emotion. The closing ceremonies and the attendant private and public functions had been reinforcing delegates' feelings for one another and their appreciation of the historic significance of the work they had now completed. The moment that destroyed the last vestige of defense against emotionalism came when the delegates presented Egan with a painting of himself.

Egan was so overwhelmed by this gesture that he broke into tears. Fischer went on to add, "At that point Egan had fifty-three other delegates for company."[10]

The emotion of the scene impressed everyone there. University of Alaska president Ernest Patty watched from the back of the room and looked to see if Muktuk Marston had been moved to tears. "If Marston is crying," the president wrote, "I've seen everything." Patty located Marston in the crowd and noted, "Finally I found him, a robust man with angles to his face that look as if they had been chiseled from granite. Tears were trickling from the corners of his eyes and he was picking them off, one by one, and throwing them on the floor. They were husky tears and I wondered if they bounced."[11]

The delegates composed themselves and gave the last word to their oldest colleague, E. B. Collins of Fairbanks. In a short speech that described the beginning and hoped for the ending of territorial rule, Collins recalled his time at the first territorial legislature in 1913 and told his friends:

> We wound up our duties with the same emotional scene as I have experienced here today. In that legislature, we formed a friendship that was enduring . . . I can see here today that the association and the friendship and the existence that are here within this convention are going to bind the personalities of each and every one of you that will endure for time to come when we enjoy the statehood of Alaska.[12]

The Alaska convention then adjourned sine die, the legend forming even as the delegates filed from the hall.

The convention adjourned in February. The next step was to place the constitution before the voters for ratification in April. When that vote came, the electorate would have another proposal before them to approve or reject. The convention had endorsed an ordinance separate from the constitution called the "Alaska-Tennessee Plan." By this plan Alaska would elect two "shadow" U.S. senators and one "shadow" U.S. representative. The "shadow" delegation would take the constitution and the dreams of the statehooders to the nation's capital and demand "Statehood Now." This plan surfaced at the convention in January with the arrival of a most amazing stranger—a wholesale refrigerator dealer from New Orleans, Louisiana, named George H. Lehleitner.

The Salesman and His Plan

Anyone doubting that the statehood battles of Alaska and Hawai'i were a product of Tom Brokaw's "Greatest Generation" need have talked only briefly to navy veteran George H. Lehleitner. Talking to Lehleitner briefly, however, was virtually impossible. The Louisianan usually spoke to all comers for at least an hour and then showed color slides of the territories he insisted must become states. Anything less, he explained, would compromise the cause of democracy for which he and others fought in World War II—and for which the nation's founding fathers strove "to create a more perfect union." When this committed veteran came to Alaska in 1955–56, he brought with him a plan he had discovered in Honolulu that he insisted would secure Alaska's admission. But just who was he, and how—and why—had he journeyed from New Orleans to Honolulu to Fairbanks?[13]

Born in 1906 in a working-class section of New Orleans, Lehleitner was the son of a cistern maker who lost his job when the city outlawed cisterns as a way to control mosquitoes and combat malaria. The family's financial situation worsened, and George left school at age fourteen to earn money for the family. He worked for a music store and then, to gain door-to-door experience, sold Real Silk Hosiery in the "red light" district of New Orleans. He soon transferred from the "red light" district to the Red Seal Records division of the Victor Talking Machine Company.

Lehleitner might have remained a record manager for the rest of his life had it not been for the advent of radio. In 1930 the Radio Corporation of America (RCA) bought Victor with the intent of phasing out its record division. Lehleitner was out of a job—momentarily. He soon decided that the electric refrigerator and the radio would be the consumer items to survive the Great Depression. In 1935, with support from some of the people he had called upon in the record business, he opened his own wholesale distributorship, George H. Lehleitner & Co. The company prospered in the late 1930s. As his own business grew, Lehleitner also financed a number of small-town merchants who became the retailers for his products. As the war approached, some friends suggested that he use his sales skills as a recruiter for the armed services. When war finally broke out in 1941, Lehleitner joined the navy and eventually became the commander of the Pacific troopship *Rotanin*.

The war years had an effect on the salesman. He became concerned with the sufferings of the men under his command and the hardships their families had to endure. Lehleitner had not been born with advantages, but he concluded that furthering his own prosperity could not remain his single-minded goal. He resolved to do something for the public good once the war was over. But what would his civic duty be?

In quiet moments at sea Lehleitner was a voracious reader of books in the ship's library. He became enthralled with a book by Clarence Streit entitled *Union Now* (1939). Streit, the *New York Times* correspondent to the League of Nations from 1929 to 1939, argued that the success of democracy against Marxism depended on some form of confederation or world government between the United States and the nations of Western Europe. As the war neared an end, Lehleitner's ship was assigned to bring a contingent of POWs to Honolulu in June 1945. The ship was in harbor only twelve hours, and the young commander never set foot on soil. Nonetheless, he was intrigued by what he saw from afar and resolved that when he got out of the navy he would take his first vacation in Hawai'i. By mid-1945 a growing desire to work for the public good, an intrigue with world government, and a view of a tropical island from a troopship all merged in Lehleitner's mind. Exactly what would become of the combination still lay in the future.

By mid-1947 Lehleitner was ready to go to Hawai'i. He contacted University of Hawai'i professor Stanley Porteus, whose recently published book *Calabashes and Kings* he had enjoyed reading. Porteus responded that he would be happy to show him around. Though the elder Porteus was still ambivalent about statehood, he introduced Lehleitner to his son, Hebden, a member of the territorial legislature and a statehood supporter who would become secretary of the 1950 Hawaii Constitutional Convention. The younger Porteus then introduced Lehleitner to Samuel Wilder King, Garner Anthony, and other leading statehooders in the islands.

From these men Lehleitner learned the full implications of territorial status. Garner Anthony explained how this status had made it possible for Congress to invoke martial law in the islands during World War II. Lehleitner became incensed at the injustice the people of Hawai'i, and by extension of Alaska, endured. He wanted to do something about it, particularly in light of his war experience to free the world of colonialism and second-class citizenship. The solution, he thought, would be simple. As he told an interviewer in 1984:

> I thought because it was so obvious that it was an injustice, and the injustice was so huge, I felt that it was going to be an easy matter convincing the Congress that Hawai'i not only

deserved statehood, but if they wanted to retain credibility with other nations of the world, they better get this potential monkey off of their back, and stop treating American citizens and American taxpayers as second-class citizens.[14]

The public good, world government, America's role in the postwar world, and Hawai'i finally merged together in the salesman's mind. George Lehleitner had found his civic duty, his first public cause. He was going to persuade Congress to admit Hawai'i, and by implication Alaska too. Lehleitner assumed that if one territory gained entry, the other would quickly follow. What argument could let one in and keep the other out?

As the injustice was so obvious, Lehleitner initially thought the cause would take only a short while. He put his company under the care of a manager and set out to convince both politicians and newspapers. He began his work locally. He convinced the editor of the *New Orleans States-Item,* George Chaplin, who had served in Hawai'i during the war, to support statehood. As his business territory also included Mississippi, Lehleitner traveled to Greenville, Mississippi, to gain the support of liberal newspaper editor Hodding Carter and the *Delta Democrat-Times.* Carter was a good prospect. He had written a Pulitzer Prize-winning editorial about the 442nd Regimental Combat Team in 1945, but had shown no interest in statehood after that. Lehleitner's visit paid off. Carter wrote a 1954 article supporting statehood that appeared not just in the *Democrat-Times* but also in the *Saturday Evening Post.*

Lehleitner also went to work on the Louisiana congressional delegation. He hoped that the war experience of some members had broadened their vision of the postwar world. Many still knew little about Hawai'i—until George arrived to make his case. He gained the support of his own New Orleans congressman, Hale Boggs, whose life would later be inextricably tied to Alaska. He then headed north to Monroe, Louisiana, to talk with navy veteran Otto Passman, who was first elected to Congress in 1946. Lehleitner had another connection to Passman. He had started Passman's career as a refrigerator retailer in the 1930s. Passman later told me that he initially knew nothing about Hawai'i and Alaska. He said he was inclined to vote against statehood until persuaded to do otherwise by Lehleitner. After Senator Russell Long told Spark Matsunaga that he did not know anyone interested in Hawai'i, he received a visit from Lehleitner. In 1953 Lehleitner arranged for Long to speak to the territorial Democratic convention in Honolulu. Lehleitner made sure the senator received the same "red carpet" tour that won him to statehood a few years earlier. Long, like Passman and Boggs, joined the pro-statehood camp. The senator told me he decided to favor statehood because he saw "no angry people" in Hawai'i. When arch senatorial statehood opponent Richard Russell of Georgia saw a picture of Long bedecked with flower leis in Hawai'i, he sighed, "We've lost Russell."[15]

Lehleitner's efforts soon expanded beyond the scope of Louisiana's politicians and newspapers. After the defeat of the Hawai'i statehood bill in 1950, Lehleitner became convinced that admission to the union was not the simple task he had envisioned in 1947. Some dramatic new tactic would be necessary to gain the attention of Congress. Salesman to the core, Lehleitner saw the need for a new marketing tactic. In 1951 he thought he had found it in a research report written for the Legislative Reference Bureau by University of Hawai'i political science professor Dan Tuttle Jr. Statehood study groups in Hawai'i and Alaska had long known that in addition to calling constitutional conventions some territories had also elected a "shadow" congressional delegation before admission. In some cases territories had elected a full slate of state officers, including a new legislature. After the 1950 defeat the Hawaii Statehood Commission asked the Legislative Reference Bureau to provide a full report. Tuttle's report indicated that five territories— Tennessee, Oregon, California, Michigan, and Kansas—had used this technique with great success. Overall Tuttle found that every territory that had used what he labeled the "force action plan" had been admitted as a state within eighteen months of the "shadow" delegation's arrival in Washington.[16]

When Lehleitner read the plan in 1951, he became convinced that this was the course of action that should be used for Hawai'i. Why had it not been adopted? There was always the underlying suggestion that a multiracial "shadow" delegation from the islands would only exacerbate the racial reservations that many congressmen held about Hawai'i. But this does not appear to be the dominant reason that held Hawai'i back. As Lehleitner met with statehood leaders—both Republican and Democrat—in the early 1950s, they reiterated that the "force action" plan simply was not needed. Holding the constitutional convention was enough. Statehood was coming; there was really no need to do anything else—particularly after the election of Eisenhower and a Republican Congress in 1952. Instead of the "force action" plan, Hawai'i decided to send a petition with over 100,000 signatures, known as the Statehood Honor Roll, to Washington in 1954. The "force action plan" simply did not attract the interest of the Hawai'i statehooders, regardless of its racial implications.

After the defeat of the 1954 Hawai'i/Alaska statehood bill, Lehleitner concluded that "waiting their turn" would never bring statehood to Hawai'i. He sensed the mood of demoralization in the islands that has been noted before. To him Hawai'i seemed to be losing its will for statehood. In addition to his concern with Hawai'i's interest in statehood, Lehleitner feared that his island friends were losing the battle because they simply did not know how to influence the Congress. He attributed this to a naïveté about the workings of the national government stemming from Hawai'i's political insularity. Lehleitner believed the islanders were too gentle, too filled with the "aloha spirit" to grab the attention of Congress. Hawai'i was not "bold enough" to adopt the force action plan. What about Alaska?

Mr. Lehleitner Goes to Fairbanks

While promoting Hawai'i in the nation's capital, Lehleitner had become aware of Alaska, but only as the "other" territory that would follow Hawai'i's lead into the union. Hawai'i was, after all, the more politically and economically mature territory. By late 1954 Alaska's people, rather than its status, attracted him more and more. He was impressed with Alaska's Bob Bartlett. The "little men" of Operation Statehood, who arrived in 1954 to support the joint statehood bill, arrested his attention. When John Butrovich and Walter Hickel effectively confronted—and angered—President Eisenhower with their demands, Lehleitner mused that these were the people who possessed the "boldness" of spirit that he thought Hawai'i lacked. When he heard in the spring of 1955 that Alaska planned to hold a constitutional convention, he wondered if he could "sell" them on the "force action" plan. To find out he first headed for the Washington office of Bob Bartlett.

Like statehood supporters in Hawai'i, Bartlett, too, was skeptical about the plan. But he was not skeptical about Lehleitner and agreed to give him an introduction to statehood leaders in Alaska. He wrote Bob Atwood that he was not completely persuaded by the plan. "However that may be," he explained, "we owe George Lehleitner a

most attentive hearing because no one in the States—not one single
individual anywhere—has sought to make the contribution to statehood that he has."[17]

Lehleitner was ready to go to Alaska in August 1955. In the tradition of the invading veterans, he decided to drive the Alaska Highway.
He timed his departure to arrive just after the election of delegates to
the constitutional convention. Lehleitner intended to win their support
along with the endorsement of the territory's newspapers.

The plan did not come as news to the delegates. As in Hawai'i, it
had been known to statehood supporters for some time. Operation
Statehood had even discussed it in 1954. But as delegate after delegate
told me, no one paid much attention to the plan until Lehleitner came
to "sell" it. At first the new delegates were cautious. Tom Stewart noted
that initially opinion was divided on the plan, with some fearing that
Congress might take offense at such boldness.

If the delegates were still cautious, Lehleitner won a total convert in
News-Miner publisher C. W. Snedden. At first Snedden was curious about
Lehleitner and even sent a query to press contacts in New Orleans "to
ascertain what kind of axe you [Lehleitner] were going to grind up
here." Even before he received a reply, Snedden became convinced of
Lehleitner's sincerity. Furthermore he decided that the *News-Miner*
would devote constant coverage to the upcoming constitutional convention. The Fairbanks publisher and the New Orleans wholesaler energized each other and became steadfast friends.[18]

Despite their reservations, the delegates agreed that they would discuss the plan at the convention. Lehleitner had now relabeled it "The
Tennessee Plan" after the first state to adopt it. Back in New Orleans,
he continued to correspond with some of the delegates and said he
would be glad to return and address the convention. Shortly before the
Christmas recess the ordinance committee decided to present the plan
to the full body in January. If adopted, it would not be a part of the
constitution but would be an ordinance recommended by the convention and placed before the people for a vote along with ratification of
the constitution. The committee extended an invitation to Lehleitner
to join them in January.

Long before the invitation arrived, Lehleitner had prepared an
extensive presentation for the delegates. He had commissioned additional research from the Library of Congress that uncovered even more
territories that had elected "shadow" congressmen. Had the appearance

of these pseudo-Senators "offended" anyone? The congressional researcher, Dr. William Tansill, reported, "At no time was such action considered revolutionary or even excessively audacious. In some quarters it was regarded as clever or unseemly or not quite cricket, but no one apparently became unduly exercised."[19]

As evidence of how the existing Congress would react, Lehleitner tested his plan on some members of Congress and elicited positive comments from Paul Douglas of Illinois and Clair Engle of California. Only Senator Clinton Anderson of New Mexico responded negatively. He claimed that New Mexico had dispatched a "shadow" delegation in 1850 that did not secure statehood. Lehleitner commissioned yet more research and explained that New Mexico's delegation had been too slow. It had arrived in Washington after the Compromise of 1850 relegated New Mexico to territorial status. California's "shadow" delegation had arrived quickly and did secure statehood. It was clear to Lehleitner that the bold must also be swift.[20]

By the time Lehleitner arrived in mid-January, the delegates themselves had become more enthusiastic about statehood and their ability to secure it. They were less shy about their boldness than in September. Bartlett wired the delegates that though he was still ambivalent about the plan, some forceful action would be needed to push the Congress. The delegates took this as an endorsement to pursue their own prerogative. In preliminary meetings Lehleitner and the delegates fueled each other's energy. On January 23, 1956, Lehleitner addressed the full convention. Short of stature and dressed with his signature bowtie, Lehleitner was not physically imposing. But few could resist him. He told the delegates that writing a constitution was not enough. Just look at what had happened to Hawai'i. Alaska must take bold action. He read letters from a host of congressmen affirming the plan. Alaska's long-time friend Dick Neuberger of Oregon, elected to the U.S. Senate in 1954, affirmed that Oregon had used the plan. Alaska should do the same.

Once Lehleitner spoke, the delegates took the lead. Only a few months before they were not sure they could draft a constitution. They had done it. Now they wanted statehood. The Tennessee Plan was the way to go. Some discussion followed. Many of the delegates now likened the "pseudo-Senators" to missionaries who would convert the Congress. Before the final vote they changed the name to the "Alaska-Tennessee Plan." The new plan passed by a 47–5 vote with three abstentions. After

the vote the oratory continued to flourish. Some said that the plan suggested the biblical boldness of Paul of Tarsus; others pointed to Patrick
Henry of Virginia. Delegate Steve McCutcheon proposed that the bold
Alaska should no longer follow the timid Hawai'i. Alaska, not Hawai'i,
should now become the forty-ninth state.

The delegates had adopted the Alaska-Tennessee Plan. Would the
people of Alaska adopt it too? The prospect of the April referendum
now consumed the thoughts of the delegates and the salesman from
New Orleans.

Ratification, Election, and a Symbolic Ride to Washington

April 23, 1956, was the date set for the vote on ratification of the constitution and on the Alaska-Tennessee Plan. In addition the convention
devised another ordinance for the voters to ponder—an ordinance that
would automatically prohibit fish traps once the new constitution
became effective—that is, once Alaska was admitted to the union. The
logic behind the fish trap ordinance was interesting.

As we have noted many times, trapped salmon was *the* emotional issue
in the postwar territory. Though the "outside" or "Seattle" interests were
not present at the convention, the "inside" or "resident" fishing interests
were definitely there. Of course, the inside delegates from southeastern
Alaska did not consider themselves interests. They saw themselves as representing the will of the people. They had secured constitutional protection for the open fishery and wanted some action on fish traps.
Protecting the open fishery was within the scope of a "model" constitution as it limited the scope of legislative action. But an act prohibiting
fish traps was clearly legislative in nature as it regulated the fishery. How
could the delegates satisfy the demands of the resident fishing interest
and protect their model constitution? Their answer was to create a separate ordinance approved by the convention that would hand the issue
to the voters—in effect, this action created the first popular "initiative."

The constitution writers had another motive in mind with the fish
trap ordinance. Despite the growing enthusiasm among the delegates
for the constitution and the Alaska-Tennessee Plan, there was always the
fear that the population at large was not as enthusiastic. Such doubts had
lingered since the modest 3–2 statehood referendum a decade earlier.
There was no real fear that the constitution would be defeated. But there
was concern about the Alaska-Tennessee Plan and about the overall

voter turnout. A low turnout—even if positive—would send the wrong message to Washington. The statehooders were always concerned with how Washington would see them.

The delegates knew that there was one issue that always brought out the voters—the fishery. We have already noted the 8–1 majority for the 1948 referendum on fish traps. In 1952 the voters had turned out with equal enthusiasm to pass an ordinance that would transfer management of the fishery from the federal government to the territorial government. The margin of victory was 7–1 with a turnout of twenty-four thousand voters. The delegates hoped that the fish trap ordinance would bring out the voters with a positive vote to abolish fish traps, ratify the constitution, and approve the Alaska-Tennessee Plan.

As the April election drew near, statehood supporters, including Operation Statehood and George Lehleitner, became worried that an insufficient effort was being made to publicize the election and generate voter enthusiasm. Lehleitner was particularly annoyed that Statehood Committee chair Bob Atwood had decided to take a trip to Europe. Fortunately there was not a long time to worry. The April election came and the voters turned out at the same twenty-five-thousand level as in years past.

All three ballot issues were approved. The constitution was ratified by a vote of 17,447 to 8,180 (2–1). As expected the Alaska-Tennessee Plan trailed the constitution. Not only was the plan a novel idea, it was considered a proxy for immediate statehood as opposed to eventual statehood at some unspecified time in the future. Nonetheless it was approved by a vote of 15,011 to 9,556 (3–2). Though the territory-wide vote was positive, the Alaska-Tennessee Plan was defeated in the southeastern judicial division where the "Seattle" interests were considered to be the strongest. True to all predictions, the fish trap ordinance led the pack with a positive vote of 21,285 to 4,004 (5–1). One wonders how a person could vote for the fish trap ordinance but against the ratification of the constitution that was necessary to effect the end of fish traps. Few people pondered this seeming contradiction of logic. The fish trap ordinance had served its function. It brought out the voters and sent the enthusiastic message to Washington that the statehooders had hoped for.

Before leaving the April vote, we should briefly note the size of the turnout. Statehooders were happy with the turnout of twenty-five thousand voters. This was roughly the same size as the turnout in 1948 and

1952. However, the overall population of the territory had grown from 120,000 in 1948 to 196,000 in 1952 to 220,000 in 1956. This growth was, of course, the result of the advent of military Alaska. Few military personnel registered as Alaska voters. This may explain why the military population was seemingly "invisible," and why the statehooders did not focus on them. The size of the voter turnout in 1956 should be kept in mind when analyzing the vote in 1958 after Congress passed the Alaska statehood bill. Though the overall population of the territory actually declined to 213,000 in 1958, the electorate would double to 48,000. But that event still lay in the future. After the April 1956 vote, the next pressing issue was the election of the Alaska-Tennessee Plan delegation.

That election was scheduled for October 9. The ordinance specified that the nominees for each party would be chosen by party conventions rather than through an open primary. Ernest Gruening announced that he wanted to run for the Senate, and the Democrats agreed to nominate him. Gruening had long admired, even idolized, the Senate and dreamed of becoming a member. There had always been one problem to his quest. What electorate would ever put him there? In 1956, at age sixty-nine, Gruening decided to stand for a vote of the people. Gruening had both inspired and annoyed many Alaskans. There was reason for this irritation. He could at times be insufferable. His books often read like a long exercise in name-dropping. Sometimes it seemed as if Gruening, by his own admission, knew everybody and everything. Even Bob Bartlett was at times annoyed by the man who had coaxed him as reluctant candidate for delegate in 1944. Bartlett mused to Bill Egan about the former governor: "It will be interesting enough in October to have answered at long last the question that has been asked so many thousands of times in Alaska: What is Ernest Gruening's actual strength with the people?"[21]

If Bartlett mused about Gruening, others mused about Bartlett. Many statehooders, particularly Bill Snedden and George Lehleitner, wanted Bartlett to run for the Alaska-Tennessee Plan senator seat while continuing to be delegate. The logic was clear. The Alaska-Tennessee Plan was supposed to send yet another message to Washington as to whom the territory would send as a permanent delegation after statehood. Many statehooders wanted Bartlett to be a part of the message. Bartlett demurred. He claimed he could not do both jobs. He may have also contemplated the anomaly of being all at once both a real and a "pseudo" member of Congress, or a member of the House and Senate at the same time. Regardless, he refused to be nominated. The Democrats chose Bill Egan as the other senatorial nominee. For the representative seat they chose Ralph Rivers, a convention delegate from Fairbanks who had been territorial attorney general.

To oppose the Democratic slate, the Republicans chose John Butrovich against Gruening and Bob Atwood against Egan. Little-known Charles Burdick opposed Rivers. Butrovich, the veteran legislator and statehooder who had angered Eisenhower in 1954, was the Republicans' strongest candidate, and the one most likely to win over Gruening. Atwood was an ardent statehooder but had never run for office. He had, in fact, accepted the nomination reluctantly.

When the votes were counted in October, the Democrats swept the slate and brought out an even bigger electorate than in April. Egan and Rivers won decisively. Gruening narrowly defeated Butrovich by a vote of 14,169 to 13,303. The former governor even admitted that if Butrovich had not run for both the Alaska-Tennessee Plan and the territorial senate, he would probably have won the Alaska-Tennessee Plan seat. Gruening's victory deserves a note of comment. Bartlett had wondered if Gruening actually had the support of the people. The voters responded that he did. Gruening could be annoying. He may well have been enchanted with the sound of his own voice and the workings of his own mind. But he had used that voice and mind to advance the people of Alaska—natives and settlers alike. At an age when many would have opted for the ease of retirement, Gruening was willing to put his ego on the line. The voters affirmed that a muckraking journalist turned New Dealer from New York could be an elected representative of the last frontier. It was an interesting message that the people of Alaska sent to Washington.

With the election decided, the statehooders (particularly George Lehleitner) were elated. There was no time to rest. The Alaska-Tennessee Plan delegation could not just slip into Washington. Their arrival must be the end point of an epic journey from the last frontier to the nation's capital. Nothing could be left to chance. Bells, whistles, ceremonies, and above all newspaper and magazine coverage must mark the journey. If the constitutional convention exuded symbolism, Lehleitner would ensure that the epic journey to Washington flowed with, even hemorrhaged, symbolism. It would be all that mid-twentieth-century marketing and public relations could make it.

Lehleitner had been planning the symbolic journey ever since the favorable Alaska-Tennessee Plan vote in April. When *Life Magazine* editorialized favorably about the plan in May, Lehleitner wrote the editor asking that he anticipate coverage of the delegation's January arrival in Washington. He insisted to the Statehood Committee that a talented public relations man be hired. John Adams, a former CBS White House correspondent, was selected for the job and was ready by October to begin work on the epic trip to the capital.

The publicity team proposed an automobile and airplane journey from Fairbanks to Washington via the capitals of the states that had previously used the Tennessee Plan. The day for departure, December 10, finally arrived. Two late-model sedans, painted white and emblazoned with a blue and gold flag, were poised at the steps of the University of Alaska building where the delegates had written their constitution a year before. The cars would carry two Alaska-Tennessee Plan delegation couples—Bill and Neva Egan, and Ralph and Martha Rivers—to Washington. Gruening preferred airplanes to motorcades and would join the two frontier wagons at various points along the route.

The travelers were given a rousing send-off in Fairbanks; their cars were packed with mementos from home. Like thousands of pioneer ladies before her, Neva Egan carried with her those household items she cherished the most. So inside the white Mercury she packed the new oil painting of her husband that had brought the constitutional convention to tears a few months before. Bill and Neva had made another symbolic act like earlier pioneers. They had decided to sell the grocery store they had run for years in Valdez. Neva told Bill she could not run the store by herself if he went to Washington. Egan wrote Bob Bartlett and told him that he was a bit scared at the thought of selling the store. Would there be a future for him after the Alaska-Tennessee Plan? Bartlett wrote and assured his friend with these words that there would certainly be a future for him:

> If you were to sell or otherwise dispose of your business and come on down here as a Tennessee Planner, there would [be] something for you in government from that time on even if the Tennessee Plan were not to go over with a rush. And the big chance always is there, namely, that the Plan will succeed at an early date. If that were the case then you would be a real, honest-to-goodness member of the first delegation to the Congress from the State of Alaska. What a wonderful honor that would be![22]

Egan took his friend's advice and sold the store. With their cars packed the Egans and the Rivers headed down the Alaska Highway. Shortly after their departure near-disaster struck when Egan's car stalled near the Alaska/Canada border at Tok. A loose battery cable was the culprit, and in minus-60-degree weather the battery froze. The party drove ahead in the Rivers's car to the nearest garage, where it took several hours for the mechanic to warm up his tow truck. By the time the rescue group arrived back at the disabled vehicle, the grease in the Mercury's differential had frozen The car had to be towed with its back end in the air! Finally the battery and the differential thawed. With secure cables the group continued down the Alaska Highway to Seattle, where they were to meet Ernest Gruening and appear at a luncheon of the Seattle Chamber of Commerce on December 17. They missed the luncheon but soon joined forces with Gruening and headed for Portland, Oregon, where the newspapers covered the progress and mishaps of the caravan. After their Oregon appearance, the delegation split up. Rivers traveled to Sacramento to touch base with yet another state whose precedent the Alaskans were following.

After spending Christmas at different locations with various relatives and friends, the three Alaska-Tennessee Plan congressmen regrouped in Nashville, Tennessee, on December 28. This was to be their most triumphal and carefully orchestrated reception. Governor Frank Clements greeted them with a reception at the state capitol where a cake in the shape of Alaska was served. After dinner at the governor's mansion, the travelers spent the night at the Andrew Jackson Hotel, hoping to capitalize on the symbolism of Tennessee's first elected representative. The *Nashville Banner* ran an editorial endorsing statehood for Alaska.[23]

On December 29 the two white cars left Nashville for Washington, D.C. Gruening headed for the capital on his own. Their journey was halted one last time by a snowstorm, the first of the trip, at Marion, Virginia, in the Blue Ridge Mountains. When the storm finally abated, the Alaskans made their way into the capital on the evening of December 30. The next day, New Year's Eve 1956, they drove to Capitol Hill. The odometer on their cars read 6,647—about as far as you could drive on a one-way trip across North America. They were greeted at the House Office Building by Bob Bartlett and the peripatetic Gruening. There they were, the Alaska-Tennessee Plan delegation—Bill

Egan, the small town merchant; Ralph Rivers, the frontier lawyer; and Ernest Gruening, the New York journalist with a Harvard medical degree, turned New Dealer turned territorial governor. Each man was different, but they now had one thing in common: they were congressmen from a state that didn't exist.

The epic journey was over. It had all been thrilling, emotional, and symbolic. But as the three men stood there on New Year's Eve, one thought went through their minds. Would it make any difference at all to the Congress of the United States? Was there any reason to think that the Eighty-fifth Congress would be any different from the previous five Congresses since 1947? The year 1957 would begin the next day; the Eighty-fifth Congress would soon convene. They would just have to wait and see.

Hawai'i and Alaska after World War II

25. *After World War II the International Longshoremen's and Warehousemen's Union (ILWU) organized both dockworkers and plantation workers as its membership rapidly rose from 900 in 1944 to 33,000 by 1946. Courtesy of ILWU.*

26. *Hawai'i was confident that it would become the 49th state soon after the end of World War II. Territorial Delegate Joseph Farrington poses in this photo with Pualani Avon for the "world premiere" in Washington, D.C. of a film advertising this hope, "The 49th state, Hawaii." Courtesy of the Hawai'i State Archives.*

27. *The 49th State theme was clearly evident at the 1950 Constitutional Convention held in Honolulu to hasten action on the Hawai'i statehood bill that was up for a vote in the Senate. The convention was held in the Honolulu Armory near `Iolani Palace. Flowers and leis were used extensively to express the "island spirit." Courtesy of the Hawai'i State Archives.*

28. *In both Hawai'i and Alaska the advent of regular and affordable air travel in the late 1940s and early 1950s encouraged "statehood delegations" to fly to Washington, D.C. and lobby for admission. In this 1954 photo a delegation from the Hawai'i territorial legislature prepares to take a petition signed by 116,000 citizens, known as the Statehood Honor Roll, to the nation's capital. Courtesy of the Hawai'i State Archives.*

29. *A Hawai'i statehood bill passed the U.S. House of Representatives in 1953, but was combined with an Alaska statehood bill in the Senate in 1954. This cartoon caricatures the combined bill that was then returned to the House for approval. The House refused to accept the combined bill. Courtesy of E. L. Bartlett Collection, Alaska and Polar Regions Department, Rasmuson Library, University of Alaska Fairbanks.*

30. *John A. Burns helped reorganize the Hawaii Democratic Party after World War II. In 1956 he was elected territorial delegate to Congress. Courtesy of Tom Coffman.*

31. *A drive to raise Congressional support for a memorial to those who died on the U.S.S. Arizona during the Pearl Harbor bombing gave John Burns a reason to call on every member of Congress during his first term. Completed in 1962, the U.S.S. Arizona Memorial is located at Pearl Harbor in Honolulu directly over the sunken hull of the battleship it commemorates. Photo by John S. Whitehead.*

32. *After World War II Anchorage, Alaska grew in population as a military headquarters for the Cold War. Young contractor, Walter J. Hickel, was a leader in that boom and a rising force for statehood in the local Republican Party. In 1951 Hickel, pictured on the left with his arm extended, invited U.S. Senator Herman Welker of Idaho, on the right, to speak at the party's Lincoln Day Dinner. After visiting the territory Welker pledged his support for statehood. In this photo Hickel clearly felt comfortable in standard business attire while the visitor from Idaho prepared for extreme Arctic conditions! Hickel would later become a governor of Alaska and U.S. Secretary of the Interior. Courtesy of the Walter J. Hickel Collection.*

Eisenhower and Alaska

Alaska's chances for statehood after World War II depended heavily on the support and opinion of President Dwight Eisenhower, who was reluctant to give his support in his first term. There are several theories about the nature of this reluctance. Some say that a 1947 visit to the territory convinced Eisenhower that Alaska could never support a state government. Others say that his concerns were partisan.

33. During his 1947 visit to Alaska General Eisenhower met a wide variety of people. In this photo Eisenhower is pictured in Nome with the native chief of King Island, Alaska. On the left is the head of the U.S. Army War College, General Grunther, and on the right is the local base commander in Nome, Col. Bodie. Photo courtesy of the Lomen Family Collection, acc# 72-71-2010, Alaska and Polar Regions Department, Rasmuson Library, University of Alaska Fairbanks.

34. In August 1947 Eisenhower also visited the University of Alaska Museum in Fairbanks, where university president Charles Bunnell showed him native artifacts. Courtesy of VF, Individuals, Eisenhower, acc# 58-1026-455, Alaska and Polar Regions Department, Rasmuson Library, University of Alaska Fairbanks.

35. Eisenhower's partisan concerns are depicted in this 1956 cartoon that shows the Republican Eisenhower wincing at the strength of the Demcratic Party in Alaska. Courtesy of the E.L. Bartlett Collection, Alaska and Polar Regions Department, Rasmuson Library, University of Alaska Fairbanks.

During his second term Eisenhower came to support statehood for Alaska as a result of the influence of his Secretary of the Interior, Fred Seaton, and Seaton's assistant Ted Stevens, then a World War II veteran and young attorney from Fairbanks.

36. After the statehood bill passed and was signed by Eisenhower, a grateful Fairbanks Chamber of Commerce awarded an honorary life membership to Secretary of the Interior Seaton. This December 1958 photo shows Seaton (right) receiving the award from Ted Stevens (left) and Mrs. Douglas Smith (center), secretary to Bob Bartlett. Courtesy of Senator Ted Stevens.

37. *Ted Stevens and Eisenhower remained friends in the years after statehood. In this 1962 photo Stevens confers with Eisenhower at his Gettysburg, PA farm. Eisenhower, who died in March 1969, lived to see Stevens appointed to the U.S. Senate in December 1968 to replace Bob Bartlett. Courtesy of Senator Ted Stevens.*

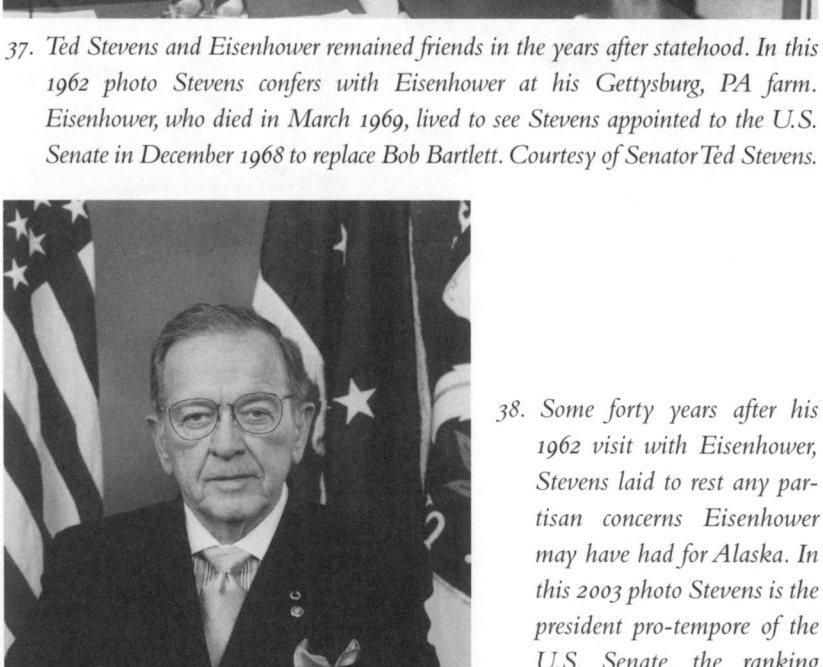

38. *Some forty years after his 1962 visit with Eisenhower, Stevens laid to rest any partisan concerns Eisenhower may have had for Alaska. In this 2003 photo Stevens is the president pro-tempore of the U.S. Senate, the ranking Republican in that body. Courtesy of Senator Ted Stevens.*

Part IV

The Needle and the Thread: Alaska and Hawai'i Complete the Union, 1957–1959

For the first decade of the Cold War, the two territories had undergone enormous changes. In the process they had hoped to join the union of states. But appeal after appeal and bill after bill had failed to move the Congress of the United States. However, in that frustrating decade of congressional inaction the two had become more and more entwined with each other. Hawai'i held a constitutional convention; five years later Alaska did the same. The bills were voted on separately and then the statehood bills were joined. It seemed as if only a miracle might ever bring the two into the union.

Then in rapid succession the Eighty-fifth and Eighty-sixth Congresses admitted Alaska and Hawai'i, respectively, in 1958 and 1959. The two were officially proclaimed states in 1959. In the process, however, the territories were turned upside down. Hawai'i had always assumed it would be the forty-ninth state and Alaska the fiftieth. By the time the two Congresses completed their work, it was the other way around—Alaska was the forty-ninth and the Hawai'i the fiftieth. When asked how this all happened, Representative Leo O'Brien, who was the floor manager for both bills in the House, explained, "Hawaii was the thread, but Alaska was the needle."

Chapter 9

"We're In": Alaska Takes the Lead as the Forty-ninth State, 1957–1959

Statehood came about in my judgment because of a unique
role of using the national news media to lobby Congress.
—*Ted Stevens, reflecting on the passage of the
1958 Alaska Statehood Bill, 1987*

The magic of the symbolic journey lasted a few more weeks for
the Alaska-Tennessee Plan delegation. On January 14, 1957, the
delegation was received in the Senate. A memorial from the constitutional convention requested that Congress seat the delegation and
accept them as members. No one expected this to happen, and it did
not. For their Senate debut they were placed in the diplomatic gallery.
Senator Spessard Holland of Florida rose to greet the delegation and
announced his own support for Alaska statehood. He asked the
Alaskans to rise in the gallery and led a round of applause from the
floor. Several other senators seconded Holland's support. The delegation was applauded, but they were not seated. Henceforth their role
would be to contact members of Congress and lobby for statehood.
They were not registered lobbyists, and they were not members of
Congress. To some extent they were sui generis—phantom congressmen from the last frontier. Soon in the session another aspect of their
status was established. Republican congressmen, as well as some
Democratic supporters of Bob Bartlett, wanted assurance that the all-
Democratic group would not be the permanent congressional delegation from Alaska. Agreement was quickly reached that after statehood
a new election would be held for the first official, rather than pseudo,
delegation from Alaska.

The Alaska-Tennessee Planners had been greeted and applauded in
the gallery. But applause from the floor was not the same as a favorable

vote from the floor. Was there any particular reason for hope with this new Congress?

The Eighty-fifth Congress and Alaska First

On the surface of things the Eighty-fifth Congress was not dramatically different from the previous Congresses that had managed to thwart, recommit, or otherwise defeat statehood. Like the Eighty-fourth Congress that had stymied statehood, the Eighty-fifth Congress had a narrow Democratic majority in the Senate (49–47) and a slightly larger Democratic majority in the House (232–199). No winds of party change gave Alaska grounds for hope. Some of statehood's oldest foes and obstructionists were gone. Senator Hugh Butler of Nebraska had died shortly after Joseph Farrington in 1954. But diehards such as Howard Smith, chairman of the House Rules Committee and author of the anti-Communist Smith Act, were as girded for battle and obstruction as ever. The southern opposition was still strong, but some important defections had occurred. We have already noted Lehleitner's efforts to win over Russell Long of Louisiana. Spessard Holland of Florida, who greeted the delegation, was also now an enthusiastic supporter.

Holland's strong support is worthy of comment. Holland had been the wartime governor of Florida and first entered the U.S. Senate in 1946. He had shown an early interest in Hawai'i statehood. Ernest Bartley, the University of Florida political scientist who had been a consultant to the Alaska constitutional convention, stoked his interest in Alaska after returning from the constitutional convention. Holland's support for Alaska, however, did not sway his Florida colleague George Smathers, who remained an opponent to the end. As we have noted before, support for statehood was so often a matter of individual choice, often based on advice from a good friend.[1]

The prospects for Alaska, as well as for Hawai'i, also hinged on the attitudes of two other Southerners in early 1957. The Eighty-fifth Congress was controlled by Speaker of the House Sam Rayburn and Senate Majority Leader Lyndon Johnson. Both Texans had been opponents of statehood in previous Congresses, though there were now indications that both Rayburn and Johnson were willing to let an Alaska bill come to the floor. Neither initially offered firm support, but they seemed willing to let the fate of statehood be decided by a vote on the floor rather than by a tactic to keep either house from voting.

To prepare those bills for the floor, statehood supporters for both Alaska and Hawai'i, including Bob Bartlett and newly elected Hawai'i delegate John Burns, met before the new Congress convened to devise a strategy. They viewed the Eighty-fifth Congress as one likely to behave like previous Congresses. They wanted to prevent any move to combine the statehood bills, as this combination had so often led to recommittal or defeat in the past. A decision was made to keep the two bills separate. A second statehood bill, either Alaska or Hawai'i, would not be debated or voted upon in Congress until both houses had passed the first statehood bill. The strategists also decided that both the Alaska and Hawai'i bills would be admission, rather than enabling, bills. Enabling bills authorized a territory to hold a constitutional convention and then apply for statehood. Both Alaska and Hawai'i had done such. So the enabling stage could now be skipped, unless Congress objected to the constitutions—which it did not. Also, admission bills could be considered "privileged" legislation that could bypass the House Rules Committee under certain conditions. With the decision made to introduce separate admission bills, the obvious next question was: Which should go first?[2]

Even before the close of the Alaska Constitutional Convention in early 1956, some Alaskans had proclaimed that the northern territory should become the forty-ninth, not the fiftieth, state. George Lehleitner's support for an "Alaska First" strategy formed in the spring and summer of 1956. Dan Tuttle Jr. of Hawai'i, the author of the first Tennessee Plan research, noted that he met with Burns, Bartlett, Lehleitner, and Bill Egan at the 1956 Democratic Convention in August. Lehleitner told Tuttle then that his primary support and effort were now behind Alaska. Hawai'i would have to follow the northern territory into the union.[3]

The congressional statehood strategists who decided on the separate admission bills gave indications that Alaska might go first in their November and December deliberations. But a firm decision may have come as late as February 1957, when the House finally announced that the Alaska bill would be scheduled first for committee action. It was in February that delegate Burns endorsed the Alaska First strategy.[4]

Alaska's ability to move ahead of Hawai'i occurred for a number of reasons. The momentum generated by the Alaska-Tennessee Plan strategy was certainly a factor. But there were other considerations. In Hawai'i the "Red Scare" just would not go away. Even as the congressional statehood strategists met in Washington during November and

December 1956, Senator James Eastland, chairman of the Senate sub-committee on internal security, held hearings in Honolulu and con-cluded that Communist conspirators still "exercise an influence on the political life of the Islands that is significant." The fear of continued Communist influence in the islands was reiterated to the Eastland com-mittee by representatives of IMUA (a Hawaiian word meaning *forward*) or the Hawaii Residents' Association, a local conservative group that had long been sounding the anti-Communist alarm. Adding further fuel to the fire was the fact that the conviction of the Hawaii Seven under the Smith Act was still under appeal. Earlier in the year Governor King had echoed the concerns of HUAC chair Francis Walter that a "con-victed Communist" was still head of Hawai'i's largest union.[5]

There was also a new relation between the territories' congressional delegates. Bob Bartlett had always assured the Farringtons and Samuel Wilder King that Hawai'i could go first. With the election of Burns, Bartlett was no longer under any prior commitment to the Farringtons. Bartlett was now the senior delegate with twelve years of congressional service. Burns was new to the Congress, and Bartlett owed him no favors.

Exactly who first pushed Alaska First is unclear. Supporters of John Burns would later say that the new delegate devised the Alaska First strat-egy as the most politically "savvy" way to gain admission for both terri-tories and suggested it to Bartlett. But there appears to be no contemporary evidence in either the Hawai'i newspapers or elsewhere to confirm this assertion. Whether the newly arrived Burns influenced the decision or merely acquiesced to the veteran Bartlett and other Democrats is unclear. What is important is that both delegates agreed to the Alaska First strategy and held to it for the duration of the Eighty-fifth Congress.[6]

While congressional statehood supporters planned the Alaska First strategy, a fortuitous change of personnel in the Executive Branch brought the recalcitrant President Eisenhower to a more favorable atti-tude toward Alaska.

The President and the Secretary

A strange quirk in the politics of the state of Oregon may well have propelled Alaska into the Union. In the summer of 1956 Senator Wayne Morse, formerly a Republican, decided to run for reelection as a Democrat. To win the seat back for the Republicans, the White House dispatched Secretary of the Interior Douglas McKay, who had been governor of Oregon, to run against Morse. With McKay's resignation, Eisenhower appointed Fred Seaton to the Interior Department position in June. Seaton had been the "appointed senator" who spoke in favor of Alaska statehood in 1952. Since that time he had become a member of the Eisenhower administration, serving as assistant secretary of defense and administrative assistant to the president.

At his confirmation hearing he was asked if he still supported Alaska statehood. He answered in the affirmative. As things turned out, Seaton did not merely support Alaska, he became one of the leading apostles of Alaska statehood. He took on a mission to convert the Republican Party and Eisenhower to the cause of Alaska. Said Eisenhower staffer and biographer William Bragg Ewald, "If Dwight Eisenhower had followed his own inclinations instead of Interior Secretary Fred Seaton's, Alaska would never have become a state while Eisenhower occupied the White House." In looking to the importance of one man in the statehood battle, we may well say that Fred Seaton's role in promoting Alaska and Hawai'i was comparable to that of Hugh Butler's in obstructing the two. What did Seaton do?[7]

The two problems Seaton faced in June 1956 were Eisenhower's concerns over strategic military locations in Alaska and the Republican Party's position on statehood at the upcoming 1956 national convention. The latter was the more pressing, as party support for Alaska was necessary if there was to be hope in the Eighty-fifth Congress. Seaton went to San Francisco for the convention in August and finally secured the party's support for Alaska with a plank pledging "immediate statehood for Alaska, recognizing the fact that an adequate provision for defense requirements must be made." Seaton gradually persuaded Eisenhower to go along with the party platform. In January 1957 Eisenhower told Congress in his Budget Message that he favored statehood for Alaska "subject to area limitations and other safeguards for the conduct of defense activities so vitally necessary to our national security."[8]

In early 1957 Seaton resolved the problem of defense requirements to Eisenhower's satisfaction. The sensitive military areas in northern and western Alaska had earlier been designated with a boundary drawn by Secretary McKay known as the McKay Line, or the Yukon-Porcupine River Line (See map 3). In 1954 proposals were made to "partition" or permanently exclude those lands from the new state. Bartlett and other Alaskans had adamantly opposed any partition. In 1955 the idea was raised that the lands would not be partitioned, but would be included in the new state subject to withdrawal in case of a defense emergency. No final solution to the partition/withdrawal issue was reached in 1955 prior to the recommittal of the Alaska/Hawai'i statehood bill. In March 1957 Seaton revived the "withdrawal idea" and incorporated it into the statehood bill under discussion in the House subcommittee on territories. If withdrawn, the lands would fall under federal legislative, executive, and judicial sovereignty, though municipalities and school districts would still operate under Alaska law. Eisenhower seemed happy with this defense solution, though he continued to doubt the economic viability of Alaska as a permanent state. Nonetheless, he deferred to Seaton's advice to support statehood for Alaska.[9]

No withdrawals have ever been made based on the McKay Line. As a result, statehooders, particularly Ernest Gruening, have belittled Eisenhower's insistence on "withdrawal." Gruening claimed there was no need for such a provision in the statehood act as the president had the power to do this in any state—though he did not say exactly how this would be done. Clearly it would be easier to make the withdrawal if it were specified in the statehood bill. Eisenhower may well have known more than he admitted. The lands designated by the McKay Line were those on which the "top-secret" DEW Line installations were being constructed. Bob Atwood claims that there were also "top-secret" plans to build silos for Minuteman missiles in the area. There may well have been several as yet unrevealed Cold War strategies in Alaska that caused Eisenhower to see the Alaska lands as more important than those in any other state.[10]

Regardless of any secret military plans for Alaska in the mid-1950s, the president's emphasis on withdrawal is important to our understanding of the potential new state. Eisenhower, almost alone, seemed to recognize and enunciate the fact that territorial Alaska was a "military territory." Take away the military and there was little else there. As noted before, "military Alaska" was in many ways invisible to the statehooders. Their concern was with the fishery and the development of Alaska's natural resources as a base for future population growth. Eisenhower recognized that what was *in* Alaska (that is, its natural resources) was not nearly as important as *where* Alaska was (that is, its strategic location). In 1957 that "where" was the closest location to the Soviet Union in the United States.

Seaton's influence on the president was only part of the role he played in rallying support for statehood. The sudden emergence of a pro-statehood Republican in the inner sanctums of the Eisenhower administration energized Alaska Republicans, who had been left out in the Alaska-Tennessee Plan delegation. Now they had a locus for their efforts. Soon after Seaton's appointment, Fairbanks publisher C. W. Snedden established a cordial relationship with the secretary. With Seaton as a supporter, Snedden decided to move to Washington and work with the secretary on the statehood cause. In addition to his own support, Snedden urged Seaton to include a former U.S. attorney in Fairbanks, Ted Stevens, as his legislative counsel in gaining support for the statehood bill on Capitol Hill. This inclusion was easy to do as Stevens had recently accepted a job with the Interior Department under Secretary McKay.

Like so many other young statehooders, Stevens was one of the "invading veterans" who came to Alaska after World War II. Born in Indiana in 1923, Stevens had served with the Army Air Corps in China from 1943 to 1946. He completed his college education at the University of California, Los Angeles, in 1947, and continued on to Harvard Law School. Finishing Harvard in 1950, he then worked for a law firm in Washington, D.C. He had always "dreamed of coming to Alaska" and in 1953 secured a job with a law firm in Fairbanks before becoming U.S. attorney later that year.

Seaton, Snedden, and Stevens (who would become an U.S. senator a decade after statehood) worked well together. In effect they became a "shadow" Republican Alaska-Tennessee Plan delegation and concentrated on Republican legislators. So emphatic for statehood did the group become that William Ewald notes, "On this cause Fred was a zealot, Ted was a fanatic. Without them, Alaskan—and Hawaiian—statehood would not have happened."[11]

While gathering support for statehood energetically in Washington, Seaton had to act somewhat cautiously in the territory itself. By early 1957 the Eisenhower administration concluded that the territorial governors of both Alaska and Hawai'i, Frank Heintzleman and Samuel Wilder King, were not advancing the Republicans' cause in either place. The Interior Department decided to replace both men. Rather than select one of Alaska's prominent Republican statehooders, such as Bob Atwood, Walter Hickel, or John Butrovich, Seaton was concerned that the appointee be acceptable both to Alaska and to the "outside" interests. To appease both sides, he chose territorial legislator Mike Stepovich of Fairbanks, a man who had not previously held a leadership position in the statehood movement. Nonetheless, Stepovich was an advance to the statehood cause over Heintzleman. Once installed as governor in May 1957, Stepovich did become a vocal statehood supporter. Seaton hoped Stepovich would be a potential Republican candidate for governor or senator.

Before leaving Seaton and the president and returning to Congress, a few last questions may well occur to the reader. Why was Seaton such a zealous supporter of Alaska? After his 1952 speech in the Senate he had not further associated himself with Alaska statehood—particularly not in his earlier jobs in the Eisenhower administration. Though I have found no definitive statement from Seaton, it is probable that Seaton, like Lehleitner and the "experts" at the constitutional convention, became infected with the enthusiasm for statehood that developed after the ratification of the Alaska constitution and the Alaska–Tennessee Plan. The support of Snedden and Stevens gave a boost to Seaton's zeal. Why Eisenhower was willing to accede to Seaton is clearer. Ewald explains that Eisenhower had the trait of choosing capable lieutenants and then acceding to their advice, even if it differed from his own personal predilection. In this way the former general-turned-president was like General Emmons in his capacity as military governor of Hawai'i. Emmons decided not to intern the islands' Japanese population because he took the advice of Robert Shivers and Kendall Fielder, his trusted intelligence advisers. In understanding the path to statehood it is important to remember that the relationship between President Eisenhower and Secretary Seaton was very much one of a former general and his trusted lieutenant.[12]

One Last Statehood Bill before the Speaker of the House

With Seaton's help, the Executive Branch was ready to accept statehood. But such support would only become critical once the statehood bill cleared the Congress. Victory there was by no means assured in early 1957. With the Alaska First strategy in play, Leo O'Brien's House subcommittee on territories first held hearings on Alaska in March 1957. The Senate Interior and Insular Affairs Committee, chaired by Henry "Scoop" Jackson of Washington State, held concurrent hearings.

The House hearings are the more important for us to examine as it would be the House bill that took precedence. The testimony at the hearings was much like that in previous Congresses. What we should note in the Eighty-fifth Congress are the final provisions of the bill—particularly its land provisions. As mentioned earlier, the Alaska statehood bill underwent a process of evolution in the postwar Congresses. Both supporters and critics emphasized that it should be an "adequate" bill that made sufficient land provisions to jump-start the territory's economy.

The bill reported by the House subcommittee contained the provisions for military withdrawal negotiated by Seaton. It also proposed an overall land grant of 182-plus million acres—substantially larger than the 100-plus million acres that Hickel and others had pushed for earlier. The huge size of the grant would likely forestall any objections by proponents or opponents that the bill was not "adequate." The 182 million acres could be selected randomly from any vacant, unreserved, and unappropriated lands in the new state. Importantly, the selections could be made from within those military "withdrawal" lands north and west of the McKay Line with the president's permission. The new state would have subsurface as well as surface rights to its land selections. And even on federal lands that the state did not select, Alaska would receive 90 percent of mineral royalties. The land offerings appeared to be a massive patrimony. One must remember, however, that the lands had only the "potential" to help Alaska's economy. There were as yet no substantial mineral discoveries—gold, oil, or otherwise—that the new state was simply waiting to acquire. The new state lands provided *hope* for economic development, but *no certainty* of it.[13]

One final note must be made on the land provisions of the House bill. The issue of native claims was not settled. Instead the bill provided that nothing in the act would prejudice the future settlement of native claims, including the eventual settlement of several land cases currently in the federal courts. In 1957 no one knew what those eventual settlements would be. Though inconclusive, the stand on native claims in the statehood act did not exacerbate the issue and retained the support of Alaska natives for the time being.

In June 1957 O'Brien's subcommittee and Clair Engle's full Interior and Insular Affairs Committee reported the bill with the recommendation that it be passed. About the same time the Senate Interior and Insular Affairs Committee reported a similar bill, which differed primarily in proposing a land grant of only 102-plus million acres. Both House and Senate committees had favorably reported Alaska statehood bills before. Would the 1957 bill get to the floor of either house? The House bill now went to the Rules Committee, where chairman Howard

Smith was adamantly opposed to statehood for either territory. In 1955 he had given an "closed" rule to a joint Alaska/Hawai'i bill. The "closed" rule meant that the joint bill could not be separated for floor debate or voting. Smith had concluded that a joint bill would never pass. Thus his rule effectively killed the bill, which was recommitted to the Interior and Insular Affairs Committee. In 1957 Smith faced a single Alaska bill. He could not simply obstruct with a "closed" rule. To kill the bill he decided to hold it in committee—forever, if necessary.

With Smith leading the obstruction, the Alaska statehood bill needed to have the support of Speaker Rayburn to get out of the Rules Committee and onto the floor. Early in the session the Speaker told Ernest Gruening that he was not inclined toward statehood for either territory, but that he preferred Alaska to Hawai'i. "Hawaii has too many Japs," the speaker explained, but "Alaska is on the continent." Despite such reservations, Rayburn said he "would not try to prevent the bill" from reaching the floor. When the bill cleared the Interior Committee in June and went to Rules, no one knew exactly what the Speaker would do.[14]

On July 25, 1957, Rayburn called Bartlett, along with Representatives Leo O'Brien and Clair Engle, to his office and promised support for Alaska statehood if they delayed action on the legislation until the second session in 1958. Later that day he met with the Alaska-Tennessee Plan delegation and repeated his pledge. According to Bill Egan, " He told us he had always opposed us previously and had helped to kill Alaska statehood legislation; that he was now *for* Alaska; that his 44 years experience dictated that this was the wrong time to press for action: that in January he knew of no other controversial legislation pending; that he would personally work to have the Alaska statehood bill called to the calendar early." Given this new level of support, the Alaskans were willing to defer to the Speaker. But exactly why had the Speaker moved from active opposition to at least non-obstructionist support?[15]

No one is exactly sure why Rayburn changed his mind. Many people emphasize Rayburn's fondness for Bob Bartlett. Gruening claimed that he asked former president Harry Truman to phone Rayburn early in the session. Truman phoned and then told Gruening, "Sam will be all right." Rayburn may also have been influenced by members of his own Texas delegation. Jim Wright became a firm supporter of Alaska statehood soon after his first election in 1954 and a visit from George Lehleitner. Wright told me that he talked with Rayburn and at least received a friendly reception. There is also the intriguing possibility that the discovery of oil in Alaska may have influenced Rayburn. The Speaker called the Alaskans to his office two days after the Richfield Oil Company drilled its first successful well on the Kenai Peninsula south of Anchorage—known as the Swanson River discovery. Alaska-Tennessee Plan representative Ralph Rivers and Hawai'i's former territorial delegate Betty Farrington later asserted that the "oil boys" in Texas wanted Alaska admitted. However, no proof of this has ever been revealed. Regardless of the reason for Rayburn's change of heart, the statehooders now had the rest of 1957 to wait until the bill could come back to the House in January 1958.[16]

While Alaska waited, supporters of statehood continued to make the rounds of congressional offices, particularly to win a positive vote from new congressmen. To aid these efforts Ernest Bartley had earlier agreed to enlist the help of the American Political Science Association in drawing up profiles of each state's congressional delegation. After the November 1956 elections Bartley compiled an analysis of the Congress to find both *where* support had come for Alaska statehood in the past—and *why*.

Bartley's survey first confirmed what had long been known—much of the opposition to Alaska was in the South. Outside of the South, support came predominantly from Democratic districts and opposition from Republican districts. The dominance of geography and party made it difficult for the analysts to draw further conclusions from other correlations they found. Urban districts favored statehood more than rural districts, but over half of the rural districts were in the South. Industrial districts tended to be more in favor of statehood than nonindustrial districts, but most blue-collar districts were outside the South and also were Democratic. Sorting through the perplexing data, the researchers made two striking observations that tend undermine any suggestion that there was an "issue-oriented" framework to the statehood struggle. They first concluded that "the most important result of this analysis . . . was the fact that there were many districts which statistically should have favored statehood, but didn't." Their second conclusion avoided statistics altogether and settled on emotion: "Probably the most important 'peculiarity' of all is the fact that there are votes which can only be explained in terms of personalities or good lobby operations. Up to now the Honorable E. L. "Bob" Bartlett has been Alaska's only really active lobbyist, but it is evident that his efforts have been very fruitful. Few persons have accomplished so much with so little."[17]

In 1987 Bartley reiterated his 1956 findings in a discussion with me. When asked about the socioeconomic typing of the districts, he responded that he did not think it proved anything one way or the other. It merely provided information for the Alaska-Tennessee Plan delegates to use in starting a conversation with a congressman. It sounded good to know something about the district. This, he said, particularly impressed freshmen congressmen. There were forty-six freshmen in the Eighty-fifth Congress. Of those, thirty-three eventually voted for the Alaska statehood bill. Those thirty-three congressmen provided a net gain of eleven votes compared to the predecessors in their districts.[18]

Bartley also affirmed that the greatest influence on House votes came from the personality of Bob Bartlett. The political scientist was almost rhapsodic in his praise of the delegate. "So many votes on the House side," he explained, "came from Bartlett's influence. His influence caused many members, I hesitate to say a majority, but at the same time I'm not sure it wasn't a majority [to vote for Alaska.]" As he thought the matter over more thoroughly, Bartley confidently asserted, "Bob Bartlett was the key to the whole operation. He was it. If Bob Bartlett had had a heart attack at the start of the battle, Alaska would not have been a state."[19]

Bartley confirmed Sam Rayburn's fondness for Bartlett and also noted that Spessard Holland's commitment was tied to the delegate. Bartlett's appeal, the political scientist explained, stemmed from the fact that he was "an all-around decent fellow" who "never raised his voice" and "never did headline grabbing stunts." Bartlett's allure then was personal. Members of Congress found it easy to like him. Possibly some of that friendship was based on the fact that, having no vote, he never voted against anyone. Bartlett did try to convince congressmen of Alaska's fitness for statehood. But it appears that this was not really their concern. They simply liked Bob Bartlett. If Bob said Alaska needed statehood, that was all they needed to know. Adding a forty-ninth star to the flag was in their mind a favor done for a good friend. This is the opinion or conclusion that comes not only from the testimony of congressmen themselves, but also from the one professional political scientist who tried to analyze them.

Privileged Legislation before the House

Once the new year 1958 began, President Eisenhower told Congress for the first time that Alaska should be admitted—no longer was there any stipulation of further defense provisions for admission. Speaker

Rayburn held true to his promise and affirmed to Bartlett that the Alaska bill would come to the floor. To reach the floor the Speaker told Rules Committee chairman Howard Smith that he wanted a rule for the bill. Smith had no interest in Rayburn's promise to Bartlett and stalled. To some extent this delaying may have strengthened Rayburn's resolve. Whether Rayburn was truly for Alaska statehood or not, he did not intend to be humiliated or bullied by Smith. Just who was in charge of the House of Representatives, Smith or Rayburn? But what power did the Speaker have over the Rules Committee?

Gimmicks and stunts like the Alaska-Tennessee Plan, drawn from research on the history of previously admitted states, were by 1958 an integral part of the statehood battle. By 1958 statehood supporters had discovered yet one more. Certain bills in the House could be considered privileged legislation. If the Rules Committee refused to report such a bill, the chairman of the committee from which the bill came could ask the House, with the Speaker's assent, to turn itself into a Committee of the Whole. The Rules Committee would be bypassed, and the Committee of the Whole would vote whether to schedule the bill for debate on the floor.

The concept of privileged legislation was not new to the House. Its use for statehood legislation was to some extent new, oddly enough because it was so old. According to George Lehleitner, statehood legislation had long been privileged legislation. Since the last states, Arizona and New Mexico, had been admitted in 1912, the inclusion of statehood legislation as "privileged" had been omitted from current editions of the House Rules book. Lehleitner told me that the parliamentarian of the Congress, Lewis Deschler, looked at earlier rules books and found the privileged designation for statehood. In February Interior and Insular Affairs chairman Engle told Smith that he would move to introduce the bill as privileged legislation if no rule was issued by mid-March. To execute such a maneuver would require the Speaker to recognize the Interior Committee chair and then guide the "privileged" proposal through any number of procedural challenges. This process itself would be quite a challenge as procedural debate pro and con would be based on who could claim that they knew the most about a little-known parliamentary procedure.[20]

No rule was forthcoming by the mid-March date. Even with Rayburn's prodding, Smith continued to stall into late April. Finally, on May 21, Rayburn agreed to recognize the Interior Committee's move to bypass the Rules Committee and turn the House into a Committee of the Whole. Obstructionists tried various maneuvers to claim that the Alaska bill was not "privileged" legislation—for example, on the grounds that it contained an appropriation. Hence it was not a "pure" admission bill. Rayburn, armed with Deschler's research, ruled that the bill was basically a statehood bill and hence was privileged. As the debate went on, the Speaker at times ruled in favor of the bill on questionable voice votes. The House, as a Committee of the Whole, finally voted to accept the Alaska statehood bill as privileged legislation. Now the bill could move out of the Committee of the Whole and onto the floor for debate and a full vote.[21]

The House debated the bill during the last week of May. Some opponents called for an amendment requiring that Alaska hold a final referendum to accept statehood. Supporters accepted this requirement. Proponents amended the lands portion of the bill to reflect the Senate's 102.5 million acres. With other specific land grants the total approached 103.5 million acres. If the House bill were to be accepted by the Senate, the land provisions needed to be the same. The "Seattle interests" were fearful that statehood would bring state management of the fishery and hence the abolition of the fish trap—as provided by the fish trap ordinance from the Alaska constitutional convention. They were able to secure an amendment (section 6e) that the fishery would remain under federal management after statehood until the Secretary of the Interior deemed the new state ready to manage it. Bartlett disliked this amendment, but Seaton told him to go along with it. The secretary promised to transfer control of the fishery quickly after statehood.

The opposition attempted other delaying tactics and amendments that were voted down on the floor. The time for a final vote came on May 28. Leo O'Brien told me that by all his calculations the votes just were not there. To help his chances he wore a shamrock tie tack given to him by Bill Egan for good luck. When the roll call was completed, the vote was 210–166. O'Brien called it a "miracle." Both parties voted affirmatively, though as expected there was a higher margin of Democratic support than Republican.[22]

The taste of victory in the House was sweet, but was there enough time to win support in the Senate? It was now the end of May. Many supporters believed that another "miracle" would have to happen—the Senate would have to accept the House bill without amendment to avoid a return to the House or a conference committee. There simply was not enough time left in the second session for any extensive deliberation. Howard Smith and his Rules Committee had certainly advanced the clock before they were pushed out of the way. Obstruction had worked before. What would now happen in the last days of the Eighty-fifth Congress?

Unamended Victory in the Senate

Time was short by the beginning of June 1958 to win a positive vote for the Alaska statehood bill in the Senate. In years past statehood had floundered for both Alaska and Hawai'i in the latter part of a congressional second session. But in June 1958 various forces were at work that created a "snowball" effect. The House had passed the bill, and the Speaker of the House had backed the unusual "privileged" legislation maneuver to outflank the Rules Committee. Secretary of the Interior Fred Seaton, a zealot for statehood, had brought the president in line. The secretary then liberally dispensed departmental patronage, particularly in the Park Service, to win votes in both houses. Public opinion was now decidedly pro-statehood, with polls reporting 80 percent in favor. The juggernaut of public relations and media pressure was in full gear. CBS had featured Alaska and Hawai'i on Edward R. Murrow's *See It Now* program in March. On that show proponents of statehood from both territories were portrayed as young and energetic; opponents were depicted as aging and inept. Widely known author Edna Ferber published *Ice Palace* in March 1958, an epic novel that trumpeted the potential glories of statehood for Alaska. Though the novel received little literary acclaim, the simple association of Ferber's name with the northern territory generated national publicity and attention.[23]

Bill Snedden and Fred Seaton were bringing an unusual form of press pressure on some recalcitrant members of the obstruction forces in Congress. If they could not persuade a congressman to vote for statehood, they had a way of silencing a negative vote. Fred called it "practical politics." Bill said it as not "all nice." Through contacts with friends who were columnists or wire service executives, Snedden and Seaton compiled a background check on "key known opponents." They used that information to effect. As Snedden later related:

> When we struck "paydirt," one of our top news men in Washington would have a casual conversation with the

individual involved, mentioning lightly what we had stum-
bled across, and inquiring what their opinion was of the
merits of Alaska statehood. This was a very delicate operation. . . . However, it worked out nicely and I am convinced
that it undoubtedly was the only way we could have accomplished the job.[24]

By May 1958 Seaton noted that Snedden had the most effective
"grapevine operation" in Washington.

Media and personal pressure were indeed needed to win the Senate.
Since January the tone of the Senate and majority leader Johnson had
been difficult to read. Early in the second session Johnson held a meeting with Bartlett, Burns, and Democratic leaders in the Senate. There
Johnson committed himself to the Alaska First strategy for the remainder of the session. Hawai'i would not be brought up during the Eighty-
fifth Congress. The majority leader pledged to prevent a Southern
filibuster but did not offer a time line for bringing the Alaska statehood
bill approved in 1957 by the Senate Interior and Insular Affairs
Committee to the floor. In February 1958 matters became murkier as
President Eisenhower and some Republican senators raised the issue of
bringing a Hawai'i bill forward with the Alaska bill. Thus little action
took place in the Senate while the "privileged" legislation in the House
went forward.[25]

Rumors that a Hawai'i bill might come forward tested John Burns's
resolve to support Alaska First. The new delegate from Hawai'i did not
waver. He announced that he would move to recommit any Hawai'i
bill that appeared in the House. He also enlisted the aid of "Big Five"
shipping officials to let Senator William Knowland of California, long
a Republican supporter of Hawai'i, know that he did not want discussion of a Hawai'i bill in the Senate until the Alaska bill passed.[26]

With the passage of the House bill in May, the Senate was now
forced to action—or by inaction to tacitly kill the bill. In June Senator
Henry "Scoop" Jackson and the Interior and Insular Affairs Committee
decided to accept the House bill without amendment and send it to
the floor of the Senate for a vote. Why was this decision made?

None of the statehooders who talked to me has been able to decipher the exact reasons for the Senate's "unamended" action. They have
suggested a number of factors to consider. If Senate statehood supporters seriously wanted to pass an Alaska statehood bill, this was the

only reasonable action that could be taken by June of the second session. The House bill had been amended to conform to the Senate's land provision. The statehood bill was clearly "adequate." And there *were* reasons why the Senate might want to pass a statehood bill. The Democratic Eighty-fifth Congress and the Republican president had locked horns on many pieces of legislation in the last two years. The Alaska statehood bill appeared to be one on which the president and Congress could agree. There are those who say that Lyndon Johnson now wanted a statehood bill as part of his emerging strategy to gain national stature in a potential run for the presidency. From a contrarian standpoint, some have noted that Southern opponents thought Republicans who favored Hawai'i would defeat an "Alaska only" bill. So bring it to the floor and let it be defeated.

To push Jackson forward, the team of Snedden, Seaton, and Stevens decided to tackle the "Seattle interests" who might hold the senator back. The Seattle papers had done little to promote statehood. Snedden knew, however, that no state was really a press island unto itself and enlisted the aid of Californian William Randolph Hearst Jr., who owned the *Seattle Post-Intelligencer.* When Jackson returned to Seattle shortly before the bill was to come before the Senate, the *Post-Intelligencer* ran Sunday front-page coverage in favor of Alaska statehood. Snedden and Hearst ensured that a number of reporters alerted Jackson to this new "interest" in Seattle. Once back in Washington, D.C., Jackson sent the Alaska bill to the floor. Hearst also came to the capital to keep the pressure on Jackson and to "work on" any lingering obstructionists. Hearst reported to Snedden in June that "two of our dedicated opponents had agreed not to actively fight, even though they did intend negative votes." Exactly what Hearst did to the recalcitrant senators remains unknown![27]

In addition to Hearst, a delegation of Republicans from Alaska, including Bob Atwood, Wally Hickel, and Mike Stepovich, arrived to help the Seaton-Snedden-Stevens team call on as many senators as possible. Evidently the group had a "no holds barred" approach to persuasion. Bob Atwood noted that some "punches" were literally exchanged in the bar at the Statler Hotel when an anti-Alaska senatorial aide approached the new group from the North and debunked the territory. The next day a senator joked with Atwood, "I understand that if I don't vote for statehood, I'll get my block knocked off."[28]

The Senate debated the Alaska statehood bill for a week in late June. As the pressure for a vote gained momentum, a number of Southern senators agreed simply to have their remarks reported in the *Congressional Record* without presenting them on the floor. The vote finally came on the evening of June 30. For reasons that are not clear, Lyndon Johnson decided to be out of town for the vote as did his Texas colleague Ralph Yarborough. In his absence statehood supporter Mike Mansfield of Montana was acting majority leader. Alaska's longtime friend Dick Neuberger of Oregon was the presiding officer of the Senate that night. No one knew exactly what the outcome would be. For luck, Leo O'Brien passed along Bill Egan's shamrock tie tack to Mansfield. The Alaska-Tennessee Plan delegation, delegate Bartlett, and other statehood supporters gathered in the Senate gallery. A little after 8 p.m. the roll call was complete—64–20 in favor of statehood. Slightly more Republicans (33) than Democrats (31) voted for the new state. A celebration erupted in the gallery and on the floor. Neuberger marked time for a while before restoring order. The Alaska delegation then followed the suggestion of Ada Wien, a delegate to the 1955–56 Constitutional Convention, and adjourned to the Capitol chapel for prayer.[29]

While the Alaskans were praying in the chapel, Bill Snedden excused himself to call Fairbanks and schedule one last act of symbolism. Snedden wanted newspaper coverage of the successful vote to first reach Congress via the *Fairbanks Daily News-Miner*. It was still afternoon in Alaska when the bill passed in Washington. Snedden's editors had already prepared a triumphal edition in anticipation that the vote would be positive. When Snedden phoned in the final tally, the presses ran in Fairbanks. Some 2,500 copies of the paper were then dispatched to Eielson Air Force Base where a plane waited for the flight to Washington. The air force plane landed at Andrews Air Force Base at 7 a.m., Washington time. By 8 a.m. on July 1 every member of Congress had a copy of the *News-Miner* on his or her desk.[30]

Of all the symbols of the statehood movement, possibly no two were more telling than the airplane and the newspaper. The airplane had modernized Alaska and made it ready for statehood. It gave the territory its defense role in World War II. The need for air bases then propelled Alaska into the Cold War. The speed of the airplane became the constant reminder that the distant territory was not that far away. The morning news in the nation's capital could come directly from the last frontier.

The newspaper, actually the vast reach of the news media, had been one of the keys in mounting support for the final statehood victory. Media coverage—and the use of media connections—had been the unending ploy of Lehleitner, Gruening, Seaton, Snedden, Atwood, and other statehooders. In commenting on the final success of the 1958 statehood bill, Ted Stevens told me in 1987, "It was the people who knew how to have the mechanisms of the press come to play on the Congress—how to have the people who were obstacles realize that if they stood in the way, the power of that press could really hit them politically."[31]

Bill Snedden's union of the airplane and the newspaper, even more than the motorcade of the Alaska-Tennessee Plan or Muktuk Marston's jade lamp, typify the modernizing forces that brought Alaska into the mainstream of American life. As such they were truly the ultimate symbols of the battle for Alaska statehood.

The Power behind the Vote: Oil, Civil Rights, the Tennessee Plan, or Just Personal

Victory in the Congress had indeed been sweet for the statehooders. But before sending the bill on to the president, it may be instructive to contemplate what forces actually led to congressional success in 1958, compared to defeat in previous years. Neither in 1958 nor in the forty-five years hence has anyone—historian or statehooder—come to a firm conclusion about the final vote. Leo O'Brien told me in 1981 that he had yet to figure out the vote after two decades of pondering it. The New Yorker said that some sixty votes he had counted against statehood were suddenly cast for it. O'Brien simply called the bill's passage a "miracle." Though we may not come to any firmer conclusion than O'Brien, let us, at least, check off some of the other reasons that have been suggested.[32]

As noted earlier, the link between the discovery of oil in Alaska in 1957 and Rayburn's support has intrigued a number of people. But no one has brought forward any substantial proof. If oil men in Texas favored statehood, they had little effect on their congressional delegation. Only two of twenty-two Texas representatives voted for statehood, and both senators were absent. Ernest Gruening noted that Senator Robert Kerr of Oklahoma was an oil man and a good friend of Kenneth Adams, chairman of the Phillips Petroleum Company. Gruening arranged for the Alaska manager of Phillips to contact Adams and persuade him to tell Kerr to vote for statehood. Adams obliged, and the Kerr vote was secured. But even Gruening did not attribute any particular connection to Kerr's support and the 1957 oil discovery. Nothing in Bob Bartlett's extensive correspondence on statehood mentions oil company support. If there was oil company influence behind the 1958 vote, it has been held secret for over forty years.[33]

A weakening of Southern intransigence on civil rights legislation in 1957 has also been cited by some as a factor in paving the way for the positive 1958 vote on statehood. Hawai'i historian Roger Bell emphasizes that the passage of the 1957 civil rights bill, albeit a weak and virtually ineffective piece of legislation, broke the back on Southern resistance to statehood. If so, few people who observed the Congress in 1957–58 attribute any particular connection between the passage of the Alaska statehood bill and any weakening of resistance by Southerners to civil rights legislation. In 1988 I specifically asked Russell Long of Louisiana if he saw his vote for statehood as part of a changing pattern on civil rights. Long answered that both he and Spessard Holland thought that statehood and civil rights could be separated and dealt with on their own merits. Their votes for statehood in no way signified a new position on civil rights. Shortly after the Senate vote Holland returned to Florida and campaigned vigorously against his challenger Claude Pepper on the grounds that Pepper was "soft" on both civil rights and Communism.[34]

In their correspondence, statehooders warned supporters in 1957–58 to keep statehood and civil rights separate. They emphasized that President Truman's linkage of statehood and civil rights had worked against passage in the late 1940s and early 1950s. In 1958 supporters were careful to prevent such a linkage. Though most of the opposition to statehood came from diehard Southern opponents, the South was by no means solid in 1958. In the Senate positive votes came from senators in Louisiana, Tennessee, Florida, North Carolina, Oklahoma, and Alabama. Though absent, both Texas senators listed themselves in favor. None of these senators noted that they were changing their minds on civil rights. It was the separation of statehood and civil rights, rather than any softening on civil rights in the Senate, that led to success in 1958.[35]

We may also ask if the positive vote for statehood was achieved as a result of the Alaska-Tennessee Plan. Again the evidence is not at all clear. Leo O'Brien told me that he could not assess the plan on a specific scale, but described the delegation as "three very able men . . . working their heads off." He particularly noted his fondness for Bill Egan, who definitely had a following among Irish Catholics in the Congress. "If we had to do it over again," mused O'Brien, "by all means have a

Tennessee Plan." Jim Wright told me that Alaska-Tennessee Plan senator Ernest Gruening was the man who impressed him the most.[36]

Delegate Bartlett was less enthusiastic than Representatives O'Brien
and Wright. Bartlett had not been an initial advocate of the plan, but
went along with it as it attracted the support of George Lehleitner and
others. By July 1957 Bartlett actually grew disgruntled with the delegation. He claimed in a private memo that neither the plan nor its delegation attracted national publicity or even concern in the Congress.
He claimed that the delegation had not done enough social entertaining to win votes. He even went so far as to say:

> To sum it up, let me say that if statehood is achieved during
> the 85th Congress, in the very nature of things the Tennessee
> Plan will be given almost exclusive credit. And my conclu-
> sion is that if statehood comes about in this Congress, the
> Tennessee Plan will have had very little to do with it.[37]

A year later statehood was achieved. Bartlett made no further comment after the victory. However, a decade later in a 1967 "personal and
confidential" letter to Thomas B. Stewart, Bartlett stated:

> I do not propose to set off the fireworks which would
> inevitably result if I were to state publicly my knowledge of
> how very, very little the Alaska-Tennessee Plan had to do with
> the achievement of Alaska statehood. As a matter of fact, I
> should go further and say that it had no impact whatsoever.[38]

What can we make of Bartlett's critiques in 1957 and 1967, particularly in light of the more favorable impression of Leo O'Brien and Jim
Wright—and the fact that all three Alaska-Tennessee Plan delegates
were elected to major offices in the new state? Bartlett's critique was
no doubt influenced by the strange situation in which the Alaska-
Tennessee Plan delegation placed him. Exactly what was the status of
these "shadow" congressmen? For over a decade the delegate had been
the *sole* elected representative of the territory in Washington, D.C. Now
there were four "elected" men from Alaska in the nation's capital—often
in Delegate Bartlett's office at the same time. Who spoke for Alaska?

The problem of "credit" for the eventual passage of the statehood bill
became a difficult and frustrating issue for Alaska's lone congressional

delegate. This problem could be particularly vexing with Ernest Gruening, who began calling himself "Mr. Statehood" in mid-1958. Professor Claus-M. Naske has explained that Bartlett's relation with Gruening reached a straining point even before the election of the Alaska–Tennessee Plan delegation. Though Gruening still considered Bartlett to be his protégé, the delegate found Gruening amazingly naïve about the workings of Congress. Neva Egan, who observed the relationships between Bartlett and the Alaska–Tennessee Plan delegation firsthand, shed further light on Bartlett's frustration in a 1986 interview:

> It was a very difficult position for Bob to be in. Here he was the official representative from Alaska, and had his office there. Well . . . they [Egan, Gruening, and Rivers] converged on Bob's office all the time . . . But, they [Bartlett and his secretary] couldn't have helped but feel resentment, because we've been here all these years and now all those people come in and get the credit.[39]

To help sort the reactions of Bartlett and get a further assessment of the Alaska–Tennessee Plan, I talked with George Lehleitner in 1986 and showed him Bartlett's letters critiquing the plan. It was the first time he had ever seen or heard of Bartlett's comments. At first I thought I had exceeded the bounds of judgment by showing him these documents. After carefully reading the letters, Lehleitner observed somewhat sadly that Bartlett had never been definite with him about the plan from their first meeting in the mid-1950s. In fact, Bartlett had resisted Lehleitner's queries in the early 1960s to write down his assessment of the statehood movement. Lehleitner then turned to me and offered his own assessment of the plan and of his friend Bartlett, who died in 1968.[40]

Lehleitner disagreed with Bartlett's view that not enough social entertaining was done by the delegation. Cocktail parties, the Southerner thought, were not the way to win votes. That had been the Farringtons' incorrect assumption, he explained. As for publicity, he noted that the plan did not push the hydrogen bomb and the Cold War from page one. But scores of newspapers and national magazines editorialized favorably on it. Lehleitner said that the importance of the plan was "the atmosphere that it created." It gave "a rebirth of enthusiasm and determination to statehood's supporters, both in Washington and Alaska."

Finally, to Bartlett's charge that the Alaska-Tennessee Plan "had no effect whatsoever" in securing statehood, Lehleitner had this response. He observed that if Bob were with us today, he would say something like this to him:

> Now, Bob, explain this to me. You entered the Congress in 1945. While you were there alone, Congress after Congress debated bill after bill for statehood and nothing happened. Then in 1957 the Tennessee Plan delegation arrived. Eighteen months later in the first Congress the Tennessee Planners met, Alaska statehood was achieved. How do you explain that, Bob? Was it all just a coincidence?

The Southerner rested his case.

From oil to civil rights to the Alaska-Tennessee Plan, the participants in the Alaska statehood battle and most of its later analysts have been at a loss to explain precise reasons for the success of the bill in 1958. As one of those later analysts who has thought about the issue for the last twenty years, I have reached no firmer conclusions. However, I do have a few observations that have particularly struck me over the years I have known and interviewed the statehooders.

The final success plan of the Alaska statehooders in 1957–58 reads like a "how to" manual for the manipulation of the U.S. Congress—particularly a closely divided Congress. No floodtide of sentiment—either domestic or international—swept the Alaska statehood bill to success. As noted many times, statehood was not a pressing issue for most members of Congress or their constituents. Jim Wright said it concerned less than 5 percent of his constituents. On the other hand there was repeatedly a positive sentiment once a statehood bill reached the floor of either house—particularly the House of Representatives. Favorable votes for both Alaska and Hawai'i statehood were recorded several times in the House. And the Senate voted *for* a combined Alaska/Hawai'i bill in 1954. In those earlier Congresses the forces of obstruction were able to defeat such positive sentiments with a bevy of procedural tactics including threats of filibuster, recommittals, the joining of statehood bills, and the refusal to produce a rule in the House.

By 1957–58 statehooders were finally able to thwart the obstructionists and, in effect, beat them at their own game. Their tactics included the Alaska First strategy, the use of "privileged" legislation, and media pressure to silence vocal obstructionists who were accustomed to getting their way. Supporters united on a strategy and then held to it. In earlier years inadvertence and naïveté on the part of supporters had let the more wily obstructionists control the Congress. The unity of the supporters in the Eighty-fifth Congress was amazing. The enthusiasm and energy that they brought to Washington trumped the obstructionists at every angle. Bob Bartlett had been there all along. After 1957 he was joined by George Lehleitner, the Alaska-Tennessee Plan delegation, Bill Snedden, Fred Seaton, Ted Stevens, Ernest Bartley, and even William Randolph Hearst Jr. In the face of such a united front one can almost hear the obstructionists saying, "Let's just let this one go through. It really doesn't matter if Alaska becomes a state."

With their united strategy the statehood supporters allowed the positive votes in Congress, which in many ways had always been there, to come forward. In watching those positive votes come forward, the most striking aspect of the statehood battle also becomes clearer. The success of the final vote appears to have been highly personal. Senators and representatives voted *for* the bill because they personally liked the other people who were *for* it. Any concrete reasons for or against Alaska's fitness for statehood seemed secondary to the fact that a representative or senator simply "liked" Bob Bartlett, Bill Egan, Ernest Gruening, George Lehleitner, or Fred Seaton. Seaton's personal hold on the president was such that Eisenhower literally went against his better judgment. If those personal reasons had not been there, it is entirely possible that the territory of Alaska might still be no more than a military defense zone today. The successful passage of the Alaska statehood bill in 1958 remains the ultimate proof of how intensely personal the U.S. Congress is—or certainly was.

The Final Say of the President and the People: We're In

The statehood bill passed by the Congress on June 30 went to the president for his signature. We will never know how enthusiastic Eisenhower actually was for Alaska statehood when he signed the bill on July 7 in a private, rather than a public, ceremony. His biographer William Bragg Ewald contends the president still thought the idea of Alaska statehood was "ridiculous." However, Ted Stevens, who watched Eisenhower at close range, told me that he thought the president finally warmed to the idea of admitting one—and then certainly two—new states to the union in his administration. Possibly Eisenhower, like many others, was torn between the symbolism and glory of a new star on the flag and the reality of admitting a far northern territory that he thought could barely support itself in the absence of federal spending.[41]

Once signed by the president, the statehood bill required one last demonstration of support. A referendum by the people of Alaska must be held. They must accept statehood as well as the boundaries of the new state and the specific conditions of the statehood bill. The statewide election, scheduled for August 26, 1958, coincided with the territory's primary election. For reasons that are not at all clear the statehooders still feared the "opposition." The *Fairbanks Daily News-Miner* expressed great concern at "rumors" being spread by unnamed sources that federal employees would lose their 25 percent cost-of-living differential if statehood passed. The action of two diehard congressional opponents to introduce such legislation caused concern that the local opposition had powerful connections. The *News-Miner's* fear mounted when it editorialized a few days later that anti-statehood talk had "spread like wildfire through the remote villages of Alaska." There "a man who swore the Eskimos to secrecy" told natives they would be put on reservations if statehood passed. Secretary Seaton quickly assured natives that no reservations were planned. Opposition rumors so concerned the *News-Miner* that the paper decided to run a series of features in advance of the vote entitled "Statehood Clinic." No doubt, as the name implied, this information would cure Fairbanks of the anti-statehood disease.[42]

When the ballots were counted on August 26, voters approved statehood in a 5–1 majority. Though this was the largest majority ever recorded for statehood in Alaska, it was less that the 17–1 majority that Hawai'i voters would give to statehood a year later. And it still trailed the 8–1 majorities in Alaska's various fish trap referenda. More impressive than the majority for statehood was the size of the electorate. Over forty-eight thousand voters, almost 75 percent more than the twenty-eight thousand in 1956, turned out for the plebiscite. Election officials had predicted a higher turnout for two reasons. The new constitution lowered the voting age from twenty-one to nineteen. Also, military personnel could now vote if they declared themselves Alaska residents. No advance registration was required; voters could do so when they appeared at the polls. The numbers, however, overwhelmed even the most optimistic projections of thirty-five thousand.

The "invisible" military personnel, who had swelled Alaska's over-all population in the 1950s, were finally in evidence at the polls. Ardent anti-statehooder Joe Vogler, who insisted that Alaska should be an independent nation, claimed that statehood was approved because of the military vote. Certainly many military people voted for the first time in this election, but there is no evidence that they altered the outcome of the election. Statehood carried by similar majorities in districts with and without military populations. There also appears to be no evidence that Alaska natives were scared by fears of being placed on reservations. The native vote varied substantially from village to village, but as a group Alaska natives approved statehood along with their non-native counterparts.[43]

The August primary also fielded a slate of candidates from each party for the new congressional delegation and the first elected governorship in the November general elections. As noted earlier, the all-Democratic Alaska-Tennessee Plan delegation was no longer linked to a new congressional delegation. But each of the Alaska-Tennessee Plan delegates announced his intention to run in the primary. Gruening and Egan filed for the Senate, and Rivers for the House. This, of course, left the issue of what Bob Bartlett would do. Many assumed that Bartlett would want to become the first governor of the new state. They thought that the first governorship was the more important position. The constitution gave the new governor the power to appoint all cabinet positions and to set the pace for the new state. But Bartlett could not make up his mind. Finally, he decided that he did not want to return to Alaska. He liked living in Washington where he had been for fifteen years. And his experience in the Congress could bode well for the new state. Bartlett announced that he would run for the Senate. Bill Egan quickly withdrew his Senate bid and filed for governor. Thus there were no upsets in the August primary campaign, and the Democrats presented a united front of veteran statehooders.[44]

The Republican slate in August was chosen simply in anticipation of the November general election as there were no intra-party challenges. Alaska Republicans, particularly Bill Snedden, had carefully nurtured territorial governor Mike Stepovich and decided to run him against the candidate most likely to beat—Ernest Gruening. Snedden had earlier used his media connections to gain Stepovich a cover picture and story in the June 2 edition of *Time* magazine. They ran their other strongest candidate, veteran statehooder John Butrovich, against

Bill Egan for governor. They made only a token attempt against Bob Bartlett with the nomination of Bob Robertson of Juneau, the only delegate to the constitutional convention who did not sign the completed document. To oppose Ralph Rivers for the U.S. House seat they chose little-known territorial labor commissioner Henry Benson.

Though Stepovich and Gruening were unopposed within their parties in the August primary, Stepovich garnered substantially more votes than Gruening. The thirty-nine-year-old governor might have beaten the seventy-one-year-old former governor in the November general election save for the fallout from further media fireworks. In early July Washington columnist Drew Pearson, an old friend of Gruening, noted in his syndicated column, "Washington Merry Go Round," that Gruening deserved credit for statehood. Mike Stepovich, he said, was a "johnny come lately" to the movement. Snedden reacted bitterly, particularly since Pearson's column ran in the *News-Miner.* He told his editor George Sundborg, long a friend of Gruening, to write an editorial criticizing Pearson and calling him the "Garbage Man of the 4th Estate." This action set off a melee between Pearson and the *News-Miner* that later resulted in a protracted legal battle. Of more consequence to the senatorial race, Snedden terminated Sundborg at the *News-Miner.* Gruening then hired Sundborg as his campaign manager. Sundborg later told me that had he remained at the *News-Miner,* Stepovich would certainly have been elected. Sundborg would have followed Snedden's edict to editorialize in favor of Stepovich. He would have been unavailable to help Gruening.[45]

During the general election campaign both Sundborg and Gruening made claims that discounted Stepovich's commitment to statehood before he became governor in 1957. Gruening nudged out Stepovich by 2,500 votes in the November election. Though Gruening had attracted controversy throughout his career in Alaska, he had obviously endeared himself to a majority of voters. By defeating his younger opponent, Gruening finally fulfilled his dream to sit in the U.S. Senate. He took the embattled Sundborg with him to Washington as his administrative assistant. In the other major races Egan, Bartlett, and Rivers won with substantial margins in a voter turnout that topped fifty thousand.

With the new state and congressional officers elected in November, only one last task remained to put the forty-ninth star on the flag. The president now must officially proclaim that Alaska had met the conditions for statehood. Admission Day finally came on January 3, 1959. The president, surrounded by a group of both Democrats and Republicans, signed the proclamation admitting Alaska as the forty-ninth state. The new forty-nine-star flag was unfurled for the first time. In both Washington and Alaska, the statehooders could now proudly shout, "We're In!"

The needle had pierced the fabric of the nation. But what about the thread? In January 1959, Alaska was in, but Hawai'i was not. To complete the union we must return to the island territory.

Postscript: The Trapped Salmon Run Free

Before moving to the islands, we should note one last transition for the northern territory. What would now happen to the trapped salmon? As noted many times, the battle to abolish fish traps always received a greater vote than the battle to abolish territorial rule. Ratification of the constitution was outvoted by the ordinance that fish traps would be abolished once Alaska became a state. However, the statehood bill left the fishery in federal control for a year after statehood or until such time as Secretary Seaton transferred control.

The fish scenario quickly ran its course. Technically, Governor Egan declared fish traps abolished in January 1959. He claimed he had jurisdiction not over the fishery but over the tidelands where the traps were located. On March 9, 1959, Secretary Seaton issued new federal regulations banning fish traps. In January 1960 Alaska finally assumed complete control of the fishery. Alaska was now saved from both colonialism and fish traps. It was the master of both its people and its fish.[46]

Chapter 10

The Last Territorial Delegate and the Admission of Hawai'i, 1957–1959

This is one of the most complicated men I have ever interviewed. He has had in his background a series of turbulent, traumatic experiences, and the result is a man of many virtues and many faults. He is a defender and fighter for the underdog. He is conscientious. He is sentimental, and at the same time he is vulgar and vindictive. His father was a drunk who used to fight with him regularly. . . . He describes his Catholic education in Kansas and the influence of certain Brothers and certain Monks on him, as being paramount in shaping his attitudes on life . . . He explained his entrance in politics and his tremendous dedication to it as a substitute for drinking . . . This man, who is full of vulgar terms in his conversation, can quote Leo and Pius and even Aristotle. This is a shrewd and complicated man.

Such were the research notes taken in November 1958 by Lawrence Fuchs in preparation for his soon to be classic account of territorial Hawai'i, *Hawaii Pono* (1961).[1] The "shrewd and complicated man" in question was John A. Burns. We have met Burns before in his capacity as Honolulu police captain in World War II, chairman of the Hawai'i Democratic Party, and territorial delegate. Shortly after Fuchs's interview Burns would acquire yet another distinction. He was about to become the last territorial delegate in the U.S. House of Representatives. Delegate Bob Bartlett of Alaska had just been elected to the U.S. Senate from the new forty-ninth state to be proclaimed on January 3, 1959. Burns won his second term as delegate in the 1958 elections. Upon his return to Washington in 1959 for the opening of the Eighty-sixth Congress, John Burns of Hawai'i would be the last in a long line that began 165 years earlier, in 1794, with the arrival of James White, territorial delegate to the Third Congress from the Territory South of the River Ohio (later the state of Tennessee). Burns's goal was to bring the fiftieth state into the union, and consequently to terminate not only his place as, but also the historical position of, territorial delegate in the Congress. Before moving to what would be a rather rapid admission of the fiftieth state in early 1959, let us first look more closely at Burns.

A Complicated "Western" Man Goes to Washington

As the last territorial delegate, John Burns truly closed the territorial frontier in Congress. This role poses the question of whether Burns was a figure from the American West or someone unique to the mid-Pacific islands. Actually Burns was much more a "western" figure than historians of the American West or of Hawai'i have previously acknowledged. Rather than an "island boy," Burns was a true child of the western frontier. He was part of that westward moving trail of mainland Americans who came to Hawai'i with the military after 1900. We have earlier sketched the military buildup of Hawai'i with the opening of the naval base at Pearl Harbor and the army installations at Schofield Barracks and Fort Shafter. Where did Burns fit in?

Though service personnel are often thought of as transient residents, there were—and still are—individuals and families in the military population who decided to make Hawai'i their permanent home by choice and at times by circumstance. A case in point was the family of army sergeant Harry Burns. Assigned to Fort Shafter in 1913, Harry Burns moved to Hawai'i with his wife, Anne, and their two sons, John and Edward. John had been born in 1909 at Fort Assinneboine, Montana; Edward arrived two years later at Fort Des Moines, Iowa. The family continued to grow in Hawai'i with the birth of two daughters, but all was not bliss for the Burns family. Harry was a drunk and a womanizer. According to various accounts, Harry left the family by 1919, never to return.[2]

Abandoned in paradise, Anne Florida Burns, a strong Catholic, decided to raise her family in Hawai'i and secured a job as the postmistress on Fort Shafter. The family lived in the poor Kalihi section of Honolulu, where Jack came to know the "brown skins" he would later champion. Jack had a troubled childhood growing up without a father in Honolulu. During his teenage years, Mrs. Burns sent Jack to live with her brother in Kansas, where he came under the influence of Catholic priests at school. After a brief stint in the army, Jack returned to Hawai'i and finally completed high school in 1930. Burns's troubled childhood left an indelible imprint on the man. The complicated personality that Fuchs spotted in 1958 was a residual product of these early years. Burns's daughter, Sheenagh, describes the legacy of that troubled period as Jack's ensuing personal struggle with what it meant to be a "father"—both to his immediate biological family and later to the extended family of "his boys and girls" in the Democratic Party.[3]

In 1930 the twenty-one-year-old Burns met a newly arrived army nurse stationed at Schofield Barracks, Beatrice Van Vleet. The couple married in 1931, moved to California for a couple of years, and started to raise a family with the birth of John Jr. They returned to Hawai'i in 1933. The next year Jack began his career in the Honolulu police department, and the couple's second child, Mary (later Sheenagh), was born. In 1935 the course of the Burns family took a new direction when Bea, while pregnant with their third child, contracted polio. She bore her third child, who died a few hours later. The polio left her permanently weakened, and Bea, like President Roosevelt, was confined to a wheelchair. In 1937 Bea was pregnant again. Though the chances of surviving the pregnancy seemed insurmountable, the couple would not consider abortion. With the help of therapy and massages from Japanese masseur Henry Seishiro Okazaki, Bea delivered a healthy baby boy whom they named James Seishiro Burns. People often called James the "miracle baby." His birth signified to John and Bea the strength of their Catholic faith.[4]

After the birth of James, the Burns family was complete. Jack's career with the police department progressed and by late 1940 he had begun the prewar liaison work between the police department and the Japanese community that we have earlier sketched. Over the next two decades Burns's life was indeed shaped in the caldron of Hawai'i politics. But his travels in his first twenty-five years on the western trail from Montana to Iowa to Hawai'i to Kansas, back to Hawai'i, to California, and back to Hawai'i again clearly put Burns in the "western" tradition of many mainland migrants to the islands. When John Burns finally came to Washington in 1956–57, he carried with him a reputation built in the islands and a heritage from the American West. Burns would need both to gain the political clout that would result in a winning vote for statehood legislation. As the first Democratic delegate since the 1930s, Burns also wanted to show that he possessed skills and abilities that his Republican predecessors somehow lacked. What did he do?

Some of Burns's chroniclers and confidants claim that the new delegate arrived in the nation's capital as a seasoned figure in national Democratic politics—thus having an advantage Mrs. Farrington lacked. His prior attendance at National Democratic conventions as chairman of the party in Hawai'i, some claim, gave him entrée into the inner circles of congressional power controlled by Sam Rayburn and Lyndon Johnson. His personal style, some said, was like that of the Texans. This was also a trait that the Farringtons could not have matched.[5]

This description is, I think, overly optimistic. I believe Burns had a more difficult entry into Washington. The now embittered Mrs. Farrington did nothing to introduce him to friends of Hawai'i in Washington. Regardless of his participation in party conventions, his standing as a Democratic candidate who could win election in the potential new state of Hawai'i was still questionable at best. He had lost more elections in the past than he had won. He finally triumphed not against a seasoned political veteran, but against the widow of the former delegate. And Burns's leadership of the rising Japanese American politicos in Hawai'i was not a role that would necessarily endear him to Southern Democrats. Burns believed, naïvely, that Southern opposition to Hawai'i's racial makeup was not based on any innate Southern racism. Instead he was convinced that previous Republican delegates to Congress and their supporters had created the racial issue and turned Southerners against Hawai'i. It is, I think, more realistic to believe that when Sam Rayburn told Bob Bartlett in early 1957 that he did not like Hawai'i because it had "too many Japs," the Speaker was expressing his own racial views rather than any prejudices suggested to him by Hawai'i Republicans.[6]

Burns faced another dilemma when he arrived in Washington. The "Alaska First" strategy withheld from him the opportunity to publicly champion statehood for Hawai'i. He would have to take a back seat while the various Alaska teams of Snedden, Seaton, and Stevens, along with Bartlett, Lehleitner, and O'Brien, pushed the Alaska bill through Congress. Ironically, only the Republican Eisenhower was initially more interested in Hawai'i than Alaska in the Eighty-fifth Congress. Placed in the position of biding his time, what did Burns do to build his own level of support for Hawai'i in the Congress?

Early in the Eighty-fifth Congress, Burns reached back to World War II to find an issue that gave him instant access to virtually every member of Congress. With the bombing of Pearl Harbor in December 1941, all of America turned westward to the mid-Pacific and wanted to know if one of "their boys" now lay entombed under the Pacific. The death toll at over two thousand connected each of the forty-eight states to Hawai'i. Fifteen years later when Burns arrived in Washington, virtually every congressman had a direct connection to Hawai'i through the Pearl Harbor disaster. And Burns had lists with the names of every one of those "boys" who formed that connection.

Burns also carried with him legislation prepared by the territory's Pacific War Memorial Commission, which he introduced as HR 5809, to build a memorial to the December 7 victims above the sunken hulk of the *U.S.S. Arizona*. The delegate now had a legitimate reason to contact every member of the Congress and to expect a response. HR 5809 passed the House in August 1957 and proceeded to the Senate. This became Burns's first legislative entrée to Lyndon Johnson. It was the Texans who lost their lives at Pearl Harbor, rather than those saved by the 442nd Regimental Combat Team in France, who attracted the Senate majority leader's attention. An August 19, 1957, letter from Burns to Johnson included the names of seventy-five Texans who died on the *Arizona*. Johnson responded to the new delegate with thanks and enthusiasm. The Senate accepted the House bill and finally passed it in March 1958. It then went to President Eisenhower who promptly signed it. After funds were raised both privately and by Congressional appropriation, the Arizona Memorial was completed in 1961 and dedicated in 1962. Thus the first piece of legislation proposed by John Burns bound Hawai'i to the nation's western military heritage. It also brought legislative success to Burns while the Alaska statehood bill was still being held captive in the House Rules Committee.[7]

The symbolism of the *U.S.S. Arizona* Memorial was Burns's calling card to Congress. It gave him a reason to make the rounds of congressional offices with a cause other than statehood. He and Bea also entertained members of Congress at home, though never specifically mentioning the potential Hawai'i statehood legislation. In that entertaining Bea had a special role. The strength and determination she exuded from her wheelchair were clearly evident to all she met and were particularly striking in the late 1950s when the nation endured several polio epidemics. Though never mentioned in any interview I

conducted, one can well imagine that Bea reminded some older congressmen of the wheelchair-bound Franklin Roosevelt.[8]

In those first eighteen months of the Eighty-fifth Congress from
January 1957 to June 1958, John and Bea Burns built a strong political
base in Washington while waiting for the Alaska statehood bill to pass.
Members of Congress, including the Texans, came to know and like Jack
Burns. In that strange caldron of Washington politics where personality
was often everything, some congressmen found a reason—new or
renewed—to like Hawai'i as they came to like Burns. While the temper
of Washington changed in those eighteen months, Hawai'i changed too.
Before picking up the saga of what would happen in Washington after
mid-1958, we must return to Hawai'i, where the Red Scare had finally
subsided and the national Republicans now worked to strengthen their
chances to win the governorship in the potential new state.

Taming the Red Scare and the Rise of Bill Quinn

If Burns had to stand back while Alaska went forward in his first eighteen months in office, this may well have been a fortunate situation for
the islands' statehood chances. Had Hawai'i gone first in 1957, it might
well have found itself ensnared in a resurgence of the Red Scare. As
noted earlier, the Red Scare flared once again in November 1956 with
the presence of the Eastland committee in Hawai'i and with the
renewed anti-Communist alarm of the local conservative group IMUA.
It has always been difficult to discern just whom IMUA represented or
how powerful it ever was. Certainly it represented an older conservative haole constituency. The support of both Walter and Louise
Dillingham, as well as former territorial governor Lawrence Judd (the
governor who presided over the Massie case), lent some credence to its
power. But no current elected officials, even those who denounced the
ILWU, were members in 1956. Its president and most prolific spokesman
in 1956, Dr. Lyle Phillips, was not a person of particular rank.
Nonetheless congressional opponents seized upon IMUA's statements
and publications to attack Hawai'i in the Congress. To counter this still-
lingering threat to statehood, several prominent islanders started a vigorous campaign to tame the Red Scare, most notably *Advertiser* publisher
Lorrin P. Thurston and one of his editors, Buck Buchwach.

Thurston's concern with Communism in the islands had long been
a source of consternation to statehooders, particularly as Thurston was a

member of the Hawaii Statehood Commission. Thurston had been a supporter of statehood immediately after the war. Both he and his paper
became particularly concerned with the ILWU and its Communist
affiliation during the sugar and dock strikes of the late 1940s. By 1950
Thurston seemed willing to postpone statehood until the Communist
issue was settled. In early 1957 he publicly supported statehood once again
and went on to claim that Communism was not an issue in the islands.[9]

In a speech before a West Coast meeting of the Democratic National
Committee in February 1957, Thurston turned his attention to the
ILWU once again. Thurston did not claim that the ILWU was free of
Communist influence. Instead he emphasized that the ILWU did not
control Hawai'i politics, particularly not since the elections of 1956.
Thurston pointed to the success of anti-ILWU candidates and to the
failure of the ILWU during the previous 1955 legislative session to repeal
the Dock Seizure Act of 1949. The publisher highlighted Samuel Wilder
King as an avowed foe of both Communism and the ILWU. Thurston
retained his earlier dislike of the ILWU and in no way tried to sever
the link of union leaders to Communism. He simply claimed that the
ILWU's opponents were strong enough to resist any takeover of the
local government. Hence statehood for Hawai'i posed no Communist
threat to the nation.[10]

Much of Thurston's stance came from information supplied to him
by Buck Buchwach. Buchwach told me in a 1986 interview that he was
particularly proud of the fact that he had been able to convince Thurston
to support statehood in 1957. Buchwach's findings were published by
the Hawaii Statehood Commission in an April 1957 pamphlet entitled
"Hawaii: Communist Beachhead or Showcase for Americanism?"[11]

Buchwach's pamphlet, like Thurston's speech, emphasized that the
ILWU was regularly rebuffed in its attempts to control local politics,
particularly in the elections of 1956. ILWU opponents were elected, and
some candidates supported by the ILWU were defeated. Buchwach
placed even greater emphasis on the patriotism of the numerous ILWU
members who had served, and in many cases given their lives, during
the Korean conflict. Some 426 "boys" from Hawai'i died in Korea—
more per capita than from any state. There were no instances of cow-
ardice or defection among Hawai'i's soldiers. Of some twenty-two
Americans who chose to stay with the Communists in Korea, not one
was from Hawai'i. Buchwach also noted that Senator Hugh Butler, one
of the early anti-Communist opponents of Hawai'i, said before his death

in 1954 that Hawai'i's service in the Korean War effectively disproved any Communist threat in the islands. The editor tried to shift attention on the ILWU from its leaders to its rank-and-file members. In emphasizing the Americanism of the union's 24,000 members, both Buchwach and Thurston reached a somewhat ironic conclusion. Communism, they said, had little chance of survival in Hawai'i because of the economic prosperity of Hawai'i's workers. Both editor and publisher acknowledged that such prosperity was the result of the union contracts negotiated by the ILWU![12]

Both Buchwach and Thurston praised Governor Samuel Wilder King as a bulwark of defense against any Communist threat to the islands. But the Eisenhower administration came to see King's stance toward the 1955 territorial legislature as more a liability than an asset. King vetoed seventy-one pieces of legislation passed by the new Democrats elected in the so-called "Revolution of 1954." Some of those vetoes were against pro-ILWU bills and other poorly crafted laws. But King's vetoes did not appear to be a simple sorting of poorly-written from well-written legislation. King seemed to oppose anything the Democrats wanted—a direct challenge to the will of the people. U.S. Interior Secretary Fred Seaton now wondered if the appointed governor stood any chance of becoming an elected governor. This consideration was more important in Washington than King's anti-Communist image.[13]

Seaton thought that the time had come to inject a new Republican face into the Hawai'i political arena, possibly one that was not so tied to the struggles of the past. Seaton did not reappoint King to a second term in early 1957. The secretary delayed for several months before making a new appointment. In July he called young Honolulu attorney and World War II veteran William F. Quinn to his Washington office. Over lunch, the secretary asked Quinn if he would like to be governor of Hawai'i. In later years Quinn admitted that he was taken by surprise with Seaton's offer and really did not know why he was asked. Betty Farrington later said that she suggested his name to the secretary. But just who was Bill Quinn—and what was new and attractive about him?[14]

In some ways Quinn was similar to John Burns, the man he would be pitted against to win the new state. An Irish Catholic mainlander like Burns, Quinn came from a middle-class family and grew up in New York and Missouri. He finished St. Louis University in 1940 and joined the navy in 1942. After the war he enrolled at Harvard Law School and graduated in 1947. He accepted a job that year with Robertson, Castle

& Anthony, a prestigious, politically liberal law firm in Honolulu. The "Anthony" was martial law critic Garner Anthony, the former territorial attorney general. The young lawyer/veteran, his wife, Nancy, and their ever-growing family migrated westward to Hawai'i, as the Burns family had done thirty-five years earlier.[15]

Quinn was an attractive new figure in Honolulu, much like the attractive young Nisei veterans who were returning from mainland law schools to build the renewed Democratic Party. Quinn, as much as Dan Inouye or Spark Matsunaga, was part of the "greatest generation." Had he gone to Alaska in 1947, he would have been part of that heralded cadre of "invading veterans." So much has been written about the return of the 442nd that little is said in histories of Hawai'i about the mainland veterans who came to the territory to build a new life after World War II. Whether Quinn represented a larger group or was seen as just an individual on his own, he attracted local attention. The affable mainlander's pleasing personality won him support within the local Republican Party. Quinn enjoyed music and sang in local theatrical productions. He readily donned an Aloha shirt and played the ukulele. In 1956 Quinn ran as a Republican for the territorial senate. Though he lost the race, he gained a reputation as an able campaigner who truly enjoyed meeting the people. When Seaton offered him the governorship in July 1957, Quinn readily accepted and took office in September.

In less than a year, from September 1957 to June 1958, Quinn emerged as a formidable political figure, in part because of his interaction with the ILWU. The union, whose power Thurston and Buchwach had insisted was on the wane in early 1957, roared back in the latter part of the year. In June 1957 the U.S. Supreme Court acquitted fourteen defendants in a Smith Act trial appeal from Los Angeles and set a precedent for the handling of the Hawai'i convictions. It seemed only a matter of time before the Ninth Circuit Court of Appeals ruled on the Hawaii Seven. In January 1958 the court acquitted Jack Hall and the other six. Though Hall had been living in Hawai'i during his appeal and continued to conduct union business, his strength as a union leader was obviously compromised while he was still under criminal conviction. With its leaders freed, the ILWU felt stronger to negotiate a major wage raise in the upcoming 1958 contract for workers in the sugar industry. Whether or not the union was convinced that the negotiations would lead to a strike, it had amassed a substantial strike fund over several years. When the initial contract talks with the Hawaiian Sugar Planters' Association (HSPA) reached loggerheads in late January 1958, the ILWU called a strike on February 1. Thus began the so-called Aloha Strike of 1958, the first major strike since 1949.[16]

The ILWU carefully cultivated the public impression that the strike was against the sugar industry, not against the entire territory of Hawai'i as had been the case in the Dock Strike of 1949. Union members participated in various community improvement projects, such as cleaning parks, while the strike wore on. But when the strike approached its third month, Quinn decided to act as its mediator. Unlike his predecessors, particularly Stainback, he did not launch into an anti-Communist, Red-baiting attack on the union. Instead he acted truly as a mediator for the good of the people of Hawai'i. As Sanford Zalburg makes clear, it was Quinn who successfully brought the strike to a close after four months in early June 1958. When both sides seemed deadlocked over a fraction of a cent, Quinn went on local radio and mounted widespread public pressure for the ILWU and the HSPA to reach an agreement. The final settlement is generally viewed as favorable to the union; the HSPA, most commentators say, remained recalcitrant too long. Quinn emerged as a peacemaker for the territory, not as an opponent or proponent of either union or management.[17]

There is yet another dimension to Quinn's settlement of the Aloha strike that requires attention. As noted in earlier chapters, there was a "colonial" quality to the strikes of 1946 and 1949. Neither local union nor management officials seemed able to negotiate a settlement. California stockholders in Honolulu firms and ILWU representatives from San Francisco were called in to settle the strike—often *outside* of Hawai'i. Quinn settled the strike with union and management officials *in* Hawai'i. He truly established himself as a commanding new presence in the islands. In less than a year Quinn rose from political newcomer to the "man to beat" in any future election for state office. Quinn's star was ascending in June 1958—just as Congress passed the Alaska statehood bill and the future of Hawai'i now came actively into play. John Burns had done his job by waiting patiently in Washington for eighteen months for his chance to win statehood. Who would now push the action in Washington—the Democratic delegate or the rising young Republican governor?

A Frustrating Intermezzo on the Potomac and in Honolulu

With the passage of the Alaska statehood bill in June 1958, many people wondered if the Hawai'i bill would now go forward. Republicans in Honolulu and Washington certainly hoped so. But Republicans were not in control of the Congress. Back in January Lyndon Johnson had told the delegation of Burns, Bartlett, and other Democrats that the Hawai'i bill would not be considered before Congress adjourned for the second session. This move was designed to ensure the success of the Alaska First strategy—not only in Congress but also in the Executive Office, where Democrats feared that Eisenhower might sign *only* a Hawai'i bill if both statehood bills were on his desk. Of course, in January no one knew when or if the Alaska bill would ever pass or be signed. Once Eisenhower signed the Alaska bill on July 7, did the "wait" on Hawai'i still hold?

Most historians and virtually all of the people I interviewed, from George Lehleitner to Leo O'Brien, concur that it was a wise policy on the part of Johnson and Rayburn to hold to the January scenario. There simply was not enough time left in the second session, most thought, for the Hawai'i bill to clear both the House and the Senate. The House Rules Committee could still attempt to stymie a Hawai'i bill. The "privileged legislation" maneuver could not be attempted until the Rules Committee had stalled for a significant time. The chance that a Hawai'i bill might fail to pass seemed too great a risk, given the fact that everyone agreed the bill would pass in the Eighty-sixth Congress. Also, both Johnson and Rayburn wanted to use the remaining time in the Eighty-fifth Congress to pass legislation other than statehood. Delegate Burns and other Democratic friends of statehood in Washington did not attempt to mount a drive to push for statehood after July. Instead they tried to assure supporters that Hawai'i would be a priority for action when the Eighty-sixth Congress convened in January 1959.

Such a strategy in Washington was not necessarily appealing in Hawai'i, particularly to the Republicans and the rising young Governor Quinn. In early July, Quinn, with the approval of Secretary Seaton, came to Washington with Sam King and Betty Farrington to mount a campaign to act on a Hawai'i bill now. The Republicans had even secured the endorsement of an editorial in *Life* magazine to this effect. It now appeared that the energetic young governor was trying to seize the statehood spotlight from Burns, who had waited so patiently.[18]

Burns tried to persuade Quinn to go home and accused him of turning the statehood fight into a partisan affair. Actually the partisan affair was not so much for the passage of the statehood bill as for the control of the new state of Hawai'i. Whoever seemed to gain "credit" for statehood would obviously be well positioned to win an elected position in the new state. Quinn persisted and managed to arrange an appointment with Lyndon Johnson. Armed with his copy of *Life,* Quinn saw Johnson after Eisenhower signed the Alaska bill and urged him to move the Hawai'i bill through Congress now. Quinn related that a furious majority leader then leaned forward and shouted, "Listen, young man, no one tells me how to run this Senate, not you, not *your* President, not *Life* magazine; that bill will be considered only when and if I want it considered, understand?" If Johnson had ever considered bringing up the Hawai'i bill in July, he certainly was not going to do so at the behest of the young Republican governor. Quinn returned to Honolulu.[19]

Upon Quinn's return, nearly all attention shifted away from Washington to Honolulu for the remainder of 1958. Hawai'i Republicans hoped they could use the intermezzo on the Potomac as a way to challenge Burns's commitment to statehood and to win back the delegateship in the November 1958 elections. They assailed his acquiescence to the Alaska First strategy and pointed out that he had brought nothing home in his first term as delegate. If Burns could be defeated, that would also augur well for a Republican victory after statehood.

While hammering at Burns on his commitment to statehood, the Republicans chose as his opponent Farrant Turner, secretary of the territory since 1953. Not only did Turner hold the "number two" appointed post in Hawai'i, he had been the organizer of the 100th Battalion in 1942 and its battlefield commander throughout much of the war until he was relieved of command in late 1943. Born in Hawai'i, Turner was part of the upper-class kama'aina tradition previously embodied by Joseph Farrington. The Republicans now hoped that Turner's "boys," who had indeed revered their wartime leader, would vote for him. Despite the efforts of the Republicans and Turner to unseat Burns, the Democratic delegate prevailed in November, defeating Turner by the same margin that he defeated Mrs. Farrington two years earlier. Though Turner was only sixty-four, he died a few months after his loss in March 1959. Both literally and figuratively, the old guard and the patrician tradition of benevolent paternalism were passing.[20]

In addition to the challenge at the polls, Hawai'i statehooders were disturbed in the July 1958 to January 1959 intermezzo by the unrelenting agitation of IMUA. The local organization continued to claim that Communism was rife in the islands. IMUA's incantations so upset George Lehleitner, now putting his entire energy behind Hawai'i, that he flew to Honolulu in September to debate IMUA's Lyle Phillips. Lehleitner emphasized that the continued sounding of the Red Scare could hurt Hawai'i's chances in the Eighty-sixth Congress. Though Bill Quinn thought Lehleitner was to some extent overreacting, both the governor and John Burns publicly applauded Lehleitner's actions.[21]

Rapid Action for the Fiftieth State

With the elections over and IMUA, to some extent, rebuffed, statehood supporters in both Washington and Hawai'i breathed a sigh of relief when the Eighty-sixth Congress finally convened in January 1959. The Eighty-sixth Congress contained substantially greater Democratic majorities in both the Senate (62–34) and the House (280–152) than did the Eighty-fifth Congress. Rayburn and Johnson retained their respective leadership roles. In addition to the support the territory had enjoyed in the Eighty-fifth Congress, Hawai'i now had the added votes of the new delegation from Alaska. By January 1959 statehood for Hawai'i had become a national media event. Not only did *Life* and other major magazines support Hawai'i, author James Michener, who moved to Hawai'i in 1958 to begin his epic novel *Hawaii*, made many statements in favor of statehood. Endorsements also came from movie stars such as Dorothy Lamour, who had appeared in several postwar films with a Pacific theme.[22]

By the time the Eighty-sixth Congress opened there was little question that the Hawai'i statehood bill would pass. With over fifty cosponsors, the bill submitted to the Senate was assured of success. Most objections to Hawai'i, such as non-contiguity, had been effectively co-opted by the passage of the Alaska bill. Once pierced by the needle, Congress could do little to hold back the thread. The only thing that surprised Hawai'i's supporters was how quickly the legislation passed.

Johnson had, of course, promised Burns that the Hawai'i bill would be a priority. Johnson knew that Eisenhower was anxious to see Hawai'i admitted. The majority leader most likely wanted to give the president the Hawai'i bill as soon as possible to gain his support on other legislation—particularly given the stalemate between the Congress and the president in the Eighty-fifth Congress. Johnson did not want to give Eisenhower an excuse to stall other legislation while waiting for a Hawai'i bill.

Both House and Senate committees began hearings in January and February. By early March the Interior and Insular Affairs committees of both houses favorably reported identical Hawai'i statehood bills. The particulars of the Hawai'i bill were not as controversial as those in the Alaska bill. The major item of note in the bill itself was a decision to limit Hawai'i's U.S. House of Representatives delegation to one member, though the territory's population justified two. A revision to two seats would have to occur after the 1960 census. Though the House Rules Committee and chairman Smith attempted to stall, it was clear that the Hawai'i bill would be presented as "privileged legislation" if Smith dawdled too long. Given the fact that Rayburn was again Speaker, Smith did not want to be embarrassed on the floor of the House a second time with Rayburn's rulings. The Rules Committee scheduled the bill for debate on March 11.[23]

Lyndon Johnson seized the initiative for first action in the Senate and announced that the bill would come to the floor for debate on the same day, March 11. Few foresaw that the vote would also come that day. One reason for such speed may have been the threat of the young Republican governor from Hawai'i, whom Johnson clearly saw as a contender for future control of the new state. When Johnson scheduled the bill for floor debate, Secretary Seaton phoned Quinn in Honolulu and told him to fly to Washington as the vote could come at any time. When Johnson heard that Quinn was on the way, he went to several Southern senators, particularly Richard Russell of Georgia and Olin Johnston of South Carolina, and asked them to withhold their dissenting speeches from the floor and to simply publish them in the *Congressional Record*. Johnson is reported to have said to some of his Southern colleagues, "That young S.O.B. Republican Governor from Hawaii is on his way now and I want to get this bill through before he gets here." The bill indeed passed minutes before Quinn's taxi brought him from the airport to the Capitol. The vote was 76 to 15. The opposition was from the South, as it had always been. But as in the case of Alaska, the South was substantially split. Stalwarts for Alaska and long-time friends of Hawai'i such as Holland of Florida and Long of Louisiana voted in favor, as did Johnson and Yarborough of Texas who had been absent on the Alaska vote.[24]

The House acted with equal speed. Leo O'Brien said the Hawai'i bill, compared to the Alaska bill, was "easy." No miracles or shamrock tie tacks were needed to win the votes. Rather than debate their House bill, O'Brien and his supporters accepted the Senate bill as a substitute and passed it on March 12 by a vote of 323–89. This was the fourth time the House had passed a Hawai'i statehood bill. The votes had always been there. Only the assured signature of the Republican president was now needed for the fiftieth state to complete the union. Eisenhower quickly announced that he would sign on March 18.[25]

The Battle for the New State of Hawai'i

Eisenhower's signing of the statehood bill had never been in doubt. The ceremony could have been a bipartisan victory celebration that signified the end of the long battle for Hawai'i statehood that had been fought by Republicans and Democrats since the end of World War II. This celebration was not to be. The Republican administration turned it into the first shot in a battle to win the new state of Hawai'i—specifically to win a Republican congressional delegation and the governorship. The Republicans had lost completely in their bid to win a single position in the new forty-ninth state of Alaska, which elected an all-Democratic delegation to Washington. They did not intend to let Hawai'i slip away. The territory had sent no Tennessee Plan delegation to Washington. Thus there was no preselection of the state's congressional delegation, as had been the case in Alaska. The Republicans wanted to win as much of it as possible. It was open season in Hawai'i.

Eisenhower signed the Alaska statehood bill in private, so as not to be seen with a room full of Democrats. The Hawai'i signing was staged as a media event with forty pressmen and photographers there. Eisenhower's office was filled with prominent Republicans, but John Burns was not invited to the signing. Nine pens were used in the signing and given to or sent to prominent Republicans including Lorrin Thurston and Bill Quinn. The pen actually used by the president was sent to Mrs. Farrington as a token of appreciation for the work that she and Joe had done over the years. Years later the former delegate pointed to the pen, framed on a table in her apartment, and told interviewer Michaelyn Chou that Burns was not "inadvertently" omitted. "It wasn't inadvertent," she said. "It was on purpose I know all about it." According to the former delegate, the president omitted Burns because "the

Farringtons did it all." Eisenhower wanted to send the message that statehood for Hawai'i had been a Republican affair.[26]

Burns said he was not initially surprised at his snubbing because he thought the signing would be a private affair as it had been for the Alaska bill. He gave no other reaction after the signing became a media event. At that moment he was probably more concerned about his own future role in the upcoming statehood elections. Would he run for the U.S. Senate, the governorship, or anything at all? Burns was in the same quandary that Alaska's Bob Bartlett had faced a year before— and he seemed as incapable as the Alaskan of making up his mind. The only thing that seemed clear in the first days after the signing was that Bill Quinn would be the Republican candidate for governor—and a candidate who would be extremely difficult to beat. Indeed, the "young S.O.B. Republican Governor," as Lyndon Johnson called him, appeared to be the leading figure in territorial politics. He was on the forefront of the Republican charge to win the battle for the new state of Hawai'i.

By all accounts, John Burns would have preferred to run for the U.S. Senate. Like Bartlett, he enjoyed Washington and the collegiality of the Congress. By 1959 he indeed had many friends, including majority leader Johnson, who had grown much closer to him in the second term of the Eighty-fifth Congress. Bea would also have preferred to remain in Washington. If any other Democrat could have run and beaten Quinn, Burns would have chosen Washington. It appeared that only Burns stood a chance to beat Quinn, and the delegate could not see turning over the first governorship to a Republican who could then make roughly five hundred initial patronage appointments. In effect, Quinn made Burns's decision to run for governor—a position to which he did not fully commit until some time in April 1959.[27]

Having opted to run for governor, Burns then decided, to the consternation of all of his supporters and all future historians, to remain in Washington until June 1959 rather than return to Honolulu in the first glow of statehood excitement and prime the Democratic charge to win the new state. Burns later talked of "duty," important sugar legislation in Congress, and discussions with Lyndon Johnson about a potential East-West Center that needed his attention. He had promised Bea that he would attend his son Jim's college graduation in late May in Kansas. Still, there would have been plenty of time to fly to Honolulu and come back to Washington. He did go to Seattle to make a speech at the ILWU convention, but not to Honolulu. Inouye and others had urged him to come back and start the bandwagon rolling. But he took his own advice.

We can only wonder what was on his mind. Did he believe he was invincible in the battle with Quinn? An April Lou Harris poll showed him trailing Quinn 2–1 in the gubernatorial battle. Did he believe that in Hawai'i, where campaigning was all-important, that he did not have to *win* the voters. If so, this was possibly the most naïve of his political assumptions—save for his unshakable belief that Southerners had no innate racial objections to Hawai'i's Asian population. Regardless of what was on his mind, he did not return to Hawai'i until June 6, 1959. The primary for the state elections, as well as a plebiscite required by the statehood bill for the people to accept statehood, was set for June 27.[28]

Burns's decision to remain in Washington was not the only miscalculation in his plans to organize the Democrats for the battle. Historians of the Democratic Party in Hawai'i make it clear that Burns's insistence on controlling the selection of local Democratic candidates while he was still in Washington posed an equal dilemma. After the 1958 legislative elections, the Democrats resumed their old habit of dividing into multiple factions. Burns could not control it all from Washington, though he felt compelled to try. He wanted to push older Democrats for the two U.S. Senate seats—namely Chinese Hawaiian William Heen and Oren Long, the former appointed governor who had been elected to the territorial legislature in 1956 and 1958. He wanted Dan Inouye to run for the U.S. House seat. However, in the confusion of Burns's absence from Hawai'i, Inouye filed for the Senate seat. Patsy Takemoto Mink, one of the few young women among the aspiring Democrats, filed for the House seat. Burns then told Inouye to file for the House, much to the upset of Mink. Burns also tried to persuade Spark Matsunaga not to run for lieutenant governor. Burns wanted Mits Kido as his running mate. All of this long-distance control antagonized members of the party. Matsunaga told me in 1988 that he and others wearied of Burns's constant desire to control their careers before, during, and after 1959. Why, Matsunaga said, had he risked his life in Europe with the 100th to come home and be told not to run for office.[29]

The fallout from the June primary was interesting. Voters, as expected, elected Burns and Kido to run for governor and lieutenant governor. For Congress, Inouye became the candidate for House. Former governor Long won a Senate nomination, but the second Senate nomination was captured by Frank Fasi, a maverick Democrat who was not in the

Burns camp. Fasi, who had come to Hawai'i from Connecticut as a marine in World War II, was something of a gadfly. He was most noted as a conservative anti-Communist critic of the ILWU and had just won his first elected office to the legislature in 1958. Nonetheless, Democratic voters chose him over William Heen, a seasoned former member of the legislature and a judge.

There was less stress in the selection of Republican nominees. As expected Quinn was the nominee for governor; his running mate was Chinese Hawaiian James Kealoha. Though it is unlikely that any Republican could have challenged Quinn for the gubernatorial nomination, any possibility of challenge vanished a few days after the statehood bill was signed with the death of Samuel Wilder King on March 24. King had definitely hoped to be a candidate for governor of the new state. He had served the territory well in its quest for statehood. It was King who as delegate to Congress had started the modern statehood battle with his 1935 Hawai'i statehood bill. It was King who had brought the first congressional committees on statehood to Hawai'i in 1935 and 1937. He had defended the loyalty of Hawai'i's Japanese Americans in Congress during the darkest hours of wartime hysteria. For this stand Betty Farrington said he earned the nickname in Washington of "Sampan Sam." He left the Congress to serve in the navy during World War II, as he had also done in World War I. He returned to Hawai'i and was elected president of the 1950 Constitutional Convention. His term as governor from 1953 to 1957 estranged many of the islands' people from him, but there is no doubt that he believed he was protecting the territory. His service to the territory and his support for statehood had been as long and as dedicated as anyone alive in 1959. He had run for and been elected to the territorial legislature in 1958, where he sat with Oren Long. Though death robbed King of his hope to become the first elected governor, it forestalled the level of squabbling within the Republican camp that afflicted the Democrats.

For the congressional delegation, voters in the Republican primary chose Chinese American Hiram Fong for the Senate. Having lost his seat in the territorial legislature in 1954, Fong had prospered in the intervening five years with his banking company, Finance Factors. He had not run for the legislature since 1954. His biographer, Michaelyn Chou, told me that Fong simply decided to give politics another try in 1959. The second Senate seat went to Wilfred Tsukiyama, a Japanese American who been in the legislature since 1946 and had been active in Republican politics since 1924. The House nomination went to Charles Silva, a Republican legislator of Portuguese background.[30]

Some historians note, seemingly with surprise, that the Republican Party, the party of the "haves," fielded a more ethnically diverse set of candidates than the "revolutionary" Democrats, the party of the "have nots." There was nothing surprising about this diversity at all. The Republicans, as noted in our discussion of the Revolution of 1954, had long been a party of opportunity for Hawai'i's Asian American population. Both Fong and Tsukiyama were seasoned politicians whose careers began while Dan Inouye, Patsy Mink, and even Spark Matsunaga were in school or college.

What is important in this slate of nominees for the first state elections is not a squabble over which party was the more ethnically progressive, but the extraordinary diversity of candidates who felt comfortable running for office in both parties. There were Chinese and Japanese Americans (both men and women), Caucasians (both those who had been in the islands for decades and newcomers like Quinn and Fasi who arrived during and immediately after World War II), and Hawaiians. Nothing like this ethnic diversity had ever happened in another state. What is truly remarkable in this story of completing the union is the fact that some of the candidates who were elected so naturally by "local custom" in Hawai'i would seem extraordinary, even revolutionary, when they reached the Congress of the United Sates.

The June primary that fielded such a diverse set of candidates for national and local office also provided the venue for the statehood plebiscite. In the August 1958 plebiscite Alaskans had endorsed statehood by a 5–1 majority. Hawai'i's voters in a record turnout endorsed statehood by a 17–1 majority: 132,938–7,854. Though numerous small rural precincts in Alaska actually voted against statehood, only the tiny and isolated all-Hawaiian precinct of Ni'ihau—out of 240 precincts—voted negatively. Seemingly everyone wanted statehood. The resounding majority of the vote appeared to belie the old fear that statehood was at least secretly opposed by conservative haoles and native Hawaiians. Sound majorities in even the most conservative haole precincts dispelled any lingering notion that IMUA was a potent force against statehood.

Predominantly Hawaiian precincts, with the exception of Ni'ihau, also voted positively. Suggestions that Hawaiians who opposed statehood did not vote seemed offset by the massive 99 percent voter turnout. Had the fears expressed by Kamokila Campbell in 1946 vanished? On March 17, five days after the statehood bill passed, Kamokila celebrated her seventy-fifth birthday with a festive party. Bedecked as usual in leis and finery, she greeted her guests with hugs and kisses and later danced a hula "that made sparks fly." During the evening she told her guests that her greatest compliment was being called a Hawaiian. Then she toasted statehood, saying, "I have always been opposed to statehood, but now it is here and many of my friends like it, I shall try to like it too." Did Kamokila's toast indicate that she and the rest of the Hawaiian community had come to terms with statehood?[31]

While Kamokila prepared for her birthday, the Reverend Abraham Akaka, minister of Kawaiaha'o Church, addressed his predominantly Hawaiian congregation the day after the statehood bill passed. Akaka supported statehood and hoped that all Hawaiians would give it a chance in the sprit of Aloha. But his message clearly acknowledged an ambivalence in the minds and hearts of his audience:

> There are some of us to whom statehood brings great hopes, and there are those to whom statehood brings silent fears . . . There are fears that Hawaii as a state will be motivated by economic greed; that statehood will turn Hawaii (as someone has said) into a great big spiritual junkyard filled with smashed dreams, worn out illusions; that it will make the Hawaiian people lonely, confused, insecure, empty, anxious, restless, disillusioned—a wistful people.[32]

A decade after statehood a Hawaiian sovereignty movement would challenge the assumption that native Hawaiians were satisfied with statehood. But in 1959 the flowering of that movement still lay in the future. Most Hawaiians, like Kamokila Campbell, seemed willing to try statehood, at least as an alternative to the territorial past. Nonetheless Reverend Akaka's message reminds us that in the midst of euphoria over multiethnic democracy and the opportunities of American life, there was, and would always be, within Hawai'i a dark cloud. He foresaw that the admission of the fiftieth state might bring the fear of irreversible loss to the original possessors of the islands.[33]

There was only a month between the primary elections on June 27 and the general statehood election scheduled for July 28, 1959. Campaigning would be the key. But Burns never seemed to take Quinn seriously. In 1958 he told Lawrence Fuchs that Quinn was "glib." Glib or not, Quinn was a vigorous campaigner. He was an attractive young candidate and a veteran—the same "greatest generation" mixture that propelled so many of Burns's AJA "boys" to victory in 1954. In contrast, neither Burns's personality nor his campaign style was a match for Quinn. As his son John Burns Jr. noted, "My father has always had this sense, that life is not something to be enjoyed . . . Life was serious business." Dan Inouye described his mentor's campaign style: "He was not the Aloha, aloha, type. He could not sing a song, he can hardly carry a tune. He was not a politician's politician, believe me. Once in a while he would try to say a joke. Inevitably it would fail." In 1959 the contest for Hawai'i's governor was between two Irishmen who could not have been more different. One took life very seriously; the other reveled in joy and song. The latter was the style that most attracted the voters of Hawai'i.[34]

To further complicate matters, the ILWU seemed more intent on defeating Fasi than on electing Burns. The demise of the union's political power announced by Buchwach and Thurston in 1957 was, like Mark Twain's death, greatly exaggerated. The union threw its support behind Republican Hiram Fong for the Senate. Like Joe Farrington, Fong had never shunned the union, but he had never taken orders from it either.

When the election results were tallied, the victors were a mixed, bipartisan lot. With ILWU support Hiram Fong won the Senate against Frank Fasi. Oren Long defeated Wilfred Tsukiyama—though Tsukiyama would soon be appointed the first chief justice of the Hawai'i Supreme Court. Dan Inouye, as everyone expected, won the House seat against Charles Silva. Quinn and Kealoha defeated Burns and Kido by four thousand votes. The delegate was stunned.

In their votes for Fong and Long for the Senate, Inouye for the House, and Quinn for governor, the citizens of Hawai'i would revolutionize the nation. Their delegation would bring the first Chinese American and the first Japanese American to the U.S. Congress. In choosing Hawai'i-born Fong, the voters reached back to the pre–World War II roots of Asian American participation in Hawai'i politics and elected one of their most seasoned legislators. With Inouye the islanders clearly opted for a "local boy" who had served with the 442nd and participated in the Revolution of 1954. In Quinn and Long the voters chose mainland immigrants to the islands. Long was part of the haole immigration of schoolteachers before and after World War I who told their Asian American students that American democracy was their right. He had been an early vice principal at McKinley High School (1919–20), where both Fong and Inouye graduated, and later superintendent of schools. In Quinn the voters elected a young veteran from the mainland who had arrived little more than a decade before.

The election results showed that Hawai'i was for a brief moment in time a vital two-party state. Both Republicans and Democrats could win state and national office. In the first state legislature elected in July, Republicans took the Senate and Democrats the House. In the victories of 1959 the voters also indicated that, Democrat or Republican, they would elect the candidates who represented the "greatest generation." Quinn and Inouye were the most obvious veterans. But Fong was actually the highest ranking officer, having served in Hawai'i from 1942 to 1945 as a major in the judge advocate division of the Seventh Air Force. He retired as a colonel. Even Long, who was far beyond draft age in World War II, served as a lieutenant in the Hawaii Defense Volunteers. In the symbolism of such multiethnic and multiparty victory, John Burns found little room for comfort. The defeated delegate had neither a state office to look forward to nor a promising career to return to. At least for the next month, he had a job—he was still a member of Congress. Until August 21 he could continue to play the historic role of last territorial delegate. Burns returned to Washington with the intention in those last three weeks of saying goodbye to old friends and introducing them to Dan Inouye, who would take his seat in the House.

The Last Territorial Delegate and the Burns Legend

Friday, August 21, was the date chosen for the president to sign the official proclamation admitting Hawai'i to the union. There had been *some* discussion over the selection of the date. Mrs. Farrington, still convinced that the "Farringtons did it all," pressured Secretary Seaton in June to set the proclamation date for October 15—Joseph Farrington's birthday. Admission Day would then be a permanent memorial to her husband. The White House seriously considered her request, but Governor Quinn did not want to wait three months after the statehood elections to launch the new state. He wanted to begin as soon as possible. Eisenhower agreed to his suggestion of the August date.[35]

By mid-August the White House had compiled a guest list for the ceremony. Once again Burns was omitted. An August 14 White House memo listed the invitees as the vice president, the Speaker of the House, Governor Quinn of Hawai'i, the newly elected congressional delegation of Inouye, Long, and Fong; and Lorrin Thurston, chairman of the Hawaii Statehood Commission. The list also included several army officers from the quartermaster corps who would assist in unveiling the new fifty-star flag. Without specifically mentioning the omission of Burns, the White House memo noted that the list of invitees "paralleled" those invited to the signing of the Alaska Proclamation in January. For that occasion delegate Bartlett had been invited as Senator-elect Bartlett.[36]

While there may have been some partisan logic in snubbing Burns at the March signing, there seems little justification for Eisenhower's action in August. The "battle for Hawai'i" was over. The Republicans had won a Senate seat and the governorship. There would be no new state elections for those positions until 1962. Why antagonize Democrats in both Hawai'i and Washington by snubbing Burns in his final hour? Eisenhower appeared to be giving the Democrats a martyr for their next election.

The Democrats definitely felt the snub. When Sam Rayburn heard that Burns would not be invited, he announced that he would not go himself. Burns, however, intervened and personally asked Rayburn to attend out of respect to the people of Hawai'i. On August 20 Burns had his own farewell ceremony with friends in the House. He gave a speech introducing Dan Inouye to the House, but was soon interrupted by friends such as Majority Leader John McCormack, who rose to praise the departing delegate.[37]

The following day Eisenhower proudly greeted the entourage in his office as he signed the proclamation and displayed the new flag. He noted that the occasion was "historic" as two new states had been admitted to the union in one year. He heartily welcomed the new state of Hawai'i to the Union and hoped that her new representatives would "find their work interesting and fruitful for all of us." If the president had focused totally on the future, the absence of the last delegate might not have been so poignant. But completing his remarks, Eisenhower announced, "The Speaker just reminds me of one fact that has great historic significance. Next Monday will be the first time in 158 years there has not been a Delegate in the membership of the Congress of the United States. The Delegates are gone and in their place we have Senators and Congressmen." Eisenhower had certainly ensured that the last territorial delegate would be gone in his office that day![38]

The president then proceeded with the customary multi-pen signing of the proclamation. When Eisenhower offered one of the pens to Sam Rayburn, the Speaker at first refused in disgust. Dan Inouye is reported to have leaned over to him and said, "Why don't you take that pen for Jack Burns." The Speaker then turned to the president and did just that. Rayburn is also reported to have said to Fred Seaton that the snubbing of John Burns was "inexcusable." Inexcusable or not, the deed was now done. The proclamation was signed. Hawai'i was now in; the new fifty-star flag was unfurled. The union was complete.[39]

When Monday, August 24, arrived, the delegates were indeed gone. There were no more territories. So our story might naturally end here. But the snubbing of Burns would reverberate to change the historical record. If the Republicans had tried to write Burns out of the statehood story, his Democratic friends would reciprocate by writing him back in and gradually writing the Republicans out. Over the next several years a "Burns Legend" would unfold that placed Burns and Burns alone at the center of the battle for Hawai'i statehood and for bringing multiethnic democracy to the islands. The saga began as soon as Burns returned to Hawai'i. Some say it had even begun on July 29, the day after the elections, as an "angry" Jack Burns and his supporters vowed to run again for governor in 1962. Soon his friends began collecting a campaign fund. The "legend" would serve as a major tool to ensure Burns's election in 1962.

Burns' friendship with Lyndon Johnson, a major plank in the Burns Legend, blossomed after the White House snubbing. Like Rayburn, Johnson was furious. He replied to a letter from a Burns supporter in Honolulu with the words: "I have known Jack Burns for quite some time. He is a big man—a very big man. I don't believe that he can be 'snubbed' because onus would fall, not upon the man who is omitted from the ceremony, but upon those who chose to omit him." The paths of Burns and Johnson grew increasingly entwined. Burns supported the Texan wholeheartedly for the 1960 presidential nomination. He joined the Johnson campaign staff and spoke around the country—though he could not bring the Hawai'i delegation to the 1960 Democratic Convention with a unanimous vote for Johnson. When Johnson became vice president in 1961, the two remained close friends as Burns prepared for a 1962 rematch with Quinn.[40]

In the years before the 1962 election Burns's admirers spoke and wrote glowingly of him. When the local Republicans erred again in omitting Burns from a November 1959 Admission Day celebration in Hawai'i, visiting congressmen Mike Mansfield and Leo O'Brien emphasized Burns's crucial role in the statehood battle. A major installment in the Burns Legend came in 1961 with the publication of Lawrence Fuchs's *Hawaii Pono*. The mainland author made no secret of his respect and admiration for the "shrewd and complicated man" he had interviewed a few years before. Author James Michener was also a major promoter of John Burns as he prepared for the 1962 run for governor.

When the 1962 elections came, Burns finally triumphed. Historians debate whether "Burns won" or "Quinn lost" in 1962. Quinn seemed to make as many errors in 1962 as Burns had done in 1959. He quarreled with his lieutenant governor, James Kealoha, who ran against him in the primary. Having been out of any political office for the previous three years, Burns had done nothing wrong that the voters could hold against him. Burns and his Hawaiian Chinese lieutenant governor, William Richardson, defeated Quinn by over 32,000 votes.[41]

Burns triumphed as governor in 1962 and again in 1966 and 1970. For more than a decade Burns presided as governor over a solidly Democratic Hawai'i. The vitality of the two-party system that we noted in 1959 quickly came to an end. The Democrats dominated the state legislature. In the Congress, Dan Inouye replaced Oren Long and moved from the House to the Senate in 1962. In the House, Hawai'i was awarded two seats in the 1962 elections and elected Democrats Spark Matsunaga and Tom Gill. Democrat Patsy Mink then replaced Gill in 1964. Only Hiram Fong in the U.S. Senate kept a solid Republican face on Hawai'i's congressional delegation. Burns's reign was cut short in 1973 when cancer so disabled the governor that his duties were assumed by lieutenant governor George Ariyoshi, whom Burns had first encouraged to run for office in 1954. Ariyoshi succeeded his mentor in the election of 1974. Burns died a few months later in 1975.

As Burns's decade in office progressed, the Burns Legend grew. The governor's relationship with Lyndon Johnson waxed stronger after the Texan became president in 1963. As America's role in Asia expanded in the mid-1960s, Johnson relied more and more on his connection with Burns as governor of Hawai'i. To keep his friend in power Johnson returned the campaign favors of 1960. He flew to Honolulu in October 1966 as part of a wider Asian tour and solidly backed Burns in his second run for governor. In a speech at the East-West Center, Johnson told his audience that his interest in both Asia and Hawai'i statehood was stoked by John Burns. "For two decades," the president explained, "I opposed its admission as a state, until at last the undeniable evidence of history, as well as the irresistible persuasiveness of John Burns, removed the scales from my eyes. Then I began to work and fight for Hawaiian statehood. And I hold that to be one of the proudest achievements of my twenty-five years in the Congress." Whether Johnson's interest in statehood and his friendship with Burns were as great in 1958–59 as in 1966 is a question historians can debate. It is clear that Johnson's 1966 speech, which he repeated in his 1971 presidential narrative *Vantage Point,* enhanced the Burns Legend.[42]

Shortly before Burns's death in 1975, the massive John Burns Oral History Project was compiled at the University of Hawai'i. The project contains interviews with most of Hawai'i's post–World War II political leaders, including John Burns. The interviewees, mainly loyal supporters of Burns, make it clear that the master politician John Burns achieved statehood. It was Burns, aide Dan Aoki explained, who thought up the Alaska First strategy. The Farringtons, many interviewees said, would never have been able to work with Democrats the way Burns did. Neither Joe nor Betty could have understood the Southerners, and they certainly could not have been friends with Johnson and Rayburn. Some interviewees even suggested that the Farringtons, particularly Betty, may not have been wholly in support of statehood. Joe Farrington's friendship with Democrat Harry Truman and his ability to persuade Southern Democrat Richard Russell to remove his objection to the naturalization of first-generation Koreans in the McCarran-Walter Act of 1952 seemed to vanish from the historical record.[43]

If Burns and Burns alone had been the architect of statehood, the legend also cast him as the architect of a pluralistic democracy for Hawai'i. It was Burns who opened the political door to Hawai'i's multiethnic population, particularly to Japanese Americans. That door, so the legend insisted, had been tightly closed by the "haole Republican oligarchy" until the Revolution of 1954. In 1985 the islands celebrated the 100th anniversary of the arrival of the Japanese in Hawai'i. In an official centennial history, author Roland Kotani clearly attributed political opportunity for the AJAs, as well as statehood, to Burns. Kotani and other legend-builders seemed not to know that in 1953 the "haole Republican oligarchy," as represented by twenty-seven Republicans in the forty-five-member legislature, included ten Japanese Americans, one Chinese American, two part-Hawaiians and one African American. There were fourteen non-haole Republicans to thirteen haole Republicans. It was difficult for the legend-builders to dismiss Republican Wilfred Tsukiyama, the first chief justice of the Hawai'i Supreme Court, but there was little indication that he was representative of any broader involvement or commitment by Japanese Americans in the Republican Party.[44]

By the time I arrived in Hawai'i in the mid-1980s to compare the statehood movements of Alaska and Hawai'i, the Burns Legend was strong. Only local political scientist Dan Tuttle and George Lehleitner, who returned to Hawai'i in 1984 for the twenty-fifth anniversary of statehood, indicated that the legend contained any degree of exaggeration. In exploring the statehood story I have challenged the Burns Legend not to lessen the contributions of John Burns. Rather my purpose has been to show that support for both statehood and a multiethnic democracy had much deeper roots that spread across a wide segment of the Hawai'i community before and after World War II. Had John Burns alone spoken for the loyalty of Hawai'i's Japanese in November 1941, his voice might well have had little effect. It is unlikely that his voice alone would have persuaded General Emmons to thwart FDR's plan to intern the entire Japanese community of Hawai'i. It is unlikely that his voice alone would have led to the creation of the 100th and the 442nd. However, Burns's voice was joined, even preceded, by many others including Charles Hemenway and Farrant Turner from the haole business community, Sam King and Joseph Farrington in the political arena, plus others in the military and FBI like Robert Shivers and Kendall Fielder, and the community liaison group members in the Emergency Service Community and the Council on Interracial Unity. It was the unique community culture of Hawai'i, embodied by both Democrats and Republicans, not simply by the lone voice of John Burns, that supported Hawai'i's Japanese community during the war and then led to the expansion of that multiethnic democracy after the war.[45]

Yet if Burns was not the exclusive voice, he was certainly among the voices. And by August 1959 he was among the few surviving voices. Farrington, King, Shivers, Hemenway, and Turner were gone. Bill Quinn could not claim a place as one of the voices from the pre–World War II past; he had not been there. Thus Burns, along with Republican

Hiram Fong, became one of the last standard-bearers of those prewar voices who saw the fifty-star flag unfurled. No wonder then that writers like Lawrence Fuchs and James Michener were so attracted to Burns. He symbolized the unique community culture in Hawai'i that offered such a compelling vision of what American democracy could be.[46]

If that unique community culture was not exclusive to Burns, John Burns's role as the last territorial delegate was his alone. In choosing to run for governor rather than U.S. senator, he forfeited a future national position that might have been the legacy of his delegateship. His protégé Dan Inouye would become nationally known. The name John Burns, however, would be known by few outside of Hawai'i as the years after 1959 progressed. The Burns Legend, largely local in origin and scope, served to secure the governorship for Burns and make him an icon within Hawai'i. But what of a national legacy or role for John Burns? Both national and western regional histories have omitted "the last territorial delegate" as surely as Eisenhower did in August 1959. But there is much more to this "shrewd and complicated man" that deserves attention.

John Burns, the last territorial delegate, was a "western man." He had "gone West" as part of the moving frontier—in his case the moving military frontier of the early twentieth century. Like westward-moving pioneers before him, family circumstances left him permanently in a land that had not necessarily been his chosen destination. Those family circumstances did not make his life particularly easy. In that new western land, he interacted with people of different races who had migrated there by other paths or had been there originally. In Burns the East truly met the West. As territorial delegate he reversed the flow and brought the West eastward. He found his way from Hawai'i to the national Congress, where he championed the diverse peoples of his far western home. In his last act as delegate on August 20, 1959, he introduced a representative of those diverse peoples, Daniel Inouye, to the Congress and quietly, without fanfare, returned home. Inouye has remained in Washington to the present day.

With Burns's departure from Washington, we may well pause and remember that Clarence Darrow had gone to Honolulu only a quarter-century before. As the mainland lawyer, who considered himself racially progressive, confronted the multiethnic jury in the Massie case, he was so dumbfounded with its complexity that he soon wrote, "They do not think as we do." A decade after Darrow's visit, millions of other

Americans went to Honolulu during World War II and also tried to understand the cultural complexity of that far western land. In 1959 it was John Burns, the last territorial delegate, who truly brought Honolulu to America and ushered in the hope that the American democracy could aspire to the level of tolerance and diversity that came so naturally in Hawai'i. He introduced the hitherto revolutionary idea that the culture of the American West could rejuvenate, even "civilize," the culture of the East. For decades historians had so often portrayed rejuvenation the other way around. In the person of John Burns, the last territorial delegate, the union was completed. The territorial frontier was closed by a very "shrewd and complicated" western man. Surely this closure too is the stuff of which legends are made—and is a legend that belongs to John Burns alone.

The Alaska Legends

39. In 1955–56 Alaska imitated Hawai'i and held a constitutional convention. In this photo William Egan, president of the convention and later first governor of Alaska, signs the completed document at a February 1956 ceremony in the gymnasium of the University of Alaska in Fairbanks. For this occasion delegate Marvin "Muktuk" Marston commissioned a jade lamp that would "light the way" for the future state. Courtesy of Ralph Rivers Collection, acc#72-049-01N, Alaska and Polar Regions Department, Rasmuson Library, University of Alaska Fairbanks.

40. There were 55 delegates to the Alaska Constitutional Convention. The number was chosen to symbolize the 55 delegates to the 1787 U.S. Constitutional Convention in Philadelphia. The group posed for this photo at the 1955–56 convention. Courtesy of the Reuel Griffin Collection, acc# 69-1078-1, Alaska and Polar Regions Department, Rasmuson Library, University of Alaska Fairbanks.

41. *The 55 delegates remained friends after the convention and formed a group called "55 Club." For the 25th Anniversary of Statehood in 1984, the remaining delegates re-assembled in Fairbanks where they had first met 29 years before. Seated fourth from the left is William Egan, president of the convention and three-term governor of Alaska. Courtesy of Jimmy Bedford.*

No single person symbolized the common cause of statehood for Alaska and Hawai'i more than George H. Lehleitner of New Orleans, Louisiana. Lehleitner became interested in statehood for Hawai'i as a result of his service in the Pacific during World War II. He encouraged Hawai'i to adopt the "Tennessee Plan" and elect a shadow Congressional delegation to lobby for statehood. When Hawai'i would not adopt the Plan he turned to Alaska.

332

42. In this 1956 photo Lehleitner addressed the Alaska Constitutional Convention and presented the Tennessee Plan, which the delegates adopted. Courtesy of George H. Lehleitner.

43. Lehleitner made many trips to Washington to win the support of Congressmen. One of his early converts in the mid-1950s was young Texas representative James C. Wright—one of only two Texas Congressmen to vote for both Alaska and Hawai'i. In this 1988 photo Lehleitner, center, reunites with Wright, left, then Speaker of the U.S. House of Representatives. The author, John S. Whitehead, is on the right. Photo by John S. Whitehead.

333

44. *Lehleitner maintained friendship with both Democrats and Republicans in Hawai'i. At the 1984 Silver Jubilee of Statehood in Hawai'i, Lehleitner greets Republican William Quinn, the last territorial governor and first state governor of Hawai'i. Photo by John S. Whitehead.*

45. *At the 1984 Silver Jubilee Lehleitner greets Democrat William S. Richardson, lieutenant governor of Hawai'i under John Burns and later Chief Justice of the Hawai'i Supreme Court. Photo by John S. Whitehead.*

We're In: The Passage of the Statehood Bills

46. The Alaska Statehood Bill passed Congress in 1958 and admitted Alaska as the 49th State. In this photo President Eisenhower signs the final Proclamation of Statehood on January 3, 1959. On his right is Vice-President Richard Nixon, on his left is Speaker of the House Sam Rayburn. Standing from left are Congressman elect Ralph Rivers, Senators-elect, Ernest Gruening and Bob Bartlett, Interior Secretary Fred Seaton, Waino Hendrickson, Alaska's last territorial governor, David Kendall, counsel to President Eisenhower, former territorial governor Mike Stepovich, and Anchorage Times publisher Bob Atwood. Courtesy of VF Addendum/Statehood, #78-114, Alaska and Polar Regions Department, Rasmuson Library, University of Alaska Fairbanks.

47. *After the signing of the proclamation at the White House, the new 49 star flag was unfurled. Anchorage Times publisher Bob Atwood holds the flag. Standing in front are from the left, Congressman-elect Ralph Rivers, Secretary of the Interior Fred Seaton, Senators-elect Ernest Gruening and Bob Bartlett, former territorial governors Mike Stepovich and Waino Hendrickson. Courtesy of VF Addendum/Statehood, acc# 90-176-449, Alaska and Polar Regions Department, Rasmuson Library, University of Alaska Fairbanks.*

48. *After the passage of the Alaska Statehood Bill, Hawai'i realized that it must now become the 50th state. A statehood delegation from Hawai'i, including (l–r) former territorial governor Oren Long, former delegate Elizabeth Farrington, territorial governor William Quinn, former delegate and territorial governor Samuel Wilder King, and Statehood Commission chair Lorrin Thurston, came to Washington in the summer of 1958 hoping to push quick action on a Hawai'i statehood bill. Courtesy of the Hawai'i State Archives.*

Once admitted as the 50th state in 1959 Hawai'i gained attention for its bi-partisan and multi-racial state and Congressional officials.

49. Chinese American Hiram Fong, a Republican, became the first Asian American elected to the U.S. Senate. Fong is pictured here in August 1959 with President Eisenhower at the signing of the Statehood Proclamation. Eisenhower is presenting Fong with the new 50 star flag. Courtesy of Hiram Fong.

50. Fong and his wife Ellyn share victory with Republican William Quinn and his wife Nancy, the first elected governor and first lady of Hawai'i. Courtesy of Hiram Fong.

51. Japanese American Daniel Inouye, a Democrat, became the first Asian American elected to the U.S. House of Representatives. Inouye is pictured here in the early 1960s with fellow Democrats President John F. Kennedy and Vice-President Lyndon Johnson. Courtesy of the Hawai'i State Archives.

52. *John Burns, who served as the nation's last territorial delegate, failed in his 1959 bid to become Hawai'i's first governor. In 1962 he won the governorship and served three terms until 1974. In this 1963 photo the newly elected Burns is flanked by President John F. Kennedy and now U.S. Senator Daniel Inouye. To secure the 1962 election and successive elections, a "Burns Legend" emerged that transformed Burns into the central figure in Hawai'i's statehood history. This photo conveys the spirit and confidence of that "legend." Courtesy of the Hawai'i State Archives.*

I'll Fly Away

The two far off and distant territories of Alaska and Hawai'i were finally incorporated into the union of states by a myriad of forces—economic, political, social, and technological. The airplane, however, was probably the ultimate symbol of the change that shrank the distance between the mainland and the far off territories. Air bases in both territories were crucial in the winning of World War II and in the permanent defense installations of the Cold War. Regular and affordable air travel made it possible for statehood delegations to fly to Washington to lobby for statehood. Once the Alaska statehood bill passed, the airplane made it possible to place copies of both the *Fairbanks Daily News-Miner* and the *Anchorage Times* on the desk of every Congressman the morning after the bill passed in the Senate at 8PM on June 30.

53. *This photo of the paired flight of two propeller planes from Hawai'i's Aloha Airlines and Alaska's Wien Airlines provides a fitting symbol for the final incorporation of the two territories into the completed union of states. Courtesy of the Vide Bartlett photograph collection, acc. #77-89-2, Alaska and Polar Regions Department, Rasmuson Library.*

Epilogue:
The Legacy of the Fifty-Star Flag

O n July 4, 1960, the new fifty-star flag, first unveiled almost a year before at the proclamation of Hawai'i statehood, became the official banner of the United States. It would fly at every school and above every public building in the nation. At the time of this writing in the summer of 2003, that fifty-star banner has flown for forty-three years. In less than half a decade—and barring any unforeseen and unanticipated act of Congress—it will have flown longer than any other flag of the nation, surpassing the forty-eight-star flag that flew for forty-seven years from 1912 to 1959. The addition of Alaska and Hawai'i appears to have set the permanent boundaries of the nation and completed the union. What the nation ultimately became is what those last two states made it. With that thought in mind, it is worth contemplating what the two new states, as well as the nation they completed, became in the ensuing half-century. What did the statehood battle mean—if anything? Did the admission of those far-off and distant territories signify anything more than the addition of two far-off and distant states? Let us take a moment to look then at the legacy or fate of the states and their statehooders, and then of the nation.[1]

The States' Fate

Neither Alaska nor Hawai'i became a significant lodestar for settlement or migration after statehood. In 1959 their populations were respectively 225,000 and 622,00. By 1980 the respective figures were 402,000 and 965,000; by 2000 the figures were 625,000 and 1.2 million. From statehood to the twenty-first century, the combined population growth of the last two states was roughly one million people, including the military. Suburbs of Los Angeles or Atlanta could claim greater population gains for the same period. However, as in the past, hundreds of thousands of people passed through the new states. Both remained major centers of military defense and became centers of tourism, particularly

Hawai'i. During any given year, there were often more transients than permanent residents in both states.

The forty-ninth state, Alaska, got off to what may have seemed a frustrating start. To some extent the excitement of the battle was now over. Bob Atwood said he suddenly felt he had no "cause" and even considered leaving Alaska. Attention now focused on the much more mundane job of actually building the state government that the new constitution had proclaimed, particularly the court system. As Atwood told me any number of times, "the monkey was on our back now. We couldn't just blame the federal government for our problems." That "monkey" indeed raised a number of perplexing issues. The statehooders had constantly asserted that Alaska could support a state government. But there were definite worries that this assertion might not prove true. The great land patrimony of the statehood act was still just a promise. Which lands should the state select and would those lands produce a wealth to finance the new government? Jay Hammond told me that in the early 1960s some members of the legislature began to wonder if statehood had been a mistake.[2]

Before such statehood doubts could reach a loud resonance, Alaska was wracked by two devastating natural disasters—an earthquake in Anchorage, Valdez, and Seward in 1964; and a flood in Fairbanks in 1967. These two disasters tested the fortitude of the state's people. But as Jay Hammond pointed out, it did something else that may well have been more important. It provided federal disaster relief funds to tide over the economy of the state until the land patrimony could be realized.

The great land patrimony of the statehood act unfurled slowly. Under Governor William Egan, the state began making its land selections. In 1964 1.5 million acres of potential oil lands were selected within the McKay Line reserve on the edge of the Arctic Ocean, the so-called North Slope, including the area known as Prudhoe Bay. In 1968 the Atlantic-Richfield Company found oil on the new land selections. The next year various major oil companies bid over $900 million for leases on state lands on the North Slope. For the first time it appeared that the new state could support itself financially.[3]

Over the next decade a complicated set of twists and turns occurred before the newly discovered oil on—actually under—the northern wastes of Alaska could be delivered to an energy-hungry world. The new state returned to the halls of Congress, where it was necessary to obtain a permit to build a pipeline. After much debate Congress granted a license in 1973 to build an eight-hundred-mile pipeline from Prudhoe Bay to the ice-free port of Valdez in south-central Alaska. Work began in 1974. For the next three years, Alaska's economy boomed with this $8 billion project. In 1977 the first oil from Prudhoe arrived in Valdez. Alaska's oil age had begun. Rather quickly, oil replaced military spending as the base of the state's economy. The statehood patrimony had been achieved.[4]

The advent of the oil age led to several other major developments. The new state had to develop a plan for dealing with the oil companies that would actually develop the resource. If Alaskans had previously bewailed the territory's impotence in the face of Seattle fish packers, they would now have to show that the state could somehow deal with the absentee interests of the world's major multinational corporations. Did they do their job well and retain, as the statehooders said they must, an adequate share of the state's resources for the people of Alaska? The literature on this subject is just beginning to be written.

As the oil age dawned, other issues left in limbo during the statehood struggle emerged. It became necessary to settle the land claims of Alaska natives to gain a clear right-of-way for the pipeline. As had been the case at the time of statehood, federal, not merely state, action was required. This resulted in the congressional passage of the Alaska Native Land Claims Settlement Act (ANCSA) in 1971 that gave natives a settlement of $962 million in cash and forty-four million acres of land. It also created thirteen new native regional corporations to administer the settlement. Over the next three decades the economic power conveyed to Alaska natives by ANCSA gave them a role of economic leadership in the state that matched their growing power in the state legislature. This role expanded the legacy of native political participation that Ernest Gruening had encouraged during and after World War II.[5]

Section 17(d)(2) of ANCSA also recommended the "review" of the remaining unreserved public lands in Alaska with the authorization to withdraw up to eighty million acres of land for inclusion in various conservation and protection units. This "review" eventually resulted in the passage of the Alaska National Interest Lands Conservation Act (ANILCA) in 1980, which set aside almost 131 million acres of land, known in Alaska as the d-2 lands, for protection as "wilderness" and "scenic" areas. As a result, the size of the National Park Service and the National Wildlife Refuge System were doubled.[6]

Though the statehooders had acknowledged the need for withdrawal and protection of some public lands in the 1955–56 state constitution, they had not envisioned "preservation" at the level of ANILCA. Their focus had been more on economic development with responsible conservation. However, in the two decades between 1958 and 1980 a number of incidents occurred that increased the interest of Alaskans and the nation in preservation and in the protection of the natural environment from potentially harmful uses, particularly from both military and nonmilitary nuclear activity.

Beginning in 1958 the Atomic Energy Commission (AEC) and Edward Teller, the nation's leading nuclear advocate, proposed a scheme for Alaska known as Project Chariot, a part of the national Project Plowshare program. Teller envisioned an underwater nuclear explosion at Cape Thompson in northwest Alaska to demonstrate the engineering capability of atomic power. The explosion would carve a man-made harbor and make possible the export of minerals from that portion of the new state. The project soon came under attack from native Alaskans who lived in the affected area and local, as well as "Lower 48," scientists who noted potential environmental hazards from radiation. In reaction to several years of protest, the AEC withdrew the project in 1962. The reaction to Project Chariot had several dramatic repercussions. Environmentalist Barry Commoner noted that his participation in the Chariot protests led to his involvement in the modern environmental movement. The environmental studies demanded by local scientists were a precursor for the Environmental Impact Statements later required by the National Environmental Protection Act of 1969. Native protest led to the creation of the first all-native newspaper in Alaska, the *Tundra Times,* and to the first unified organization of Alaska's different native groups, the Alaska Federation of Natives.[7]

Though Chariot was abandoned, the use of Alaska as a nuclear test zone was not. The lonely uninhabited island of Amchitka in the Aleutian chain, which had been a fortified defense post in World War II, was chosen by the Department of Defense and the AEC to test nuclear warheads considered too large for detonation at the Nevada test site. Three major tests were conducted, in 1965, 1969, and 1971. The latter test, known as "Cannikin," aroused the protest of environmentalists and native groups. One group of protesters, who arrived on a ship named *Greenpeace,* soon formed an environmental activist group by the same name. The 1971 blast at Amchitka proved to be an ending rather than an acceleration of nuclear testing in Alaska. From 1958 to 1971 and thereafter events in the new forty-ninth state were vital components in the growing national concern over environmental pollution and protection. Alaska helped fan the nation's environmental movement and was also a staging area for major native political movements.

Those protest movements of the 1960s as well as the new state's quest for economic development set the stage for the passage of ANCSA and ANILCA. There were now more forces at play than had been the case in the 1950s. Still, all the forces were part of that quest for an "adequate lands bill" that had been such a priority of the statehooders. With the passage of ANCSA and ANILCA, along with the 1958 statehood bill, the lands issue—at least in terms of distribution, ownership, and classification—had largely been settled. Alaska's 365 million acres, the bulk of which had been "vacant, unreserved, and unappropriated" in the 1950s, were now divided between the state, native corporations, and the federal government. Private ownership was still only a minuscule part of the total. Not since Thomas Jefferson contemplated the use and expanse of 530 million acres (828,000 square miles) in the Louisiana Purchase in 1803 had such a massive lands issue confronted the nation and absorbed so much of its energy. Even into the first decade of the twenty-first century, the amalgam of developmental and environmental land issues in Alaska, such as the right to drill oil in the Alaska National Wildlife Refuge (ANWR), still commands the attention of the nation.

By 1980 the completion of the pipeline, along with the passage of ANCSA and ANILCA, set the direction for Alaska's future. Beginning in the late 1970s and dramatically escalating in the early 1980s, the state of Alaska was awash in oil revenues coming from its royalty share of North Slope production and other taxes on the oil industry. It decided to save roughly 25 percent of those revenues in a dedicated fund known as the Alaska Permanent Fund and to distribute the fund's earnings as an annual per capita "dividend" to all state residents. The remaining 75 percent of annual oil revenues was still so great that in 1980 the state abolished the personal income tax that Gruening had labored so long to enact. In the ensuing two decades, as oil revenues waxed and waned like flood and famine, Alaska sought to reenact an equitable tax structure. At the time of this writing in 2003, this structure still seems to be as elusive as it was to Gruening more than a half-century earlier.

The oil bonanza initially resolved a major question in the minds of many Alaskans—certainly of the statehooders. Statehood had been a success. The state's twenty-fifth anniversary observation in 1984 was truly a cause for celebration. The statehooders returned to Fairbanks, where they had written their constitution, and rejoiced. Delegates to the convention, members of the Alaska Statehood Committee, and a few others were awarded medallions as Founders of the State of Alaska by Governor William Sheffield. Who was still there in 1984 to join in the celebration? What had happened to the statehooders in the ensuing quarter-century?

Some had passed on, but many were still around. Bill Egan, the president of the convention and first governor, was there. He had served two consecutive terms (1959–66) and later a third term (1970–74) in the executive office. The delegates praised him in 1984 as they had done at the convention in 1956. Sadly, it was his last hurrah. Egan died of cancer a few months after the celebration.

Walter Hickel was there too. He succeeded Egan as governor in 1966 and pushed plans for the development of Prudhoe Bay oil before becoming U.S. Secretary of the Interior in 1969. He ran for governor again upon his return from Washington, but was bested twice in 1974 and 1978 by Jay Hammond—the young marine who arrived in 1946, opposed statehood, and then was elected to the first state legislature. Hickel succeeded in becoming governor again from 1990 to 1994 and refined the relationship between the state and the oil companies—including various issues of taxation. In 2003 Hickel could still be found at his office in Anchorage, ready to talk of visions for Alaska and the North. His frequent opponent, Jay Hammond, was also ready for conversation at his home in remote Lake Clark.[8]

Alaska's original congressional delegation was not present in 1984. Bob Bartlett died while serving in the Senate in December 1968. Governor Hickel then exercised his power to appoint Bartlett's successor and named Ted Stevens. Though Stevens had worked valiantly for statehood, his appointment in 1968 was not so obvious. After returning to Alaska in 1961, he served in the state legislature. But he lost bids as a Republican contender for Ernest Gruening's Senate seat in both 1962 and 1968. Nonetheless, Hickel concluded that Stevens would be a "survivor." The assumption was correct. Stevens went on to be elected and reelected to the Senate. In 2003 he became president pro-tempore of the U.S. Senate—replacing Strom Thurmond of South Carolina, an ardent opponent of statehood!

By the time Stevens arrived in the Senate, the other members of the "SSS" statehood team, Fred Seaton and C. W. Snedden, had returned to run their newspapers in Nebraska and Alaska. Seaton died in 1974, and Snedden in 1989.

Ernest Gruening's fate also changed in 1968. Gruening had been reelected to the Senate in 1962 and seemed to retain the support of Alaska's people. He increasingly directed his attention to international events, particularly his 1964 vote against the Gulf of Tonkin resolution that escalated the Vietnam War. He was eighty-one years old in 1968. For reasons that have never been fully explained, Gruening was defeated in the Democratic primary that year by Mike Gravel, an Anchorage real estate dealer and state legislator. Gravel hammered away at Gruening's age and portrayed himself as a war veteran—even though he was only fifteen when World War II ended. After his defeat Gruening remained in Washington, D.C. Upon his death in 1974, his ashes were spread on Mount Gruening near Juneau. In 1980 his grandson Clark Gruening, a member of the state legislature, defeated Mike Gravel in the Democratic primary for U.S. Senate but lost in the general election to Republican Frank Murkowski. Murkowski served for almost twenty-two years before being elected governor of Alaska in 2002. As governor, he then used his power of appointment and selected his daughter Lisa, a member of the state legislature, to fulfill his Senate term until the 2004 election. Gruening's Senate seat has thus acquired a dynastic, familial aura.

The lone house seat revolved more rapidly in the first statehood days. Ralph Rivers served until 1967, moved out of Alaska, and died in 1976. He was succeeded by Howard Pollock, an Anchorage legislator, who served until 1971 and, like Rivers, left Alaska. Pollock's successor, Nick Begich, an Anchorage teacher and state legislator, attracted the support of Hale Boggs of Louisiana, the majority leader of the U.S. House of Representatives, whom George Lehleitner first won to statehood in the 1950s. Boggs came to Alaska to campaign for Begich in the 1972 election. On the night of October 16, they took a flight in a small plane from Anchorage to Juneau. The plane disappeared and supposedly crashed. No trace of the plane, Boggs, or Begich was ever found. Both men were reelected in absentia to their congressional seats, but were subsequently declared or presumed dead. In special elections held in March 1973 Boggs was succeeded by his wife, Corinne (Lindy), who served from 1973 to 1991. Begich was succeeded by Republican Don

Young. Young ended the revolving door for Alaska in the House of Representatives and in 2003 remained Alaska's lone member of the House of Representatives. A decade after their death, the U.S. Forest Service commemorated the union of Boggs and Begich with the dedication of the Begich, Boggs Visitor Center at Portage Glacier in the Chugach National Forest outside of Anchorage.

Of more direct attention at the twenty-fifth anniversary were the surviving delegates to the constitutional convention. Of the original fifty-five, thirty were still living. The delegates had maintained their relation with each other over the years through an organization they called "55 Club." In addition to providing a forum for reunions and reminiscing, "55 Club" had a special mission: to preserve the constitution. The constitution they wrote contained a provision that every ten years the question "Shall there be a constitutional convention?" should be placed on the general election ballot. The same question was in the Hawai'i constitution. In the island state, new conventions had been called in 1968 and 1978. The Alaskan delegates, however, concluded that never again could a constitution be written that was not influenced by outside interests. So the delegates coalesced to lobby against the passage of the ballot question. They almost lost in 1970, but through a technicality had the results nullified with another vote scheduled for the next election. In 1972 the question was again on the ballot, and went down to defeat by a 2 (no) to 1 (yes) margin. The delegates won again in 1982 with a similar negative vote. They were thus in jubilation in 1984 and clearly proud that their legendary achievement still set the tone for the state.

In the years since 1984, the delegates have dwindled away. In 1991–92 there was a particularly strong movement to call another convention. Some Alaskans were concerned that only a new convention could deal with such issues as legislative term limits. The surviving delegates, twenty-one in early 1991, once again proclaimed that never again could a convention like theirs take place. They were the right people, at the right time, at the right place. Such a situation could never be repeated, they claimed. Despite the concerns of their opponents, the delegates still prevailed with a negative vote in November 1992. A decade later, in 2002, only six of the fifty-five were still alive. But the furies over the constitution had subsided. The 2002 ballot proposition rejected a new convention with a resounding vote. One of the prime legends of statehood, Alaska's model constitution of 1955–56, had survived into the twenty-first century. It might one day survive the statehooders themselves.[9]

The fiftieth state, Hawai'i, entered the union with few of the uncertainties of Alaska. As had always been the case, there was little concern with the viability of the new state's economy. This had, of course, been the claim of Hawai'i statehooders since 1935. Military defense continued, as in Alaska, to be a major factor in that economy, particularly with the escalation of the Vietnam War in the 1960s and 1970s. Tourism soon became the main civilian component of the economy and quickly eclipsed plantation agriculture in revenue. The arrival of the first jet flights from the both the West Coast of the United States and the Western Pacific (Australia) in 1959 turned the tourist economy from the luxury tourism of the prewar territory to mass tourism. By 1972 tourist revenues of $840 million surpassed even military spending of $732 million. In 1979 four million tourists arrived in Hawai'i. A construction boom to service both the growing tourist industry and an enhanced military infrastructure propelled Hawai'i into an economic boom in the 1960s and early 1970s that surpassed the economic growth rate of the nation at large.[10]

In that booming economy the ILWU remained a strong force, though the radical union and its leaders gradually seemed to become a part of the "establishment." Jack Hall became a director and vice president of the Hawai'i Visitor's Bureau before his death in 1971. Any concern over the union's Communist heritage seemed to vanish with time. In the 1970s and 1980s union leaders remained reticent to speak of their Communist past and its influence on both union and political activity. Possibly future historians may one day discover if that radical union heritage had a lingering impact on the life of the islands, which came as close as any American state to having a European-style "labor party."

The principal "cause" the new state faced after statehood was the "cause" of John Burns. We have already traced the building of the Burns Legend that resulted in Burns's election as governor in 1962. As noted earlier, Burns served for over a decade until cancer cut short his political career in 1973–74. George Ariyoshi then succeeded his mentor and served as Hawai'i's and the nation's first Japanese American governor from 1974 to 1986. The legend set not only the post-statehood tone for Burns's personal role, but also the idea that Burns and his Democrats, who controlled the state legislature throughout his and Ariyoshi's governorship, would bring a greater social and economic democracy to the islands. Not only would the leadership of the state reflect wider racial and ethnic diversity, but the distribution of economic resources would also be much broader than what was perceived to have been the case in the supposedly "oligarchic" period before statehood with a few "haves" and many "have-nots." The economic boom of the 1960s and 1970s certainly gave the appearance of a wider prosperity in the islands.

As Hawai'i approached its twenty-fifth anniversary, the island state, like Alaska, had reason to celebrate. The Silver Jubilee Celebration featured a display of Hawaiian music and dance. It focused less on the state-hooders than did the celebration in Fairbanks. Governor Ariyoshi presided, and it was clear to the audience that the Burns Legend was still alive. There were few formal speakers, though George Lehleitner, whom only a few remembered by 1984, spoke glowingly of Hawai'i's multiracial society and its positive impact on the nation. Only one former governor was alive in 1984, Bill Quinn.

Quinn was still jovial in 1984, though he had returned to a business/legal career after 1962 with little further involvement in politics. He attended the celebration and was given a token acknowledgment during the program. The former governor, however, still had media appeal. Unbeknownst to those present at the celebration in Honolulu's Blaisdell Arena, Quinn received an extensive television interview at intermission by local station KITV. Still brimming with enthusiasm, Quinn continued to exude the image that had so attracted the voters in 1959. Thus it becomes, I suppose, a media question of whether Quinn was featured in the 1984 celebration. If one were at the live performance, the answer is No. If one watched at home on television, Quinn was a star. But there was no intent of a further political future for the first governor. Quinn continued to mind his legal practice. In the summer of 2003 he and his wife, Nancy, continued to live in Honolulu.[11]

Nineteen eighty-four provides a vantage point to comment on the fate of other Hawai'i statehooders. We have already noted that many died shortly before or after statehood. The delegates to the constitutional convention, unlike their legendary counterparts in Alaska, had been forgotten by the mid-1950s. But there was a continued vibrancy in the congressional delegation. As noted earlier, Daniel Inouye has remained in the U.S. Congress since John Burns first introduced him in August 1959. As of the summer of 2003, he had been in the Congress for forty-four years and in the Senate, which he joined in 1963, for forty years. He was third in Senate tenure to Robert Byrd of West Virginia and Edward Kennedy of Massachusetts. Republican Hiram Fong held his Senate seat until 1977 and was not a candidate for reelection in 1976. Fong returned to Honolulu to pursue his business interests. Fong has thrived and in summer of 2003 still lived with his wife, Ellyn, in Honolulu at age ninety-six.

Fong was succeeded in the Senate by Spark Matsunaga, who had served in the House of Representatives since 1963. In 1977 Matsunaga thus joined the Senate chamber with Russell Long of Louisiana, who had told the young veteran in 1950 to find someone in Louisiana who was interested in Hawai'i. Matsunaga served in the Senate until his death in 1990. Matsunaga was succeeded with the appointment of U.S. Representative Daniel Akaka, younger brother of the Reverend Abraham Akaka who uttered those fateful lines in 1959 about statehood and the future of native Hawaiians.

Hawai'i's two seats (since 1962) in the U.S. House of Representatives have changed hands a number of times in the ensuing half-century—in many cases to those not necessarily connected with the statehood movement. We have already noted Inouye's and Matsunaga's service in the House. One other long-time member with roots in the pre-state-hood days deserves mention. Patsy Takemoto Mink was one of the few "girls" in Burns's early cadre of young AJA Democrats. She was probably more "revolutionary" than her mentor or any of the "boys" in the greatest generation. After serving in both the territorial and state leg-islatures, she was elected to the U.S. House of Representatives in 1964 and served there until 1977. Reelected in 1990, she served until her death in 2002 due to complications from adult chicken pox. While in Congress, Mink pioneered legislation for women of all races and eth-nicities, most notably the famed Title IX legislation requiring equal treatment of women athletes in American colleges and universities.

Mink's death in the House certainly conjures up memories both of Joseph Farrington and of Mink's female predecessor in the House, Elizabeth Farrington. We have already noted Mrs. Farrington's frustra-tions after her defeat in 1956 and her continuing efforts to belittle John Burns and to claim that statehood belonged to the Farringtons. She continued this line, as evidenced in her interview with Michaelyn Chou, after Burns's death in 1975 and until her own passing in 1984. One can possibly understand that devotion to her husband drove her to this stand. The two had fought the good fight from that night in Madison, Wisconsin, when Joe proposed and told her that the struggle for statehood would be their life. But she simply could not reconcile herself to the fact that the torch passed in the last lap to Burns. By continually belittling Burns, she elicited a reaction that relegated Joe to a political patrician past of ineffectiveness. As such, Mrs. Farrington did more than any other person, I believe, to blur the political history of Hawai'i and the contributions of Joseph Farrington to the people of Hawai'i and the nation.

So much for the fate of the statehooders before and after 1984. What of the fate of Hawai'i and its statehood legends? Though the Silver Celebration lauded the Burns Legend and its accomplishments, there were emerging signs of cracks in the armor. University of Hawai'i ethnic studies professor Noel Kent first challenged the democratic legend in 1983 with his book *Hawaii: Islands under the Influence*. Kent claimed that Hawai'i still had a dependent, colonial economy characterized by exploitation. His unabashed Marxist approach left many unconvinced. However, two years later the widely respected historian Gavan Daws and his legal partner George Cooper gained a wider audience with the publication of *Land and Power in Hawaii* (1985). Cooper and Daws claimed that Hawai'i's most precious and finite resource, land, was no more equitably distributed in 1985 than in the period of the oligarchy. They went on to note that many Democratic politicians, often AJAs, had managed to use their new connections to gain a major stake in the power of land. Cooper and Daws implied that social and economic democracy in the islands had changed little, except for the color of the faces in the boardrooms and the political chambers of Hawai'i's elite. Hawai'i was still characterized by "haves" and "have-nots."

The alarms sounded by Kent and Cooper/Daws were occasioned to some extent because of Hawai'i's post-statehood success. Ethnic diversity in the leadership of the state was no longer a goal, but a given fact of life. There was now less concern with the diversity of those in the boardroom and more concern with what they were doing. This revelation often came slowly to visiting mainlanders still looking for Fuchs's "promise of Hawaii." As numerous friends in Hawai'i told me, "We're so tired of mainland sociologists coming over and proclaiming Hawai'i a racial paradise. We have real racial and ethnic tensions as well as social and economic problems here."

Among those tensions was the perception that native Hawaiians had not shared in the post-statehood economic prosperity. Most social indices indicated that Hawaiians fell far behind other ethnic groups in the islands in terms of income and education; they were overrepresented in the prison population and in the vital statistics for suicide and disease. There were definite overtones of Kamokila Campbell's 1946 plea to Congress and Abraham Akaka's fears on the eve of statehood. The so-called Modern Hawaiian Movement had begun in 1970 when a group of low-income Hawaiian families, practicing a traditional rural lifestyle, were forced from lands they leased to make way for a modern suburban development called Hawai'i Kai. The movement had gained further momentum by the time of the Silver Jubilee. The direction of the movement was at times splintered, but it was based on a revival of native Hawaiian culture and a quest for some form of native sovereignty, ranging from "nation within a nation" status similar to that of some American Indian tribes to a restoration of an independent Hawaiian nation. Two sisters, Mililani and Haunani-Kay Trask, emerged as leaders of the sovereignty cause. The movement also focused on various land issues. Hawaiians sought to end the military use of the island of Kaho'olawe as a navy bombing site. They also called for a return of the so-called "Ceded Lands," former royal lands that were taken over by the federal government in the 1898 annexation, to the Hawaiian people. The Hawaiian Movement remained quite alive in the summer of 2003. Some issues, such as the bombing of Kaho'olawe have been resolved, while others remain undecided.[12]

The challenges from academic leftists, lawyers, and native Hawaiians to the Democrats' post-statehood order gained conservative Republican support as the 1990s progressed. Charges of corruption in both state politics and the management of the state's largest landed philanthropic trust, the Bishop Estate, swelled toward the end of the century. Elections for governor were close. The Democrats held on with the election of Hawaiian John Waihe'e in 1986 and 1990, and of Filipino Ben Cayetano in 1994 and 1998. The Democrats' post-statehood world finally reached the breaking point in the general election of 2002 with the election of Linda Lingle as governor, a Republican woman who had been the mayor of Maui. Even before Lingle's victory, newspapers, both locally and on the mainland, announced that several former Democratic politicians were in jail. The New York Times noted, of all things, that "feuding factions" were now rampant in the Democratic Party![13]

Had the multiracial dream of the statehooders gone sour—or had it ever been as idealistic as the Burns Legend purported? Historians and social scientists are just beginning to sort this question out. As the story unfolds, I think that one constant from the statehood period will emerge.

A look at Hawai'i is always a look at the future. Fuchs and Michener looked to Hawai'i in the late 1950s as the land where racial and ethnic diversity had first taken hold. Hawai'i was what, they hoped, a future America might become. Historians of the twenty-first century may now find that Hawai'i shows how a multiracial society operates once inclusion is no longer an issue. The issue of the future will be what the "included" do, not merely who they are. As the first state in which no racial or ethnic group holds a majority of the population, Hawai'i continues to be the window on what the larger nation may one day become and how it may act.

So much for the fate of the states. Did the admission of those distant lands affect the nation in any way at all?

The Nation's Fate

Many congressmen said the admission of Alaska and Hawai'i made little difference at all to their constituents. Did the admission of these two states then make any difference at all to the progress or posture of the nation? There were, I believe, certainly two crucial ramifications—one international and the other domestic.

The admission of Alaska and Hawai'i moved the western boundaries of the nation deep into the mid-Pacific and within miles of the Siberian coast. This had resounding international repercussions. The *Christian Science Monitor* had been right in January 1946. A decision by Congress on the admission of Hawai'i—and by extension of Alaska—would serve as a statement of America's world policy. Billy Mitchell's 1935 statement to Congress that control of Alaska was the key to any world system of security made the same prediction. One might have thought that World War II itself had permanently turned the nation toward Asia and the Pacific. But Congress had been slow to recognize such a permanent world focus until at least a decade into the Cold War.

In 1966 President Lyndon Johnson explained this belated congressional vision and its effect on Hawai'i in a speech at Honolulu's East-West Center. As noted earlier, Johnson said that until the 1950s he had seen "America's destiny almost entirely in relation to Europe. My forebears came from Britain, Ireland and Germany. People in my section of the country regarded Asia as totally alien in spirit as well as nationality. We therefore looked away from the Pacific, away from its hopes as well as its great crises." Johnson tied his eventual support for Hawai'i statehood to his realization of the Pacific's role in America's future. The admission of Alaska and Hawai'i was thus a culmination, possibly more a turning point, in the development of the nation's international policy that had been evolving from the 1930s through the Second World War and into the Cold War. Alas, for Johnson, his new Asian vision became a fatal vision. As he spoke in 1966, the nation's involvement in Asia and Vietnam was in the process of becoming the "quagmire" that brought his administration to an end. In hindsight it is ironic that it was Ernest Gruening of Alaska who tried to warn Johnson against the direction of his new vision with his 1964 vote against the Gulf of Tonkin Resolution.[14]

The role of Alaska and Hawai'i as a defense zone in the Pacific has remained strong in the days since statehood. The union or "twinness" of the two states has become even more apparent in this regard—particularly at the congressional level. Possibly no stronger bipartisan connection exists in the U.S. Senate than the union of Senators Inouye (D–HI) and Stevens (R–AK) to maintain that Alaska/Hawai'i defense zone. The union of the two Pacific states was made even more emphatic in 1989 when the Alaskan Command was placed under CINCPAC (Commander in Chief Pacific), headquartered in Honolulu. Pacific defense functions in non–U.S. locations have increasingly been transferred to the Alaska/Hawai'i defense perimeter. For example, the eruption of Mount Pinatubo in 1991 and the subsequent closing of Clark Air Force Base and Subic Bay Naval Base in the Philippines led to the transfer of training and medical operations to Alaska.

The role of Alaska and Hawai'i as the nation's mid-Pacific boundary has carried a role much greater than simply military defense. National actions toward the distant states have often been a proxy for the nation's attitude toward Asia. The nation's treatment of the Japanese in Hawai'i has long been an indicator of its attitude toward Japan. Actions and attitudes in Alaska and Hawai'i have also widened the parameter and nature of thought about Asia and the Pacific. In Hawai'i people talk differently than they do on the mainland about Asia. It is a much closer, more intimate locus of endeavor for both business and travel. In Alaska people talk differently about Russia. Walter Hickel told me that when he was Secretary of the Interior, the talk in Washington about Russia was of a land half a world away. But in Alaska, Hickel pointed out, people talk of Russia as a neighbor, as a land they can see on a clear day across Bering Strait. As the mood of Congress changed in the 1950s toward a greater acceptance of America's Pacific role, the argument of non-contiguity against Alaska and Hawai'i began to change. Gradually the two territories were no longer seen as separate, floating appendages in the middle or end of nowhere, but as bridges connecting the mainland nation to a wider Pacific world. If any change in the mood of Congress occurred in the 1950s that facilitated statehood, it was a change in the attitude of the nation's place in the Pacific. Alaska and Hawai'i became the new markers of that place and role.

While statehood pointed to a wider international role for the nation, it also raised the domestic issues of race relations and civil rights. Over and over we have noted that the nation added two diverse multiracial societies with the admission of Alaska and Hawai'i. The statehood battle has been linked by many to the domestic civil rights movement, particularly as some of the major opponents of statehood were Southerners who were desperate to prevent a change in the racial patterns of their region. Earlier in my discussion of the passage of the Alaska statehood bill, I argued that a softening or change in the attitude of Congress toward civil rights—if such occurred at all in the mid-1950s—was not the major factor in the achievement of statehood. Southern congressmen told me they were able to separate the two issues and support statehood while maintaining a hard stand on segregation or civil rights within their region. I hold to that argument and suggest that readers refer to it. If statehood and civil rights were not necessarily linked in the passage of statehood legislation, did the admission of these two multiracial societies affect the nation and its civil rights attitudes at all?

In the broadest definition of "civil rights," the admission of Alaska and Hawai'i advanced the national agenda by ending "colonialism" in the two territories. The discriminations against all the people of the two territories and their right to full political participation were ended by statehood. In 1935 the clamor for statehood gained force in Hawai'i because of congressional discrimination against Hawaiian sugar. The nascent statehood commission organized by Joseph Farrington first called itself the "Equal Rights Commission." George Lehleitner and Ernest Gruening both defined the "justice" they wanted to achieve for the nation as an end to colonialism. This is what Truman meant, I believe, when he linked statehood to other "civil rights" issues in 1948. It quickly became obvious that many members of Congress, particularly Southerners, did not accept this broad definition of "civil rights" and narrowed the definition to racial discrimination.

Joseph Farrington foresaw the potential dilemma of linking statehood to civil rights shortly after hearings on Hawai'i statehood began in 1949 and explained:

> We are part of the so-called civil rights program whose adoption has been strongly recommended by the president . . . I agree that civil rights is involved in the issue, but not in same sense that it is involved in other parts of the program. I do not believe that statehood for Hawaii is a race question and certainly it has no relationship to the problem which prompted proposals for anti-lynching and anti-poll tax legislation which are part of this program.

The statehooders tried to circumvent such a linkage between their cause and southern racial issues by limiting the name of their cause to "statehood" and eschewing any connection to "rights." The Hawaii Equal Rights Commission had already changed its name to the Hawaii Statehood Commission by 1947.[15]

However, once statehood was achieved, that broad definition of civil rights still had a power. Within a year of the admission of Hawai'i, Congress passed the twenty-third amendment to the Constitution giving residents of the District of Columbia the right to vote for presidential electors. Though the territories were gone after 1959, the statehood movement had a ripple effect in continuing that "broad" discussion of "civil rights" in the remaining dependent or less than equal sections of the nation from Puerto Rico, Guam, American Samoa, and the Virgin Islands to the District of Columbia. In the 1970s and early 1980s federal law permitted non-voting delegates from the latter four places to sit in the U.S. House of Representatives, along with the non-voting "resident commissioner" from Puerto Rico who had sat in the House since 1901. The rights and privileges of those non-voting members were also increased. In the 1980s and 1990s "statehood" movements in both Puerto Rico and the District of Columbia were mounted, but they eventually proved ineffective.[16]

In that narrower definition of civil rights, did statehood for Alaska and Hawai'i affect racial discrimination in the nation—regardless of the efforts of statehood proponents to distance themselves from the word "rights"? It definitely had an effect in terms of racial discrimination against Asian Americans. Mainland discrimination against Asians before

World War II was extreme, as evidenced in the internment of mainland Japanese. The role of Hawai'i in World War II, the refusal of General Emmons to intern Hawai'i's Japanese, and the war record of the 100th and 442nd (composed predominantly of Hawai'i, not mainland, AJAs) turned the tide for the nation. After the war, there was little continued discrimination against the Japanese. The McCarran–Walter Act of 1952, which lifted the centuries-old ban against naturalization for Japanese immigrants, may well be considered the first major piece of civil rights, anti-racial-discrimination legislation passed by the postwar Congress. Even Southerners voted for this act—and overturned Truman's veto. But as the act was clothed in anti-Communist garb, it somehow did not appear to be "civil rights" legislation. The Congress seemed willing to pass such "civil rights" acts as long as they were not called such and did not directly impact a congressman's district.

The admission of Hawai'i brought Asian American representatives to the Congress for the first time. The very presence of those men rallied the spirit of Asian Americans throughout the nation. As historian Roger Daniels has noted, "It would be hard to overstate the importance of Senators Fong and Inouye . . . in terms of their impact on Asian American self-image and confidence . . . Hawaiian statehood, which triggered this process, was thus important to Asian Americans everywhere, not just to those in the islands." A little more than fifteen years after Asian Americans first entered the Congress from Hawai'i, S. I. Hayakawa and Norman Mineta from California joined their Hawai'i counterparts in the Senate and House of Representatives. The "promise of Hawai'i" had been exported to the mainland.[17]

Statehood definitely affected racial discrimination against Asian Americans. But did it have any effect in easing discrimination against African Americans on the mainland in general, and principally in the American South? Many of the World War II and Cold War stories of Alaska and Hawai'i have dealt with the interactions of African American and Caucasian, as well as Asian American, people in civilian and military roles. There was interracial cooperation in the building of the Alaska Highway. Charlayne Hunter-Gault went to her first "integrated" school in Anchorage in 1954. Discrimination in public places was eliminated by law in Alaska in 1945. Historians regularly note the number of Southerners who advanced the cause of racial tolerance in Hawai'i for both Asian Americans and African Americans. FBI chief Robert Shivers was from Tennessee, as was territorial governor and U.S. Senator Oren

Long. Scores of Southerners came to Hawai'i before World War II to teach in the public schools. Spark Matsunaga told me that he was first motivated to aspire to first-class citizenship and run for the U.S. Senate because of his high school civics teacher, Robert Clopton of Alabama.

It is clear that mainlanders reacted differently—and more tolerantly—to race while they were in Hawai'i and Alaska. But did this reaction have an effect when they returned home? Hawai'i and Alaska certainly affected Southerners, but did they affect the South? This is the infinitely more difficult question to answer. It is truly in Winston Churchill's words a "riddle wrapped in a mystery inside an enigma." I, like many others who have thought on the issue, muse that certainly something must have changed. On the other hand the very non-contiguity of Alaska and Hawai'i may argue that this new racial tolerance on the part of mainlanders occurred only when they were "out there." Historians and social scientists often use the concept of "liminality" to explain the actions of mainland Americans who went to Hawai'i at different historical times. Social behavior, according to this theory, changes when people are distant from the social and cultural restraints of their home. Liminality has been used to explain the lack of sexual restraint on the part of American sailors who came to Hawai'i in the early nineteenth century. Freed from the cultural restraint of nineteenth-century New England, they formed sexual liaisons with local women unimagined back home. Similarly "liminality" might be applied to mainland Americans who went to Hawai'i and Alaska during World War II and the Cold War. Freed from the cultural restraints of their home, they practiced a level of racial tolerance unimagined on the mainland—and which they could not imagine when they returned home.[18]

Lawrence Fuchs hoped that the "promise of Hawai'i" would set a new tone of racial tolerance for the nation. In *Hawaii Pono* he described a Caucasian army couple from Mississippi who praised an African American teacher in their child's elementary school. The principal of the school then asked if this would not be a good thing for Mississippi. Fuchs went on to relate:

> The Army wife was horrified and exclaimed, "Why no, we would not stand for such a thing in Mississippi!" When asked why she tolerated and even warmly endorsed the teacher in Honolulu, the mother shrugged her shoulders and said,

"When you're in Hawaii, you do what you are supposed to do in Hawaii." [19]

The riddle still remains wrapped in the mystery. Possibly future historians and social scientists will find more precise ways to decipher the ramifications of these racial experiences.

The ultimate riddle of statehood and civil rights remains to be solved. But as to the fate of the nation we can certainly say that the admission of Alaska and Hawai'i widened the nation's boundaries and ushered in an expanded world role. It eliminated the stigma of colonialism attached to territorial rule and ended racial discrimination against Asian Americans—a feat unimagined before 1940. Statehood also brought two multiracial societies into the union of states where mainlanders experienced a different scenario of racial tolerance—at least for a while. No wonder then that Leo O'Brien saw statehood, more than space flight, as the most important accomplishment of his congressional career. The nation that flew the fifty-star flag was simply not the same as the one that flew only forty-eight.

Journey's End:
A Personal Note

When I began the journey in the introduction of this book, I was on my way in the summer of 1981 to see Leo O'Brien in Albany, New York. It all seemed like a wonderful summer gambit for a young professor—an expense-paid trip to "find the statehooders." And, of all things, I could make a recommendation on the potential "secession" of the state of Alaska. Was this all a dream from which I would soon awake? Or had I fallen down the hole behind Alice into Wonderland? Was finding the statehooders worth that much thought? After all, it was contract research. I would hand in my report, and it would be over by September. Little did I know what lay in store as I interviewed the statehooders, first in Alaska and then in Hawai'i. There was a force in the postwar statehood movement that left an impact on everything and everybody it touched. By mid-summer I would never be the same again. "We can't just stop at one interview," George Lehleitner insisted. "You must come again to New Orleans. And then we'll need to go to Honolulu. And of course, we need to see Jim Wright and Russell Long in Washington." And we did.

Suddenly I found myself in an unending time warp. No, it would not end in September. George recreated the world of the 1940s and 1950s and the people in it. Sitting at home on a winter evening in Fairbanks, the phone would ring. Would it be George? Did I have two hours to talk? It was cold. What else did I have to do? On one call, George said he had just found a shoe-box full of editorials on the Tennessee Plan. Bob Bartlett had been wrong that the Tennessee Plan did not achieve national publicity. Would I like the box? "Certainly," I replied. Another time, George called with a few more facts about Speaker Rayburn's ruling on the "privileged" Alaska statehood bill. The Speaker had put his ruling in a hundred-year time capsule in the Capitol. George said it would be opened sometime in the early 2060s. I won't be there. Possibly a college student reading this today will be able to discover in retirement if this was all true.

If the call was not from George, it was from the statehooders, from "55 Club." Could I come to the twenty-fifth reunion of statehood? Then could I come to the thirty-fifth reunion of the convention? The debates from the convention never seemed to end. We really should have tried a unicameral legislature, one delegate insisted. How many times, I wondered, could the democratic faults or virtues of initiative and referendum be rehashed. On one question, however, there was no real debate. There would never be another convention like theirs.

As I interviewed politicians, the discussion of statehood always seemed to change the tone of their demeanor. By training I was supposed to be suspicious of politicians. Whatever else they had done, whatever compromises or political deals they had made, it all seemed to take a back seat to their memory of statehood and the day the vote was cast. There was talk of politics as I sat with George Lehleitner in the office of Speaker of the U.S. House of Representatives, Jim Wright, in March 1988. George praised the Speaker for the speech he had made on the House floor for Alaska back in 1958. "Is the United States finished with growing?" the young congressman had asked thirty years earlier. Just as the mood of that bygone time began to fill the room, Wright suddenly announced that another commitment required that he leave us right away. But in a parting moment with a decidedly wistful look in his eye and a reminiscent tone in his voice, he said to George, "In those days I had time to think and sit down and write speeches and polish them so that they said precisely what I felt. Sadly I have that opportunity no longer." There was no doubt in my mind that he meant it. None of us in the Speaker's office that day imagined that in a little over a year Wright's thirty-five-year congressional career would come to an end as the result of a partisan attack. By phone George and I lamented the fate of Speaker Wright, but we concurred that statehood had been one of his finest hours.

After more than a decade of wandering the halls of Congress, attending the reunions of "55 Club," and talking in the homes and clubs of Honolulu, I realized that I was not on a summer gambit that I could soon forget. Something about the statehood movement, and in particular the statehooders, was unlike anything else I had ever encountered. I now knew what John Bebout and Emil Sady meant when they described their experience at the Alaska Constitutional Convention. Something totally irresistible had overcome them. I knew why Ernest Bartley, on contract research like Bebout, Sady, and myself, could not simply hand in his report in 1956 and go back home. He had to stay on with statehooders, analyze the Congress for them, and call on his friends in the American Political Science Association.

So it had been for Lawrence Fuchs and James Michener during their stay in Hawai'i in the late 1950s as they became enthralled with the "promise of Hawai'i." "This is one of the most complicated men I have ever interviewed," or "I have just had a magnificent talk with . . ." were the lines Fuchs used to begin his interview notes. Something extraordinary was in the air of Hawai'i. Tom Coffman and Dan Boylan reported the same kind of experience when interviewing John Burns and his circle in the 1960s and 1970s. Much of the long-lasting force behind the Burns Legend came from the simple fact that the words of their interviewees were so compelling. In the 1980s and 1990s Tom Brokaw also succumbed to the force of the "greatest generation" of which the statehooders were so much a part. I was relieved to know that I was not the only one who had felt that force.

From journalists to academics seemingly everyone who began the journey with the statehooders reported one extraordinary experience after another. One of the most memorable for me was an afternoon in Washington, D.C. After visiting Speaker Wright, my wife, Patty, and I asked George Lehleitner if he would like to drive out to Mount Vernon. He said he had been there many times. But certainly it would be nice to go again. As we wandered the grounds of Washington's home, a certain serenity seemed to overcome George. He lingered a while at Washington's grave, seemingly in deep thought and contemplation. As we drove back to the city, George thanked us for taking him. He suddenly said, "You know I actually hadn't been there since the 1920s on a school trip from New Orleans. I hadn't been out there since statehood. It was such a wonderful opportunity to be able to . . ." His voice trailed off and I didn't exactly hear what he said. Somehow I thought he said, "to talk with Mr. Washington." And well he might. One George had started the union; the other had completed it. That afternoon at Mount Vernon would be the last time I would ever see George. He returned to New Orleans; we talked by phone and corresponded. But we just could not find another way to get together before he died in early 1993.

Does it sound now as if I too have been "touched by my experience," like Bebout and Sady? I often wondered this myself. It took me some time to understand the nature of that "force" or the "ecstasy" that

I described in the introduction. After examining newspapers and congressional documents to see if I had somehow been misled by the words of the statehooders, I finally realized that the "force" was the ultimate historical reality of the postwar statehood story. It was the glue that held so many disparate people together for a considerable period of time. It explained Fred Seaton's conversion to the statehood cause after a talk with Ernest Gruening and Joe Farrington. It explained Sam Rayburn's final commitment to Bob Bartlett and John Burns on the floor of the House of Representatives. They all found something compelling in the words and convictions of the statehooders and their cause. Historians are not usually trained or advised to use the phrase "Believe it" to convince readers of their findings. But like the political scientists who joined the statehood cause, I finally realized that "believe" was the only verb that could adequately convey the words that the statehooders repeated so many times.

With such a realization I started to plan the nature of the book that I would write to join those volumes written by others before me. But the phone continued to ring from the statehooders. One day in the spring of 1996 I got a call from Bob Atwood. He was having "55 Club" to his house in Anchorage and invited me to come down and talk about my experiences in Hawai'i. He thought the delegates would enjoy the comparisons. Bob and Evangeline Atwood's houses in Anchorage were famous. General Buckner and Admiral Theobald had argued over the course of the Aleutian War in one. In another, the battles and strategies for statehood had been formed in the 1950s. That house then slid into a crevasse and was smashed into thousands of pieces in the 1964 earthquake. Bob and Evangeline then rebuilt to revive the spirit of Anchorage after the earthquake. I was headed to that new third house.

Bob greeted me heartily at the door. Eight of the fourteen living delegates to the convention were there. Tom Stewart, who had planned the convention, also came. Neva Egan, Bill's widow, was there with memories of the good times. Ted Stevens dropped by to wish everyone well. At age eighty-nine Bob seemed in amazingly good spirits. I would not have blamed him if he had been sad that evening. Evangeline, with whom he had literally built Anchorage, had died in 1987. Then, in 1994, his elder daughter, Marilyn, died from circumstances that never seemed clear. He had earlier told me that her death really "took the wind out of my sails." And by 1996 the *Anchorage Times,* the great paper of statehood, was also gone—the victim of various newspaper wars, both locally and nationally, in the 1990s. In the presence of the statehooders there was not a sad line in Bob's face that evening. At dinner he turned to me and said, "John, it's been an amazing life for those of us here this evening. We came here when there was nothing. We wanted a city. We wanted a state. And it happened. We had it all. We were the lucky ones."

I gave my talk, and a good time seemed to be had by all. Soon I had to leave and take a plane back to Fairbanks. This would be the last time I would see Bob or "55 Club." Bob died unexpectedly in January 1997 and within two years I retired and returned to my childhood home in Georgia. My journey with the statehooders was coming to an end. But what a time I had with them. How much they had told me! Did I get it all down? The time had come to write while I could still check quotes with the surviving statehooders. As I said good bye to Bob and "55 Club" in Anchorage that night, I knew the shape my volume would take. I have tried, like Brokaw, Fuchs, Michener, and others, to tell the story of the statehood generation. I have tried to convey that sense of force and hope that they offered from their far distant posts to shape the postwar nation and create a more perfect union. My story is secondhand and hence second-best. But in making sure that their memories live on, possibly I can say that I too played a bit part in the battle for statehood. On that last night with "55 Club," I knew I was one of the lucky ones too.

Notes

Introduction

1. Interview with Leo O'Brien, August 1981, by John S. Whitehead, in Claus-M. Naske, John S. Whitehead, and William Schneider, *Alaska Statehood: The Memory of the Battle and the Evaluation of the Present by Those Who Lived It: An Oral History of the Remaining Actors in the Alaska Statehood Movement* (Fairbanks: Alaska Statehood Commission, 1981).

2. Interview with Robert Oshiro, 1974, by Dan Boylan, John A. Burns Oral History (hereafter JBOH), University of Hawai'i Mānoa, 11.

3. John E. Bebout and Emil J. Sady, "Staging a State Constitutional Convention," paper delivered to the Annual Meeting of the Southern Political Science Association, Gatlinburg, Tennessee, November 8, 1956 (typescript in author's possession).

4. The northernmost point is Pt. Barrow, Alaska. The southernmost point is Ka Lae, Hawai'i. The 180th meridian bisects the Aleutian Islands of Alaska, thus creating the easternmost and westernmost points.

5. Interview with Russell B. Long, March 15, 1988, by John S. Whitehead. Long's statement is repeated in an interview with Spark Matsunaga, July 15, 1988, by John S. Whitehead, Oral History Collection, Rasmuson Library, University of Alaska Fairbanks.

6. George M. Gallup, Public Opinion News Service, August 29, 1956. As a sample of constituent correspondence I checked the senatorial papers of Spessard Holland, University of Florida Library, and Richard Russell, University of Georgia Library. I found no constituent correspondence on statehood in 1958 or 1959 in Holland's papers. In Russell's correspondence for 1958 I counted nine letters from Georgia constituents expressing a view on Alaska statehood (two for, seven against). There were eleven letters from elementary or high school students requesting information on Alaska statehood for civics classes or debates.

7. CBS Television, "Alaska-Hawaii Statehood," *See It Now,* March 1958, videotape in Rasmuson Library, University of Alaska Fairbanks. For response to the program see *Honolulu Star-Bulletin,* March 6, 1958.

8. *Congressional Record,* 85th Cong., 2d sess., vol. 104, pt. 7, p. 9507.

9. For the findings and recommendations of the Alaska Statehood Commission, see Alaska Statehood Commission, *More Perfect Union: A Preliminary Report* (Fairbanks: Alaska Statehood Commission, January 19, 1982); Alaska Statehood Commission, *More Perfect Union: A Plan for Action, Final Report* (Fairbanks: Alaska Statehood Commission, January 1983).

10. The normal course for admission is to first secure enabling legislation, which authorizes a territory to hold a constitutional convention. Once the constitution is presented to Congress, an admission bill would be passed to admit the new state to the union. However, if a territory holds a constitutional convention before gaining congressional authorization and ratifies a constitution, it is possible to initiate the statehood process with a direct admission bill, thus bypassing the enabling process. This latter course was followed by Alaska and Hawai'i.

11. John S. Whitehead, "Alaska and Hawai'i: The Cold War States," in *The Cold War American West, 1945–1989,* ed. Kevin Fernlund (Albuquerque: University of New Mexico Press, 1998).

12. Interview with delegates to the Alaska Constitutional Convention, Fairbanks, February 1996, as recorded in Fernlund, *The Cold War American West,* 197–98. As many oral historians have found, interviewees usually respond directly to the questions they are asked. At times they may expand on the question and provide connections and analogies that did not occur to the interviewer. But in most cases, the interviewer must ask if there is a connection to get a response.

13. Tom Brokaw, *The Greatest Generation* (New York: Random House, 1998), xviii.

14. For Neuberger's role in the statehood vote, see Ernest Gruening, *The State of Alaska,* rev. ed. (New York: Random House, 1968), 504.

15. Interview with James C. Wright, March 15, 1988, by John S. Whitehead; George Lehleitner to the author, November 17, 1981 (in author's possession).

Chapter 1

1. "Hawaii: Sugar Coated Fort," *Fortune* 22 (August 1940): 31.

2. For a full description of Hawai'i's prewar development as a military encampment, see Brian McAllister Linn, *Guardians of Empire: The U.S. Army and the Pacific, 1902–1940* (Chapel Hill: University of North Carolina Press, 1997).

3. The literature on the events leading to the Revolution of 1893 and the subsequent annexation to the United States is extensive and controversial. The best starting place for interested readers is Tom Coffman, *Nation Within: The Story of America's Annexation of the Nation of Hawai'i* (Honolulu: Epicenter Press, 1998).

4. Norman Meller, "Hawaii: The Fiftieth State," *Parliamentary Affairs* 13 (1960): 494–96. The 1787 Northwest Ordinance was written by the Congress of the Confederation to establish a governmental framework for the territories to be carved from the Northwest Territory, which included the future states of Ohio, Indiana, Illinois, Michigan, and Wisconsin. It also provided the mechanism for these territories to become states. Once a territory's population reached sixty thousand, it could then petition the Congress for admission as a state—equal to the other states. The 1787 Ordinance pertained only to the territories in the Old Northwest. However, it served as a precedent for other areas that were created as territories and admitted to the Union. Except in a few cases, such as California and Texas, the precedent of the Northwest Ordinance was followed for the admission of nearly all the states in the American West. The best modern source on the Northwest Ordinance is Peter S. Onuf, *Statehood and Union: A History of the Northwest Ordinance* (Bloomington: Indiana University Press, 1987).

5. Ray Lyman Wilbur, "Statehood for Hawaii," *Atlantic Monthly* 166 (1940): 495.

6. For population statistics of Hawai'i, including military population, I have relied on Robert C. Schmitt, *Historical Statistics of Hawaii* (Honolulu: University of Hawai'i Press, 1977).

7. "Haole" is a Hawaiian word meaning "foreigner" or "stranger." It was originally applied to any stranger to the islands. Today it is used in Hawai'i as a racial description for Caucasians of American or northern European origin. It is not used to describe Portuguese Caucasians who migrated to Hawai'i primarily from the Portuguese islands of Madeira. The Portuguese, however, formed the majority of Caucasians in the prewar period. Racial statistics often list the haoles as "other Caucasians."

   The term "Hawaiian," as a noun, always refers to native Hawaiians. The term part-Hawaiian refers to people with both Hawaiian and non-Hawaiian parentage. In the prewar period, non-Hawaiian parentage was most often haole or Chinese, sometimes listed as Chinese Hawaiian.

8. Figures for territorial legislators in 1941 were based on a check by the author of the legislative journals of the 1941 territorial legislature.

9. For Baker's three articles, see Ray Stannard Baker, "Wonderful Hawaii—A World Experiment Station, I. How King Sugar Rules in Hawaii," *American Magazine* 73 (November 1911); "II. The Land and the Landless," *American Magazine* 73 (December 1911); "Human Nature in Hawaii: How the Few Want the Many to Work for Them," *American Magazine* 73 (January 1912). For a discussion of Baker's views of Hawai'i and of other pre–World War II journalist opinions, see John S. Whitehead, "Western Progressives, Old South Planters, or Colonial Oppressors: The Enigma of Hawai'i's Big Five, 1898–1940," *Western Historical Quarterly* 30 (Autumn 1999): 295–326.

10. For the best treatment of the 1920 strike and the Japanese "conspiracy," see Masayo Umezawa Duus, *The Japanese Conspiracy: The Oahu Sugar Strike of 1920* (Berkeley: University of California Press, 1999).

11. The Massie case has an extensive literature. For full-book treatments, see Theon Wright, *Rape in Paradise* (New York: Pyramid Books, 1966); Peter Van Slingerland, *Something Terrible Has Happened* (New York: Harper and Row, 1966). For Clarence Darrow's personal account, see Clarence Darrow, *The Story of My Life* (New York: Charles Scribners Sons, 1932). For territorial governor Lawrence Judd's account, see Lawrence M. Judd, *Lawrence M. Judd and Hawaii* (Rutland, Vt.: Charles F. Tuttle Co, 1971). For a fictionalized account that also appeared as a CBS miniseries for television, see Norman Katkov, *Blood and Orchids* (New York: St. Martin's Press, 1983).

12. Darrow, *Story of My Life,* 458.

13. Ibid., 460.

14. Ibid., 462, 479. Darrow was incorrect in noting that there were Japanese on the jury. Six members of the jury were haoles and one was Portuguese. Darrow did not acknowledge that the majority of the jury was Caucasian.

15. For the Richardson report, see U.S. Senate, 72d Cong., 1st sess., document 78, *Law Enforcement in the Territory of Hawaii,* April 4, 1932 (Washington: Government Printing Office, 1932). For Lawrence Judd's opinion of the report, see Judd, *Lawrence M. Judd and Hawaii,* 204–5.

16. For the quote by Lorrin Thurston and other aspects of the pre–World War II moves toward statehood, I have relied on, in addition to standard secondary sources, an unpublished document by Joseph R. Farrington, "Chronology of Hawaii Statehood Campaign and Role of Joseph R. Farrington." This document can be found in the papers of Joseph R. Farrington (Archives of Hawaii, Farrington, Del.: Statehood file, Eighty-third Congress, 1952).

17. Michaelyn Chou, *Interview with Elizabeth P. Farrington, Delegate to Congress from the Territory of Hawaii, 1954–57* (1978), Special Collections, Hamilton Library, University of Hawai'i Mānoa.

18. Farrington, "Chronology of Hawaii Statehood Campaign."

19. For the prewar statehood hearings, see U.S. Congress, House Committee on Territories, *Statehood for Hawaii Hearings,* before the subcommittee of the Committee on Territories, HR 3034, 74th Cong., 1st sess., October 7–18, 1935 (Washington, D.C., 1936); U.S. Congress, Joint Committee on Hawaii, *Statehood for Hawaii Report,* S. Con. Res. 18, 75th Cong., 2d sess., October 6–22, 1937 (Washington, D.C., 1938).

Chapter 2

1. Jean Potter, *Alaska under Arms* (New York: Macmillan Co., 1942), ix, 1.

2. Ibid., 31.

3. Ibid., 8, 74, 104.

4. Ibid., 149, 168, 177.

5. The "neglect thesis" can be found throughout many writings on Alaska history. For its earliest presentation see Jeannette Paddock Nichols, *Alaska: A History of Its Administration, Exploitation and Industrial Development During Its First Half Century under the Rule of the United States* (Cleveland, Ohio: Arthur H. Clark Co., 1924). Ernest Gruening extended and expanded the "neglect thesis" in *The State of Alaska: A Definitive History of America's Northernmost Frontier,* rev. ed. (New York: Random House, 1968). (Gruening's first edition was published in 1954.) For accounts of post-purchase Alaska that downplay the neglect thesis, see Ted C. Hinckley, *The Americanization of Alaska* (Palo Alto, Calif.: Pacific Books, 1972); and particularly Stephen Haycox, *Alaska: An American Colony* (Seattle: University of Washington Press, 2002).

6. For the best background on the canned salmon industry and the regulation of the fishery, see Richard Cooley, *Politics and Conservation: The Decline of Alaska Salmon* (New York: Harper and Row, 1963). Princeton University undergraduate David Felsenthal produced an excellent 1992 senior thesis, "The Alaskan Salmon Fishing Industry: A History of Exploitation and Depletion, 1912–45," which is in the author's possession. I am indebted to Felsenthal for expanding my knowledge of the Alaska fishery. In all discussions of the Alaska fishery, the standard statistic for measuring the size of the annual salmon catch is the number

of packed cases of salmon. A case of canned salmon equals forty-eight one-pound tins.

7. For Gruening's critique of the 1884 act, see Gruening, *The State of Alaska,* 46–70.

8. The classic account of the Klondike gold rush is Pierre Berton, *The Klondike Fever* (New York: Alfred A. Knopf, 1958). For a more recent treatment that covers the development of the entire Alaska/Canada Yukon Basin in the gold rush era, see Melody Webb, *Yukon* (Lincoln: University of Nebraska Press, 1993).

9. For the best treatment of Alaska's 1900–1910 industrial development, see Elizabeth A. Tower, *Icebound Empire: Industry and Politics on the Last Frontier, 1898–1938* (Anchorage: Publication Consultants, 1996).

10. Gruening, *The State of Alaska,* 177.

11. For the best treatment of the Alaska Railroad, see William H. Wilson, *Railroad in the Clouds: The Alaska Railroad in the Age of Steam* (Boulder, Colo.: Pruett Publishing Co., 1977).

12. Gruening, *The State of Alaska,* 309; Potter, *Alaska under Arms,* 33.

13. Gruening, *The State of Alaska,* 311.

14. For the best source on John Green Brady and his travails, see Ted C. Hinckley, *Alaskan John Green Brady* (Oxford, Ohio: Miami University, 1982).

15. The best treatment of Wickersham and the governors he came in contact with is Evangeline Atwood, *Frontier Politics: Alaska's James Wickersham* (Portland, Ore.: Binford and Mort, 1979).

16. For Tower's view on Wickersham and the syndicate, see Tower, *Icebound Empire,* 147–57, 268–70. Historians Stephen Haycox and the late Morgan Sherwood are less sympathetic to the syndicate. However, both have confirmed in conversations with me that they know of no specific reason Wickersham objected to the syndicate except that he failed to get the general counsel job. Prior to that moment Wickersham had been pro-syndicate.

17. For Sutherland's career, his handwritten autobiography is fascinating. It has been edited by John S. Whitehead and published as "Dan Sutherland: Gold Rush Pioneer and Politician," *Alaska History* 10, no. 1 (Spring 1995).

18. For the details surrounding Gruening's ousting in Washington, see Gruening's own version in Ernest Gruening, *Many Battles* (New York: Liveright, 1973) and a more critical perspective in Robert David Johnson, *Ernest Gruening and the American Dissenting Tradition* (Cambridge, Mass.: Harvard University Press, 1998), 151–54.

Chapter 3

1. Daniel K. Inouye, *Journey to Washington* (Englewood Cliffs, N.J.: Prentice-Hall, 1967), 54–55. We may well wonder if Inouye and his family actually heard of the attack on the radio at 7:55 a.m. as his narrative states. Most sources claim that radio reporting of the attack was not made for another hour.

2. Ibid., 56.

3. Ibid., 57.

4. J. Garner Anthony, *Hawaii under Army Rule* (Palo Alto, Calif.: Stanford University Press, 1955). Portions of the volume are drawn from several law review articles written by Anthony during the period of martial law. However, the bulk of the book was written in the early to mid-1950s when Anthony was particularly concerned with the specter of anti-Communist activity. Anthony saw a great similarity between anti-Communist activity and the precedents set by the army in Hawai'i a decade earlier. My discussion of martial law in Hawai'i is drawn mainly from Anthony. For other sources on this period, see United States Commission on Wartime Relocation and Internment of Civilians, *Personal Justice Denied* (Seattle: University of Washington Press, 1997); Gary Okihiro, *Cane Fires* (Philadelphia: University of Pennsylvania Press, 1991), 209–49; Gwenfread Allen, *Hawaii's War Years* (Honolulu: University of Hawai'i Press, 1950), 35–37, 170–83; Roger Bell, *Last among Equals* (Honolulu: University of Hawai'i Press, 1984), 84–91; Blake Clark, *Hawaii the 49th State* (New York: Doubleday, 1947), 183–210.

5. Allen, *Hawaii's War Years*, 36.

6. Though the Report of the Roberts Commission cited no acts of disloyalty, Chief Justice Roberts nonetheless told Secretary of War Henry Stimson upon his return from Hawai'i that he still doubted the loyalty of the islands' Japanese and Japanese American population. See *Personal Justice Denied*, 59.

7. George Chaplin, *Presstime in Paradise* (Honolulu: University of Hawai'i Press, 1998), 206.

8. Anthony, *Hawaii under Army Rule*, 118.

9. Ibid., 108.

10. Okihiro, *Cane Fires*, 209; Anthony, *Hawaii under Army Rule*, 121.

11. Allen, *Hawaii's War Years*, 145. Of the seven AJA members in the 1941 legislature, two had been interned by the 1942 elections. The other five did not run for reelection to the territorial house. The term *AJA*, or

American(s) of Japanese Ancestry, is a term specific to Hawai'i for the Nisei, or Japanese Americans. It appears to have originated during World War II as a way of emphasizing the "Americanization" of the Nisei. Its origins are murky. Honolulu police captain, and later territorial delegate, John Burns claims he coined the acronym while working with the Nisei during the war. Gwenfread Allen and other newspaper writers of the time used the term, but did not attribute its origins to Burns. The term is widely used in current literature about Hawai'i, though the terms *Nisei* and *Japanese American* are also used. I have never seen the term *AJA* used in the discussion of the Japanese population of the mainland United States, where the terms *Nisei* or *Japanese American* are the standard usage.

12. Delos Emmons, "Brief Personal History from Memory," Hoover Institution, Stanford University, Palo Alto, Calif., 8. There is no date on the fifteen-page transcript, and it appears that a few additional pages may be missing. The last mention of a date is February 1947. However, Emmons indicates that he is aware of "one book" on martial law. That is likely to be Anthony's *Hawaii under Army Rule,* first published in 1955. Emmons died in 1965. I am indebted to Honolulu political writer and historian Tom Coffman for bringing the Emmons typescript to my attention.

13. Emmons, "Brief History," 9.

14. Ibid., 10.

15. Neither Emmons nor Anthony make any mention of speaking to each other or corresponding. Anthony reissued his book in 1977, again with no mention that he had corresponded with Emmons in the time between 1955 and 1965, when Emmons died. In contrast to the reams of scholarship on military rule during the Reconstruction period in the American South, little writing exists on military rule in territorial Hawai'i. Garner Anthony's slim volume remains the crucial published document from one of the civilian participants. Emmons's "brief history" is our only look into the "military mind." The subject deserves closer scrutiny by modern scholars.

16. For the numbers of Japanese and Japanese Americans taken into custody and interned, see Okihiro, *Cane Fires,* 267; Allen, *Hawaii's War Years,* 37, 134–37, 141; and the recently published Tetsuden Kashima, *Judgment without Trial: Japanese American Imprisonment during World War II* (Seattle: University of Washington Press, 2003), 69–72, 78–80, 86. Okihiro sets the total number of internees transferred to the mainland at 1,875 while

Kashima ups the number to 2,092 with 300 additional internees remaining in Hawai'i. Even with Kashima's higher numbers the proportion of the population interned remains under 1.5 percent. The Japanese population figure of 158,000 is based on the 1940 census figure. For the best description of the process by which the FBI selected those taken into custody, see Tom Coffman, *The Island Edge of America: A Political History of Hawai'i* (Honolulu: University of Hawai'i Press, 2003), 52–53, 60–65. Of the roughly 1,500 taken into custody over the course of the war, approximately 475 were arrested in the first three days after the Pearl Harbor attack.

17. For information on Sanji Abe, see his obituaries in the *Honolulu Star-Bulletin,* December 1, 1982, and *Honolulu Advertiser,* December 2, 1982. Abe technically was a dual citizen of the United States and Japan, a common situation for many Nisei.

18. For Thomas Sakakihara, see his obituary in the *Honolulu Advertiser,* March 3, 1989; *Honolulu Star-Bulletin,* March 18, 1976; *Honolulu Advertiser,* February 26, 1942.

19. Emmons, "Brief Personal History," 11. For Emmons's stalling tactics, see Ted T. Tsukiyama and Ellen Godbey Carson, "A Tale of Two Generals and Japanese Americans," *Honolulu Star-Bulletin,* December 2, 1991, A-15; Roland Kotani, *The Japanese of Hawaii: A Century of Struggle* (Honolulu: Hawaii Hochi, 1985), 98–101; *Personal Justice Denied,* 262, 265, 269–77; Coffman, *The Island Edge,* 76–80; and Kashima, *Judgment without Trial,* 75–81.

20. Emmons. "Brief Personal History," 7; Tsukiyama, "A Tale of Two Generals," A-15.

21. For the role of Hemenway in persuading Fielder and Shivers not to relocate the Japanese, see Ted T. Tsukiyama, *Charles Reed Hemenway, 1875–1947* (Honolulu, 1995), pamphlet in Special Collections, Hamilton Library, University of Hawai'i Mānoa. For the role of Burns, see Inouye, *Journey to Washington,* 64; and Dan Boylan and T. Michael Holmes, *John A. Burns: The Man and His Times* (Honolulu: University of Hawai'i Press, 2000), 37. For Shivers's direct links to the Japanese community, see Roland Kotani, *The Japanese of Hawaii,* 90. The role of General Emmons in forestalling the implementation of Executive Order 9066 is emphasized in *Personal Justice Denied,* but no mention is made of the role of Shivers or Fielder in influencing Emmons.

22. Coffman, *The Island Edge,* 49–51; Ted Tsukiyama, "A Tale of Two Generals." In addition to Shivers, Fielder, Burns, Hemenway, and

Dillingham, Tsukiyama also acknowledges the efforts of military intelligence officers Col. George Bicknell and Capt. Frank Blake; Honolulu community leaders Leslie Hicks, John H. Midkiff, and Charles Loomis; *Star-Bulletin* editor Riley Allen, Territorial Delegate Joe Farrington, University of Hawai'i Professor Andrew Lind, Territorial Secretary Oren Long, and Hung Wai Ching, director of the University YMCA. For detail on Walter Dillingham and his wartime role, see H. Brett Melendy, *Walter Francis Dillingham, 1875–1943: Hawaiian Entrepreneur and Statesman* (Lewiston, N.Y.: Edwin Mellen Press, 1996), 246–51.

23. Tom Coffman, *The Island Edge,* 47–48. For the prewar views of the army in Hawai'i on the Japanese, see also Brian Linn, *Guardians of Empire,* 152–53, 156–57.

24. Emmons, "Personal History," 10–11. Kashima, *Judgment without Trial,* emphasizes the labor situation as a motivating factor in Emmons's actions, but Coffman, *The Island Edge,* downplays the labor need. Kashima does not appear to have used Emmons's typescript memoirs.

25. Inouye, *Journey to Washington,* 65–67.

26. For the 1976 story on wartime internment in Hawai'i, see *Honolulu Star-Bulletin,* March 18, 1976. This coverage by the *Star-Bulletin* was not only prompted by President Ford's repeal of Executive Order 9066, but by the release of the national television documentary "Farewell to Manzanar," which detailed a well-known mainland internment camp. I find no reference to Emmons's work in forestalling the evacuation until the publication of *Personal Justice Denied* in 1983.

27. Emmons, "Brief Personal History," 11; Kotani, *The Japanese in Hawaii,* 108.

28. Emmons, "Brief Personal History," 11; Ted T. Tsukiyama, "A Salute to One Puka Puka," in *Go For Broke 1943–1993* (Honolulu: N.p., 1993), 18.

29. For the split between the Nisei and Caucasian officers, see Kotani, *The Japanese in Hawaii,* 108.

30. Masayo Duus, *Unlikely Liberators: The Men of the 100th and 442nd* (Honolulu: University of Hawai'i Press, 1987), 44–45.

31. For the best background on the evolution of the 442nd, see Tsukiyama, "Origins of the 442nd"; Duus, *Unlikely Liberators;* Kotani, *The Japanese in Hawaii;* and most recently Coffman, *The Island Edge of America.*

32. Tsukiyama, "Origins of the 442nd," 14–15; Duus, *Unlikely Liberators,* 58. In his memoir Emmons makes mention of his role in the organization of the 100th and the Varsity Victory Volunteers, but not of the 442nd.

33. Duus, *Unlikely Liberators,* 59. For Elmer Davis's editing of FDR's speech, see Tsukiyama, "The Origins of the 442nd," 15. The designation of FDR as "Dr. Martial Law and Relocation" and "Dr. Go for Broke" is my own.

34. For statistics on the casualties suffered by the 442nd, see Duus, *Unlikely Liberators,* 217; Kotani, *The Japanese in Hawaii,* 121–22. In addition to the books cited on the 442nd/100th, interested readers may also want to consult the 1951 MGM movie *Go for Broke* starring Van Johnson. The movie widely sung the glories of the 442nd and its connection to Texas. Johnson played a young Texan infantry lieutenant who was assigned to lead a platoon of the 442nd. At first he made it clear that he wanted no part of the Japanese Americans and yearned to be transferred to his old unit, the 36th. As the movie progressed, the young lieutenant grew increasing fond of his men. By the time the unit arrived in France, the lieutenant's loyalty was firm. He even slugged his old drill sergeant from the 36th for calling the AJAs "Japs." The rescue of the Lost Battalion forms the sensational climax of the film.

35. For the various listings of the number of awards received by the combined 100th/442nd until 1946, see *Honolulu Advertiser,* special supplement, March 21, 1993. For the Medal of Honor upgrades in the year 2000, see "Medal of Honor" supplement to *Hawaii Herald,* July 7, 2000. Upgrades went to a total of twenty-two men of Asian descent. Twenty were AJA members of the 442nd/100th, including Daniel Inouye. The two others were a Filipino American and a Chinese American who were not in the 442nd/100th. Filipino American Rudolph Davila joined the six members of the 442nd/100th at the June 21, 2000, ceremony.

36. Inouye, *Journey to Washington,* 179–80, 185.

37. Ibid., 185.

38. The AJAs comprised about 50 percent of all those who served in the military from Hawai'i. An equivalent number of other islanders served abroad in a wide variety of units. Many individuals from Hawai'i gained distinction for their service, but no others were so consciously grouped and identified with Hawai'i as the AJAs in the 442nd/100th. And no other unit was so consistently publicized by the army itself as a showcase of American ideals. It should also be noted that not all AJAs who served in the war were with the 100th/442nd. A substantial number, particularly those thought to have Japanese language ability, served with the Military Intelligence Service.

39. Allen, *Hawaii's War Years,* 185. The classic description of the impact of World War II on Hawai'i is the previously cited Gwenfread Allen,

Hawaii's War Years (1950). Allen covers both the effect of the war on Hawai'i and on the workers and service personnel who came to Hawai'i from the mainland. Writing over forty years later, Beth Bailey and David Farber (*The First Strange Place: The Alchemy of Race and Sex in World War II Hawaii* [New York: Free Press, 1992]) rely on Allen's overall analysis of the impact of Hawai'i on the mainland workers and service personnel, and add numerous vignettes of specific individuals who were affected.

40. For overall population statistics during the war, see Schmitt, *Historical Statistics of Hawaii*, 10.

41. Allen, *Hawaii's War Years*, 219.

42. Ibid., 239.

43. Allen, *Hawaii's War Years*, 246. Farber and Bailey, *The First Strange Place*, also place much emphasis on the level of complaining among workers and service personnel in Hawai'i.

44. Inouye, *Journey to Washington*, 208.

Chapter 4

1. The story of KFAR and the Pearl Harbor news is well told in Potter, *Alaska under Arms*, 110–18. The KFAR station, newly built in 1939, still stands in Fairbanks (as of 2003) in the middle of the golf course for the Fairbanks Golf and Country Club.

2. For year-by-year population statistics for World War II and George Rogers' analysis of the economic changes brought by the war, see George W. Rogers, *The Future of Alaska: Economic Consequences of Statehood* (Baltimore: Johns Hopkins University Press, 1962). Readers can find the same "Military Alaska" section in David T. Kresge, Thomas A. Morehouse, and George W. Rogers, *Issues in Alaskan Development* (Seattle: University of Washington Press, 1977), 35–45. For other overall assessments of the impact of World War II and the military on Alaska, see Fern Chandonnet, ed., *Alaska at War, 1941–45* (Anchorage: Alaska at War Committee, 1995); Penny Rennick, ed., "World War II in Alaska," *Alaska Geographic* 22, no. 4 (1995); Jonathan Nielson, *Armed Forces on a Northern Frontier: The Military in Alaska's History, 1867–1987* (New York: Greenwood Press, 1988); U.S. Army, *Alaska, The U.S. Army in Alaska*, USARL Pamphlet 360–5, 1972 (previous editions in 1969 and 1965 appear as *The Army's Role in the Building of Alaska* and *Building Alaska with the Army*). An extensive photo collection of the military buildup in the Aleutians as well as in other parts

of Alaska can be found in the multivolume series by Stan Cohen et al., *The Forgotten War* (Missoula, Mont.: Pictorial Histories, 1981). See also the videos *Alaska at War* (Alaska Video Publishing, 1993) and *Aleut Evacuation: The Untold War Story* (Aleutian /Pribilof Islands Assn., 1992).

3. The are three leading sources for the Aleutian war. The first and indispensable source is Samuel Eliot Morison, *A History of United States Naval Operations in World War II,* 15 vol. (Boston: Little, Brown and Co., 1947–62). Morison divides his discussion of the Aleutians between volume 4, *Coral Sea, Midway and Submarine Actions, May 1942–August 1942* (1949), 74–76 and 160–84; and volume 7, *Aleutians, Gilberts and Marshalls, June 1942–April 1944* (1951), 3–66. Morison is crucial for understanding both Japanese and American intentions in the Aleutians. His treatment, however, emphasizes naval operations rather than ground and air operations. Brian Garfield (*The Thousand Mile War: World War II in Alaska and the Aleutians* [New York: Doubleday, 1969]) greatly expands Morison's treatment with a large number of interviews with participants in the Aleutian campaign. John Haile Cloe (*The Aleutian Warriors* [Missoula, Mont.: Anchorage Chapter—Air Force Association and Pictorial Histories Publishing Co., 1990]) corrects many of Garfield's assertions and theories. Cloe's volume, however, concentrates on the 11th Air Force to the relative exclusion of naval operations. All three historians should be read for a full overview. Two very recent additions to the Aleutian literature, published after the completion of my manuscript, are Galen Roger Perras, *Stepping Stones to Nowhere: The Aleutian Islands, Alaska, and American Military Strategy, 1867–1945* (Vancouver: University of British Columbia Press, 2003); and Otis Hayes Jr., *Alaska's Hidden Wars: Secret Campaigns on the North Pacific Rim* (Fairbanks: University of Alaska Press, 2004).

4. There is a good bit of speculation about the relation of Doolittle's raid to the Aleutian campaign. Garfield, *The Thousand Mile War,* 6, notes that the Japanese command was aware of the presence of aircraft carriers from which the raid could have been launched, but suggests that some in the Japanese command still conjectured that the planes came from the Aleutians. The Japanese were not aware of any airfields there, but thought that Doolittle's early childhood in Nome, Alaska, argued for a connection. Cloe, *The Aleutian Warriors,* 80–81, states emphatically that the Japanese were sure that Doolittle's planes came from an aircraft carrier and flatly rejects that there was any speculation that the attack came from the Aleutians. Morison, *History of United States Naval Operations,* 7:75, also

asserts that the Japanese knew that Doolittle's planes probably came from an aircraft carrier, but suggests that some in the high command thought the planes might have come from Midway. As both American and Japanese commanders in the Aleutian campaign accepted and rejected their own intelligence reports, it may well be that all the speculations about Doolittle's raid were held by someone in the Japanese command.

5. At the onset of World War II there was no unified military command in Alaska. Hence the separation of command for the navy from Honolulu (Pacific Command) and the army from San Francisco (Western Command). See chapter 7 for the origins of the first unified command in Alaska.

6. My students have always insisted upon debating whether Attu and Kiska were the first pieces of American soil to be occupied during World War II. The Philippines was still an American colonial possession when it was occupied earlier in 1942. Alaska was not a state in 1942, but it was an incorporated territory that stood in a position to become a state. Thus I think it can be stated that Attu and Kiska were the first parts of the incorporated United States to be occupied.

7. On June 7 there were ten men at the U.S. Navy weather station on Kiska. On Attu there were forty-two Aleuts and two Caucasian school-teachers.

8. The Japanese were able to slip through the blockade because of an amazing piece of luck. Several American ships had been diverted from the Kiska blockade in July 1943 as part of an intriguing story known as the Battle of the Pips. An American surveillance plane thought that its radar detected seven enemy ships southwest of Attu. When the American ships diverted from Kiska reached the area, they began firing and the radar "pips" disappeared. However, in searching the area no evidence of any wreckage was found. Immediately after the incident the "pips" were attributed to an atmospheric interference with radar. Samuel Eliot Morison suggested that the pips were radar "echoes" from the mountains of Amchitka Island (*History of United States Naval Operations,* 7:60). In more recent years some have attributed the pips to large flocks of migratory water birds. See Garfield, *Thousand Mile War,* 280–90; and Rennick, "World War II in Alaska," 37.

9. Morison, *History of United States Naval Operations,* 4:162. See chapter 7 for a description by General Delos Emmons that the army in no way "forgot" the Aleutians after 1943 and had substantial plans for their use if Russia entered the war against Japan.

10. David Price, "*Williwaw:* Gore Vidal's First Novel," in *Gore Vidal, Writer against the Grain,* ed. Jay Parini, 37–55 (New York: Columbia University Press, 1992). Born in October 1925, Vidal was eighteen when he went to Alaska; he was twenty when *Williwaw* was published. Though rarely mentioned today as one of Vidal's best works, *Williwaw* received favorable reviews when it was published and was widely read for a brief time. I found anecdotal insight into the reception of *Williwaw* on the "Date Due" slip on the first-edition copy I borrowed from the Athens, Georgia, public library. The book was checked out seven times in 1946–47 and another seven times from 1949 to 1951. In the ensuing half-century only three users borrowed the book.

   For the significance of the later raids on the Kuriles, see the subheading "General Emmons's Alaska" in chapter 7.

11. Morison, *History of United States Naval Operations,* 7:3; Cloe, *The Aleutian Warriors,* 323. The Aleutian Campaign was one of the first joint U.S./Canadian operations. Hence Cloe's reference to the loss of Canadian lives. Huston's film was nominated for an Academy Award as the best documentary of 1943.

12. The length of the Alaska Highway is at best a floating target. It changed even during construction as civilian road crews straightened portions built only a few weeks before by the army. As first laid out, the proposed length was nearly 1,700 miles. By the time the pioneer highway was opened in November 1942 the length was closer to 1,600. With continued straightening, the highway today is officially 1,520 miles, though *Milepost* notes that the driving distance is only 1,488 miles.

   The best single source on the Alaska Highway from the American perspective is Heath Twichell, *Northwest Epic: The Building of the Alaska Highway* (New York: St. Martin's Press, 1992). Twichell, an army officer also trained as a historian, was the son of Heath Twichell, an army engineer who worked on the Alaska Highway. The senior Twichell began collecting notes for a history of the highway and writing his memoirs before his death in 1973. The junior Twichell used those notes and memoirs to complete the work his father began. For a western Canadian perspective, see K. S. Coates and W. R. Morrison, *The Alaska Highway in World War II: The U.S. Army of Occupation in Canada's Northwest* (Norman: University of Oklahoma Press, 1992).

13. Both Routes "A" and "B" began near Prince George, British Columbia, where they could connect to existing highways south to Vancouver and on to Seattle. Route "B" would go to Fairbanks via Dawson City, the

historic town of the Klondike gold rush. Though Route "A" initially went through Dawson City, it was revised in the late 1930s to turn into Alaska and bypass Dawson. The 1938 commission was not the first approved by Congress. In 1930 it created a commission to study building an Alaska Highway. Though there was publicity for the highway, the Depression made the chances of construction unlikely.

14. Cohen, *The Forgotten War*, 1:154.

15. For Twichell's analysis of black soldiers, see *Northwest Epic*, 97–98, 130–47.

16. The senior Heath Twichell became commander of the 95th Engineer Regiment in July 1942. For the change in his attitude toward the ability of black soldiers, see *Northwest Epic*, 179–84.

17. For ALSIB see Twichell, *Northwest Epic*, 277–88; "Fairbanks," *Alaska Geographic* 22, no. 1 (1995): 26–27; and Alexander B. Dolitsky, "The Alaska-Siberia Lend-Lease Program," in Chandonnet, *Alaska at War*, 333–39. For an excellent description of the Russian troops in Fairbanks, see Dermot Cole, *Fairbanks* (Fairbanks: Epicenter Press, 1999). The procurement of luxury products in Fairbanks was aided by the fact that Alaska was exempt from the wartime rationing program that restricted such goods in the "Lower 48."

18. For the best background to CANOL and General Somervell, see Twichell, *Northwest Epic*, 148–66. From his Washington, D.C., office, Somervell was in charge of both the construction of the Alaska Highway and CANOL.

19. For the Truman Hearings, see Twichell, *Northwest Epic*, 257–76.

20. For Twichell's assessment of the futures of Truman and Somervell after the CANOL hearings, see Twichell, *Northwest Epic*, 273–76.

21. For the story of the Aleut evacuation, see Kohlhoff, *When the Wind Was a River*; Commission on Wartime Relocation, *Personal Justice Denied*, 317–59. See also the video *Aleut Evacuation: The Untold Story*.

22. For Gruber's assessment of the Aleuts in 1941, see Kohlhoff, *When the Wind Was a River*, 25. For Gruber's personal account of her time in Alaska, and her other activities in World War II, see Ruth Gruber, *Inside of Time: My Journey from Alaska to Israel* (New York: Carroll and Graf, 2003).

23. For comparison we might look to the evacuation of other groups in Alaska during World War II. Military spouses and dependents were evacuated after Pearl Harbor as they were under the authority of the military. Japanese and Japanese Americans were evacuated under the authority of Executive Order 9066.

24. Some sources, see especially the video *Aleut Evacuation,* claim that the evacuation of the Aleuts was racially motivated, like the evacuation and internment of Japanese Americans. Kohlhoff (*When the Wind Was a River,* 184) and Commission on Wartime Relocation (*Personal Justice Denied*) 464, downplay such racial claims and emphasize the mandate of the army to protect civilians in a war zone. Not all Aleuts were evacuated, only those living on islands west of Unimak. Those living on Unimak were undisturbed.

25. For mortality statistics see Kohlhoff, *When the Wind Was a River,* 114.

26. The final reparations settlement of 1988 (Public Law 100-383, August 10, 1988) created a trust fund of $5 million to be managed by the U.S. Treasury for the Aleut evacuees and their dependents. In addition the sum of $1.4 million was paid as compensation for damaged church property. Individual evacuees who were still alive at the time of the settlement (about four hundred) received $12,000 each. As the island of Attu was never resettled but placed in the National Wilderness Preservation system, a sum not to exceed $15 million was authorized to be paid to the Aleut Corporation, one of the ANCSA (Alaska Native Claims Settlement Act) native corporations created in 1972. The federal government also agreed to clean up the remaining World War II debris on the islands. For more detail on the settlement, see Kohlhoff, *When the Wind Was a River,* 186–87; Commission on Wartime Relocation, *Personal Justice Denied,* 465–67; and "The Aleutian Islands," *Alaska Geographic* 22, no. 2 (1995): 66–67.

27. For comments on the political awakening, see Kohlhoff, *When the Wind Was a River,* x, 176–87; and "Islands of the Seals: The Pribilofs," *Alaska Geographic* 9, no. 3 (1982): 84–85. The Pribilofs did not achieve full self-governing status until 1966 with the passage of the Fur Seal Act of 1966, sponsored by Senator Bob Bartlett. The act finally transferred land ownership from the federal government to the Pribilovians and allowed the communities of St. Paul and St. George to incorporate as municipalities.

28. The best sources for Gruening's life are his own autobiography, *Many Battles,* and the more recent biography by Robert David Johnson, *Ernest Gruening and the American Dissenting Tradition* (Cambridge, Mass.: Harvard University Press, 1998). Claus-M. Naske, *Ernest Gruening: Alaska's Greatest Governor* (Fairbanks: University of Alaska Press, 2004) is forthcoming.

29. For Gruening's early involvement with the NAACP, see Johnson, *Ernest Gruening,* 14–17; and Gruening, *Many Battles,* 65.

30. Johnson, *Ernest Gruening,* 5–6.

31. For "Alaska Hire," see Gruening, *Many Battles,* 287–90.

32. For Gruening's "battle" with the 1941 legislature, see Gruening, *Many Battles,* 297–301; Johnson, *Ernest Gruening,* 157–58.

33. For the possibilities of martial law and other procedures to curtail civilian authority in Alaska, see Kohlhoff, *When the Wind Was a River,* 29–32; Johnson, *Ernest Gruening,* 159–62.

34. For Gruening and censorship, see Gruening, *Many Battles,* 312–14.

35. Marvin R. "Muktuk" Marston, *Men of the Tundra: Eskimos at War* (New York: October House, 1969), 47.

36. Marston, *Men of the Tundra,* 58; for the view that Buckner did not like Marston, see Gruening, *Many Battles,* 309–10.

37. Marston organized the guard in the western half of the territory. The guard in the eastern half was organized by Capt. Carl Scheibner. The eastern Alaska Territorial Guard served ably but has not been publicized as well as the Eskimo Scouts. "Rusty" Heurlin (1895–1986) came to Alaska in 1916 and became one of the most noted artists in the territory/state. For information on Heurlin and other artists who recorded wartime life in Alaska, see Kesler E. Woodward, *Painting in the North: Alaska Art in the Anchorage Museum of History and Art* (Seattle: University of Washington Press, 1993), 89, 100–115; and "Painting in Alaska," *Alaska Geographic* 27, no. 3 (2000): 91–92.

38. For the political development of the Eskimo Scouts, see Rennick, "World War II in Alaska," 66–71, as well as Marston, *Men of the Tundra.*

39. For the status of discrimination against natives, see Gruening, *Many Battles,* 318–22; Marston, *Men of the Tundra,* 131–39; and Terrence Cole, "Jim Crow Segregation in Alaska: The Passage of the Alaska Equal Rights Act of 1945," *Western Historical Quarterly* 23 (November 1992): 429–49.

40. Most accounts note that Gruening's appeal to Roosevelt over discrimination at military events severely strained the governor's relationship with Buckner. Gruening, Marston, and Twichell all refer to Buckner's "southern racial prejudices." It is thus ironic that so much racial progress was made in both the military and civilian front in the area Buckner commanded.

41. The bill to expand the legislature required congressional approval but did not require endorsement by the territorial legislature. According to Dimond's biographer, Dr. Mary Mangusso, Dimond's original bill called for a Senate that was also based on proportional representation rather than on equal "at large" representation from each of the four judicial districts.

42. Alaska's native population is usually divided into six distinct groups—Aleuts, Eskimos, Athabascans, Tlingits, Haidas, and Tsimshains. Though collectively called "Alaska natives," the different groups are definitely seen as separate and have their ancestral homes in different parts of Alaska.

43. For Gruening's "meddling" with Bartlett in 1944, see Gruening, *Many Battles*, 325–26; and Claus-M. Naske, *Edward Lewis "Bob" Bartlett of Alaska: A Life in Politics* (Fairbanks: University of Alaska Press, 1979), 50–55.

44. Evangeline Atwood, *Anchorage: All-America City* (Portland, Ore.: Binford and Mort, 1957), 42.

45. Talley's later residence in Alaska is well worthy of mention. In the 1970s, 1980s, and 1990s he was a regular attendee at Alaska Historical Society meetings. In the 1990s he entranced my students at University of Alaska Fairbanks with his presentations on the building of air bases in the Aleutians. His ingenuity led to the development of three-dimensional or "stereoscopic" mapping. He also designed a binocular device to read such maps. He demonstrated this in my classes. After interviewing him for *The Thousand Mile War*, Brian Garfield said of Talley that his "only fault has been in insisting that credit for the remarkable engineering achievements in the Aleutians belongs to everyone but himself."

46. Marston, *Men of the Tundra*, 171–72.

Chapter 5

1. For Stainback's testimony, see U.S. Cong., House, Committee on Territories, *Statehood for Hawaii: Hearings before the subcommittee of the Committee on Territories, on HR 236*, 79th Cong., 2d sess., January 7–18, 1946 (Washington: Government Printing Office, 1946), 10–20. Cited hereafter as *Larcade Committee Hearings*.

2. *Larcade Committee Hearings*, 19.

3. The presentation of Kamokila's testimony and the reaction to it are drawn from my article "The Anti-Statehood Movement and the Legacy of Alice Kamokila Campbell," *Hawaiian Journal of History* 27 (1993): 43–63. For the full text of her testimony, see *Larcade Committee Hearings*, 481–503. Alice Kamokila Campbell was such a well-known figure in Hawai'i that she was frequently referred to in the press by the single name Kamokila—much in the fashion of royalty.

4. For an analysis of the 1947 vote, see Bell, *Last among Equals*, 127–28. A majority of Republicans voted *for* statehood (141–56), but only a

minority of Democrats voted *for* statehood (55–77). Notable also is the number of House members who did not vote: 94.

5. For a background to Stainback's 1947 anti-Communist crusade, see T. Michael Holmes, *The Specter of Communism in Hawaii* (Honolulu: University of Hawai'i Press, 1994), 43–52; Sanford Zalburg, *A Spark Is Struck! Jack Hall and the ILWU in Hawaii* (Honolulu: University of Hawai'i Press, 1979), 195–98; and H. Brett Melendy, *The Federal Government's Search for Communists in the Territory of Hawaii* (Lewiston, N.Y: Edward Mellen Press, 2002), 21–33. For the Reinecke hearing, see Holmes, *The Specter of Communism*, 68–122.

6. The best general background for labor history in Hawai'i is Edward Beechert, *Working in Hawaii: A Labor History* (Honolulu: University of Hawai'i Press, 1985).

7. Australian-born Harry Bridges was the West Coast head of the ILA during the 1934 San Francisco strike. After the strike Bridges argued with the East Coast leadership of the union. In 1937 he took his West Coast longshoremen out and joined with warehousemen to form the ILWU, which then became an affiliate of the CIO. Though the name and organization of the union changed, Bridge's 1934 West Coast ILA and the 1937 ILWU were effectively the same union.

8. John Burns interview by Lawrence Fuchs, November 1958. Lawrence Fuchs published his classic work *Hawaii Pono* in 1961 (New York: Harcourt Brace Jovanovich). He conducted extensive interviews in Hawai'i in 1958 and 1959. Transcripts of the Fuchs interviews can be found in box 5 of the Melendy Collection at the University of Hawai'i Mānoa. Zalburg (*A Spark Is Struck*, xiv, 199) confirms Hall's membership in the Communist Party as well as the fact that Burns knew about it before and during the war. See Holmes, *Specter of Communism*, 24–26, for Hall's membership in and use of the Communist Party; and Melendy, *The Federal Government's Search for Communists*, 7–20, for early investigations by the FBI of Communists in Hawai'i.

9. The wartime wage freeze is widely cited as a principal motivator for the surge in union activity after World War II. See Beechert, *Working in Hawaii*, 285–87; Allen, *Hawaii's War Years*, 310–12, 326; and Thomas Kemper Hitch, *Islands in Transition* (Honolulu: First Hawaiian Bank, 1992), 151. Hitch also explained the wage freeze and its impact on unionization in a January 1959 interview with Lawrence Fuchs.

10. Thomas Hitch worked for President Truman's Council of Economic Advisers before coming to Hawai'i in 1950 as the director of research

for the HEC. He remained in Hawai'i until his death four decades later. Hitch explained the organization of the HEC in *Islands in Transition,* 153–55. Hitch presented the same explanation to Lawrence Fuchs in his January 1959 interview. Both Zalburg (*A Spark Is Struck,* 42, 117) and Beechert (*Working in Hawaii,* 298) emphasize labor's sponsorship of the HERA but make no reference to management's support of the bill through the HEC.

11. Zalburg, *A Spark Is Struck,* 155–56, notes that ILWU negotiators in San Francisco got along well with James Blaisdell in his San Francisco days. Blaisdell did not get along with Jack Hall as well as he did with the San Francisco negotiators.

12. Robert McElrath interview by Chris Conybeare, in *Perspectives on Hawai'i's Statehood* (Honolulu: Oral History Project, SSRI-UH, June 1986), 113. McElrath became involved in union activities in the late 1930s. He was also a suspected Communist. By 1947 he was in charge of all ILWU organizing activities in Hawai'i. He was also information director for the union. On the Borthwick affair, see Zalburg, *A Spark Is Struck,* 165–70; and Holmes, *The Specter of Communism,* 38–39.

13. For Thurston's opposition to Farrington, see George Chaplin, *Presstime in Paradise,* 227–31.

14. For Stainback's ouster of Hall, see Holmes, *The Specter of Communism,* 39–40.

15. Zalburg, *A Spark Is Struck,* 195–98, 226.

16. Ernest Gruening, *The Battle for Alaska Statehood* (Fairbanks: University of Alaska Press, 1967), 5–7; videotape, *See It Now,* 1958.

17. For the best overall discussion of Butler and his opposition to Hawai'i statehood, see Justus F. Paul, "The Power of Seniority: Senator Hugh Butler and Statehood for Hawaii," *Hawaiian Journal of History,* 1975, 140–47. James Coke wrote on November 24, 1947, to R. A. Van Orsdel, vice president of the Chesapeake and Potomac Telephone Co. in Washington and friend of Butler. He asked that his letter be forwarded to Butler. Van Orsdel did so on November 28. Butler responded on December 2, that he was delighted with Coke's letter. He indicated at the time that he was already of the mind not to recommend the bill until his committee went to Hawai'i. The Coke–Van Orsdel–Butler correspondence is in the Hugh A. Butler Papers, box 241, Hawaii Statehood 1947, Nebraska State Historical Society, Manuscripts, Lincoln, Nebraska.

18. For Butler's early statements on statehood, see Paul, "The Power of Seniority," 141; for Kamokila Campbell's 1948 testimony, see Holmes,

Specter of Communism, 126. See references in footnote 17 for James Coke. For Cordon's findings on Communism, see Bell, *Last among Equals,* 155.

19. For both the Millikin and the Knowland Resolutions, see Bell, *Last among Equals,* 130–31.

20. U.S. Congress, Senate, Committee on Interior and Insular Affairs, *Statehood for Hawaii: Communist Penetration of the Hawaiian Islands,* 80th Cong., 2d sess., June 1949. For detail on Butler's time in Hawai'i, see Melendy, *The Federal Government's Search for Communists,* 45–62.

21. Butler to James L. Coke, June 11, 1949, Butler Papers. By 1949 Coke and Butler were corresponding directly without the intermediary of Van Orsdel.

22. Chuck Mau interview by John S. Whitehead, January 8, 1986. Tape in author's possession. James Coke to Hugh Butler, June 1, 1949, Butler Papers.

23. Both Zalburg (*A Spark Is Struck,* 243–44) and Holmes (*The Specter of Communism,* 141) confirm the last-minute fifteen- vs. sixteen-cent negotiations. Beechert, *Working in Hawaii,* makes no mention of anything except the official twenty-one- vs. twelve-cent offers. Zalburg is the prime source for information on the Dock Strike of 1949.

24. Spessard Holland papers, box 316, 1949, Eighty-first Congress, University of Florida, Gainesville. There were ten letters to Holland on the Dock Strike. Holland had a sister, a brother-in-law, and two nephews who lived in Hawai'i. He was noncommittal in letters in 1948 and 1949 about his stand on statehood. He became a supporter in the mid–1950s after University of Florida professor Ernest Bartley, a consultant to the 1955–56 Alaska Constitutional Convention, talked with him.

25. The tactic to discharge the bill from the Rules Committee was a rule agreed to by the House in the Eighty-first Congress and then repealed in future Congresses. If the Rules Committee failed to act in twenty-one days on a bill approved by another house committee, that first committee could petition the Speaker to discharge the bill from the Rules Committee and bring it to the floor. For details on the discharge petition and its use on the Alaska and Hawai'i statehood bills, see Bell, *Last among Equals,* 172–73; and Claus-M. Naske, *A History of Alaska Statehood* (Lanham, Md.: University Press of America, 1985), 134–35. In 1950 the victory for Hawai'i was more substantial than in 1947 because (1) more members of Congress voted and (2) a majority of House Democrats and House Republicans voted for Hawai'i, though the Republican

majority was more substantial. The overall vote for Alaska was smaller because more House members abstained.

26. My discussion of the 1950 convention is taken from my previous research report, John S. Whitehead, *Completing The Union: The Alaska and Hawaii Statehood Movements,* Alaska Historical Commission Studies in History no. 198, June 1986. See also Norman Meller, *With an Understanding Heart: Constitution Making in Hawaii,* National Municipal League, State Constitutional Convention Studies no. 5 (New York: National Municipal League, 1971); and Richard Kosaki, "Constitutions and Constitutional Conventions in Hawaii," *Hawaiian Journal of History* 12 (1978): 120–38.

27. The delegates used a manual put together by the Legislative Reference Bureau of the University of Hawai'i (LRB) and the Hawaii Statehood Commission. The LRB and the Statehood Commission in turn used the National Municipal League guidelines.

28. Chuck Mau interview by John S. Whitehead, January 8, 1986. Clearly the leadership positions at the convention went to the established Old Guard. But at the time of the convention elections there was a great deal of excitement about the advent of newcomers in politics. A total of 243 candidates filed for the 63 seats. At a primary election in February, 18 candidates were elected outright and 90 others competed in the March runoff election for the remaining 45 seats. John Burns did not make the cutoff in the primary. After the March runoff the newspapers proudly announced the number of "novices" who were elected and the number of "old timers" who were defeated. Of the 22 members of the 1949 legislature who ran, only 12 were elected to the convention. Nonetheless, the convention quickly gained a reputation as an Old Guard rather than a "newcomers" affair.

29. *Honolulu Star-Bulletin,* March 24, 1950.

30. For Kageyama's ousting, see Whitehead, *Completing the Union,* 1986, 44.

31. For Silva's ousting, see Whitehead, *Completing the Union,* 1986, 45–46.

32. For Larsen and Anthony's discussion on Silva, see Whitehead, *Completing the Union,* 1986, 47–48. Silva did appear before the committee, but took the Fifth Amendment. Union leader Robert McElrath told Sanford Zalburg that almost no one at the convention had a clue what the word "contumacious" meant. Zalburg, *A Spark Is Struck,* 298–99.

33. Editorial, *Honolulu Star-Bulletin,* April 22, 1950. The other ILWU delegate to the convention, Frank Luiz, specifically asked to be appointed to the eleven-member special committee that investigated Silva. That

committee returned a unanimous decision to disqualify Silva. When the convention finally voted to disqualify Silva, Luiz was one of three delegates not voting. Silva was replaced by another ILWU candidate, Matsuki Arashiro. Silva's and Kageyama's expulsions were not a cause of further concern in 1950 or in later times. In 1985–86 I interviewed a number of people who had been present at the convention. All of the interviewees answered that the oustings of Silva and Kageyama were not important events. I interviewed Kageyama, who had no bitterness about his time at the convention. Though he remembered the convention well, he insisted that he had not been expelled. See Whitehead, *Completing the Union*, 1986, 49–50, for the legacy of the Silva/Kageyama expulsions

34. The ILWU protested the absence of initiative and referendum in the constitution and the fact that so few officials were elected outside of the legislative branch. Silva's ousting was not cited as a reason for opposition. In later years ILWU leader Robert McElrath said the union changed its position on initiative and referendum and agreed that the two Progressive measures were banes to efficient lawmaking. Interview with Robert McElrath in *Perspectives on Hawaii's Statehood* (1986), 121–22.

35. See Bell, *Last among Equals*, 175–79, for the best description of the Southern filibuster and Truman's efforts to secure statehood in the summer and fall of 1950.

36. For more on the oblivion of the convention, see Whitehead, *Completing the Union*, 1986, 21–22.

Chapter 6

1. "Hawaii Constellation: How Would Statehood Affect U.S. Role in the Pacific?" *Christian Science Monitor*, January 14, 1946, section 2.

2. Lyndon B. Johnson, *The Vantage Point: Perspectives of the Presidency* (New York: Holt, Rinehart, Winston, 1971), 360.

3. Schmitt, *Historical Statistics of Hawaii*, 10 (table 1.4), 661 (table 26.3), and 668 (table 26.7). Comparative statistics on military personnel are confusing because of changing statistical methods. Before 1950 only shore-based personnel were counted. After 1950 shore-based and naval personnel afloat on ships based in Hawai'i were counted.

4. For Tom Coffman's characterization of Hawai'i's political parties, see *The Island Edge of America*, 9–14. For the postwar Democratic Party, see Paul Phillips, *Chasing the American Dream* (Lanham, Md.: University Press of America, 1982); Fuchs, *Hawaii Pono*, 308–53; Dan Boylan and T. Michael

Holmes, *John A. Burns: The Man and His Times* (Honolulu: University of Hawai'i Press, 2000); and Tom Coffman, *Catch a Wave* (Honolulu: University of Hawai'i Press, 1973), 19–22. The massive John Burns Oral History Project (JBOH) at the University of Hawai'i Mānoa, includes extensive interviews with members of the Burns faction.

5. The term "shambles" is used repeatedly by Daniel K. Inouye in his 1975 interview in the JBOH, p. 9. Boylan and Holmes (*John A. Burns,* 69) also use the term though with no direct attribution to Inouye.

6. In his radical critique of twentieth-century Hawai'i, *Islands under the Influence* (1983), 134–39, Noel Kent suggests that the ILWU did have a radical agenda to create a socialist-workers state in Hawai'i. He thus criticizes the ILWU for its failure to do so and for betraying its original radical goals by accommodating to bourgeoisie capitalism. However, it appears that such a socialist-workers state is what Noel Kent would have liked the ILWU to do, rather than a plan that the ILWU ever envisioned. Kent cites no ILWU sources with a radical plan for the future.

7. For the origins of "The Five" and their decision to back the Democrats, see Tom Coffman, *Catch a Wave,* 19–20; and Boylan and Holmes, *John A. Burns,* 70–71.

8. Interview with John Burns by Lawrence Fuchs, November 1958, Melendy Collection, University of Hawai'i.

9. Nearly all sources on Burns note his devout Catholicism and the influence of Benedictine priests at a series of Catholic high schools that Burns attended in Kansas where his uncle lived. Also nearly all sources note the expressed opinion by Burns and Inouye that the Democratic Party had to rid itself of its radical/ILWU tinge (for example, see Phillips, *Hawaii's Democrats,* 20–21).

10. For details on Inouye's decision to join the Democratic Party, see the 1975 interview with Daniel Inouye in the JBOH, p. 8; and Inouye, *Journey to Washington,* 207–11. It is not clear if Inouye joined the party because of Burns or got to know Burns once he was in the party. The JBOH interview says he did not know Burns in 1947, but first met him in 1948. In *Journey to Washington* Inouye says that Burns signed him up in 1947.

11. For the 1950 Democratic convention, see Boylan and Holmes, *John A. Burns,* 95–98; and Phillips, *Hawaii's Democrats,* 21–22.

12. See Coffman, *The Island Edge of America,* 145, for Burns's comments on Shivers as governor.

13. For Long's appointment, see Boylan and Holmes, *John A. Burns*, 99–101; and Phillips, *Hawaii's Democrats*, 22–24. Regardless of whether Long was the "obvious choice," both Johnny Wilson and Delbert Metzger wanted the job in 1951 and were disappointed, even bitter, not to get it. The Burns group also considered Hawaiian Ernest Kai but preferred Long. It is my observation that the appointment of governors, both Democrat and Republican, in Hawai'i left more party members discontented than did any ensuing election of governors.

14. Gruening, *Battle for Alaska Statehood*, 7.

15. For Kawano's testimony and Mau's involvement, see Zalburg, *A Spark Is Struck*, 304–10; Boylan and Holmes, *John A. Burns*, 101–5; and Holmes, *The Specter of Communism in Hawaii*, 178–89.

16. For the best coverage of the Smith Act Trial, see Zalburg, *A Spark Is Struck*, 324–65.

17. Interview with Daniel Inouye, 1975, JBOH, 28–29.

18. Metzger would lose his judgeship as a result of his ruling on the Reluctant 39. He was not reappointed when his term expired in September 1951. He was replaced in June 1952. For the best description of Metzger, who came to Hawai'i from Kansas in 1899 and helped organize the local Democratic Party, see H. Brett Melendy, "Delbert E. Metzger, Hawai'i's Liberal Judge," *Hawaiian Journal of History* 35 (2001): 43–63.

19. Fuchs, *Hawaii Pono*, 321. The party affiliations of members of the territorial legislature are clearly listed in the various legislative directories for the prewar period. I am indebted to Tom Coffman and Wendell Marumoto for a comprehensive list of AJA legislators. Fuchs used a number of assistants in compiling his research. Their errors extended not merely to an incorrect assumption of party affiliation for Hawai'i's AJAs, but to listing territorial legislators who were never elected. Thus Fuchs claims that Democrat AJA James Murakami was elected to the legislature in 1948 and 1950. There was never a James Murakami in the legislature. There were sixteen AJAs elected in 1952, not seventeen as Fuchs states.

20. Interview with Daniel Inouye, 1975, JBOH, 24–25.

21. Chou, *Interview with Elizabeth P. Farrington, Delegate to Congress from the Territory of Hawaii, 1954–57*, 19.

22. For the best discussion of the 1951–52 statehood legislation for Alaska and Hawai'i, see Bell, *Last among Equals*, 195–201; and Naske, *A History of Alaska Statehood*, 161–67.

23. For the early history of the Walter Resolution, see *Honolulu Star-Bulletin,* August 29, 1950. My discussion of the legislative history of the McCarran-Walter Act is based on Honolulu newspaper coverage.

24. For the number of people naturalized in Hawai'i after 1952, see *Honolulu Star-Bulletin,* June 29, 1957. For Matsunaga's comments, see *Honolulu Star-Bulletin,* June 27, 1967.

25. For Butler's change of heart, see Paul, "The Power of Seniority," 143–45.

26. For the legislative mechanics of the 1953–54 Hawai'i statehood bill, see Bell, *Last among Equals,* 201–7.

27. For Farrington's last day in Washington, see Drew Pearson, "Washington Merry-Go-Round," *Honolulu Star-Bulletin,* August 17, 1954.

28. *Honolulu Advertiser,* June 22, 1954.

29. For local coverage of Farrington's funeral, see *Honolulu Advertiser,* June 27–28, 1954; *Honolulu Star-Bulletin,* June 28, 1954.

30. Chou, *Interview with Elizabeth P. Farrington, Delegate to Congress from the Territory of Hawaii, 1954–57,* 21.

31. Bell, *Last among Equals,* 218; For Anthony's eulogy, see *Honolulu Star-Bulletin,* June 28, 1954.

32. For King's desire to "appoint" Mrs. Farrington, see Boylan and Holmes, *John A. Burns,* 123–24.

33. Pearson, "Washington Merry-Go-Round."

34. George Ariyoshi, *With Obligation to All* (Honolulu: Ariyoshi Foundation, 1997), 37.

35. For the Bergman-Nagoshi poll, see Phillips, *Hawaii's Democrats,* 34–35.

36. Inouye, *Journey to Washington,* 241. Inouye first returned to Honolulu in 1947 and graduated from the University of Hawai'i in 1950. In the fall of 1950 he departed for George Washington University Law School in Washington, D.C., and returned in 1952. The failure of the Republicans to employ the AJA lawyers is emphasized by Big Five executive Malcolm McNaughton in "Oral History Interview with Malcolm McNaughton, October 31, 1984," in *Perspectives on Hawaii's Statehood* (Oral History Project, SSRI, University of Hawai'i Mānoa, June 1986), 50–51.

37. Daws, *Shoal of Time,* 379.

38. Ariyoshi, *With Obligation to All,* 39.

39. Inouye, *Journey to Washington,* 244.

40. Members of the 1953–54 legislature who were not retained in the 1955–56 legislature included five Republican AJAs, six Republican haoles, one Republican Chinese American, one Democrat Chinese

American, one Republican Hawaiian, and one Democrat AJA. Only in the fourth district of Oʻahu did anything approaching an ethnic/party "revolution" take place. In 1953 the fourth district had six haole male Republicans. Only one was reelected in 1954. The other five were replaced by four Democrat AJAs and one Hawaiian woman.

41. For Sakakihara's charges, see *Honolulu Advertiser*, October 31, 1954; Inouye, *Journey to Washington*, 246–49; Ariyoshi, *With Obligation to All*, 40–42.

42. Bell, *Last among Equals*, 227–29. When Alaska and Hawaiʻi were eventually admitted in 1959, the addition of two new representatives raised the size of the House to 437 members for the Eighty-sixth and Eighty-seventh Congresses. A reapportionment based on the 1960 census returned the House to 435 members for the Eighty-eighth Congress elected in the fall of 1962.

43. Bell, *Last among Equals*, 225.

44. "Interview with Elizabeth Farrington," 1977, JBOH, 20.

45. Chou, *Interview with Elizabeth P. Farrington, Delegate to Congress from the Territory of Hawaii, 1954–57*, 76.

46. *Honolulu Star-Bulletin*, March 26, 1951.

Chapter 7

1. Gruening, *The Battle for Alaska Statehood*, 2.

2. Unless otherwise noted, all references to Emmons's career are from Delos C. Emmons, "Brief Personal History," unpublished manuscript in the Hoover Library, Stanford University, Palo Alto, California.

3. Emmons's role in trying to reverse DeWitt's internment of the Japanese is confirmed in Commission on Wartime Relocation and Internment of Civilians, *Personal Justice Denied*, 230–31. *Personal Justice Denied* confirms that Emmons initiated a process for internees to apply to return to their homes, and that approximately 1,485 internees were back in the Western Defense Command by the end of 1944, several months after Emmons left.

4. Some historians claim that the creation of a separate department deemphasized Alaska's importance by removing it from the Western Defense Command. There is nothing in Emmons's memoir that would indicate this. Why would the army send a three-star general to command a department it had downgraded—and why would Emmons want to command it? I hold with the impression given by Emmons

that the new department indicated a continued importance for Alaska. Emmons made the recommendation for a separate department before the Kiska invasion.

5. Bob Atwood, *Bob Atwood's Alaska* (Anchorage: Marilaine Publishing, 2003), 68–69. Atwood does not indicate how he eventually learned of the secret Pentagon plan for Alaska aside from his observation of planes returning to Anchorage. Atwood had been working on his memoirs when he died in January 1997. His daughter Elaine edited and published the memoirs in 2003.

6. I cannot explain the lack of attention given to Emmons by historians in Alaska. When I made informal inquiries to a number of historians in 2001, the response was either (1) they had never heard of Emmons or (2) his posting to Alaska must have been a demotion. I can only imagine that this impression has come from a lack of sources on Emmons. The "brief personal history" discovered by Tom Coffman in the Hoover Institution is the extent of information on the general.

7. Evangeline Atwood, *Anchorage: All America City* (Portland, Ore.: Binford and Mort, 1957), 42.

8. Gruening, *Many Battles,* 341.

9. WASPs could ferry ALSIB planes to Great Falls, but could not fly further north, supposedly because toilet and rest facilities for women were not available. For the story of Joe and Claire Fejes, see Claire Fejes, *Cold Starry Night* (Fairbanks: Epicenter Press, 1996), 12–13. Claire Fejes became a nationally recognized painter of Alaskan scenes of native life. For Hammond's decision to come to Alaska and his dramatic arrival, see Jay Hammond, *Bush Rat Governor* (Fairbanks: Epicenter Press, 1994), 53–58.

10. For the postwar growth of Anchorage, see Evangeline Atwood, *Anchorage: All America City,* and Bob Atwood, *Bob Atwood's Alaska.* For Hickel's arrival and early business career in Anchorage, see Walter J. Hickel, *Who Owns America* (Englewood, N.J.: Prentice Hall, 1971), 53–68.

11. Bob Atwood, *Bob Atwood's Alaska,* 117–18.

12. The analysis of the 1946 plebiscite and the opposition to statehood is drawn from John S. Whitehead, "Anti-Statehood and Its Legacy in Alaska and Hawaii," in *Completing the Union: The Alaska and Hawaii Statehood Movements* (Alaska Humanities Forum, December 1988), 3–10.

13. For the best treatment of Cap Lathrop's business views and practices, see Elizabeth A. Tower, *Mining Media Movies—Cap Lathrop's Keys for Alaska's Riches* (privately printed, 1991).

14. In 1936 Congress had allowed Alaska's municipalities to acquire bonded indebtedness up to 10 percent of the community's assessed property value without congressional approval. Anchorage grew so rapidly in the 1950s that its need for municipal bonds exceeded that value. Thus the need for congressional approval that so annoyed Atwood. Bob Atwood reiterated this fret about bonded indebtedness to me repeatedly.

15. For Hammond's position against statehood, see John S. Whitehead, "The Governor Who Opposed Statehood," *Alaska History* 7, no. 2L (Fall 1992).

16. For Sutherland's career history, see his autobiography edited by John S, Whitehead, "Dan Sutherland, Gold Rush Pioneer and Politician," *Alaska History* 10, no. 1 (Spring 1995). For data on the number of fishermen, see Cooley, *Politics and Conservation,* 53. For the idea that miners had been fishermen before coming to Alaska, see James H. Ducker, "Gold Rushes North: A Census of the Yukon and Alaskan Gold Rushes, 1896–1900," *Pacific Northwest Quarterly* 85, no. 3 (July 1994): 82–92.

17. For Hoover's interest in the Alaska fishery and his "reserve" plan, see Herbert Hoover, *The Memoirs of Herbert Hoover: The Cabinet and the Presidency, 1920–33* (New York: Macmillan Co., 1952), 150–51. See also Ray Lyman Wilbur, *The Hoover Policies* (New York: Charles Scribner's Sons, 1937), 241–44. For Sutherland's reaction, see Whitehead, "Dan Sutherland," 30. For the provisions of the White Act see Cooley, *Politics and Conservation,* 119–25.

18. For Sutherland's 1936 testimony to Congress, see U.S. House of Representatives, 74th Cong., 2d sess., *Fish Traps in Alaskan Waters, Hearings before the Committee on Merchant Marine and Fisheries, on HR 4254 and HR 8213,* January 15 and 16, 1936, 36–38.

19. For the best summary of territorial taxes on the fisheries and Walstein's Smith's testimony, see U.S. House, *Fish Traps in Alaskan Waters,* 152–70. The four-cent-per-case tax was technically levied by the federal government and then turned over to the territory.

20. For the 1948 vote, see "Official Returns—Territorial Canvassing Board, General Election, October 12, 1948." The precise wording of the ballot proposition was "The practice of fishing by means of fish traps within the Territory should be gradually abolished over a ten year period by appropriate legislation."

21. "Alaska Steamship Company Interview with D. E. Skinner, April 4, 1986," by William S. Schneider. Oral interview in Oral History Collection, Alaska and Polar Regions Department, Rasmuson Library,

University of Alaska Fairbanks, 12–13. After World War I Skinner and Eddy began buying salmon canneries in Alaska. In the 1930s Skinner and Eddy organized the Northland Transportation Company as a competitor to the Alaska Steamship Co. With the 1944 purchase of Alaska Steam, the two companies were merged under the name of Alaska Steamship Company, thus giving Skinner and Eddy a virtual monopoly on water transportation.

22. Gruening, *Many Battles,* 351–53.

23. Bob Atwood, *Bob Atwood's Alaska,* 32.

24. For the saga of Gruening's 1949 U.S. Senate confirmation, see Gruening, *Many Battles,* 354–60; Johnson, *Ernest Gruening,* 172–74; and Claus-M. Naske, "Governor Ernest Gruening's Struggle for Territorial Status: Personal or Political?" *Journal of the West* 20 (1981): 34–36.

25. For Gruening's fate in Mexico and Puerto Rico, see Johnson, *Ernest Gruening,* 48–53, 138–48. Readers of the governor's autobiography *Many Battles* can easily detect Gruening's own tendency to dismiss the opposition.

26. Gruening, *Many Battles,* 360–61.

27. Gruening, *Many Battles,* 360; Johnson, *Ernest Gruening,* 176.

28. The impact of the Cold War military buildup in Alaska is taken from my chapter "The Cold War States: Alaska and Hawai'i," in Fernlund, *The Cold War West.* For specific economic and population data, see also George W. Rogers and Richard A. Cooley, *Alaska's Population and Economy: Regional Growth, Development and Future Outlook,* vol. 2, *Statistical Handbook* (College: University of Alaska Press, 1963).

29. The "arming" of Alaska natives with binoculars was told to me by Fairbanks resident Glenn Wilcox, who was an Episcopal priest in northwest Alaska during the 1950s. According to Wilcox this was a "secret" project. Though many native families had the air force–issued binoculars, they were told not to tell each other.

30. Charlayne Hunter-Gault, *In My Place* (New York: Vintage Books, 1992), 89–106. Hunter-Gault was not the only Georgian in Alaska. I am constantly amazed at the number of people I meet who were in Alaska with the military in the 1950s. On my small two-block street in Athens, Georgia, two families had such a connection.

31. Daniel T. Kresge, George W. Rogers, and Thomas H. Morehouse, *Issues in Alaska Development* (Seattle: University of Washington Press, 1977), 45. For further discussion of "Military Alaska" see also George W. Rogers, *The Future of Alaska: The Economic Consequences of Statehood*

(Baltimore: Johns Hopkins University Press, 1962). The "greater" urban population figures obviously refer to the city and suburbs. In addition both Fairbanks and Anchorage constantly redrew their municipal boundaries to include the new residents.

32. Interview with Fortieth Reunion of Constitutional Convention Delegates, Fairbanks, February 4, 1996. Notes in author's possession.

33. William Bragg Ewald Jr., *Eisenhower The President: Crucial Days 1951–60* (Englewood, N.J.: Prentice Hall, 1981), 201–2.

34. For the full legislative history of each Alaska statehood bill, see Claus-M. Naske, *A History of Alaska Statehood* (Lanham, Md.: University Press of America, 1985). For Bartlett's changes on the size of the land grant in 1947–48, see also Claus-M. Naske, *Edward Lewis Bob Bartlett of Alaska: A Life in Politics* (Fairbanks: University of Alaska Press, 1979), 122–27.

35. In the House the committee handling statehood legislation was named the House Public Lands Committee for the years until 1951, after which it was renamed the House Interior and Insular Affairs Committee. In the Senate the relevant committee was the Senate Public Lands Committee until 1949, when it was renamed the Senate Interior and Insular Affairs Committee.

36. Naske, *A History of Alaska Statehood*, 145. The Department of the Interior had mentioned such a deviation from the township system in 1947–48, but it had not been incorporated into a statehood bill until after Arnold's 1950 testimony.

37. For Hickel's recommittal meeting with Taft, see Hickel, *Who Owns America*, 72–74; Walter Hickel, *Crisis in the Commons: The Alaska Solution* (Oakland, Calif.: Institute for Contemporary Studies, 2002), 45–49.

38. Calculating the size of the statehood land grants is an imprecise affair. Central to every bill was a "general" land grant from the unappropriated, vacant, and unreserved federal lands in the territory to be used for any purpose. This grant often ranged from twenty million to one hundred million acres. In addition smaller specific grants—usually less than one million acres—were made from specific lands, for example, lands in national forests to be used for specific purposes. In the various revisions of bills the specific grants would often be rolled into the general grant. Thus the later statehood bills with their general and specific grants totaled approximately 103 million acres—usually a few hundred thousand acres more—though the general grant was less than 103 million acres.

39. The seventeenth amendment to the U.S. Constitution (Popular Election of Senators) provides that the legislature of a state may

empower the governor of a state to appoint a U.S. senator to fill a vacancy occasioned by death or resignation. Most states follow this process rather than calling for an immediate election, which the amendment also allows. The appointment option is not available to vacancies that occur in the House; a new election must be held. During the postwar statehood battle approximately thirty appointed senators took their seats. There were additional appointees who did not take their seat because some senators were appointed late in the term of a previous senator but could not be sworn in because Congress was not in session. In other situations (for example, Richard Nixon) a senator was elected in November, then appointed to fill the unexpired term of his predecessor (for example, Sheridan Downey), who subsequently resigned before the end of his term. The number of appointed senators in any one Congress ranged from three (Eightieth and Eighty-fourth) to eight (Eighty-first and Eighty-third). Three senators were appointed in the Eighty-sixth Congress but after Hawai'i was admitted in March 1959. I did not include them in the thirty. There was no particular pattern between appointment and future service as a senator. One-half, like Seaton, did not stand for election. Of the half who stood for election, about one-third were elected and two-thirds defeated. Source: *Biographical Directory of the United States Congress* (Washington, D.C.: Joint Committee on Printing, 1989).

40. Gruening, *The Battle for Alaska Statehood*, 57–59. Gruening's story of his encounter with Seaton was confirmed to me in a 1988 interview with George Sundborg, who was with Gruening in Washington in 1952 as director of the Alaska Development Board.

41. Naske, *A History of Alaska Statehood,* 175.

42. For Hickel's meeting with Eisenhower, see Hickel, *Crisis in the Commons,* 60–62; George H. Lehleitner of New Orleans remembered that Hickel said, "Mr. President, you're nuts." Lehleitner's role in the statehood movement is explained in chapter 8.

43. Hickel, *Crisis in the Commons,* 62.

Chapter 8

1. Unless otherwise cited, my discussion of the Alaska Constitutional Convention comes from my earlier 1986 research report *Completing the Union: The Alaska and Hawaii Statehood Movements.* This report can be found in the library of the University of Alaska Fairbanks and other

Alaska libraries. All reference to the "1981 interviews" can be found in Naske, Whitehead, and Schneider, *Alaska Statehood: The Memory of the Battle and the Evaluation of the Present by Those Who Lived It*. This document can be found in the University of Alaska Fairbanks library and other Alaska libraries. For primary source records on the convention, see *Alaska Constitutional Convention Proceedings* (Juneau: Alaska Legislative Council, March 1965). For secondary accounts of the convention, see Victor Fischer, *Alaska's Constitutional Convention* (Fairbanks: University of Alaska Press, 1975); and Gerald E. Bowkett, *Reaching For A Star: The Final Campaign for Alaska Statehood* (Fairbanks: Epicenter Press, 1989).

2. Stewart describes his role in organizing the convention in an unpublished memo, "Notes on the Making of the Alaska Constitution." My discussion of his role is based on this memo and on an extensive interview with Stewart, January 24, 1986. The memo and tapes are in the author's possession.

3. Snedden described his role in the statehood movement in a long letter to George Lehleitner, May 7, 1964, copy in Bartlett Papers, "Statehood File—Tennessee Plan 1958–67," Rasmuson Library, University of Alaska Fairbanks.

4. Johnson, *Ernest Gruening*, 191.

5. The voting requirement to read or speak English was eliminated by a constitutional amendment in 1970 based on federal rulings to make voting requirements less restrictive.

6. The state provides funding for schools throughout the state. The schools are administered through a series of local school districts at the borough level and special rural education authorities in unorganized areas.

7. Alaska may have drawn inspiration for the "state" as the central focus of government from Hawai'i, though I have never seen this stated. Both territorial Hawai'i and the state of Hawai'i have been noted for the central function of state. This central function was derived from the Kingdom of Hawai'i. Hawai'i does have counties. But it maintained one centralized school system, without local school districts, from territorial days into the new state. Only recently have local school districts been created. The Hawai'i state constitution confirmed a central state function from the precedent of the past. The Alaska constitution created a central state function from the vacuum of the past.

8. Robertson left the convention a few days before the signing and submitted a letter of resignation. The letter arrived after the convention adjourned, so he was still considered a member of the convention at

the time of signing. Four years later, in 1960, Robertson asked to sign the constitution a few days before he died.

9. Press release, *Operation Statehood,* April 18, 1956, in Operation Statehood Papers, folder 24, Rasmuson Library, University of Alaska Fairbanks. Marston also described the jade lamp in *Alaska Constitutional Convention Proceedings,* 3950.

10. Fischer, *Alaska's Constitutional Convention,* 164–65.

11. Ernest N. Patty, *North Country Challenge* (New York: David McKay Co. 1969), 252.

12. *Alaska Constitutional Convention Proceedings,* 3982.

13. Unless otherwise cited, the discussion of George Lehleitner and the Tennessee Plan is drawn from my 1986 Alaska Historical Commission study *Completing the Union: The Alaska and Hawaii Statehood Movements,* noted in note 1. I interviewed Lehleitner first in 1981 for the Alaska Statehood Commission study noted in note 1. I conducted further interviews with Lehleitner in 1984, 1986, and 1988 and kept in touch with him by telephone and correspondence. I also traveled with Lehleitner to Hawai'i and Washington, D.C. Lehleitner's story has also been described by former U.S. House of Representatives Speaker Jim Wright in *You and Your Congressman* (New York: Coward McCann, 1963), 209–15.

14. Interview with George Lehleitner by Chris Conybeare and Warren Nishimoto, *Perspectives on Hawai'i's Statehood* (Honolulu: Oral History Project, SSRI, University of Hawai'i Mānoa, June 1986), 13.

15. Lehleitner arranged for me to meet and interview Passman, Long, and Lindy Boggs, wife of Hale Boggs. Hale Boggs died in a plane crash in 1972 while campaigning in Alaska for Representative Nick Begich. Lehleitner also won the support of Louisiana representative Edward Hebert. He could not convince the state's senior U.S. senator, Allen Ellender, to support statehood.

16. Daniel W. Tuttle Jr., *"State" Elections Prior to Admittance into the Union,* Report no. 1-1951 (Honolulu: Legislative Reference Bureau, 1951).

17. E. L. Bartlett to Robert B. Atwood, August 3, 1955, Operation Statehood Papers, "Correspondence with Bartlett."

18. For Snedden's initial impression of Lehleitner, see C. W. Snedden to G. H. Lehleitner, May 7, 1964, Bartlett Papers, "Statehood File— Tennessee Plan."

19. William Tansill, "Election of Congressional Delegations Prior to the According of Statehood," mimeograph (Washington, D.C.: Library of Congress—Legislative Reference Service, October 7, 1955), copy in Egan

Papers, "Tennessee Plan-Feasibility" Rasmuson Library, University of Alaska Fairbanks. The additional states using a variation of the Tennessee Plan included Vermont, Texas, Kansas, Iowa, Minnesota, and New Mexico.

20. We may well wonder if the tardiness of New Mexico's delegation did affect the Compromise of 1850. However, Lehleitner was not really interested in the 1850s or in New Mexico. He merely wanted to rebut any charge from Anderson that might compromise the adoption of the plan for Alaska in 1956.

21. E. L. Bartlett to William Egan, June 27, 1956, Egan Papers, "Tennessee Plan—Correspondence," Rasmuson Library, University of Alaska Fairbanks.

22. E. L. Bartlett to William Egan, May 9, 1956, Egan Papers, "Tennessee Plan—Correspondence."

23. Jackson had not been a "shadow" representative. The Tennessee territorial legislature had chosen William Blount and William Cocke to be its "shadow" senators. The territory did not stage an election for a "shadow" representative. After Tennessee was admitted as a state, the U.S. Senate refused to confirm Blount and Cocke. This refusal set the precedent that the Congress would not recognize the election of "shadow" members. The new Tennessee state legislature then elected Blount and Cocke as its U.S. senators. Jackson, elected by the people as U.S. representative, then joined the two as part of Tennessee's first congressional delegation.

Chapter 9

1. Holland's support for Alaska had been stoked by Ernest Bartley. See interview with Ernest Bartley in Naske, Whitehead, and Schneider, *Alaska Statehood: The Memory of the Battle and the Evaluation of the Present by Those Who Lived It—An Oral History of the Remaining Actors in the Alaska Statehood Movement*. Hereafter all interviews in this volume will be cited as "1981 interview with . . ."

2. Honolulu newspapers offered continuous coverage of these November and December meetings. In addition to Burns and Bartlett, the important strategists included Rep. Clair Engel of California, chairman of the House Interior and Insular Affairs Committee, and Rep. Leo O'Brien of New York, chairman of the subcommittee on territories. O'Brien would be the manager of the Alaska statehood bill on the floor of Congress.

3. Dan Tuttle Jr., "Vignettes of Hawaii Politics, 1953–73," unpublished draft. Copy in author's possession. Lehleitner later told me that he did not go to the Democratic Convention, but may well have been in Chicago for a wholesalers' convention. He confirmed that his support had shifted to Alaska by that time.

4. Honolulu coverage of the strategy meetings clearly mention the possibility of Alaska First in November and December. But Bartlett and Burns then "tossed a coin" and designated the Hawai'i statehood bill as HR 49 and Alaska as HR 50. I find Burns's first official acceptance of Alaska First in the February 9, 1957, edition of the *Honolulu Star-Bulletin*.

5. For the best contemporary assessment of the Red Scare in 1956–57, see Buch Buchwach, *Hawaii, U.S.A.: Communist Beachhead or Showcase for Americanism?* (Honolulu: Hawaii Statehood Commission, April 1957). The strength of the Red Scare issue in 1956–57 can be debated. Dan Boylan asserts in *John A. Burns: The Man and His Times* (Honolulu: University of Hawai'i Press, 2000) that the scare was over by 1956 (142). However, Hawai'i statehooders issued pamphlets such as Buchwach's in 1957 and 1958 in an attempt to counter the Communist fear. For King's statements, see *Honolulu Star-Bulletin*, February 12, 1956.

6. See chapter 10 for further discussion of why it became necessary to give Burns a leading role in initiating the Alaska First strategy.

7. William Bragg Ewald, *Eisenhower the President: Crucial Days, 1951–60* (Englewood, N.J.: Prentice Hall, 1981), 201.

8. Claus-M. Naske, *A History of Alaska Statehood*, 238–39, 247.

9. For the development of the "withdrawal" provision, later known as section 10 of the statehood bill, see Naske, *A History of Alaska Statehood*, 213–16, 248.

10. For Gruening's dismissal of the importance of "withdrawal," see Gruening, *The Battle for Alaska Statehood*, 95. For Atwood's comments, see Bob Atwood, *Bob Atwood's Alaska*, 132. Atwood talked with Eisenhower in 1954 about the defense lands. Exactly how he knew about the Minuteman silos is unclear. He claims the project was so secret that the president could not tell him about it. Atwood alludes to the fact that the *Times* was "speculating" about such secret plans.

11. Ewald, *Eisenhower the President*, 203. Snedden described his long involvement in the statehood movement, particularly his relation with Seaton and Stevens, in a long letter to George Lehleitner in 1963. C.W. Snedden to George H. Lehleitner, May 7, 1964, folder "Tennessee Plan,

1958–67," Bartlett Papers, Rasmuson Library, University of Alaska Fairbanks. Stevens's account of his tenure with Seaton is drawn from my interview with Senator Ted Stevens, December 30, 1987. A copy is in the Rasmuson Library, University of Alaska Fairbanks.

12. Ewald, *Eisenhower the President,* 201.

13. See section 6 of the Statehood Act for the final land provisions. On the withdrawal lands, the wording read, "That no selection hereunder shall be made in the area north and west of the line described in section 10 without approval of the president or his designated representative." Most people interpreted this as a positive for selection in the withdrawal area with the president's approval.

14. Gruening, *Many Battles,* 388.

15. William A. Egan to George McLaughlin, July 29, 1957; William A. Egan to C.W. Snedden, July 27, 1957; both in Egan Papers, Rasmuson Library, University of Alaska Fairbanks.

16. For Rayburn's relation to Bartlett, see Naske, *A History of Alaska Statehood,* 251; Gruening, *Many Battles,* 388; Jim Wright interview by John S. Whitehead, March 15, 1988, in Oral History Collection, Rasmuson Library, University of Alaska Fairbanks; Ralph Rivers interview by Claus-M. Naske, December 30, 1969 (private collection of Claus-M. Naske); Chou, *Interview with Elizabeth P. Farrington, Delegate to Congress from the Territory of Hawaii, 1954–57,* 31–32. In the interview Mrs. Farrington claimed that former Alaska governor Walter Hickel had confirmed her story of oil influence while he was Interior Secretary. I asked Hickel in a March 1988 conversation if he remembered confirming Farrington's story. He remembered Mrs. Farrington well, but had no recollection of her story about Texas and Oklahoma oil men.

17. Bartley's 1956 political analysis carried the authorship of his graduate student, Robert G. Kelsay, "Research Activity Preparatory to Operations Favoring Alaska Statehood in the 85th Congress," Colloquium Report, University of Florida, November 15, 1956, copy in Egan Papers, Rasmuson Library, University of Alaska Fairbanks.

18. Interview with Ernest Bartley by John S. Whitehead, May 18, 1987, Oral History Collection, Rasmuson Library, University of Alaska Fairbanks. The net gain of eleven freshmen votes was computed by my student assistant Beverly St. Sauver. She compared the final 1958 vote on Alaska statehood with Bartley's 1956 classification of each House district as positive or negative for statehood.

19. "1981 Interview" with Ernest Bartley and George Lehleitner, July 31, 1981. Bartley's 1981 opinion was reiterated in 1987.

20. Conversations with George Lehleitner, March 25, 1986, February 14, 1988, November 6, 1988, March 5, 1989 (notes in author's possession). Lehleitner was able to work with Deschler because Deschler's son had done legal work for Lehleitner. Deschler's research was done at the behest of Clair Engle. Deschler discovered that though statehood legislation as "privileged" had been omitted from the rulebook after 1912, it had never been abrogated.

21. Deschler told Rayburn that many "privileged" statehood bills had contained an appropriation. No challenge to "privileged" status based on the inclusion of an appropriation had ever been sustained. Lehleitner said in his March 5, 1989, conversation with me that Rayburn was so proud of "overruling" Howard Smith on this procedural challenge that he placed a copy of his ruling in a time capsule in the cornerstone for a new East Wing of the Capitol.

22. "1981 interview" with Leo O'Brien.

23. See the introductory chapter, "Apathy and Ecstasy," for more on the Murrow show. Gruening took credit for influencing Ferber to write her Alaska novel. He claimed he had known her since the 1920s when he wrote a book on Mexico. Gruening, *Many Battles,* 389–90. Ferber had won the Pulitzer Prize for her novel *So Big* in 1926. In 1952 her novel *Giant* attracted national attention for her emphasis on racial prejudice against Mexicans in Texas.

24. C. W. Snedden to George Lehleitner, May 7, 1964, Bartlett Papers/Tennessee Plan 1958–67, Rasmuson Library, University of Alaska Fairbanks.

25. For a full description on the early 1958 Senate maneuverings, see Naske, *History of Alaska Statehood,* 259–60.

26. For Burns's adherence to the Alaska First strategy, see Bell, *Last among Equals,* 248; Boylan and Holmes, *John A. Burns: The Man and His Times,* 150–51.

27. Snedden to Lehleitner, May 7, 1964.

28. Bob Atwood, *Bob Atwood's Alaska,* 143.

29. Johnson's absence from the Senate has led statehooders to endless speculation on the majority leader's true intentions. If he was in favor of statehood, why did he leave? Or had he always hoped that he could say he brought the bill to the floor where it was defeated? No one is certain of Johnson's motives. He did, however, indicate in the *Congressional*

Record that he was absent, but in favor of statehood. This statement has been interpreted by many as a show of sentimentality and affection for Bob Bartlett.

30. Snedden to Lehleitner, May 7, 1964. Bob Atwood also arranged for copies of the *Anchorage Times* to be flown to Washington. I do not know which paper arrived first.

31. Interview with Ted Stevens, December 30, 1987.

32. "1981 interview" with Leo O'Brien.

33. Of the two Texas votes, Jim Wright attributed his support to George Lehleitner. The other Texan to vote for statehood was Lindley Beckworth, a freshman in the Eighty-fifth Congress. Other Texas representatives such as Walter Rogers adamantly opposed statehood. For Gruening's interaction with Oklahoma oil men, see Gruening, *Many Battles,* 391. Though Kerr of Oklahoma voted for statehood, Senator Monroney was a bitter foe. Phillips Petroleum had an office in Alaska, but it was not one of the companies involved in the 1957 Swanson River oil discovery. The 1957 Swanson River discovery produced only nine hundred barrels a day by 1958. It was not on the scale of the Prudhoe Bay discovery a decade later.

    The most recent author on oil in Alaska, Jack Roderick (*Crude Dreams: A Personal History of Oil and Politics in Alaska* [Fairbanks: Epicenter Press, 1997]), cites no direct link between oil company support and the congressional vote. Roderick would likely have known if such support had existed because he was involved in the Alaska oil industry in 1958.

34. For the connection between the 1957 civil rights bill and statehood, see Bell, *Last among Equals,* 239–43. For Long's comments, see my interview with Russell Long, March 15, 1988. For Holland's 1958 campaign against Claude Pepper, see Holland Papers, University of Florida Library, particularly "Speech given on WFLA-TV, July 23, 1958" (box 603, folder 41). Claude Pepper served as senator from Florida from 1936 to 1951. He was defeated in the Democratic primary of 1950 by George Smathers in a bitter campaign. After failing again in a bid for the Senate against Holland in 1958, he ran successfully for the House of Representatives in 1962. He served in the House continuously from 1963 to 1989.

35. Southerners voting *for* statehood in the Senate included Long (LA), Holland (FL), Kerr (OK), Hill and Sparkman (AL), Kefauver (TN), Jordan (NC). Yarborough and Johnson of Texas were absent but in favor.

36. "1981 interview" with Leo O'Brien; interview with Jim Wright, March 1988.

37. "An Evaluation," July 1, 1957, Bartlett Papers, "Statehood file— Tennessee Plan 1957." The "evaluation" was clearly written by Bartlett.

38. E. L. Bartlett to Thomas B. Stewart, January 19, 1967, Bartlett Papers, "Statehood file—Tennessee Plan 1958–67."

39. For Naske's perceptive analysis of the "father-son" relationship between Bartlett and Gruening, see Naske, *Ernest Lewis Bob Bartlett: A Life in Politics,* 201–28. Naske noted that the tension between the two increased in the years after 1959 when both men advanced to represent Alaska in the Senate. Bartlett's 1967 letter to Stewart may reflect his continuing tension with Gruening in the Senate. Neva Egan interview by John S. Whitehead, February 28, 1986, Oral History Collection, Rasmuson Library, University of Alaska Fairbanks.

40. Lehleitner's reaction to Bartlett's letters comes from a series of conversations with Lehleitner, March 23–27, 1986 (notes in author's possession).

41. Ewald, *Eisenhower the President,* 202; interview with Ted Stevens, December 30, 1987. For the issue of the "private ceremony" with the suggestion that Eisenhower did not want to be photographed in a coterie of Alaska Democrats, see Naske, *A History of Alaska Statehood,* 271.

42. *Fairbanks Daily News-Miner,* August 8, 9, 13, 14, 1958. Federal employees retained their 25 percent cost-of-living deferential after statehood.

43. I checked the precinct-by-precinct vote of the August plebiscite and found no major variations among the vote given by the military, natives, and the general public. There were certain missing gaps in the manuscript returns but they did not affect the overall count. Anti-statehooder Joe Vogler continued to champion independence for Alaska years after it became a state. He organized the Alaska Independence Party and regularly ran for governor on the independence platform—often gaining about 5 percent of the vote. Vogler maintained his stance until his death in 1993.

44. For Bartlett's ambivalence before the August 1958 primary, see Naske, *Ernest Lewis Bob Bartlett,* 163–67. Egan and Rivers faced Democratic opposition in the primary, but won the nomination readily. Gruening and Bartlett were unopposed within the party.

45. Sundborg described the Drew Pearson controversy and his role in a May 16, 1988, interview with John S. Whitehead. Copy of the tape in

Oral History Collection, Rasmuson Library, University of Fairbanks. Pearson sued the *News-Miner* for libel. The case dragged on until September 1964, when Fairbanks Judge Everett Hepp ruled that Pearson was a "public figure" who was not entitled to the same libel protection as a "private individual." Sundborg became editor of the *News-Miner* in 1957. He had followed Snedden's plan to publicize Stepovich and had written Stepovich's 1957 inaugural address as governor.

46. For the fishery transfer, see Gruening, *State of Alaska,* rev. ed., 1968, 532–33.

Chapter 10

1. Interview with John Burns by Lawrence Fuchs, November 1958, Melendy Collection University of Hawai'i Mānoa, box 5, folder: Fuchs Interviews.
2. For basic information on the Burns family, see Boylan and Holmes, *John A. Burns,* 7–27; Sheenagh M. Burns, "Jack Burns: A Daughter's Portrait," *Hawaiian Journal of History* 24 (1990): 163–83. Boylan/Holmes and Sheenagh Burns differ on many details of the Burns family. Sheenagh Burns calls her grandmother Anne, while Boylan/Holmes insist she was known as "Flo." Boylan/Holmes have Harry Burns arriving at Fort Shafter in 1911 with the family following in 1913, while Sheenagh has the entire family arriving in 1913. The two accounts also differ on the precise scenario by which Harry Burns left the family. Also see note 4 of this chapter for further differences in the two accounts.
3. Burns, "Jack Burns: A Daughter's Portrait," 181–83.
4. Boylan/Holmes and Sheenagh Burns offer differing accounts of the circumstances surrounding James's birth. Boylan/Holmes present the story of the massages from Dr. Seishiro Okazaki based on interviews with Beatrice Burns. Sheenagh Burns does not include the story of Okazaki and also states that James's middle name was Stanton, not Seishiro. The story of the massages by Professor Okazaki is widely accepted in Hawai'i and repeated in many other accounts of John and Bea Burns's life, notwithstanding the account of Sheenagh Burns.
5. For Burns's initial strength in Washington and his attitude toward Southern politicians, see Boylan and Holmes, *John A. Burns,* 142–50. See also "Interview with Dan Aoki," JBOH, University of Hawai'i Mānoa, 1975.

6. Burns's belief that previous delegates fanned Southern racial prejudice against Hawaii is clear from a series of letters written by Burns to: Nelson Doi, August 15, 1957; Peter Fairfax Meyer, January 11, 1958; Oren Long, March 13, 1958, John A. Burns Papers (hereafter Burns Papers), Hawai'i State Archives.

7. John A. Burns to Lyndon Johnson, August 19, 1957; Lyndon Johnson to John A. Burns, August 21, 1957, LBJA Congressional File, container 47, LBJ Library, University of Texas. See chapter 3 for the story of the 442nd and the rescue of the "lost" Texas battalion.

8. I can attest to Mrs. Burns's personal charisma as the result of an August 1984 visit.

9. For Thurston's changing position on statehood, see George Chaplin, *Presstime in Paradise* (Honolulu: University of Hawai'i Press, 1998), 235–39.

10. Lorrin P. Thurston, "Communism Does Not and Never Will, Control Hawaii," speech to a meeting of the Democratic western states (western division of Democratic National Committee), San Francisco, February 16, 1957, typescript in Hamilton Library, University of Hawai'i Mānoa.

11. Interview with Buck Buchwach by John S, Whitehead, January 10, 1986. Buchwach was executive secretary of the Hawaii Statehood Commission from 1950 to 1955. He returned to the *Advertiser* in 1955 as city editor.

12. Buck Buchwach, "Hawaii: Communist Beachhead or Showcase of Americanism?" Hawaii Statehood Commission, April 1957, 3, 4, 27.

13. For King's vetoes, see Boylan and Holmes, *John A. Burns,* 129–30. Some commentators suggest that King's favor in Washington waned after the death of his prime supporter, Robert Taft, in July 1953. Given that Seaton followed the same strategy of ousting a seemingly unelectable governor in Alaska, it is more likely that King's potential as a candidate rather than any attachment to Taft led to his ousting.

14. For Quinn's surprise at his appointment, see interview with William F. Quinn by H. Brett Melendy, September 25, 1980 (copy in author's possession). For Farrington's statement that she suggested him, see "Interview with Elizabeth Farrington," JBOH, 1977, 21. Mrs. Farrington claimed that Seaton actually wanted her to be governor. She said she declined and submitted a list of six names, one of which was Quinn. While Seaton delayed, King continued to serve as a "lame duck" governor.

15. For background information on Quinn, see Melendy, 1980 interview; interview with William Quinn, JBOH, 1984; and Mary C. K. Richards, *No Ordinary Man: William Francis Quinn, His Role in Hawaii's History* (Honolulu: Hawaii Education Association, 1998).

16. For the acquittal of the Hawaii Seven and the origins of the Aloha Strike, see Sanford Zalburg, *A Spark Is Struck* (Honolulu: University of Hawai'i Press, 1979), 399–408.

17. For Zalburg's analysis of Quinn's role in the strike, see *A Spark Is Struck,* 405–8.

18. For Quinn's account of his July 1958 trip to Washington, see William Quinn, "The Politics of Statehood," *Hawaiian Journal of History* 18 (1984): 1–12.

19. Ibid., 7–8.

20. Farrant Turner was born in Hilo in 1895 and educated at Punahou School in Honolulu and Wesleyan University in Connecticut. He was vice president of one of Honolulu's elite haole business firms, Lewers & Cooke. He never held elected office but was appointed secretary of the territory in 1953, the position he still held in 1958. Most accounts indicate that Turner was relieved of his command of the 100th in late 1943 because of age (forty-eight) and health. Masayo Duus, *Unlikely Liberators,* 100, indicates that he was no longer emotionally fit to be a front-line commander. This, however, does not seem to have affected the devotion of his men for their commander. When he ran for delegate in 1958, many of his campaign workers were men from the 100th. Turner left the 100th in late 1943. The younger Nisei in the 442nd Regimental Combat Team did not merge with the 100th until mid-1944. Thus they never served under Turner.

21. For Lehleitner's concerns with IMUA and his debate with Phillips, see *Honolulu Star-Bulletin,* September 18, 19, 1958; *Advertiser,* September 25, 1958.

22. For Michener's involvement with Hawai'i, see A. Grove Day, *Mad about Islands* (Honolulu: Mutual Publishing Co., 1987), 245–55.

23. For particulars on the scheduling of the bill in the House and Senate, see Bell, *Last among Equals,* 271–76.

24. Quinn, "The Politics of Statehood," 11–12. Of the fifteen Senate negative votes cast, fourteen were from Southern Democrats. Republican John Butler of Maryland cast the other negative vote. The Southern Democrats were not consistent in their votes for Hawai'i and Alaska. Long (LA), Holland (FL), Kefauver (TN), Jordan (NC), and Kerr (OK) voted for both

Hawai'i and Alaska. Sparkman and Hill (AL) voted for Alaska, but against Hawai'i. Ervin (NC) voted against Alaska but for Hawai'i. Smathers (FL) voted against Hawai'i, but was absent on Alaska. Johnson and Yarborough (TX) were for Hawai'i but absent on Alaska. Gore (TN) was absent on both votes. Monroney (OK) was for Hawai'i but against Alaska.

25. Interview by John S. Whitehead with Leo O'Brien, August 1981 (1981 interviews). In the House tally, the bulk of the negative votes were from Southerners combined with a few die-hard anti-Communists in the northeastern states such as John Pillion of New York. The votes of Senators Yarborough and Johnson had little impact on the Texas delegation in the House. Only five of twenty-two Texas representatives voted for Hawai'i—Jim Wright and Lindley Beckworth, who voted for Alaska, and Olin Teague, William Poage, and Clark Thompson. Teague had previously voted against statehood three times, but he was the most decorated war veteran in the House. In an April 22, 1958, letter to Oren Long, Burns predicted the positive votes of all five. He also predicted the potential positive votes of an additional five Texans who voted *No*. Burns Papers, chronological file, Hawai'i State Archives.

26. For the signing ceremony, see *Honolulu Star-Bulletin,* March 18, 1959; Michaelyn Chou, *Interview with Elizabeth Farrington,* 28.

27. For Burns's quandary over which office to pursue, see Boylan and Holmes, *John A. Burns,* 153–61.

28. Boylan and Holmes, *John A. Burns,* 161. Burns held firmly to his view of Southerners and told George Lehleitner, who had tried to persuade Burns otherwise, in late April 1959 that "I still can't agree with you as to the Southern problem." John A. Burns to George Lehleitner, April 20, 1959, Burns Papers, chronological file, Hawai'i State Archives.

29. Boylan and Holmes, *John A. Burns,* 160–61; Phillips, *Hawaii's Democrats,* 53–55. Interview by John S. Whitehead with Spark Matsunaga, July 15, 1988, 6–9.

30. Conversation with Michaelyn Chou, December 28, 2002, Honolulu.

31. For Kamokila Campbell's reaction, see *Honolulu Star-Bulletin,* March 19, 1959; *Advertiser,* March 23, 1959; and Whitehead, "The Anti-Statehood Movement," 53.

32. Abraham Akaka, *"Aloha Ke Akua," March 13, 1959* (Honolulu: University of Hawai'i Press, 1959).

33. For the emergence of the Modern Hawaiian Movement, see Haunani-Kay Trask, "The Birth of the Modern Hawaiian Movement: Kalama Valley Oahu," *Hawaiian Journal of History* 21 (1987): 126–53.

34. Interview with John Burns by Lawrence Fuchs, November 1958; Interview with John Burns Jr., JBOH, 1979; Interview with Daniel Inouye, JBOH, 1975, 26.

35. Elizabeth Farrington to Wilton B. Persons (assistant to the president), June 17, 1959; Wilton Persons to Fred Seaton, June 23, 1959; Anthony Lausi to Fred Seaton, June 26, 1959; Fred Seaton to Elizabeth Farrington, July 1, 1959, Seaton/Farrington correspondence, Melendy Collection, University of Hawai'i.

36. "Memorandum for the President" from Robert E. Merriam, August 14, 1959, Eisenhower Papers, Eisenhower Library, Abilene, Kansas. Quinn could not come, as he would be sworn in as governor in Honolulu that day. He requested that State Secretary Edward Johnston be substituted. The White House agreed.

37. For Rayburn's reaction, see Boylan and Holmes, *John A. Burns,* 166–67. For Burns's last day in Congress, see Ed Rohrbough, "The Making of a Governor," *Honolulu Star-Bulletin,* November 20, 1962.

38. Press Release by White House press secretary James C. Hagerty, August 21, 1959, "Extemporaneous Remarks by the President on the Signing of the Proclamation Admitting Hawaii...." Eisenhower Papers, Eisenhower Library.

   Eisenhower's reference to the Speaker's suggestion that Monday will be the first day in 158 years there has not been a delegate in Congress is not entirely correct. One hundred fifty-eight years would refer to 1801. The first territorial delegate arrived from the Territory South of the River Ohio in November 1794 for the second session of the Third Congress and remained in the Fourth Congress until June 1796, when Tennessee was admitted as a state. There was no territorial delegate in the Fifth Congress, 1797–99. A delegate returned in the Sixth Congress (1799–1801) to represent the Territory Northwest of the River Ohio (later the state of Ohio). In the Seventh Congress (1801–3) there were delegates from both the Territory Northwest of the River Ohio and the Mississippi Territory. Actually it would have been 165 years (since 1794) or 160 years (since 1799) since there had been no delegate— depending on whether you start before the first delegate arrived or after the 1797–99 interlude when there was no delegate.

39. Rohrbough, "The Making of a Governor"; Boylan and Holmes, *John A. Burns,* 167.

40. Lyndon Johnson to Emmet Cahill, September 2, 1959, LBJA subject file/Statehood, Lyndon Johnson Library. For Burns's links with Johnson,

see Rohrbough, "The Making of a Governor," *Honolulu Star-Bulletin,* November 21, 1962; and Boylan and Holmes, *John A. Burns,* 171–74.

41. For the 1962 election, see Boylan and Holmes, *John A. Burns,* 178–82; and Phillips, *Hawaii's Democrats,* 60–70.

42. Johnson, *Vantage Point,* 360. I corresponded with Johnson presidential aide Walt Rostow in 1992. Rostow told me by phone that he believed it was Burns, more than anyone else, who convinced Johnson to support statehood for Hawai'i in 1958 as Johnson became convinced that Asia would be more important in the future.

43. The John Burns Oral History at the University of Hawai'i was compiled by Stuart Gerry Brown, Paul A. Hooper, and Dan Boylan over the period from 1974 to 1977 with a few succeeding interviews.

44. Kotani, *The Japanese in Hawaii,* 143–61. Kotani does mention that some Japanese had been successful as Republicans but does not provide a list of those in office. He does mention Tsukiyama, but primarily as a successful lawyer appointed to the court, not as a successful Republican legislator throughout the postwar period. Kotani emphasizes that Tsukiyama would not run against Burns for delegate in 1958. Kotani's volume was published as "The Official Booklet of the Oahu Kanyaku Imin Centennial Committee."

45. For Tuttle and Lehleitner's challenge of the legend, see *Honolulu Star-Bulletin,* August 21, 1987, A-4.

46. Two voices from the prewar period did outlive the others, including Burns. Hiram Fong, who served as U.S. senator from 1959 to 1977, is still alive and active in the summer of 2003 at age ninety-six. Hung Wai Ching of the Council on Interracial Unity is generally credited with creating the Varsity Victory Volunteers. Ching survived until 2002, when he died at age ninety-six. After the war, he devoted his energies to business and organized, among other projects, Aloha Airlines. Ching was a 1924 graduate of McKinley High School, along with Hiram Fong, and a 1928 graduate of the University of Hawai'i. Like Fong, Hung Wai Ching was a Republican; his younger and equally successful brother, Hung Wo Ching, was a Democrat. See *Honolulu Star-Bulletin,* February 22, 2002, for his obituary.

Epilogue

1. New flags become official on the July 4 after a statehood proclamation is made. The forty-nine-star flag became official on July 4, 1959. The

Hawai'i statehood proclamation was made on August 21, 1959. Thus the fifty-star flag became official on July 4, 1960.

2. Bob Atwood, *Bob Atwood's Alaska,* 177–78; Whitehead, "The Governor Who Opposed Statehood."

3. For the best introduction to Alaska's oil lands and the state's relation to oil companies, see Roderick, *Crude Dreams: A Personal History of Oil and Politics in Alaska.*

4. For the controversy, environmental and congressional, over the Trans-Alaska Pipeline, see Peter A. Coates, *The Trans-Alaska Pipeline Controversy: Technology, Conservation, and the Frontier* (Bethlehem, Pa.: Lehigh University Press, 1991).

5. For an introduction to ANCSA at the time of its enactment, see Robert D. Arnold, *Alaska Native Land Claims* (Anchorage: Alaska Native Foundation, 1976). For an assessment of ANCSA after thirty years of operation, see Stephen Haycox, *Frigid Embrace: Politics, Economics and Environment in Alaska* (Corvallis: Oregon State University Press, 2002).

6. For a classic assessment of ANILCA at the time of its enactment, see "Alaska National Interest Lands," *Alaska Geographic* 8, no. 1 (1981). The guest editors for this volume were Celia Hunter and Ginny Wood. For a view in 2002, see Haycox, *Frigid Embrace.*

7. The story of Project Chariot is well told in Dan O'Neill, *The Firecracker Boys* (New York: St. Martin's Press, 1994). See also my chapter "Alaska and Hawai'i: The Cold War States" in Fernlund, *The Cold War American West.*

8. For Hickel's assessment of his role as governor and his vision for the future of Alaska, see Walter Hickel, *The Alaska Solution* (Oakland, Calif.: Institute for Contemporary Studies, 2002).

9. For information on "55 Club," I am indebted to Katie Hurley of Wasilla, Alaska. Ms. Hurley was the clerk to the constitutional convention in 1955–56. She has organized its reunions and kept careful track of its members.

10. For Hawai'i's post-statehood economic boom, see Thomas Kemper Hitch, *Islands in Transition: The Past, Present, and Future of Hawaii's Economy* (Honolulu: First Hawaiian Bank, 1992), 181–86.

11. The author was present at the 1984 Hawai'i Silver Jubilee celebration and later obtained a videotape of the KITV presentation.

12. For an introduction to the issues in the Modern Hawaiian Movement, see Haunani-Kay Trask, *From a Native Daughter: Colonialism and Sovereignty in Hawai'i* (Monroe, Me.: Common Courage Press, 1993);

and Michael Kioni Dudley and Keoni Kealoha Agard, *A Call for Hawaiian Sovereignty* (Honolulu: Na Kane O Ka Malo Press, 1990).

13. John M. Broder, "Death and Scandal Leaving Democrats in Chaos in Hawaii," *New York Times,* October 19, 2002, A1, A12.

14. Johnson, *The Vantage Point,* 360. For the entire text of the East-West Center Speech, see *Honolulu Advertiser,* October 13, 1966.

15. *Honolulu Advertiser,* February 15, 1949.

16. The "delegate" from the District of Columbia entered Congress in 1971 (Ninety-second Congress); the delegates from Guam and from the Virgin Islands entered in 1973 (Ninety-third Congress), and the delegate from American Samoa entered in 1981 (Ninety-seventh Congress). In the 1980s and 1990s several plebiscites in Puerto Rico failed to gain a majority vote for "statehood." In 1998 Congress passed a bill calling for yet another plebiscite to determine the future political status of Puerto Rico. The 1998 legislation was sponsored by Representative Young and Senator Murkowski of Alaska. In the December 1998 plebiscite, statehood received a 46 percent vote. The overall winner in 1998, with 50.2 percent of the vote, was "none of the above." Given that the 3–2 majority for statehood in Alaska in 1946 was considered a weak mandate, the likelihood for Puerto Rican statehood is slim. Puerto Rico's people are yet to be united on statehood.

In 1978 Congress passed a constitutional amendment giving the District of Columbia the same congressional representation as a state. The amendment failed to be ratified by the required three-quarters of the states (only sixteen of the needed thirty-eight did so) and was rendered moot in 1985. The District of Columbia adopted a "Tennessee Plan" in 1990 and elected Jesse Jackson as a "shadow senator." However, the Congress has yet to authorize a "statehood" plebiscite for the district. There is, in my opinion, less chance of statehood for the District of Columbia than for Puerto Rico. The simple reason is that the District of Columbia was consciously created as something "other" than a state. There continue to be plans to bring a greater degree of self-determination to the district's residents. In the summer of 2003 there were discussions in Congress to give the district a voting seat in the House of Representatives. There have also been discussions to make the district a part of Maryland for purposes of congressional representation. For a good discussion of these plans, see John Steele Gordon, "A Senator from D.C.?" *Wall Street Journal,* January 14, 2004, A12.

For the gradual enhancement of the rights of the non-voting members from Puerto Rico, Guam, the Virgin Islands, and the District of Columbia, see William R. Tansill, "The Resident Commissioner to the United States from Puerto Rico: An Historical Perspective," *Revista Juridica de la Universidad de Puerto Rico* 47 (1978). The delegate from American Samoa was authorized after Tansill's article was published. Though the rights and privileges of these non-voting members have been increased, there has been no move to designate any of these non-states as "incorporated territories."

17. Roger Daniels, *Asian Americans* (Seattle: University of Washington Press, 1988), 311.

18. My understanding of the term "liminality" in reference to Hawai'i has been enhanced by conversations with Jennifer Fish Kashay, whose book *Savages, Sinners, and Saints* is forthcoming.

19. Fuchs, *Hawaii Pono,* 448.

A Guide to Sources and Orthography

Oral History Sources and Other Interviews

This book began as a set of oral history interviews conducted in the summer of 1981 for the Alaska Statehood Commission. Formal oral histories differ from simple interviews in a number of ways that should be noted. An oral history is conducted with the intent of creating an archive that can be used by the general public, not merely by the interviewer for a specific purpose. The interviewee signs a release form indicating his/her approval for the interview to be accessed by the general public or with specific limitations to that access. At minimum the taped interview is deposited in an archive. When funding exists, there is also a verbatim transcript. In other cases a written interview summary and an index to the tape are often available. I created a number of formal oral histories, used other archived oral histories, and also conducted a number of traditional non-archived interviews for the project. The major oral histories and interviews are as follows:

Oral History of the Remaining Actors in the Alaska Statehood Movement

Conducted in the summer of 1981 by Claus-M. Naske, John S. Whitehead, and William Schneider for the Alaska Statehood Commission, this collection contains some fifty-four interviews. The tapes, along with tape indexes and tape summaries, are deposited in the Oral History Collection, Alaska and Polar Regions Department, Rasmuson Library, University of Alaska Fairbanks. There are no transcripts to this collection. A report of this project was published by the Alaska Statehood Commission as *Alaska Statehood: The Memory of the Battle and the Evaluation of the Present by Those Who Lived It* (Fairbanks: Alaska Statehood Commission, 1981). Copies of the publication are on deposit in most libraries in Alaska. Interviews in the collection conducted by the author include:

Robert Atwood
Ernest Bartley
Carl Brady
Seaborn Buckalew
Jack Coghill
William Egan
Walter Hickel
Herb Hilscher
George Lehleitner
Steve McCutcheon
Ralph Moody
Leo O'Brien
George Rogers
C. W. Snedden
Barrie White

John Burns Oral History

The John Burns Oral History at the University of Hawai'i Mānoa was compiled by Stuart Gerry Brown, Paul Hooper, and Dan Boylan over the period from 1974 to 1977, with a few succeeding interviews. The John Burns Oral History contains sixty six interviews with most of Hawai'i's post–World War II leaders. Full transcripts of these interviews are located in the Special Collections of the Hamilton Library, University of Hawai'i Mānoa.

Other Oral Histories Used in Hawai'i

Elizabeth Farrington—An in-depth oral history of Elizabeth Farrington with a full transcript conducted by Michaelyn Chou is available in the Special Collections, Hamilton Library. The title is *Interview with Elizabeth P. Farrington, Delegate to Congress from the Territory of Hawaii, 1954–57* (1978).

Perspectives on Hawai'i's Statehood (1986)—The Oral History Project in the Social Science Research Institute of the University of Hawai'i Mānoa-conducted nine interviews on the subject of statehood in 1984–85. The interviewers were Warren Nishimoto and Chris Conybeare. Those interviewed were George H. Lehleitner, John S. Whitehead, Thomas P. Gill, Malcolm McNaughton, Hiram Fong, Robert Hogan, Robert McElrath,

Daniel Tuttle Jr., and Dan Aoki. The full transcripts of these interviews are available in most public libraries in Hawaiʻi.

Individual Oral Histories Conducted by John S. Whitehead

As part of a grant from the Alaska Humanities, I conducted a number of formal oral history interviews in 1987–88. Full transcripts are available in the Oral History Collection, Alaska and Polar Regions Department, Rasmuson Library, University of Alaska Fairbanks.

> Jay Hammond
> Russell Long
> Spark Matsunaga
> Ted Stevens
> James C. Wright Jr.
> Ernest Bartley (tape only)
> George Sundborg (tape only)

Informal Interviews: Tapes and Interview Notes in Author's Possession

Hawaiʻi
> Dan Boylan, 1988, and other times
> Buck Buchwach, 1986
> Beatrice Burns, 1984
> James S. Burns, 1988
> George Chaplin, 1986, 1988
> Hiram Fong, 1986
> Richard Kageyama, 1986
> Richard Lyman, 1985
> Chuck Mau, 1986
> Norman Meller, 1985
> Hebden Porteus, 1985
> William Richardson, 1985, 1988
> Bud Smyser, 1985, 1988
> Haunani-Kay Trask, 1988
> Daniel Tuttle Jr. 1985, and other times

Alaska
>   Rolland Armstrong, 1982
>   Robert B. Atwood, 1986
>   Neva Egan, 1986
>   Jim Hurley, 1985
>   Tom Stewart, 1986

Louisiana and Washington, D.C.
>   Corinne (Lindy) Boggs, 1984
>   Mrs. Hodding Carter, 1984
>   Mrs. Frank Church, 1988
>   George H. Lehleitner, 1984, 1986, 1988, and other times
>   Mrs. George H. Lehleitner, 1984
>   William Tansill, 1988
>   Jack Todd, admin asst. to Russell Long, 1986

Manuscript Collection and Newspapers

Hawai'i

In preparation for the book I was greatly aided by Professor Brett Melendy, formerly of the University of Hawai'i and San Jose State University. In preparation for three books on Hawai'i (*Walter Francis Dillingham, 1875–1963: Hawaiian Entrepreneur and Statesman* [1996]; *Hawaii: America's Sugar Territory* [1999]; and *The Federal Government's Search for Communists in the Territory of Hawaii* [2002], all published by the Edward Mellen Press), Melendy and an assistant made a large photocopy collection of a vast number of archival sources and put them into one collection for the statehood era. Melendy photocopied the papers of John A. Burns when they were still in the hands of the Burns family. The Burns Papers are now housed in the Archives of the State of Hawai'i. In addition to the Burns Papers, I also used copies of the Farrington Papers, also now in the Archives of the State of Hawai'i. Melendy's collection also included many helpful pieces from both the Lyndon B. Johnson Papers, the Eisenhower Papers, and the Hugh Butler Papers. I have cited the primary location of the papers I used in applicable notes.

Melendy also copied interviews compiled by Lawrence Fuchs for *Hawaii Pono*. Fuchs conducted over 155 interviews in 1958–59, a portion of which were copied by Melendy. The Fuchs interviews are in the style commonly compiled by historians rather than oral histories. Basically the interview is a written narrative by Fuchs of what the interviewee said and what Fuchs thought of the interviewee, not a transcript. These interviews form one of the best snapshots of Hawai'i at one point in time, 1958–59. Many of Fuchs's interviewees (for example, John A. Burns, Daniel K. Inouye) went on to become leaders of the state of Hawai'i. The Fuchs interviews thus give a preview for the oral histories in the John Burns Oral History conducted fifteen years later.

Melendy's collection, including the Fuchs interviews, has been deposited in the Special Collections, Hamilton Library, University of Hawai'i Mānoa, where they are available for use by other researchers.

Hawai'i Newspaper Morgue

There is a microform collection of both the *Honolulu Advertiser* and the *Honolulu Star-Bulletin* as well as other state newspapers at the Hamilton Library, University of Hawai'i Mānoa. Until the early 1980s the Hawai'i newspapers maintained a clipping service. In my early research I used files of clippings on the constitutional convention. Currently all of those clippings have been placed on microform and are housed as the Hawai'i Newspaper Morgue in the Hamilton Library, University of Hawai'i Mānoa. The "morgue" is a boon to all researchers. For example, one can trace the entire political career of AJA legislator Thomas Sakakihara from his first run for office in the 1920s until his death in the 1970s based on fifty years of clippings on a few microforms in the "morgue."

Alaska

Bartlett Papers—The outstanding manuscript collection for a study of Alaska statehood is the delegate papers and correspondence of Delegate Bob Bartlett in the Alaska and Polar Regions Collection, Rasmuson Library, University of Alaska Fairbanks.

Egan Papers—Many of Governor William Egan's papers were destroyed in the 1964 Earthquake, but his papers as Alaska-Tennessee Plan delegate are available in the Alaska and Polar Regions Department, Rasmuson Library, University of Alaska Fairbanks.

Ralph Rivers Scrapbook—A scrapbook of memorabilia collected by Ralph Rivers as an Alaska-Tennessee Plan delegate is housed in the Alaska and Polar Regions Department, University of Alaska Fairbanks.

Gruening Papers—The papers of Territorial Governor Ernest Gruening are now housed in the Alaska and Polar Regions Department, Rasmuson Library, University of Alaska Fairbanks. During the initial years of my research the papers were in a constant state of flux and disarray with several recatalogings. Gruening's three books (see list below), however, cover virtually any information to be found in his papers.

Private Papers of Tom Stewart—Tom Stewart, secretary of the Alaska Constitutional Convention, allowed me to use his private papers, including his "Notes on the Making of the Alaska Constitutional Convention," along with letters to the convention consultants. These papers are still in Stewart's private possession in Juneau, Alaska.

Proceedings of the Constitutional Conventions

Full transcripts of both the Alaska and Hawai'i constitutional conventions have been compiled and deposited respectively in the public libraries of Alaska and Hawai'i. The full titles are:

Alaska Constitutional Convention Proceedings (Juneau: Alaska Legislative Council, 1965).

Proceedings of the Constitutional Convention of Hawaii 1950 (Honolulu: State of Hawai'i, 1960).

Prior Research Reports

In the course of research for this version of *Completing the Union*, several research reports were issued along the way that contain more detailed and comparative information on specific aspects of the statehood story.

A grant from the Alaska Historical Commission in 1986 supported interviews and research for a comparative study of the two constitutional conventions and the Tennessee Plan. It was published as John S. Whitehead, *Completing the Union: The Alaska and Hawaii Statehood Movements,* Alaska Historical Commission Studies in History no. 198, June 1986. It is available in the main public libraries of the state of Alaska.

A grant from the Alaska Humanities Forum in 1987–88 provided support for more interviews and research on the anti-statehood movement and the actions of congressmen toward statehood. Oral history transcripts from those interviews are listed above. Two research reports, "The Anti-Statehood Movement in Alaska and Hawaii" and "Congressman and Statehood," were produced. These reports are not publicly available, but are in the possession of the author and the Alaska Humanities Forum. Two published articles on anti-statehood were drawn from the reports. "The Anti-Statehood Movement and the Legacy of Alice Kamokila Campbell," *Hawaiian Journal of History* 27 (1993); and "The Governor Who Opposed Statehood: The Legacy of Jay Hammond," *Alaska History* 7, no. 2 (Fall 1992). The bulk of "Congressmen and Statehood" is incorporated into chapters 7, 9, and 10 of *Completing the Union*.

Published Works

The published works on Alaska and Hawai'i that I used are discussed thoroughly in the notes following each chapter. There are a handful of books on each state that deserve special mention for setting the tone of the times. These volumes were generally written by participants in the statehood movement or by observers on the scene at the time of the statehood battle. These books are "musts" for anyone who wants an introduction to the temper of the times in both territories.

Hawai'i

Allen, Gwenfread. *Hawaii's War Years.* Honolulu: University of Hawai'i Press, 1950.

Allen was a reporter for the Honolulu *Star-Bulletin* during World War II and became the official territorial historian for the war years. Her volume is one of the best histories of the domestic scene during World War II—and particularly the domestic scene in the city where the war began.

Anthony, J. Garner. *Hawaii under Army Rule.* Honolulu: University of Hawai'i Press, 1955.

Anthony was Hawai'i's attorney general during World War II and a strident opponent of martial law. Anthony was later a delegate to the 1950 Hawai'i Constitutional Convention. The volume is simply the best depiction of the curtailment of democratic government in the United States in the twentieth century.

Fuchs, Lawrence. *Hawaii Pono.* New York: Harcourt Brace Jovanovich, 1961.

This book is often called the "classic" history of territorial Hawai'i. The volume is more valuable as a "classic" statement of the hope one mainland academician placed on Hawai'i as an example of a tolerant multiracial society in the 1950s. As such, it became one of the bulwarks forming the Burns Legend. It is a capsule snapshot of Hawai'i in the late 1950s.

Inouye, Daniel K. *Journey to Washington*. New York: Prentice Hall, 1967.
    Though written after Inouye became a senator, the book still captures Inouye's "coming of age" as an aspiring Japanese American who became the first Asian American member of the U.S. House of Representatives.

Alaska

Atwood, Robert B. *Bob Atwood's Alaska*. Anchorage: Marilaine Publishing, 2003.
    Bob Atwood's memoirs were published by his daughter, Elaine, some six years after the Anchorage publisher's death. The memoirs begin with Atwood's arrival in Anchorage in 1935 and continue until his death in 1997. There is no better single source of the growth of Anchorage from a frontier railroad outpost of 2,200 in 1935 to a metropolis of over 250,000 sixty years later. Atwood was at the "center of it all" from the day of his arrival to the day of his death.

Fischer, Victor. *Alaska's Constitutional Convention*. Fairbanks: University of Alaska Press, 1975.
    Fischer was a delegate to the 1955–56 convention and was one of the youngest (age thirty-one) and most "intellectual" delegates. He was the city planning director for Anchorage in 1955 and became vice president of Operation Statehood. The volume is part of a National Municipal League series on state constitutional conventions. On the surface, this is a dry, technical analysis of the constitution writing process in Alaska. But Fischer well conveys the seriousness of purpose that surrounded the delegates in their quest to produce a constitution that would attract national attention and confirm Alaska's readiness for self-government.

Gruening, Ernest. *The State of Alaska*. 2d rev. ed. 1954; New York: Random House, 1968.
———. *The Battle for Alaska Statehood*. Fairbanks: University of Alaska Press, 1967.

————. *Many Battles: The Autobiography of Ernest Gruening.* New York: Liveright, 1974.

I have often thought that Gruening did not want to risk leaving the story of his life to historians. These three volumes truly capture the Gruening style. The *State of Alaska* was written to win a reluctant Congress and nation to the cause of statehood. It ably portrays Gruening's "muck-raking" style of Progressive journalism that he developed in the early years of the century. *The Battle for Alaska Statehood* gives Gruening's view of the workings of Congress and also Gruening's sense of knowing almost every-one of political consequence on the national scene. *Many Battles* is Gruening's autobiography written after his Senate defeat in 1968. Readers will readily grasp Gruening's "sense of himself" and his tendency to dis-miss those opposed to him. These three volumes readily show why Gruening was both deeply admired and deeply resented.

Marston, Marvin R. "Muktuk." *Men of the Tundra: Eskimos at War.* New York: October House, 1969.

A superb narrative by a man who came to Alaska during World War II and found a true "mission" with the native people of the territory. Marston then became part of the band of "veterans" who remained in the territory after the war and built the new state.

U.S. Congress

Wright, James C. Jr. *You and Your Congressman.* New York: Coward McCann, 1963.

There is a "Mr. Smith Goes to Washington" tone to Congressman Wright's book about his first decade in Congress. But Wright devotes sev-eral pages to his relationship with George Lehleitner and Alaska statehood. This section well explains the bond between the two.

Alaska Geographic Magazine

A last invaluable source that should be noted is the thirty-year run of *Alaska Geographic Magazine.* From its first quarterly issue in 1972 on the future of the North Slope of Alaska, the magazine became the single best source on the progress and controversies surrounding the "lands issue" in Alaska. Some 122 quarterly editions have touched every corner of the forty-ninth state. Different volumes have dealt with the development of Alaska's cities, its national parks and monuments, and its various peoples and industries. The various guest editors have brought a vast spectrum of thought and opinion to the printed page. Some of the volumes are classic sources on and by the people discussed in *Completing the Union*. Two issues deserve special note in this regard: (1) Vol. 8, no. 4, 1981, "Alaska National Interest Lands," by guest editors Celia Hunter and Ginny Hill Wood. Hunter and Wood were the two WASPs who came to Fairbanks in 1946 and became vital actors in the environmental history of the new state. This is their introduction to the changes wrought by the passage of ANILCA. (2) Vol. 25, no. 1, 1998, "Steve McCutcheon's Alaska." Born in Alaska in 1911, McCutcheon experienced the life of the early territory and then became an integral part of the statehood movement as a delegate to the 1955–56 Constitutional Convention. He was by profession a photographer and captured the territory, the statehooders, and the new forty-ninth state on film as no one else did. This volume is the ultimate photographic record of the Alaska portion of *Completing the Union*.

In the early fall of 2003, *Alaska Geographic* abruptly ceased publication. Its editors, Penny Rennick and Kathy Doogan, wrote the magazine's subscribers, "There's little left to cover that would be new to members. *Alaska Geographic* as a publication has reached the end of its natural life." As such, that life in its 122 volumes constitutes the single most important archive on the development of the forty-ninth state. The volumes can be found in most Alaska libraries as well as in many private collections.

A Note on Orthography

Over the twenty years that I have been engaged in research for this book, a major change has occurred in orthography in Hawai'i. This change began as part of the Modern Hawaiian Movement to reinvigorate Hawaiian culture and included the reintroduction of the glottal stop between certain vowels in words such as *Hawai'i* and *O'ahu* and the addition of the macron over vowels in words such as *Kūhiō, Kalākaua,* and *Mānoa*. The use of these Hawaiian spellings first began in articles on native Hawaiian culture. Over time the new spelling was gradually adopted by most newspapers and publishers in Hawai'i and was also authorized by state law. These diacritical marks are regularly used *except* when a word (for example, *Hawaii*) is directly quoted from a source that did not use the marks or when it is part of the title of a historic term that did not use the punctuation (for example, Hawaii Statehood Commission).

For readers interested in a more extended discussion of these changes in Hawaiian orthography and language, see Albert J. Schutz, *The Voices of Eden: A History of Hawaiian Language Studies* (Honolulu: University of Hawai'i Press, 1994).

Index

Note: Page numbers in italics refer to illustrations.